People on the Move

A United States History

Published as a complete one-volume text and *in two volumes:*

Complete (hardbound):

PEOPLE ON THE MOVE—A UNITED STATES HISTORY

Two-volume (softbound):

PEOPLE ON THE MOVE—A UNITED STATES HISTORY (TO 1877)
PEOPLE ON THE MOVE—A UNITED STATES HISTORY (SINCE 1860)

PEOPLE ON THE MOVE

A United States History since 1860

RAY GINGER
The University of Calgary

with the aid of
VICTORIA GINGER

Allyn and Bacon, Inc.   Boston

PRINTED IN THE UNITED STATES OF AMERICA

"After Apple Picking" by Robert Frost, from *The Poetry of Robert Frost* edited by Edward Connery Lathem. Copyright 1930, 1939, © 1969 by Holt, Rinehart, and Winston, Inc. Copyright © 1958 by Robert Frost. Copyright © 1967 by Lesley Frost Ballantine. Reprinted by permission of Holt, Rinehart and Winston, Inc.
From "The Love Song of J. Alfred Prufrock" by T. S. Eliot, from *Collected Poems 1909–1962*, by permission of Harcourt, Brace, Jovanovich, Inc.

LIBRARY OF CONGRESS CATALOGING IN PUBLICATION DATA

Ginger, Ray.
  People on the move: a United States History.

  Bibliography: p.
  Includes indexes.
  CONTENTS: [1] To 1877.—[2] Since 1860.
  1. United States—History. I. Title.
E178.1.G54   1975b   973   74-22212

ISB#   0-205-04733-5

Contents

Preface

Often in the middle of the night I reach for some printed words that do not require much attention. This kind of junk reading, whether Westerns or mysteries or science fiction, helps to cross the abyss between alertness and full sleep. It serves a need. But the present book is intended to meet quite different needs. What is said here is not, so far as I am aware, written down in any sense of those words. It is aimed by two adults at other adults. Frequently it uses analogies from our own lives in an attempt to illuminate what happened at earlier times and in separate places; this mode of comparison is a type of thinking that we all use whether we observe our actions or not. Here it is made explicit. Readers are entitled to some advance warning about other features of this volume that might seem unusual.

1. THE NARRATIVE. These pages try to tell a story. They assume that a portrait, however brief, of John Fitch or Benjamin Franklin or the Kennedy brothers, can help you to understand some salient traits of human nature as exposed in the American experience. But this work tries to reach farther yet. It tries to make sense of the lives that people have struggled through in the United States. Facts, like persons, do not carry their meanings on their sleeves. Out of the mists of the past, a historian must select certain events because he cannot tell it all, even if he knew it all, which he does not. But his standards of selection he should try to state clearly. Here are some of mine.

The main theme of this study is put down in the title. Americans more than any other nation known to me have been *People on the Move.* Whatever criterion be chosen—whether geographical or socioeconomic or ethical—we have hustled. Perhaps the most unAmerican of all traits is contentment. Beneath this broadest rubric, however, subcategories can be discerned. Recognizing that the most pervasive American symbol is the moving van, let us list other topics that will recur repeatedly below:

a) *Technology and its applications.* Almost everybody would believe that development of the automobile has been a socially desirable innovation even though it results in air pollution and so many traffic deaths. But can an affirmative verdict be given on the space program that first put men on the moon?

b) *Economic institutions and their evolution.* Using a lackadaisical vocabulary, some historians have characterized Americans as a "materialistic" people. The same writers, in their hope of wiping out the enemy with a questionable epithet, do not heed the types of organization that have helped to make a specific country—so far—the most productive in the history of the earth. To give three examples, they have vaguely opined that money and banking has been important in American history, but they have not tried to explain clearly just what these devices do and have done. They have written about labor relations chiefly in terms of trade unions, which are only a marginal piece of the tale. They have not even tried to look closely at the psychology of leaders who fabricated industrial empires. The following pages try to remedy these ailments.

c) *The phrase "think ethnic"* is unquestionably a great one in its application to American history. But it has been applied chiefly to political events, with some attention to social ones. Here an effort is made to roam into the significance of immigration for economic growth. Obviously if each individual invader from Europe had been forced to make it on his own, he would never have made it at all. But considering the population as a whole, and ignoring the influx of people including the importation of slaves prior to 1860, would the United States now have a Gross National Product of $100,000,000,000 had it not been for the influx of peoples in the last hundred years?

d) The last question opens the realm of *social changes*. The inquiry starts with alterations in birth rates, in death rates, in distributions of the population by age and by sex. But the problems do not end with demography narrowly construed. The structure of American families has altered enormously from Puritan times to the present; indeed, the child-centered entity has emerged in the last hundred years. As infant mortality has fallen, the care lavished on individual offspring has risen rapidly. One of the most searching essays of recent years explores the meaning for character formation of a society that is so affluent that each member of the family can have a private room. The rise of cities has meant manifold revision of male-female relations.

e) *Life of the mind.* The shifting attitudes of the common man have found some of their most intense expressions in the work of intellectuals. Writers and painters and musicians have tried to evoke the hidden meanings of their contemporary ambience. Speaking of the most profound artists, it seems too trite to say that they tried to touch the pulse of their own times: they reached through the skin to reach the heart that drove the pulse. These pages try to give a fair sampling of American achievements in belles lettres and other exalted crafts. Attention will be paid to the ways in which architects, by their design of dwellings as well as of public buildings, have reflected the values of their age. Although knowledge is widespread about the emergence in the twentieth century of native American music, remarks will be made about lesser known aspects of this achievement. Finally, it will be argued that photography and its derivatives are the most significant new departure in the arts since 1800.

f) *Constitutional and political conflicts.* The social and economic tensions of a country also are exposed by the struggles for control of its governments. From the Kansas-Nebraska Act to black power, from the National Association of Manufacturers to trade unions with their Political Action Committee, the clashes have gone on. For twenty-five years after World War II, the fashionable school of historians chose to depict the United States as a nation of consensus, where we all agreed that free-enterprise and republican government were the be-all and end-all. Stated in this form, the view should not be brushed aside. But it must be strictly qualified. American politicians are not pantywaists or paper tigers; they play a body-contact sport. The United States has not been noted for its Christian brotherhood—at least not when power is at stake. The American attitude in the strife for control and use of government has been: I can take you, Buster, so I will.

g) *Foreign policy.* Official attitudes toward the rest of the world have been shaped above all by the stresses within the United States. To cite one example, Washington's Farewell Address cannot be understood without knowing the domestic problems that prompted it. The Monroe Doctrine was a brilliant exploitation of the home difficulties, not of the United States, but of England. In 1914–18 the English found a means to reverse the exploitation: whereas earlier John Quincy Adams had used British power to accomplish American goals, now Sir Edward Grey used American power to carry out British intentions.

h) *Military affairs.* Warfare has been a central element in the history of the United States. From the days of the English colonies in North America to the present, the musket, the Gatling gun, or the hydrogen bomb have been kept close to hand. This brute fact has been pervasive: on the economy, on constitutional relations, on psychology, even in some respects on religion. To speak thus is not to assert that Americans have been "militaristic"—a charge that is about as senseless as to say that they have been "materialistic." Quite the contrary. The United States from earliest days until World War II put its reliance on a civilian militia. The country never bothered to mobilize a fighting force until a war had started, but its advantage was that it held in reserve a devastating capacity that had not been frittered away on the maintenance of a standing army.

i) *The total man.* These pages insist that history is about human beings, and that man is a highly complicated animism. They urge that the diverse facets of man's activities cannot be segmented cleanly from each other. At the same time, however, the making of historical categories can be carried beyond the point of usefulness as requisite tools for our thinking; artificial categories can also betray some connections that existed in other times. In any case, historians do not know enough to reveal all of the linkages that occurred in the past, and I cheerfully although regretfully concede that I have only a part of the knowledge that is owned by the totality of the historical guild. Thus nobody will find this book compartmented by a system of self-contained topics in which one chapter talks about railroads and the next talks about money and banking, while the foresaid topics never touch on one another. The connections I have asserted often fluctuate—a complexity that seems to be dictated by reality. Chapter 3 ties international commerce to the transplantation of culture, suggesting that the movement of goods meant also the movement of ideas from the same parts of the Old World. But two centuries later, in Chapter 14, intellectual tides are joined not to economic ones but to social ones.

This ebb and flow of complications can be avoided only by tactics that are simplistic in the extreme. To quote a great French historian:

> Only a divine mind could make a whole of the infinite variety of aspects of history. . . . Whoever pursues religious history must not neglect economic history, because it is the same man who believes in some religion and is also part of an economic system, or a legal, or a political one. I think that this idea of the concrete historic man is what joins together all the special fields, and gives historical research its full richness.

j) *Mobility.* While these subthemes keep emerging through the book, it should be emphasized that the main motif is mobility. Some three generations of American scholars have gone to the skeet ranges to shoot down Frederick Jackson Turner. But he remains, together with that nonesuch visitor Alexis de Tocqueville, one of the two greatest commentators on the American story. To say that Turner did not know everything is hardly a devastating rebuttal. Fine research has shown that he neglected the stimuli provided by towns and cities in the settlement of the frontier. No analyst of the westward movement would today leave out the pioneers who came westward across the ocean from Europe. The fringes of settlement were not the seedbed of egalitarianism that Turner thought them to be. But few philosophers—Plato, Machiavelli, Marx-Engels, Lincoln—have provided a platform from which we can soar higher. For those interested in American history, Turner's writings, slender though they are, remain the springboard.

k) *What we don't know.* It may seem dogged and even bullheaded, but large parts of this volume are a confession of ignorance. Large and vital parts of American history are still uncharted ground. The maps of our coast lines and rivers that were done in the eighteenth century evoke more confidence than we can feel in charts of portions of the national life which were made two centuries later. One instance is the dubious picture of the origins of political parties in the United States. Several books have appeared recently that purport to deal with the administrations of Washington and Adams. But when they try to explain how the nation arrived at a mode of managing its government that was not approved by any powerful man of the age, no existing work offers a picture that is convincing.

Some portions of history need not remain as befogged forever as they are today. Where a hiatus appears, I have tried to identify it. Where I had an idea of methods that might fill the gap, I have stated them.

[For the author's full discussion of the other features of this text, see the complete preface as printed before Chapter 1 of the alternate editions. Briefly they are as follows—*Notable events:* To free the text of clustered dates and events, many related items are listed at the ends of chapter summaries. *Documents:* A lively selection of significantly related documentary quotations is added to each chapter. *Ways to Study History:* Each chapter is followed by a brief account of how a particular historian pursued a problem in finding and evaluating new evidence. *Illustrations:* First-rate artistic achievements in America are displayed and analyzed in a representative balance by era, region, genre, and suitability for reproduction. *How Did It Work?* Key technological achievements are highlighted in special explanatory sections. *Maps.* The focus of these has been kept sharp and simple for important demographic, geographic, and political features. *Charts and Graphs:* Most of these are to clarify relationships of quantifiable data; some are to provide simple conceptual models of economic relationships. *Bibliographies:* A general list and one for each Part is provided, limited arbitrarily to fifty books for each unit, and focused on major works on important subtopics in each area. *Three Indexes:* A separate glossary index of key terms, as well as a more general subject index, and a name index are provided.]

People on the Move

A United States History

PART IV

Sectional Smiles, but Social Strife: *1860–1898*

Civil War and (Non-) Reconstruction

The Civil War can be seen from several vantages. It might be viewed as a campaign for Southern suicide. It affirmed Herman Melville's vision of the implacable cruelty in the world (Document 16-1). For those few thoughtful persons who were still trying to rejoice with the Enlightenment, it stomped on the jaunty faith that progress was inevitable.

The secession process needs no close-grained treatment here, but some generalizations about it can be ventured. As one might guess, the first state to leave the Union was South Carolina on 20 December, 1860, by unanimous vote of a specially elected convention of 169 members. By 26 January, 1861, all of the Gulf states from Florida to Louisiana had seceded. These were the six states that convened to establish the Confederate States of America. Before they completed their constitution on March 11 they were joined by representatives from Texas even though Governor Sam Houston of that state opposed secession and was deposed from office for his loyalty. Texas was further distinguished by being the only state to submit its resolution of secession to a popular vote; elsewhere the matter was carried by a newly chosen convention.

Soon, of the fifteen slave states another four would join the Confederacy: Arkansas, Tennessee, North Carolina, Virginia. The new federal government had a constitution that was largely modelled on and often copied from the basic document of its parent. But, again as one might guess, the Confederate constitution placed even more weight on the rights of states. During the brief existence of the new government it was chronically beset by separatist movements.* The center of white disaffection was the same upcountry zone in the Carolina Appalachians that had spawned the Regulator movements (Chapter 4) a century earlier. From the peckerwood districts of the Carolinas and Georgia came a good many volunteers for the Union armies. East Tennessee produced a president of the United States, if not a distinguished one. These centrifugal impulses in the Confederacy came to their ultimate in Virginia when the mountainous western reaches split away altogether to form a new loyal state admitted to the Union in 1863.

The difficulties of the rebellion involved not only institutions but also personalities. The emergent polity erred badly in its choice of leaders. Jefferson Davis had graduated from West Point and had served in the army for several years. He had been secretary of war and a senator. But one suspects that he was elected president of the Confederacy because he and his brother owned as many slaves on their Mississippi plantations as did any family in the South. Along with (because of?) his elegant airs he was crude and imperious. He was repeatedly embroiled in quarrels with his congress. He chronically interfered in unwise ways with his field commanders, to the point of sending them detailed instructions about battlefield tactics when he could not possibly know what the specific situation was. Lincoln too had troubles with his Congress; he too spent years of trial and error seeking generals on whom he could rely. But when he found them—particularly Grant, Sherman, George H. Thomas—he left them to manage the conduct of campaigns.

Perhaps it is inevitable that the typical human will downgrade the difficulties he faces; if we did not, we might be inert. This self-deceit is especially apparent at the onset of war. An illustration can be given almost at random: in October, 1776, a British officer wrote from Westchester County, New York "I think that June next will bring us back to London. . . ." But the next May he wrote that he hoped "to visit you before Christmas." A bare three months later he amended: "I hope our Son and Daughter are in perfect health, they will have grown so tall & so old, I fear, before this War is over that we shall be greater Strangers when we meet than, I trust, we shall be ever after." But even if we try by such analogies to keep matters in perspective, who today can avoid a macabre smile at the reactions of American statesmen to the outbreak of hostilities in 1861? The Confederate hawks were confident that the

---

*A central theme of American history from the beginning has of course been the conflict of tendencies toward union and toward separatism. The latter urges can be traced at least back to the Reformation and would embrace, among other things, everything from Antinomianism to our contemporary divorce courts.

superior valor of their cavalier gentry would quickly ride over the mudsills. Similarly Lincoln, three days after the enemy on April 12 had fired on the Union's Fort Sumter in Charleston, South Carolina, called forth "the militia of the several States of the Union, to the . . . number of seventy-five thousand." He might have expected that the doughty yeomen of his free society could waltz into the Confederate capital at Richmond, but he would live to smell

> *the patriotic gore*
> *That flecked the streets of Baltimore.*

A fashion has persisted for speculating that Lincoln, by his efforts to supply the garrison at Sumter, deliberately provoked the secessionists into cannonading the fort and thus starting the war. This fad should stop. It is even more obscene than the speculations that Roosevelt wanted the Japanese to attack Pearl Harbor. The circumstances are clear. Lincoln had taken an oath to maintain federal property. The fort belonged in that category. He had no alternative to what he did. But a similar claim cannot be made for another decision he took. President-elect Lincoln made his worst judgment about policy—possibly his only serious blunder about policy—before he entered the White House. On 18 December, 1860, the Crittenden Compromise was put forward by a senator from Kentucky. This proposal for Amendments to the Constitution of the United States was a sober try at reconciliation.* It would have reconstituted the line of the Missouri Compromise at 36° 30′ in the federal Territories, with slavery allowed below, banned above. Each state would be allowed to set its own provincial policy on the question. Northern states would be asked to repeal their personal-liberty laws that conflicted with the Fugitive Slave Act of the federal government. It seems likely that Congress could have been persuaded to vote this package. But the personal intervention of Abraham Lincoln killed it.

His line of argument in reaching this verdict is not known for sure. Many historians have asserted that the Crittenden Compromise was merely a stopgap, that it could not have survived, that war was bound to come. This is almost certainly true, but at times it is wise to defer a war, if only for five or ten years. If compromise was useful to the Union in 1850, it would also have been useful a decade later. Crittenden's proposals were manifestly perpetuating an injustice to 4 million slaves, but we may doubt if that was Lincoln's reason for rejecting them. Vital to his opposition was the proposal to allow slavery expansion south of 36° 30′. A hunch whispers that he thought the showdown had come, and that it had best be faced when Abraham Lincoln was commander in chief rather than another doughface like Pierce or Buchanan. Even so, it seems that rejection of the Crittenden Compromise was at best

---

*One clause in the proposition still seems gravely defective: Article Six provided that the preceding Amendments could not themselves be amended. Sound reasons still exist for adhering to the creed of Paine and Jefferson that no generation in a republic can legitimately exercise the power to bind its successors.

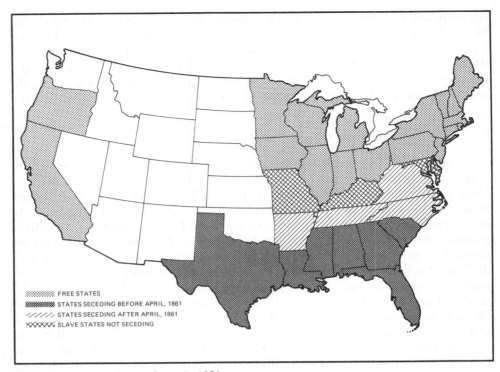

FREE STATES
STATES SECEDING BEFORE APRIL, 1861
STATES SECEDING AFTER APRIL, 1861
SLAVE STATES NOT SECEDING

FIGURE 16-1. *The United States in 1861*

dubious statesmanship. Another mode of averting a civil war was also suggested. Lincoln's secretary of state, William H. Seward (appropriately on April Fool's Day, before the clash at Fort Sumter) proposed that he start a donnybrook with European powers that would hopefully lead to a foreign war, thus healing the domestic cleavage. The president spurned this option.

We must try to confront problems as they came upon the president. He quickly learned that 75,000 militia would not be adequate to the job. After two demoralizing defeats at Bull Run, the Union settled in for a wearing attrition. An inefficient but *de facto* draft was established by the militia act of 1862. In that same year, 27 September, the Confederacy passed its second conscription act, but the Northern Congress did not enact a similar measure until 3 March, 1863. It was immediately and violently resisted. The worst anti-draft riots occurred in New York City, especially by Irish immigrants. Hatred of conscription undoubtedly was a factor, but the explosion was aggravated when paddy longshoremen went on strike and were replaced by blacks as scabs. A provision by which the wealthy could buy their way out of the army was a further contribution to resentment. The Confederacy had an analogy: any overseer of twenty slaves (later fifteen) was exempt from conscription.

Mobilization of manpower by the Union must include the recruitment of leadership. In spite of Seward's lapses into miserable advice, he was an able man, and so were other members of the cabinet. While the civilian slots were filled with expedition and judgment, the military command was a persisting headache. For nearly three years President Lincoln experimented with field commanders in the East. He tried five—McDowell, McClellan, Burnside, Hooker, Meade—and found all deficient. But it is hard to see what alternative to trial and error the president had. He inherited a peacetime army plus a tradition of anti-militarism, of a civilian army. But slowly, while great masses of stolid soldiers were slaughtering each other in the brief march between the rival capitals at Richmond and Washington, the three generals who would do the most for the Union cause were rising to prominence in the Mississippi valley. It is gross error to assume that the South had the more competent generals: Grant, Sherman, and Thomas could rank with any trio of the Confederacy (Lee, Jackson, and Joseph E. Johnston?).

Such fallacies can become popular because few of us have bothered to think about warfare as an institution. An honorable exception to this aspersion is historian T. Harry Williams. In his masterly *Americans at War* (1960) he underscores the need to distinguish among the (a) tactics that determine battles, the (b) strategies that influence campaigns, and the (c) policy that often determines who will win the war. Considering the American War for Independence in this schema, for instance, it would have availed the British little if their strategy and tactics had been brilliant (they were not) because their policy was so bad.* Williams goes on to argue that the military genius of the Civil War was the president of the United States. This contention, while true, is so startlingly unusual as to need explication. Everybody knows the pointed maxim of Karl von Clausewitz that war is the continuation of politics by other means. So far, all right. But Clausewitz also wrote: "The *offensive* . . . has for its absolute object not so much *combat* as the *taking possession of something.*" We have all seen the United States generally accept this formula whereby the key to national security allegedly is to hold strategic points in the world. Lincoln promptly and decisively rejected this approach. His objective was not to capture Southern soil but to destroy Confederate armies.

Apart from Clausewitz, the reigning theoreticians of warfare in 1861 were Frenchmen such as Napoleon I and Antoine Henri Jomini. From their battles and treatises American officers had drawn the preachment that military force should be concentrated at a single point. But this principle had been derived in the relatively limited geographical areas of Europe. Lincoln swiftly saw that it did not apply to his problem. His strategy was to take the offensive simultaneously in many different theaters, to hit and hit and hit again, almost heedless of cost. And the cost was terrible. With the invention of the Gatling gun and the improvement of artillery, the advantage in battle had swung to defensive alignments, and attempts to dislodge enemy positions cost both

---

*The same conclusion applied with equal force to engagement of the United States in Viet Nam.

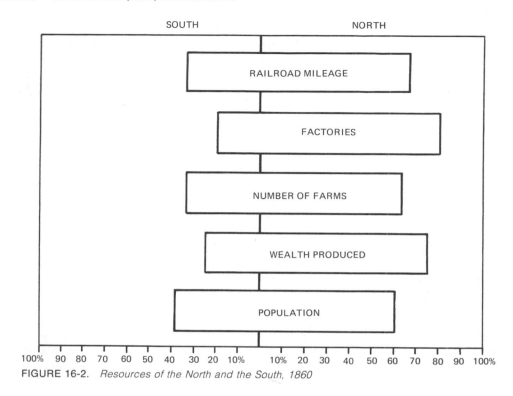

FIGURE 16-2. *Resources of the North and the South, 1860*

sides dearly in blood. Even today the figures are numbing: in a nation of 31 million souls, 600,000 lives came to a stop.

But the president knew that his cause could pay the ghastly price. When the war started the distribution of power was dreadfully lopsided. In manpower, in transportation, in its ability to produce uniforms as well as guns, the greater heft was in the North. The president, intuitively grasping the importance of economic warfare, wrenched the balance further by imposing a total blockade on Southern ports. Soon the South was deficient in vital supplies; a fascinating book tells how the shortage of salt prevented her from preserving meat. It has been common to argue that since the South had the interior position, she was benefited by having shorter lines of supply. Logistically the point should be heard, but it does not take full account of the facts. The chief iron and munitions factories of the Confederacy were in Richmond. Six railroads entered that city. No two of them connected. For rail and road communications the North had far better facilities.

Which brings us to another frequent distortion of the situation during the war. Lincoln's desire to hold the loyalty of the border states, particularly Kentucky and Missouri, is widely known, but a crucial reason for that desire is often ignored. More vital to the Union than any other pathway for moving men and matériel was the Ohio-Mississippi basin. He had to keep this channel open. Thus when John Charles Frémont, the general commanding in St. Louis, proclaimed on 30 August, 1861, that all slaves within his command were emancipated, the president at once revoked the order. A Republican senator from Maine called Lincoln's action a "weak and unjustifiable concession to the Union men of the border states." A concession it was, but we question the epithetical adjectives. The president said, "I hope to have God on my side, but I must have Kentucky." It is relevant too that more than 250,000 Union soldiers were recruited from the border slave states during the war.

On the question of slavery the president was caught in an incessant crossfire. Probably Lincoln knew from the start that the issue of emancipation could not be evaded forever. But he could not afford to admit that, so he presented his every action as a war measure done to save the Union (Document 16-2). Snide remarks have also been made that the Emancipation Proclamation, when it took effect on New Year's Day of 1863, did not free a single slave since it applied only in still rebellious areas where it could not be enforced. Such comments show little charity to a great statesman. Lincoln's task was literally impossible: to lead a self-contradictory nation to fight a bloody war for a revolutionary objective that nobody believed in. Yet he achieved it. In one sense he was probably lucky: he was assassinated at the right moment. Speculations have been rife about whether the troubled era of Reconstruction would have gone better if Lincoln had lived to tackle its problems. The answer clearly is No. The nation was hopelessly divided on many questions, and these rifts were concentrated in Washington. Congress had been at the president's throat from the moment he took office, and this internecine fray was not about to cease at the request of any chief executive.

The full extent of these antagonisms became clear between December, 1863, and July, 1864. First Lincoln announced his plan. It assumed that the rebellious regions had not left the Union at all. When the residents of a state equal in number to 10 per cent of the electorate in 1860 had taken an oath of loyalty, they could elect new members of Congress. A crucial feature of the procedure was the pardoning power of the president. But in Congress, where each house has the power to determine whom it will seat, the new men returned from the South were rejected. Congress summed up its opposition to the president's plan in the Wade-Davis bill. Here was what is called "Congressional Reconstruction." Whereas Lincoln's proposal had referred to a decimal of the electorate, this measure was predicated on a majority. Moreover, it barred from the polity all who had held office "under the rebel usurpation" or who had carried arms against the Union.

While politicians squabbled, some Union armies ground forward. The war was decided by two crucial events that occurred in the first four days of July in 1863. The difference between those two events illuminates the war's true nature, so often concealed by microscopic accounts of this battle and that battle. The first decision was made at Gettysburg where the clash killed 50,000 men in three days and ended a stalemate. The entire war in the East, over those dreadful bloody miles—a mere hundred—between the rival capitals, had been a stalemate. Nobody won; both sides lost in appalling measure. Since the North could better afford to waste men as well as matériel, these wicked engagements tilted the sectional balance still further. Second, the war was won in the Ohio-Mississippi valley. On Independence day, after a siege of six weeks, the Confederates at Vicksburg surrendered to Grant. Soon a decisive win by Thomas at Chattanooga opened the way for Sherman's subsequent invasion of Georgia. From this day forward the Confederacy had no chance for victory in the field.

By now, too, the schism within the North about the nature of the war had been stoutly expressed. Sherman took Atlanta on 2 September, 1864. Fearing a counterattack and desiring to shorten his lines, he ordered the city cleared of all civilians. The mayor protested that, with winter approaching, the evacuation would be inhumane to the aged and the ill. Sherman would not bend.

> We must have peace, not only at Atlanta, but in all America. To secure this, we must stop the war that now desolates our once happy and favored country. To stop war, we must defeat the rebel armies which are arrayed against the laws and Constitution that all must respect and obey. . . . I cannot discuss this subject with you fairly, because I cannot impart to you what we propose to do, but I assert that our military plans make it necessary for the inhabitants to go away, and I can only renew my offer of services to make their exodus in any direction as easy and comfortable as possible.
>
> You cannot qualify war in harsher terms than I will. War is cruelty, and you cannot refine it; and those who brought war into our country deserve all the curses and maledictions a people can pour out. I know I had no hand in making this, and I will make more sacrifices to-day than any of you to secure peace. But you cannot have peace and a division of our country. . . .
>
> We don't want your negroes, or your horses, or your lands, or any thing you have, but we do want and will have a just obedience to the laws of the United States.

Having departed from the benign eighteenth-century code of combat (Chapter 5), Sherman approached the doctrine of total war that has haunted mankind in modern times. But his commander in chief continued to advocate mercy, as he had exemplified in his Proclamation of Amnesty and Reconstruction.

Probably Grant in his attitude stood closer to Sherman than to Lincoln. But recognizing the differences among these three men should not blind us to their similiarities. In a revealing passage published in 1952, Benjamin P. Thomas focused on the conference among them at Hampton Roads, Virginia on 28 March, 1865. In a quiet way, Thomas came as close as anybody to defining what the Civil War was all about: "All three were Midwesterners, though Lincoln came of Southern origin. None of them could have come close to the top except in America. War had made them comrades of a sort; each trusted the others to do their job." While the conjunction of these men on this occasion might well symbolize the American experience, two of them saw the immediate future as forbidding: Grant and Sherman thought that another bloody battle must be fought. The president hoped not. As often, Lincoln was right. Lee surrendered on April 9; Johnston conceded for the other main Confederate army on April 18. In the interim the president was shot to death.

He was succeeded by Andrew Johnson of Tennessee. The very selection of a loyal senator from a Confederate state as the vice presidential nominee on the Union ticket in 1864 tells how perilous the president thought his position was. It also reflects how much importance he attached to the border states, and it shows his outlook toward getting the secessionists back into the Union. But because of his temperament, Johnson was not a happy choice. Some historians have emphasized his upbringing in the lower middle class (he was a tailor by trade), his fondness for booze, his crabbed mentality. He was fuzzy both intellectually and emotionally. He envied the deposed planters, which is to say that he both hated them and looked up to them. Looking always backward, he found his idols in Jefferson and Jackson, who had also looked backward.* Earnestly trying to improve the status of the white yeoman, he did not realize how many of his pets shared his sympathy for the old social order incarnate in the ex-slaveholders. About the blacks, free or slave, he cared nothing.

The new president did want to abolish slavery as a legal institution. But he did not seek to revamp the total structure in which slavery was the linchpin. Several congressmen disagreed. They deemed it essential that Union force should be used *promptly* to *reconstruct* the South. Any realistic chance for this kind of accomplishment was always most unlikely. It could not be achieved without use of the army, and the commander in chief was the hostile president. Not only was Johnson at best indifferent to any use of military strength to enhance the position of Southern blacks, he also regarded the status of the erstwhile governing class in the defeated provinces as a personal rather than a political problem; he wanted the subjugated to feel indebted to him as an individual rather than to a benign government. Lincoln would have granted a general amnesty; Johnson insisted on private applications to the president for a pardon. By September, 1867, he had granted about 13,500 such pardons, each signed personally.

Going further yet, he appointed many former Confederates to Union offices. The ex-foes heard their cues distinctly. In the summer and autumn of 1865, secessionist states seriatim passed their Black Codes. The intent was clear: to keep all blacks in a condition of servitude. Perhaps they would no longer be slaves at law, but in fact they would be suppressed, repressed, and depressed. Each slaveholder had lost his private property, but, as one senator said, "the blacks at large belong to the whites at large." The president made no protests.

---

*Here is another superb unexploited subject for a doctoral dissertation: the role of nostalgia in shaping the values of successive generations of Americans. Two facets of the topic are treated with insight by Henry Nash Smith, *Virgin Land* (1950) and by Marvin Meyers, *The Jacksonian Persuasion* (1957).

But a potent faction in Congress stood for a radically opposed policy. By the end of 1865 Johnson had given up hope of reconstituting the South; six months earlier some percipient congressmen had given up hope that he would do otherwise. The most forceful spokesman for this position was Thaddeus Stevens, Representative from Pennsylvania, although Senators Charles Sumner (Mass.) and Benjamin F. Wade (Ohio) held higher official positions. It is worth while to compare Stevens to Lincoln. The former was guilty of unfortunate rancor. The two differed not only in temperament but also in position: a representative can opt for an extreme that is denied to a president. But the two agreed in devotion to the welfare of the ordinary, aspiring citizen. Maybe the chief disparity is that Stevens was more willing to extend his dedication to all commoners, regardless of color. He left a clear testament; his will, decrying the ubiquity of all-white cemeteries, provided that he should be buried in a graveyard with blacks.

The irreconcilables in Congress seldom wield a majority. Even when he voted with his peers, Stevens was a far-out voice in a much broader chorus. They won some victories. The Freedmen's Bureau and an accompanying bank were created by Congress in 1865 and played a useful part for four years (see below on changes in the South). From 1865 to 1870 three Amendments were added to the Constitution, ostensibly to advance the rights of black people; their application was never more than haphazard. The reasons for this ambivalence will be viewed promptly below, and the tortuous course of judicial constructions will be examined at appropriate places thereafter. The Reconstructionists also carried Civil Rights Acts in 1866 and 1875 that would serve for a century as the main platform in federal courts for legal efforts to elevate the station of blacks. Repeatedly the insurgents had to carry their reforms by two-thirds majorities following a veto by the president. This fact may suggest that Andrew Johnson should carry much, perhaps most, of the blame for the failure of Reconstruction.

But to argue so would be mistaken. In his views of blacks, the president was undoubtedly closer to most voters than was Stevens. The latter might well declare, "This is not a 'white man's government.' To say so is political blasphemy, for it violates the fundamental principles of our gospel of liberty. This is man's government; the government of all men alike." This rhetoric was merely stating an ideal, an ideal that he held almost alone. The reality was put bluntly by a Republican representative from Indiana: "The real trouble is that *we hate the negro.* It is not his ignorance that offends us, but his color." That tells the story. American blacks had no keener white friend in 1865 than Thomas Wentworth Higginson of Boston. He was one of the Secret Six who financed John Brown's venture at Harper's Ferry. When the other conspirators tried to weasel out of their complicity, Higginson publicly avowed his. He was colonel of a black regiment during the war. But his reminiscences of that experience are larded with a condescending tone.

The vast majority of whites would not accept any black as equal socially, neither for a friendly beer nor for the connubial bed. But political rights were another matter. The Republicans won sweeping gains at the congressional polls in 1866, and they had an obvious interest in enfranchising the freed blacks. Whether their policy was supported by most Northern whites still seems a moot question. Ulysses S. Grant, even though he was a conquering general, won the presidency in 1868 only by reason of 700,000 black votes. Two years later the Fifteenth Amendment forbade discrimination in the suffrage at federal elections "on account of race, color, or previous condition of servitude—" But the issue had already been resolved in the negative. At various times in human affairs, one type of relation dominates others and in the postwar South economics would undermine politics.* At least a billion dollars in property, the slaves, had been cancelled. Major cities had been flattened. Railroads were disrupted. One farm animal in three had been killed. The labor force, particularly the managerial segment, had been greatly reduced, and what remained was chaotic. In such circumstances, the man who could first gain an independent livelihood would rule over the polity.

Contemporaries understood this. When black leaders met in Savannah just before the war ended, their word was "The way we can best take care of ourselves is to have land, and . . . till it by our own labor." Even earlier, a member of a commission appointed by the secretary of war to investigate the South had counselled: "No such thing as a free, democratic society can exist in any country where all lands are owned by one class of men and cultivated by another." Here too Thaddeus Stevens was clear. The plantations had been "nurseries of the Rebellion"; they "must be broken up and the freedmen must have the pieces." His plan envisaged confiscation of about 400 million acres (eight times Kansas) owned by 70,000 slaveholders, only 5 per cent of the South's white families. "The whole fabric of southern society *must* be changed," he declared, "and never can it be done if this opportunity is lost. How can republican institutions, free schools, free churches, free social intercourse exist in a mingled community of nabobs and serfs? . . . If the South is ever to be made a safe Republic let her lands be cultivated by the toil of the owners, or the free labor of intelligent citizens. This must be done even though it drive her nobility into exile." But the president opposed any redistribution of land among the freedmen. On the Sea Islands along the Georgia-Carolina coast General Sherman launched a program of granting not more than forty acres per black family; "40 acres and a mule." Johnson restored most of these lands to their former owners. He invalidated another program in Mississippi. By the time Stevens died in 1868, land reform and the economic independence of blacks were dead also.

But the spats of president with Congress had not abated. Quite properly, the Reconstructionists were provoked by the flagrant prejudice of Southern

---

*I have no desire here to lay down any universal law of history. The reverse may be true in other circumstances. The campaign for school integration, in spite of its prominence, did not accomplish much in the twenty years after 1954. The true revolution of that time was the enfranchisement of black voters. Political power can be a necessary prerequisite to economic power, as well as the reverse.

conservatives. The Black Codes were vainglorious in their bias: the South Carolina law, for instance, defined a vagrant as a person lacking "some fixed and known place of abode, and some lawful and reputable employment." A vagrant "of color" could be apprehended by a magistrate, tried by him in conjunction with five freeholders, and sentenced to a maximum of one year. He could then be hired out for the length of his term to do hard labor for any landholder. Thus originated the convict-lease system that, as shall be seen, produced some of the vilest crimes in American history. But even this was not the ultimate evil. The Black Codes at least were adopted under color of law, and some effort was made to administer them by judicial processes. But they were quickly supplemented by the extralegal Ku Klux Klan, by floggings and murders, by race riots in urban centers.

Congress met force with force. By the First Reconstruction Act it established a military occupation of the South, which was divided into five Army districts. Adult males, regardless of color, not disqualified for participation in the rebellion, would elect delegates to write a new constitution in each state and to form a new government. Johnson vetoed the bill, and Congress then passed it over his opposition. Congress promptly curbed the president in two other respects. The Tenure of Office Act forbade him to dismiss members of the cabinet without senatorial consent. A second statute hobbled the president's control of the armed forces. Johnson understandably was infuriated. These Congressional measures brought a showdown. The president sought to replace the secretary of war. The Senate declined its assent. Johnson persisted. In 1868 the House of Representatives for the first time exercised its power to impeach the chief executive for "the violation of a law of Congress and other offenses."

Although the trial of Johnson continues to create sensations, it had meager results. The evidence leading to this conclusion is varied. The Senate required a two-thirds majority to remove the president from office, and it failed of this margin by only one vote: 35 for conviction against 19. In spite of frequent assertions to the contrary, postbellum presidents were not "intimidated" by Congress: Grover Cleveland for instance distributed vetoes like confetti—as some deserved to be. The failure of Reconstruction was already clear, so the trial could hardly determine that topic. Congress had already stipulated the terms on which members of a seceded state would be seated: ratification of three Amendments to the Constitution of the United States, plus the Civil Rights Acts. By the end of 1868 six former Confederate states had been re-admitted to Congress.

In any case, the impeachment of Johnson, whatever its outcome, was trivial compared to realignments in society and its politics. The nation underwent a colossal shift in its political configuration. From 1875 to 1889, there was not an instant when the same party controlled the White House and both branches of Congress. Presidential elections were determined by a handful of votes. Thus if we focus on Washington we can talk seriously about a two-party system. But in most localities one party or the other had a stranglehold. Up to 1876 the Republicans needed the votes of Southern blacks to check Democratic challenges for the presidency. But the soaring population of the Old Northwest (the seven states from Ohio to Minnesota) altered the situation. Prior to the Civil War this area had rather consistently been Democratic. During the War its southerly portions had bristled with Copperheads, as the Confederate sympathizers in the North were called. But Republican strategists (think of Lincoln) helped to effect a massive switch. They had new groups of voters to appeal to: especially immigrants from Germany. They could impugn the opposition for disloyalty. The secessionist departure from Congress made it possible for them to enact some vote-getting laws to be examined later—the Homestead Act, a protective tariff, appropriations to improve rivers and harbors, a measure to establish land-grant agricultural colleges. In eleven presidential contests beginning with 1868, these seven states were all Republican eight times. Four of the states did not vote Democratic a single time, Illinois and Wisconsin once each, Indiana thrice.

The meaning of such developments in the North was obscured until recently because historians of the late nineteenth century were preoccupied with politics, either in Washington or in the state capitals during (non) Reconstruction. Most overviews of the United States during that epoch halted abruptly with "the end of Reconstruction" in 1877 and resumed, also abruptly, with "the farmers' revolt" of the 1890's or even as late as the twentieth century and "the Progressive movement." The ascribing of categories is doubtless essential, but ill-chosen and loose rubrics can mislead historical understanding for generations. And surely nothing is gained by minimizing three of the most volatile decades in American history: the years from 1865 to 1895.

Surprisingly, the section of the country that has received the most study was the one where the least was changing—the South. Too much attention has been paid to governments, not enough to social structure, to economic life, to the daily routines that claimed the multitudes. Prosecutors and champions of the new black-white states have alike offered unbalanced judgments. Let us begin with two topics: schools, and venality. Only in this century have scholars generally recognized that public schools in the region had their origins during Reconstruction; Georgia, for example, by its constitution of 1868 declared for a "thorough system of general education to be forever free to all the children of the state." This ambition was not achieved anywhere in the former Confederacy. The dreadfully impoverished area could not afford teachers or classrooms or books. Parents could ill afford to release their children from productive labor, usually in the fields. The Freedmen's Bureau did start 4,000 schools to educate blacks. Many teachers were white imports from the North who hastened to meet the hunger of Southern blacks for learning. Few black teachers were available to be hired even where money was available to hire them; at the end of the century the historian W. E. B. DuBois would point out that black colleges to train black teachers had to precede primary and secondary schools in building an educational system for the South. The total funds granted to higher education in nine Southern states in 1903 did not equal the income that year of Harvard University.

On the other hand, until about forty years ago the received tradition among scholars amounted to a gross distortion of the nature and degree of peculation in the Reconstruction states. Crookedness among black office-holders, carpetbaggers (Northern whites who held Southern posts), and scalawags (Southern whites who endorsed the Northern occupation) was unquestionably common. But insight cannot be gained unless the phenomenon is seen in comparative terms. How typical was jobbery besides that in ante-bellum Southern regimes? How typical in postbellum Northern states and cities? in the federal government? in the post-Reconstruction Southern oligarchies commonly known as the Bourbons or the Redeemers (suggesting the restoration of local rule)? These questions must be asked, but they cannot now be answered with precision. Thieves notoriously like to work in the dark; bagmen do not demand receipts; the surviving evidence is perhaps no more than a fragment of what once existed. Incidents have lately been produced to suggest that many Redeemers did not earn a reputation for purity. In 1873 a Bourbon state treasurer in Virginia was indicted for embezzlement; he escaped trial on the grounds of insanity. The equivalent official in Georgia in 1879 was impeached for defalcation; he restored the funds and avoided punishment. The state treasurer of Tennessee skipped with $400,000 in 1883. The treasurer of Alabama dropped from sight only three weeks later, but he took only half as much.

These cases do not demonstrate individual culpability so much as social calamity. Whether white or black, a Southerner after the Civil War could hardly inherit wealth or marry it; the stuff was not there. So if he wanted it he had these choices: work for it, or steal it. Perforce, most of the available loot was in the public coffers. When blacks had access to the civic till—and let us never forget that these occasions were seldom—some dipped their fingers. With whites, who had the chance more often, likewise. Nothing is likely to be learned by trying to make distinctions here. But in other respects, discriminations can be made. Blacks might sell, but they could not buy, railroad franchises. Perhaps even more significant in the short run for the acquisition of wealth in an impoverished society, they could be victimized by, but they themselves could not victimize by use of the convict-lease system. In the exploitation of prisoners the collusion was statewide rather than federal, as four jurisdictions will illustrate. In Georgia a senator (sometime redneck, sometime governor) owned coal mines. He paid the state for a 20-year lease that guaranteed him 300 able-bodied laborers. He paid the treasury about 8 cents a day for each man. In Alabama the warden of the state penitentiary "grew rich in a few years on $2,000 a year." In Arkansas in 1881 the death-rate among convicts was said to be 25 per cent. Thus it seems that one result of the prisoner-lease arrangement was to wipe out the prisoners. But that was not so beneficial to taxpayers as to wipe out the prison but keep the convicts. In 1883 the Tennessee Coal, Iron, and Railroad Company leased from that state all 1,300 state inmates, for a charge approximating 20 cents a man per day. It will not do to underestimate the degree to which an entire society can be lured into iniquity.

The procedures of selling or hiring your own chain gang had beneficiaries both north and south of the Mason-Dixon Line. Similarly with the purchase and sale of licenses to build railroads. These were various, from a mere authorization to operate a line, to grants of so many acres of land for each mile of track installed, to guarantees by cities and states of bonds sold to private investors. The last arrangement approached in fact if not in form the outright grant to the Canadian Pacific by the new Dominion of Canada of $25 million in addition to 25 million acres. This resemblance should be especially remarked, along with the reasons for it. Whether in Canada or in the former Confederacy, transportation could be improved only by seducing in capital from the American North; neither region had private funds within its confines to do the job. The handicaps of the slave states have already been summarized; the handicap of Canada was a population in 1881 of 4.3 million versus the projected line of 2,500 miles, through almost unpopulated territory, over often impassable terrain. The goal in one region was to rejuvenate a war-raped land, in the other to extend and preserve a foundling nation. Each found, as have many other peoples, that its noble aim did not reduce the high price to be paid for outside help. The perspective being underscored here is entwined in the essence of economic growth. If the ex-Confederacy or Canada wanted railroad development from 1870 to 1880, it would have to barter in a vicious market. Every culture at certain times has been forced to rely heavily on child labor; what then of free public schools? The existence of company towns and company stores need not mean that the company is fiendishly gouging; perhaps in a capital-rare district it had to use these devices to remove the timber or the minerals at all.

All of this leads us to the economic institutions of the postbellum South; here are some:

convict-lease system
crop-lien or crop-mortgage system
landlord-owned stores giving credit at high rates
sharecropping

The sole alternative to this infernal machinery had disappeared within three years of war's end: Forty Acres and a Mule. When that was gone, only sin was left. Except for the convict-lease system, the modes listed above can be described superficially as varieties of free contract. But they were only the flinty fragments—the talus, scree, and detritus—of the Enlightenment.

When one party to a negotiation has almost no bargaining power, the agreement is not free. The South had no money with which to lubricate its own economy. To get it, Southern businessmen were forced into onerous terms by Yankees; in Arkansas, for instance, the commissioner of immigration was given control of publicly held lands and instructed to use them to attract "northern capital and labor to the state." Six months after the war ended it was estimated that half of the stores in downtown Charleston were controlled by Northerners. Two men from Ohio, both Union soldiers, went into business in Tennessee after they were dismissed from service. They became prominent in coal and iron mining, iron furnaces, a portland cement plant, a cotton mill, a bank. Yankees did not need to invade the South in order to tap its economy: even in New York they could sell the shipping services and insurance and warehousing needed to move the cotton crop to Fall River and Liverpool. In the words of C. Vann Woodward, "The merchant was only a bucket on an endless chain by which the agricultural well of a tributary region was drained of its flow."

Southern promoters, then, could hire the funds of Boston and of Europe by pawning part of the future of their economy. But how could they hire workers? Even blacks were no longer vulnerable to the crude coercions of slavery. Would-be employers had no cash to pay wages. The ensuing accommodations involved a medley of barter, credit, and governmental manipulations. Sharecropping could involve a huge range of divisions of the product between landlord and tenant; if the cropper furnished his own tools and perhaps a draft animal he might get half of the proceeds. Under the crop-lien system the landlord in his turn might go into hock, mortgaging off a crop that was not grown in exchange for working capital. Then he might try to grab back a portion of what he had spent but not yet earned by requiring his sharecroppers to buy their provisions at a store that he owned and where he got inflated prices in exchange for the credit he granted. Crucial to the survival of this maze of credit was the overpowering fact of the state: judges and sheriffs would enforce the inequitable contracts. Historians of generally Marxist persuasion have done more than any other group in analyzing the role of government in what they call "the primitive accumulation of capital." In a poor culture, normal patterns of trade simply do not yield substantial profits. The sanctions of the state must be invoked to tip the balance of price-bargains, whether the precise shape be the war contracts of Thomas Hancock, licensed privateering and the courts of admiralty that passed on naval prizes, or the new weapons of exploitation that replaced slavery in the South.

Freedmen were badly fitted to survive in this competitive milieu; that they did so is a marvel of fortitude and adaptability. Subject at every turn to written words, to contracts and laws, most could not read. Subordinate to the rights of property, most owned none. Seeking to sustain themselves in a society ruled by political power, they had little. They knew their weakness. At the constitutional convention of South Carolina in 1868, an ex-slave declared: "I believe, my friends and fellow-citizens, we are not prepared for this suffrage. But we can learn. Give a man tools and let him commence to use them, and in time he will learn a trade. So it is with voting. We may not understand it at the start, but in time we shall learn to do our duty." But in the next thirty years the opportunity to learn civic responsibility be exercising it was stripped away from Southern blacks.

A good deal is now known about economic institutions and political realities in the postbellum South. But when we turn to social relations we find ourselves on uncertain ground. For decades the body of lore about the family patterns of blacks was unchallenged. Since man-wife ties under slavery were unstable both legally and factually, so the received argument ran, the black family after emancipation tended to be dominated by a matriarch. Recent research has at the very least forced us again to question this conclusion. A similar doubt surrounds another vital problem: the personal backgrounds of the whites who ruled the South after the war. Was the ruling class ex-slaveholders and their descendants? Or was it a new medley of self-made men who had pushed forward through virtual anarchy? A question of this sort can be studied systematically; we have revealing surveys of several other groups: leading executives in various industries, for instance. Somebody should take the 300 eminent citizens of each Southern state in 1880 or 1900 and tell us where they came from. Only by such methodical techniques will we improve our understanding of the processes that operated in the past.

To secede from the United States, the rebellious South followed procedures copied from those that had originated the Union seventy years earlier. Only Texas of the eleven departing states submitted the issue of secession to a popular vote; the others decided the matter by specially formed conventions. For the first two years of the War, the Confederacy seemed to be holding the Union to a stand-off, at times doing better than that. The superiority of the North then began to tell. This dominance had several facets. It was quantitative: more soldiers, more war matériel, more free productive workers. It was qualitative: better transportation networks, and, on balance, better leadership. If the two contestants were equal in terms of their generals, they were far from equal in terms of statesmen; a decided edge lay with the Union. The fray was the bloodiest by far in American history, and it taught parts of the nation the meaning of "total war." Although four years of conflict did preserve the United States and abolish slavery, they did not result in a social revolution in the defeated section. No white man was willing to accord sweeping equality to the freedmen. Congress would not even grant to blacks the chance that might have come from confiscating the plantations of slave-holders and using them to give each former bondsman forty acres and a mule. Indeed, from a longer view of postbellum society we might argue that the Civil War wrote more alterations in the structure of Northern culture than of Southern.

SOME NOTABLE EVENTS

1860   South Carolina secedes, Dec. 20.

1861   Confederacy formed, Feb. 4, at Montgomery, Alabama.
       Morrill Tariff Act passes, March 2.

Fort Sumter fired on, April 12.
First federal income tax.
First transcontinental telegraph.
Frémont's proclamation emancipating slaves, Aug. 30.

1862   U.S. government issues greenbacks.
Homestead Act passes, May 20.
Morrill Act passes to establish land-grant colleges, July 2.
Congress abolishes slavery in District of Columbia and the Territories.

1863   Emancipation Proclamation, Jan. 1.
National Banking Act, Feb. 25.
Battle of Gettysburg, July 1–3.
Grant takes Vicksburg, July 4.
Lincoln's Proclamation of Amnesty and Reconstruction, Dec. 8.

1864   National Bank Act, June 3.
Wade-Davis bill passes Congress; Lincoln vetoes it, July 8.
Sherman, May–Dec., sweeps from Tennessee through Atlanta to Savannah.

1865   Hampton Roads Conference, Feb. 3.
Freedmen's Bureau created; Freedmen's Savings and Trust Co. chartered, March 3.
Lee surrenders, April 9.
Lincoln dies; Andrew Johnson becomes president, April 15.
Johnson's Proclamation of Amnesty and Reconstruction, May 29.
Blacks convene at several sites to protest their treatment, May–Oct.
All-white legislatures in ex-Confederate states adopt Black Codes, summer–autumn.
Ku Klux Klan formed, Pulaski, Tenn.
13th Amendment to Constitution.

1866   Fisk University chartered for blacks, Jan. 9.
Civil Rights Act passes over president's veto, April 9.
ex parte Milligan case limits power of military courts over civilians.
Riot in Memphis, May 1.
Report of Joint Committee on Reconstruction, June 20.
Tennessee restored to Union, July 24.
Riot in New Orleans, July 30.

1867   Congress starts investigation of the president, Jan. 7.
First three Reconstruction Acts, March 2, March 23, July 19.
Union League begins to organize Republican politics in South, spring.
Constitutional conventions meet in former Confederate states, fall.

1868   Impeachment of Johnson begins, March 4.
Fourth Reconstruction Act becomes law, March 11.
Impeachment vote taken in Senate, fails to convict, May 16.
Arkansas restored, June 22.
Omnibus Bill restores North Carolina, South Carolina, Alabama, Florida, and Louisiana.
14th Amendment added to Constitution, July 28.
Thaddeus Stevens dies, August 11.
Georgia legislature expels its black members, Sept. 3.

1869   Conservatives win Tennessee, Oct. 4, and Virginia, Oct. 5.
Texas v. *White.*

1870   Virginia restored, Jan. 26, and Mississippi, Feb. 23.
Hiram R. Revels of Mississippi, first black senator, takes his seat, Feb. 25.
15th Amendment added to Constitution, March 30.
Texas restored, March 30, and Georgia, July 15.
Conservatives win North Carolina, Nov. 3.
Joseph H. Rainey of South Carolina, first black representative, takes his seat, Dec. 12.

1871   Conservatives win Georgia, Nov. 1.

1872   Colored National Convention, at New Orleans, Frederick Douglass presiding, April 15.

1873   Conservatives win Texas, Jan. 14.

1874   Conservatives win Arkansas, Nov. 10, and Alabama, Nov. 14.

1875   Civil Rights Act, March 1.
Conservatives win Mississippi, Nov. 3, and South Carolina, Nov. 12.

1877   Conservatives win Florida and Louisiana, Jan. 2.
Electoral Commission rules for Hayes, sets stage for troop withdrawal from South, Feb. 8.
Wormley House bargain, Feb. 26.
U.S. troops withdraw from South Carolina as arranged, officially ending reconstruction, April 10.

Ways to Study History XVI

Take a world view. Too often American history has been looked at with provincial or even parochial spectacles. We have already seen ways in which the Civil War has been distorted because some of its major aspects have not been taken into account: the vital importance of the Ohio-Mississippi river basin, the significance for military events of policy in addition to strategy and tactics. That event has also been interpreted largely in terms of its significance for the United States and for Americans. In point of fact the Civil War was "the last best hope" of all mankind.

David M. Potter, arguing along lines anticipated by Alexis de Tocqueville and Abraham Lincoln, emphasized that developments in the United States have revealed several paths that civilizations would come to follow in other parts of the world. In a brilliant essay, Potter wrote, ". . . here are two things which the Civil War did: first, it turned the tide which had been running against nationalism for forty years, or ever since Waterloo; and second, it forged a bond between nationalism and liberalism at a time when it appeared that the two might draw apart and move in opposite directions."

The war preserved the nation *unum,* but it likewise left it *pluribus.* To exemplify his thesis, Potter contrasts Lincoln to Otto von Bismarck, Chancellor of Prussia. While we could argue whether Lincoln created a national state or merely saved one, undoubtedly Bismarck was head architect in the fusion of German sovereignty. But conversely, in spite of wartime infractions against civil liberties, the United States that emerged from the war was a country where individual citizens had personal freedoms which never appeared in the centralized Germany of the Hohenzollerns.

Thus one merit of Potter's essay is that he underscores what might be called the global meaning of our Civil War. Another is that he does so in a form that is lucid, without pretensions, and takes only eleven pages.

Document 16-1

Herman Melville published "Shiloh" in 1866 in *Battle-Pieces and Aspects of the War.* This first horrendous clash on the Western front involved a Confederate force led by Albert Sidney Johnston and a Union army commanded by Ulysses S. Grant. In two days of fighting (April 6–7, 1862), over 23,500 men were killed or wounded.

Shiloh   *A Requiem*   *(April, 1862)*

Skimming lightly, wheeling still,
The swallows fly low
Over the field in clouded days,
The forest-field of Shiloh—
Over the field where April rain
Solaced the parched ones stretched in pain
Through the pause of night
That followed the Sunday fight
Around the church of Shiloh—
The church so lone, the log-built one,
That echoed to many a parting groan
And natural prayer
Of dying foemen mingled there—
Foemen at morn, but friends at eve—
Fame or country least their care:
(What like a bullet can undeceive!)
But now they lie low,
While over them the swallows skim,
And all is hushed at Shiloh.

Document 16-2

Clearly Lincoln's two most famous speeches are the Gettysburg Address and the Second Inaugural. They deserve fame. But in being succinct, lucid—and humane—this open letter to Horace Greeley, editor of the nation's most influential newspaper, approaches them in quality. The date is 22 August, 1862, just before the battle of Antietam.

I have just read yours of the 19th. addressed to myself through the New-York Tribune. If there be in it any statement, or assumptions of fact, which I may know to be erroneous, I do not, now and here, controvert them. If there be in it any inferences which I may believe to be falsely drawn, I do not now and here argue against them. If there be perceptable in it an impatient and dictatorial tone, I waive it in deference to an old friend, whose heart I have always supposed to be right.

As to the policy I "seem to be pursuing" as you say, I have not meant to leave any one in doubt.

I would save the Union. I would save it the shortest way under the Constitution. The sooner the national authority can be restored; the nearer the Union will be "the Union as it was." If there be those who would not save the Union, unless they could at the same time save slavery, I do not agree with them. If there be those who would not save the Union unless they could at the same time destroy slavery, I do not agree with them. My paramount object in this struggle is to save the Union, and is not either to save or to destroy slavery. If I could save the Union without freeing any slave, I would do it; and if I could save it by freeing all the slaves I would do it; and if I could save it by freeing some and leaving others alone I would also do that. . . .

I have there stated my purpose according to my view of official duty; and I intend no modification of my oft-expressed personal wish that all men every where could be free.

Document 16-3

Seventy years after the Civil War ended, the Federal Writers' Project of the WPA (Works Progress Administration; see mid-Chapter 27) interviewed hundreds of ex-slaves. An old person's memories of childhood are often inaccurate, but they can also be quite vivid about some episodes. The lad has accompanied his father to a hamlet in South Carolina in December 1864 to pick up the mail for the plantation. They watch a Confederate troop train en route to Savannah to help defend against Sherman's army.

I stand wid my pappy near de long trestle, and see de train rock by. One enjine in front pulling one in de back pushing, pushing, pushing. De train load down wid soldier. They thick as peas. Been so many a whole ton been riding on de car roof. They shout and holler. I make big amaze to see such a lot of soldier—all going down to die.

And they start to sing as they cross de trestle. One pick a banjo, one play de fiddle. They sing and whoop, they laugh; they holler to de people on de ground, and sing out, "Good-bye." All going down to die.

And it seem to me dat is de most wonderful sight I ever see. All them soldier, laughing light, singing and shouting dat way, and all riding fast to battle.

One soldier man say in a loud voice: "Well, boys we going to cut de Yankee throat. We on our way to meet him and he better tremble. Our gun greeze up, and our bayonet sharp. Boys, we going to eat our dinner in hell today." . . .

De train still rumble by. One gang of soldier on de top been playing card. I see um hold up de card as plain as day, when de luck fall right. They going to face bullet, but yet they play card, and sing and laugh like they in their own house . . . All going down to die.

De train pull 'cross de trestle. I stand up and watch um till he go out of sight 'round de bend. De last thing I hear is de soldier laugh and sing . . . All going down to die.

Capitalists, Workers, Farmers

The effulgence of the American economy after the Civil War suggests several theses, but perhaps we should begin with a protagonist. Andrew Carnegie admitted as a young man that he was pushy. Brought by his parents from Scotland to Pittsburgh when he was only twelve, he learned to send teletype. This craft, plus charm, made him personal secretary to Thomas A. Scott, who was superintendent of the Pennsylvania Railroad in the area. Railroad construction was the chief outlet for iron products at the time, so Carnegie's contacts here were indispensable later. As Scott climbed the ladder, so did Andy, becoming division supervisor himself. Early in the war he was an administrator of transport for the Union. Back in Pittsburgh, he worked for the railroad while also investing in the new oil fields of northwestern Pennsylvania. His investment in that sphere, $11,000, showed a profit of nearly $18,000 in the first year. He entered a syndicate that bought drilling rights on a specific farm for $40,000; their ultimate take was over $5 million. Andrew

Carnegie was only 27 years old when he was conscripted for the Union army, and he had to pay $850 for a substitute to go in his stead. He could afford to pay.

The juxtaposition of a popular tune with the financier's own words will emphasize the context in which Carnegie made his fortune. As a boy in Scotland he heard his father, a weaver, sing:

> To the West, to the West, to the land of the free,
> Where the mighty Missouri rolls down to the sea;
> Where a man is a man even though he must toil
> And the poorest may gather the fruits of the soil.

Before he was eighteen, Carnegie had written from America: "Our public Lands of almost unlimited extent are becoming settled with an enterprising people. . . . Pauperism is almost unknown. Everything around us is motion— mind is freed from superstitious reverence for old customs, unawed by gorgeous and unmeaning shows & forms. . . ."

If everybody was in motion, and the number of bodies was growing swiftly, obviously the transportation net would be both thickened and stretched. Carnegie could have settled down to grow with the Pennsylvania Railroad. But he did not. He went, so to speak, behind and beneath the operation of trains, into bridge building, telegraphy, manufacture of sleeping cars. In 1872 he embarked upon the construction of a completely new steel mill. His formulas for managing a company were precise. He emphasized a steady reduction in costs of production: if you succeeded in that sphere, profits were certain. Knock down the charges you paid to railroads for hauling your iron ore and coal and finished steel. Be ready to scrap any equipment, however new, if a tool becomes available that will cut costs per ton of output; in 1898 it was estimated that Carnegie's steel mills were replacing their entire capital plant every three years. He kept the salaries of his executives low, rewarding them by giving out small shares in the ownership. But he always kept a majority interest for himself. If any other administrator tried to thwart his policies, he was forced to withdraw from the firm.

He also had good luck. An omniscient executive might have embarked in the 1870's on a policy of vertical integration, by which a steel mill would have become self-sufficient by owning ore fields and fabricating its own finished products and so on. But Carnegie came to this strategy late and accidentally. He also profited immensely from the boom of the American economy at the close of the century. As late as 1898 the profits of Carnegie Steel were only $10 million. Then came the Klondike gold rush and the Spanish-American War. For 1899 the profits more than doubled. The projected figure for 1900 was $40 million. When Carnegie sold the company as the basis of the new United States Steel in 1901, his 58.5 per cent share brought him $255,639,000. He insisted that it be paid to him in 5 per cent first-mortgage gold bonds.

This concern for payment in *gold* became an obsession with groups of Americans in the last third of the nineteenth century. The preoccupation began during the Civil War. Americans have never been willing to pull their belts tight enough to finance a war while they are fighting it. An inevitable consequence was massive deficits because the federal government was spending more than it collected by taxation. A further result was inflation. Often after a war it has happened that the cost of living has achieved some degree of stability rather quickly. But after the Civil War this did not happen. The runaway inflation was reversed into a sharp drop in the value of goods and services; that is, into a rise in the value of money. In contrast to other postwar epochs, the deflation persisted for decades. Allowing for the fluctuations around this long-term trend—the shorter swings are usually called business cycles and last seven-ten years from trough to trough—the drop in prices continued for about thirty years: 1866–1897.

Part of the explanation of this secular trend lies in the monetary policies of the federal government. The justification of those policies was the need of the wartime Treasury for funds to pay soldiers and buy matériel. Conditions were indeed grim. Two slaughters of Union troops at Bull Run were strong warrant that the conflict would not be brief or easy. So Congress, unwilling to raise taxes to the level necessary to support military procurement, sought for a palatable bundle of fiscal devices. Government became entangled with politics.* The Republicans came to power in 1861 as a fledgling party and a minority party. They had to reach out vigorously to a diversity of groups, while also confronting the fiscal requirements of the sectional division. Even before Lincoln took office, Congress seized on the departure of its Southern members to pass a high protective tariff. The measure can be defended as wartime finance, but it was more than that; it enticed into the Republican fold both managers and workers of the iron industry in Pennsylvania. Having tossed a plum to that sizable voting bloc, the party proceeded to take apples away from them in order to placate other interest groups. The Homestead Act, by which any head of family could receive free 160 acres of federal land if he could meet simple tests, had long been blocked by a coalition of Southern congressmen (who wanted to sell the public lands to raise federal revenue so that the import duties could be kept low) with Eastern industrialists (who wanted to keep a large labor supply in their home counties). In 1862 Congress passed the bill. Giving away public assets instead of selling them was a peculiar way to finance a war, but it was an effective way to build a party.

It was a time of slippery alliances. Search as we may, we cannot see any majority in the entire land that could agree on the urgent issues of the period. Consider the desires for instance of the congressional delegation from Pennsylvania. In general they wanted

---

*Politics and government are always related in a republic, but it is not wise to confuse the two. A statesman as distinguished from a placeman may take an action that will hurt him at the polls. Conversely a deed may be done to help a party even though it will harm the nation.

high tariffs
easy or cheap or soft money
Radical Reconstruction

On the first they had their way; on the other two they did not. Their significance in the Republican party, while great, was not overriding. Or consider the Midwestern Democrats. From the days of Andrew Jackson their party had stood for hard money: now they drifted into the opposite stand and shouted for paper money, "shinplasters."

Paper money there was during the war; the Treasury required it to pay its bills with. True, the federal debt in 1865 that can be laid against the war came to $2.6 billion, whereas the issue of greenbacks was only a sixth of that amount. But this ratio tells nothing about whether the specific purchases made with the paper money were essential to the Union cause, and of course once put in circulation the bills were spent many times. We do not know, but a guess seems plausible. We do know that military necessity swayed many congressmen into voting for the issue of greenbacks which passed as legal tender; that is, sellers were required by law to accept them at their face value, and prices quoted in greenbacks could not legally be higher than prices quoted in gold. Many of the legislators who voted for the measure did so reluctantly. On principle they despised the idea of any paper money that would not be redeemed in solid coin, either gold or silver. Paper money (and the bank or government that issued it) was *per se* crooked. To this type of mind, money could not be separated from morality. Greenbacks were sterile. Decades earlier, a correspondent of Andrew Jackson had condemned the Second Bank of the United States on the grounds that it "had never raised a single bushel of wheat, nor even a single head of cabbage nor a single pumpkin, potato or turnip during its whole existence, nor never will." The Civil War greenbacks continued in circulation until 1879, while the metaphors mounted. Wrote one man: "Paper money is the sum of all iniquity: specie is philosophy, morality and religion." A prominent weekly financial journal fulminated about "a connection between irredeemable paper money and the growth of financial dishonesty since the war."

Clearly, thought congressmen of this ilk, a source was required that could emit money that would be stable in value and redeemable in specie. The result was the National Banking Act of 1863, amended a year later. This structure would be the essence of the country's monetary system for the next half century. Its details are not our concern, but the grave defects must be noted. One was its sectional inequities. To secure a federal charter, a bank had to have at least $100,000 in capital, and twice that in large cities. These conditions were far easier to meet in the East than in Midwest or South. In consequence the volume of bank notes in circulation—and therefore the degree of deflation—varied greatly in different areas. For 1863–1865, the dollars per person circulated in seven Midwestern states averaged $6.36, whereas in New England and New York the circulation was about five times as

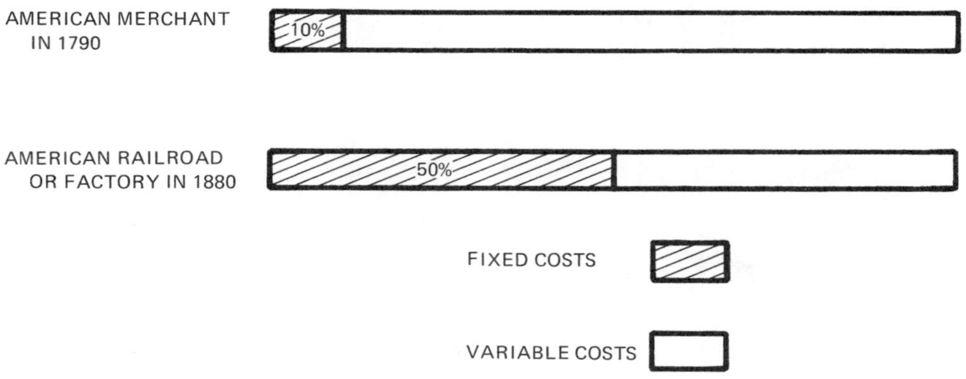

AMERICAN MERCHANT
IN 1790

10%

AMERICAN RAILROAD
OR FACTORY IN 1880

50%

FIXED COSTS

VARIABLE COSTS

FIGURE 17-1. *Fixed and Variable Costs*

The relations charted here are meant to be representative and to signify a shift in proportions (a) over time, and (b) from one type of activity to others. These percentages emphatically do not speak for any specific company, but my researches lead me to think that they are broadly typical of the type of enterprise named. Strangely enough, it is easier to give precise figures for the merchant in the late eighteenth century than for an industrialist in the late nineteenth. Merchants left ledgers that clearly distinguish office expenses and value of ship from value of cargo and pay to crew. In contrast, Standard Oil put up huge refineries and wrote off the entire expenditure as an operating expense; in modern language, the firm did not keep a separate capital account.

Variable costs are those that fluctuate as the output varies. For instance, under slavery the purchase and maintenance of the slaves was not a variable cost; it was a sum that had to be paid no matter what happened to the price of cotton or to the produce of a plantation. But with free labor, wages became a variable cost. Purchase of certain services such as banking and insurance and transportation might also come in this category. Conversely, fixed (otherwise called sunk or overhead) costs must be paid even if the level of production falls to zero. In the early railroad systems, interest on borrowed money was the vital element; repeatedly a company could not pay it and thus was forced into bankruptcy. But salaries to valued managers or indispensable maintenance of physical property are also normally an overhead cost.

The shift from variable to fixed costs is a clear index of the changing structure of business. The importance of the transition was aggravated by improvements in transportation; see Figure 17-4.

FIGURE 17-2. *Frederick Remington,* Fight for the Waterhole

Fight for the Waterhole by Frederic Remington imparts a curiously nostalgic aroma. Done in 1908, the painting seems to be a recollection of glorious days when giants roamed the earth. Partly this effect derives from almost unworldly chiaroscuro contrasts of light and shadow. (The desert indeed can be eerie with such stark lighting.) Also the artist used a large canvas, 27″ × 40″, perhaps to contribute to awareness of the vastness of the landscape.

This interpretation seems to fit the shape of Remington's brief career (1861–1909). Born to a well-to-do family in upstate New York, he was sent to military school and then sent to Yale to study fine arts. A college drop-out at nineteen, he headed for the Great Plains. He worked with trail crews and became adept with horses. The advent of railroads chilled his sense of romance. "I knew the wild riders and the vacant land were about to vanish forever, and the more I considered the subject, the bigger the *forever* loomed. . . . I began to try to record some facts around me, and the more I looked, the more the panorama unfolded." His attempts to immortalize facets of his transient present resulted in more than 2700 pictures. He had been a crony of Theodore Roosevelt, Rudyard Kipling, and Owen Wister, author of *The Virginian* ("When you call me that, smile."). When publisher Hearst sent him to Cuba to portray the Spanish-American War, he wired back that he couldn't find any war. Hearst's answer proved out for both men: "You furnish the pictures; I'll furnish the war."

The subject of this picture is also of special interest. Perhaps no Easterner can truly understand what water means in the West. For a rancher, even the federal land policy that had been devised for great. Seemingly by 1866 the disparity had become worse: $77 for Rhode Island, less than $6 for Illinois. The injustice of the situation was exaggerated because the newer areas needed more national bank notes than the seaboard, not less; the Midwest had not yet progressed nearly as far as the East in using bank deposits and checks as a form of money.

Another defect of the National Banking Act was its class inequities. Discussion of this topic can be subjected to many refinements that are not advisable here, but some usable angles can be suggested. Let us start with two groups within the business community: manufacturers, and bankers. The former had benefited immensely from the wartime inflation; they repeatedly bought raw materials and hired their laborers at a lower level of prices than the one prevailing when they sold their output. Their profits soared. For bankers, this situation might even be reversed; they often made loans in more valuable money than the form that was later repaid to them. After the war, when the level of prices was falling, we encounter a turnabout: bankers win, industrialists lose. Now the latter must buy their inputs at higher prices than what they can get for their outputs. In consequence, as the example of Andrew Carnegie illustrates, they faced a remorseless pressure to cut their costs of production. But for them this strategy became ever harder to implement because a growing percentage of their costs were fixed costs rather than variable costs (see Figure 17-1).

Meanwhile the bankers were in clover. With prices falling, loans they had made earlier were constantly being repaid in more valuable dollars than those they had loaned. Naturally they wanted to preserve this situation. They proclaimed: No repudiation of public debts. No cheap money. All the while, money became more dear. The bankers needed a line by which they could sell to millions of voters a policy that violated the interests of millions of debtors. So the fatcats talked about morality. Listen to a New York banker, son of Albert Gallatin, himself a New York banker who had been a great statesman:

> The demoralization of society progresses steadily under the blighting influence of an irredeemable legal tender paper money. Religion, virtue, and honor decline. Vice becomes fashionable. Gambling prevailes in the marts of trade and the financial centres, from the very necessities of the case, because the slow process of honesty, prudence, forethought and plodding industry are impracticable in occupations subject to the licentious reign of such paper money.

The Gospel of Work was virtually unchallenged in the nation. Man was born to do his duty, and his chief obligation was to drive himself relentlessly.

---

the prairies would not suffice on the plains—not enough water, not enough forage. New federal laws were enacted; a full section of land (640 acres) was taken to be a minimum. Colorado in 1862 had already put through a law regulating the diversion of water from streams into irrigation ditches; other states soon followed. Wyoming in 1888 hit the nail on its head: the water goes wlth the land.

The sanctified traits were three: be industrious, be sober, be frugal (Save). The original sin was sloth. This was the true American creed of our great-grandparents. Before we proceed with an explication of other major features of American industrialization, it might be well to confront some misleading notions. One is embodied in the phrase "social Darwinism." It implies that significant numbers of people thought of society in the vocabulary of biological evolution, thought in terms of the "survival of the fittest," believed it was right that weak people should be stomped under, and disapproved of any public program aimed at aiding the helpless. No evidence has been found to show that many businessmen reasoned in this way. Their self-justification was the right of private property: This company is mine and I'll manage it as I please. It is true that countless Americans regarded poverty not as a social maladjustment but as a penalty for personal vice; this creed, by no means extinct today, did not require an elaborate conceptual apparatus stemming from the evolutionist Charles Darwin.

Another, more complex, question is posed in the title of an article by Thomas C. Cochran: "Did the Civil War Retard Industrialization?" The literature bearing directly on this problem is extensive, and after perusing it I think the answer is definitely No. This judgment applies strictly to the United States as a whole. For the South the war clearly had a negative effect. Much of its productive capacity in farming was nullified. Its labor system was disrupted. Many of its workers, including a sizable segment of its managerial talent, were killed or wounded. Railroads and factories were smashed. Not until the new century would the South overcome the adverse consequences of the conflict. But in North and West the results generally were the reverse. There physical damage to resources was marginal. Secession freed the federal government to launch a series of policies that immensely aided large-scale private enterprise: the National Banks, improvements to rivers and harbors, protective tariffs, subsidies to trans-Mississippi railroads, the Morrill Act for providing research and scientific training to agriculture. But even these policies of the federal agencies seem to pale beside one overwhelming influence: The Civil War produced an unprecedented concentration of liquid capital in the hands of a small number who were determined to make it multiply. They were far from the first who wanted to make a dollar grow into two: it was the scale of their breeding program that commands attention. Today a few connoisseurs may think of the late nineteenth century by recalling outstanding writers or painters, but most Americans will think of Rockefeller's oil refineries and Carnegie's steel mills. Even these titans do not symbolize the age until we take account of Standard Oil profits grasping out in countless directions toward the end of the century. The symbol is J. P. Morgan's access to liquid wealth, to countless numbers of paper counters, to money. Large-scale production needs large-scale investment, and it was a few investment bankers like Morgan who could raise the funds.

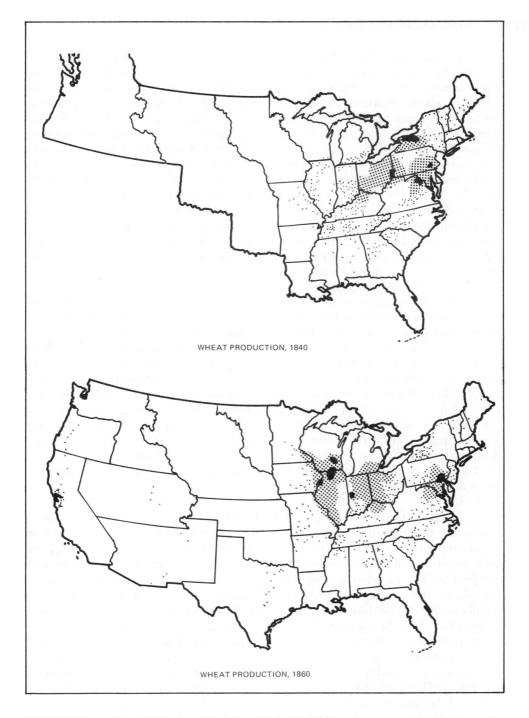

WHEAT PRODUCTION, 1840

WHEAT PRODUCTION, 1860

FIGURE 17-3. *Major Wheat-producing Areas, 1840 and 1860*

Considering the full span from 1865 to 1897, the main groups victimized by the economic-political developments were clusters of farmers. Exceptions to this generalization might well be noted before we diagnose the plight of most agrarians. Well-to-do owners of substantial holdings in the Midwestern area from Pennsylvania to Iowa, for instance, did well right through the hard times; the diary of the proprietor of a mixed farm (mainly corn and hogs) in Illinois reveals him gaily junketing to the Chicago World's Fair during the bleak days of farm depression in 1893. Also, as Henry Nash Smith has demonstrated, Americans remained committed to the ideal of the "family farm" long after it had ceased being practical. This commitment produced some favorable legislation. In spite of all the abuses that occurred, the Homestead Act did enable thousands of men to better themselves on the land. But probably few of these beneficiaries had been poor earlier; they were solid Ohio types who moved to Iowa and became more solid. Likewise the already privileged were those most likely to use the facilities of the new agricultural land-grant colleges.

The dilemma of many farmers began during the Civil War, when the normal American reasons for mechanization were aggravated by the wartime shortage of labor. Operations that could not raise the capital to buy a reaper felt they had to buy one anyway, on credit. The axe did not immediately fall on these downcoming victims at war's end. In 1868 the Democrats sought to win power by appealing to the farm vote. That they did not win was due in part to hatreds lingering from the conflict, in part as already noted (Chapter 16) to the votes of blacks, but also in part to their failure to win enough rural districts. The price of wheat in the election year was $1.46 a bushel—a peak never reached again until 1914. Buoyant prosperity could mitigate where it did not conquer the grievances of the yeomen: concentration of National Bank notes in the East, the power of grain elevators and railroads that reached monopoly in some districts (see Figure 17-4).

If the National Banking policy played a vital part in the long waves of prices, the fluctuations in railroad construction were the chief single factor in the shorter-run business cycles. Wherever a railroad was built, it wrenched the local economy into a new set of occupations. In certain areas it cut sharply into the profitability of what had long been a staple crop; in others it immensely stimulated the production of a crop relatively new to the locale. The first phenomenon can be diagnosed in western New York, where wheat was a staple by the time of the Revolution. But the Genesee valley lost out when the prairies of Minnesota and the Dakotas began to pour into Eastern markets swelling floods of cheap grain. A farmer in Monroe County, New York, estimated that the value of his land had fallen at least 25 per cent in about four years because the rate policies of the railroads favored his Western competitors; to ship identical freight from Rochester to New York City cost more than from Chicago. Bell County, Texas shows how the railroad could virtually create an

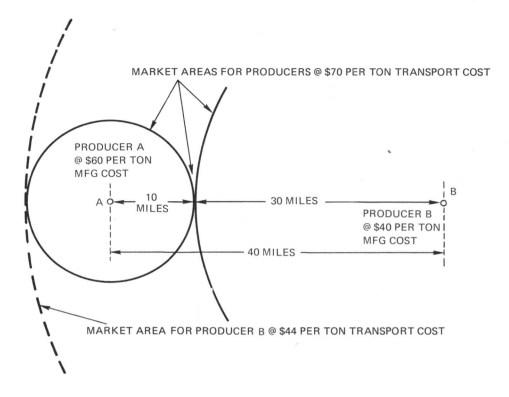

FIGURE 17-4. *Transportation Costs and Scale of Production*

This chart will illustrate the revolutionary effects of the railroad (as a great reducer of shipping costs) on other industries, whether in agriculture or manufacturing. Suppose that independent steel mills are located at A and B, forty miles apart. Since both are located within the United States, we need not allow for tariff or import duties. For mill A the cost of production is $60 a ton, for mill B $40, including a satisfactory profit for each. Transportation is by wagon, and the cost is $1 per ton-mile. The market areas will meet ten miles from mill A, for at that spot each mill can deliver steel at a price of $70 per ton.

Now imagine a railroad built, with the result that shipping costs for iron fall at once to ten cents a ton-mile. Now for only $44 a ton mill B can deliver steel at the doorstep of mill A. The market area of mill B will extend westward even beyond mill A, engulfing almost all A's market area. The latter is driven out of business. But the expansion of mill B will go further yet. Now it is selling more steel. This may open to it what are technically called economies of scale. Perhaps it can afford to buy more efficient machinery, as Carnegie did. Perhaps it can hire higher-priced but more competent executives, as Carnegie did not. Certainly it can drive better bargains in procuring raw materials and workers. Then it might begin to cut its prices. Then it might benefit from what economists call elasticity of demand; that is, as price per unit falls, volume of sales rises more than proportionately. By such processes a world market for steel was created.

industry. In the late seventies the farmers there grew what breadstuffs they used, having them ground into flour at local gristmills. Their cotton crop was small—too expensive to haul by wagon to ports on the Gulf since their community was some 115 miles northeast of Houston. Then came the railroad. In ten years the county's production of wheat fell 75 per cent. To buy flour milled in Minneapolis, the farmers grew and sold cotton; output grew four times in a decade.

No mileage would be gained by clogging this discussion with tables of figures, but it is valuable to show as precisely as may be the wild deviations in the pace at which the railroad network was extended. Here is the rundown on miles of track in operation:

1866	36,801	1879	86,556
1867	39,050	1880	93,262
1868	42,229	1881	103,103
1869	46,804	1882	114,677
1870	52,922	1883	121,422
1871	60,301	1884	125,345
1872	66,171	1885	128,320
1873	70,268	1886	136,338
1874	72,385	1887	149,214
1875	74,396	1888	156,114
1876	76,808	1889	161,276
1877	79,082	1890	166,703
1878	81,747		

Note especially the rate of construction fell markedly when the Philadelphia bank of Jay Cooke overextended itself in promoting the Northern Pacific Railroad and was forced to close in 1873 (Document 17-2). The ensuing depression lasted five years. Then came a huge surge forward: nearly 5,000 miles of new line in 1879, more than 6,000 the next year, 10,000 the next, a record 11,000 the next. Given the resources then available to American society, this table summarizes an unbelievable achievement.

The problems that had been solved were many. Routes had to be located. In this regard the federal government helped; many of the early surveys were done by the Corps of Engineers of the army. Then ownership of those routes had to be contested; the supply was small, and the avenues staked out then across desert and mountain are the ones used now by interstate highways and piggyback trains. The worst bottlenecks were the passes through the Rockies and the Sierras, and a company that seized one in strength could exclude everybody else. Right of way had to be set and rails to be laid, using human muscle rather than bulldozers and jackhammers. Readers who have driven across those arid reaches and craggy ranges in their 300-horsepower cars on freeways that afford them each hour a strawberry soda or a cup of coffee should still entertain a vague appreciation of the skill and valor shown by their forebears a century ago.

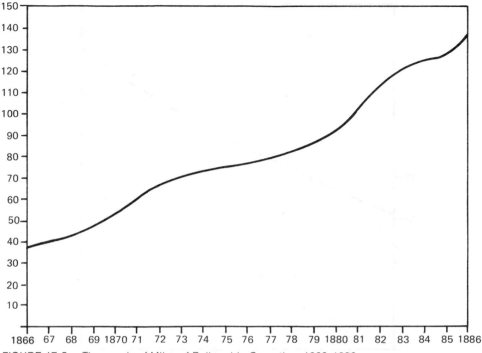

FIGURE 17-5. *Thousands of Miles of Railroad in Operation, 1866–1886*

The task of building railroads could probably not have been accomplished without the twice-blessed immigration from Europe from the Civil War to World War I. This matter will be discussed again in Chapter 19, but one consideration might enter here. Repeatedly these pages have asserted that the economic development of the United States was inevitable, given the psychology of the Europeans who emigrated plus the resources of their new environment. We must push this assertion further. Immigration from the Old World in the late nineteenth century constituted an immense annual subsidy to the growth of the New. In 1877 the population of the nation was 47 million; by 1893 it had grown by 20 million backs, 40 million hands (see Figure 17-6). In most years at least a third of the increase was immigrants. These newcomers were not a cross-section of their homelands, nor of their adopted country either. Year after year more than 60 per cent of the arrivals were male, more than two thirds were aged 15 to 40 (see Figure 21-3). The United States did not receive aged, infants, infirm. It got hearty workers who had been nurtured and educated for years at the expense of some other economy, and had then fled from their patrons to do the bidding of American employers. Socially and

413

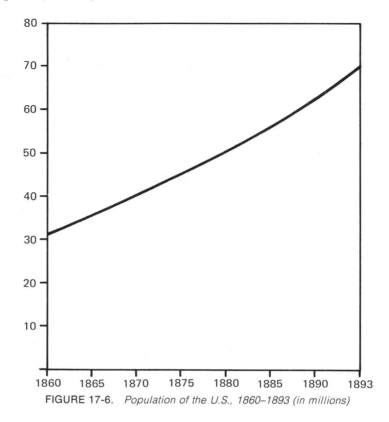

FIGURE 17-6. *Population of the U.S., 1860–1893 (in millions)*

psychologically there are handicaps in being a nation of fugitives, but as a formula for economic growth this pattern cannot be beaten.*

The matter should be stated carefully. Many economists have written as if the phrase "labor shortage" was simply meaningless. By this contention the ultimate reality that could be measured was relative levels of wages; if the hourly or daily rate was increased, the supply of workers would rise. But obviously this argument is silly if we want to consider specific skills; for example, no society early in the twentieth century had any supply of television repairmen, at any level of wages, and so at mid-century workers for the new electronics industries would be hard to find. We also know now by evidence from other cultures that any increase in the hourly wage may be followed by a reduction in the number of hours worked; many a laborer earns what he regards as a traditional day's wage and then goes fishing. Probably the most sweeping generalization that is valid is this: until about the Civil War, the

---

*The gains are greater if your immigrants are above the average in education, as with West Germany since World War II.

chief impact of expensive labor in the United States was to stimulate the substitution of machinery for men, a so-called deepening of capital. Thereafter a cumulative change occurred in the comparative costs of labor and capital, with immigration driving down the value of labor, while massive expenditures in railroads and building construction drove the value of capital upward. This process encouraged a widening of capital; the new facilities being built were identical with the old in that the capital-labor ratio of inputs remained fairly fixed.

In fabricating the railroad net, it was not topography or climate or governmental obstacles or manpower shortages that was most likely to prove lethal; it was usually capital droughts and organizational defects. The business cycles in railroad building recorded above are attributable mainly to attitudes on Wall Street, on State Street (Boston), in the City (London), and in Hamburg and Amsterdam. The collapse of empires like Cooke's could turn the financial markets into dust bowls. New expansions could not be undertaken in panicky times like 1873–1878; the continuation of any construction at all was rather a febrile dance to gain some profit from investments already made. In retrospect, it is clear that most trans-Mississippi trunklines never had a chance to show a profit. There were exceptions. John Murray Forbes with his group based on the Burlington and James J. Hill with his Great Northern showed their genius in creating stable companies that helped to develop countless resources. Hill stated the core problem: You cannot make money hauling empties. The transport web of North America faced difficulties that did not confront the ones of Europe; it built into regions that had no people. Forbes' solution was to link cities: Chicago to Minneapolis, Chicago to Denver. Hill's solution was virtually to return to the technique of the American railroad promoters before the Civil War: to see his roadbed as a feeder into the Twin Cities and to push it forward foot by foot while he was toiling to aid farmers in the regions it serviced. But the exceptions were that. If we added together the interest and dividends paid by all American railroads, and subtracted from that all funds spent by citizens to buy bonds and stock, we almost surely would end with a negative figure. Why were investors so loony, not once, but over and over? Some railroad companies went into receivership a half dozen times, repeatedly writing down the book value of their "securities" (how is that for an ironical word?), not only in the United States, but in the "sophisticated" exchanges of Europe. The best answer now available to us points to the New World as incarnating the Myth of the Garden—an infinite market, beckoning from an idealized world of infinitely expanding frontiers for the rugged-individual family farmer (Chapters 14 and 15).

A major innovation of the railroads, then, was to raise unprecedented amounts of capital, and to tie much of it up in fixed costs (see Figure 17-1). But how could you put together an operation that could meet the claims against that capital, able to pay those fixed costs? Answers devised in other industries

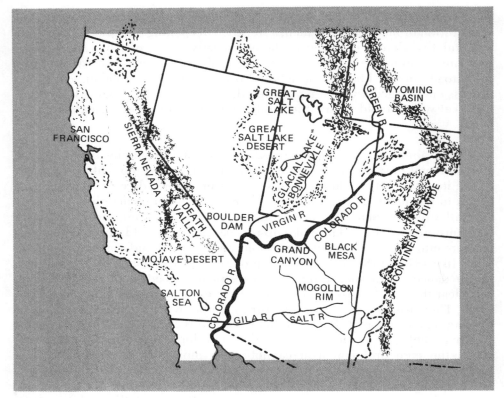

FIGURE 17-7. *The Colorado River System*

were not suitable for enterprises stretching over thousands of miles. Carnegie, for instance, had his producing facilities concentrated around Pittsburgh. He lived in New York where he got detailed reports often; he also made frequent visits to his factories. Seemingly only two of his ranking subordinates had exceptional talents. Standard Oil was at the other pole from this one-man rule. Certainly John D. Rockefeller was the first among equals, but he had a dozen partners who specialized in a phase of the business. An indication of their individual competence is that several of them went on to form their own empires that had nothing to do with petroleum (see mid-Chapter 21 on trusts and conglomerates). For one thing, the geographical sprawl of the company got to be immense, with the site of the oil fields leaping westward from Pennsylvania to the Lima fields in Ohio to the Spindletop well that inaugurated the Texas strikes in 1901. For another, the chief product of the organization was kerosene for lighting—goodbye to whale-oil lamps—and most of it was sold abroad (Document 20-1). Refineries migrated to the seaboard, and a distribution mechanism had to be maintained in Europe and China (Document 21-2). Standard Oil came to be run by a galaxy of committees. But in a significant respect it was not yet "modern"; by current standards its system of accounting must be labelled primitive. In the typical manufacturing firm, the managers still did their jobs by making on-the-spot inspections of the operation.

Even the railroads tried to preserve this principle. But a large system might be running thousands of miles of track. What to do? It was the railroads that pioneered in large-scale organization, and more specifically it was the Pennsylvania that first tried to tackle the problems systematically. One step was to divide the system into geographical divisions about 100 miles long. A superintendent was set over each. No employee could be given instructions by anybody except his immediate superior. Next an adequate breakdown of costs had to be achieved, in terms described by a railroad manager of the time:

> In the consideration of the subject of the cost of railroad transportation it is of the greatest importance to discriminate between the expenditures which vary with the amount of work performed and those which are entirely independent thereof. The latter form so large a proportion of the total operating expenses of railroads that it becomes impossible to make the *amount of work performed* a criterion or measure of the cost.

Thus emerged, but ever so gradually, such crucial ideas in accounting as the discrimination of fixed from variable costs, of capital budget from operating expenses (Figure 17-1). Further innovations in corporate organization and the correlate accounting will be examined in Chapter 21.

The myth of rags to riches has also been subjected to solid investigations. This problem has been studied from two perspectives: How far was the myth believed? How far was the myth an accurate rendition of reality? The answer to the first question is clear: Very far. Unless we are willing to believe that most people are fools, and I am not, the fact of its currency suggests that the desire to become a self-made man had considerable foundation in fact. But the research of the last twenty-five years shows that we should not exaggerate this substance. The poor lad from the farm was far less likely to make good than the middle-class boy in the city. One study took 190 corporate executives of 1900. When these men were born, about 1850, 83 per cent of all Americans lived in rural areas, but only 40 per cent of the executives were born and reared in that setting. Businessmen or professionals had been the parents of 86 per cent of the leaders of 1900. Nearly one of two in the general population had at least one foreign-born parent; among the sample, one in five. Four of every five business leaders were of British ancestry, and the majority were of old American families. Another survey treats only of the presidents of textile firms (note that this office was usually honorific, as the chief executive officer was normally the treasurer). The Civil War marks a rather sharp break. Before the conflict, if a man did not become president of a company by age 45, he was not likely to reach that goal at all. He was probably a rich Boston merchant who had diverted some of his capital into textile stocks, and the chances were that he stayed active in other forms of enterprise—in short, he was a general entrepreneur. For this industry at least, the postwar pattern was changed. Half of the presidents after the war did not gain that eminence until they had passed age 55. Often such men had inherited their fortunes. They were not smuggled into textiles from the general business community but had risen within the industry. Typically they had retired from active business concerns, and did not often take a hand in managing the firm over which they honorifically presided.

Many companies could ride favorably through stormy economic forces if they enjoyed crucial counterbalances in the struggle against the sagging level of prices. On the supply side, probably the two most important forces driving prices downward were the rapid advance of technology and the growing number of firms that competed fiercely. But on the demand side, consumers were present in growing numbers. More important, they not only had money but they were accessible because they were concentrated in cities as never before. Metropolises in the East grew rapidly: Manhattan from 1,911,692 in 1880 to more than 2.5 million in 1890; in the same decade Philadelphia from 847,170 to 1,046,964. But the real boom towns were in the Midwest:

	1880	1890
Chicago	503,125	1,099,850
Minneapolis	46,887	164,738
St. Paul	41,473	133,156
Kansas City	55,781	132,710
Denver	35,029	106,773

In ten years each of these cities except Chicago approximately tripled, while that metropolis doubled and would do so again by 1900.

We still do not have an adequate conceptualization of the processes involved in such headlong urban development. But we might hazard a few guesses, partly to illustrate how the Turner thesis—that the frontier experience has been the dominant theme in American history—does not limit its application solely to rural areas and farmers. What confronts us here is a phenomenon that has been aptly labelled "sequential growth." Many areas were opened long before a sturdy yeoman went near them, by a military post, by a mining venture, a lumber camp, a railroad junction point. A commercial-residential town appeared to sell goods and services to these first settlers. Then, and perhaps only then, farmers moved in to provision the town. Any new region offers quite a few opportunities for "one-for-all investment": roads and civic buildings, business centers, housing subdivisions. Opportunities are present for bankers and real-estate men, doctors and lawyers, scoundrels eager to dip to their elbows in any old public coffers. Land values might grow even more rapidly than population, and consequent profits can be reinvested in processing plants. This company builds a sawmill, that one a smelter; another begins to package oatmeal. Extension of job options will suck in more people. The sequence feeds on itself. Literally, a city reaches the stage when it grows because its inhabitants take in each other's washing. How do we identify that stage? Again, we do not yet know. For the late nineteenth century, my hunch whispers that about 50,000 people was the starting point for "take-off."

The expansion of demand was also spurred by what today's economists call the multiplier. Some students claim to have a hard time grasping the idea, but it is quite simple. Start from a government that spends money to buy goods and services (Government Expenditures, GE) or a company that buys new plant or equipment (purchases of second-hand goods do not count; Investment, I). These outlays will be income for others. They will spend in turn a portion of their increased receipts. So will the next round of recipients, and so on. Before these increments have flattended out to zero, the first I or GE will have been multiplied several times through a number of transactions. For the United States since World War II, a consensus holds that the multiplier has fluctuated around 3. This figure is probably valid for the late nineteenth century also. To comprehend how this statement can be made, an additional consideration must be introduced. Statisticians define Savings (S) simply: if you take Income (Y) and subtract from it the portion spent in the current time period for consumer goods and services (C), the balance is S (note that if your grandfather leaves a bequest that you put in your savings account, this is not a saving of personal income over consumer expenses, and so you have not committed S). It seems reasonable to assume that as income is distributed more equally, C will increase and S will decrease: poor people do not save as high a proportion of their income as do rich people. The best available studies conclude that in the United States, the distribution of personal incomes after taxes has not changed much if at all in the last fifty years. Maybe this ratio cannot be projected backwards in time indefinitely, but the proposition remains to be proved, and it is likely that the raw materials do not exist to reach a conclusive answer—ever. We can say this: in dollar terms, even the spending for railroad extension was less than that for construction of buildings. As these initial payments worked through the economy, their impact multiplied.

What is vital here is to grasp for a hold on the interaction of these processes, one with another. Manufacturers, for instance, would have been in a tighter vise without the rapid multiplication of urban buyers. So would farmers: the 10,000 acre bonanza farms growing wheat in the Dakotas would have made no sense whatever in an economy of self-sufficient yeomen (Figure 29-3). Each of these segments was affected in a contradictory way by the inauguration of a national railway network. The fall in transportation costs enabled an industrialist to reach out farther for more customers; it also exposed him to new competitors from distant locations. A Texas planter could specialize in cotton, at great economies of scale, but he also had to fight in the markets of the world against cotton from several other countries.

419

It remains to look at some effects of these developments on employees, especially industrial workers. Again, a couple of preliminary generalizations seem advisable. Although some solid investigations have been made, particularly since World War II, the study of the history of American laborers has been rather wretched. Basic difficulties stem from the influence of the so-called Wisconsin School, at the state University there. Some of their work is still useful; no scholar in the field can ignore the ten-volume *Documentary History of American Industrial Society* (1910–1911), but their efforts to theorize were deplorable. First, they concentrated on the history of trade unions, even though the significant question about American labor until the last forty years is the reverse: Why were so few unions organized? Then too, though substantial impediments lay in the path of industrialists' desires, they wrote of fifty years as if they were an unrestricted "age of the employers." In this milieu, they argued, the watchwords of the unions were three: More. Here. Now. They contended that this "business unionism" with its narrow focus on higher wages and shorter hours and job security was the ultimate in wisdom; never think of tomorrow, only of today. In plain truth, such business unionism before World War II had nothing to offer to the great majority of employees.

It is true that in times of crisis, capitalists could sometimes invoke the overpowering force of some government. We might begin with a famous episode—the Haymarket bombing in Chicago, because it was both sensational at the moment and also had repercussions that resounded for decades. The city, as the railroad hub of the nation, was also a booming industrial center. Its magnates tended to be hard-nosed; its laboring elements had a vociferous anarchist wing. Labor relations were tense and often approached violence. In 1886 a lockout occurred at the huge McCormick Harvesting Machine (reapers) factory. It reopened with new, non-union labor. Former employees continued to picket the gates. A widespread movement was trying to win an eight-hour day and had set May Day as the deadline for enforcement of the demand; it was estimated that one of every eight residents of Chicago was participating in the campaign. At the McCormick plant on May 3 a riot started. Police came. Two men were killed. A meeting to protest the police action was called to assemble at a square near downtown, the Haymarket. Affairs were peaceable. But nearly 200 police marched up in serried ranks. Somebody tossed a bomb among them. The police then fired into the crowd. Of the officers, the bomb killed seven, wounded 67. The toll among the audience is not known. Subtle discriminations are not made in times of panic. A police dragnet hauled in every anarchist to be found, plus many who were quite innocent. Eight men were brought to trial for the bombing. All were convicted. One committed suicide in his cell. Four were hanged. Three were imprisoned, and of them I shall tell more later (early Chapter 20 on Governor Altgeld).

This stark recital of a noisy and tragic episode should not obscure the fact that urban workers were not being ruthlessly crushed by some juggernaut of capitalists allied with governments. Laborers had their defenses, ways of fighting back. Also they had ways of evening the score; probably the most important of these was theft. Doubtless many employees at all times and places have stolen from the boss. This topic so far as I know has not been systematically studied, but there are many areas where it could be. We find numerous instances in the putting-out system of eighteenth-century Britain; slaves indulged in it; a famous book told of *White Collar Crime* in the United States (How was anybody ever so naive as to think that you are more likely to steal if you have a black face, or a blue collar?); soldiers have always thought that public property was fair game; the incentive to pilfer becomes more intense when a small electronics part can be sold in the black market for hundreds of dollars; in two major cities a ring of police has been caught with a warehouse filled with television sets.

Workers had more public weapons. The researches of Herbert Gutman have revealed their variety, especially in smaller industrial or mining towns. A case study is presented by Paterson, New Jersey. In 1877, after four gruelling years of depression, the silk-ribbon mills announced a 20 percent wage cut and other irritating stipulations. This brought the largest strike in the record of the town; 2,000 workers shut down the plants. The local Board of Trade, controlled by the biggest owners, screamed that "the laws of the land are treated with contempt and trampled upon by a despotic mob." One employer offered to pay for a private militia; another proclaimed that the strike leaders should be "taken out and shot." This bluster availed little. Shopkeepers gave credit to strikers and raised funds for them. While the newspapers were critical of the strikers also, they urged the employers to use "conscience as well as capital." With this tone in the community, public officials did not yield to the demands of the owners. The mayor with exemplary discretion used his police force only to prevent open violence. He owned a small spindle factory himself, and headed a local bank. The aldermen were skilled craftsmen, professionals, retailers, no workers or big owners. Even though they were mostly Democrats while the mayor was a Republican, they commended his "wise and judicious course." Similarly local courts stalled in deciding cases brought against strikers. After the shutdown had lasted for ten weeks, it was settled by a compromise in which the companies rescinded the wage reduction. Likewise in many other towns, owners could not always have their own way.

Especially fortunate workers did not even need to form a trade union in order to find a hothouse within which they could grow. Let us take as an example again the McCormick works in Chicago. Save for a brief period when the Knights of Labor penetrated its walls, the only organization was among the molders who were a mere 10 per cent of the labor force. This small band with a developed skill won repeated advances in their conditions. Remarkedly, these gains spread to the less skilled, unorganized employees. Just before the Haymarket episode the molders' union was destroyed in a strike, and the craftsmen were replaced by common labor using automatic molding machines. But the wages of unskilled employees did not fall; just the contrary. Their hourly rate remained at 15 cents while the cost of living declined. Real wages in 1896 for this group were more than double what they had been in 1860. Two influences seem to explain this notable result: The firm's executives feared that pay cuts might bring a return of unions. Perhaps more vital were the attitudes of the founder's widow, who held a major interest in the company. She feared that an earlier series of violent strikes had harmed her family's "good name" in the community; she wanted no more. Her pressure was frequently toward peace.

The above case studies should be taken as indications that local conditions could vary greatly. But they must be seen as qualifications. The generalization is simple: The late nineteenth century knew an enormous disparity in bargaining power. Speaking of collective disputes as a genus, employers nearly always had the upper hand, a topic to which we will return in Chapters 20 and 23. Even the gradations we have outlined show only that employees could often neutralize the power of the state; almost never could they use it to serve their own ends.

Nor should the relation of molders to semiskilled at the McCormick factory be understood as typical. In the sphere of labor history that I have studied the most closely—the railroad brotherhoods—the companies consistently pinched back from the pay envelopes of the less skilled what they had previously bestowed on the "aristocrats of labor." This label was applied to the locomotive engineers, who in many junction points strutted about with their gold chains across their serge vests, ranking with the banker and the lawyer and the doctor as the leading citizens in town.* At the other pole, the switchmen and the gandy dancers often did not earn enough to maintain their families in decency. Another useful insight into the railroad brotherhoods is to remember that they did not begin as collective-bargaining agents at all; they originated as fraternal and burial societies. They are classic instances of associations that originated for certain purposes and later were diverted to another function altogether. An analogy will be seen in the Patrons of Husbandry, commonly called the Grangers (see Chapter 20). Burial societies were likewise common in black neighborhoods: if a person cannot live with dignity, he should get some when he dies.

By this devious route we return to the central if usually ignored question raised above: Why were so few unions organized? (Dissenters can wave airily at the brotherhoods and the cigarmakers and the carpenters, but the staggering truth remains.) The core of the answer is surely that ancient cliché: the opportunities of American life. Most men, given a plausible chance to make good on their own, see no reason to make personal sacrifices in a common

---

*The shortage of many skills coupled with the new superabundance of unskilled workers brought immense differences in pay. At the Homestead works, the typical laborer got at most $1.50 a day, a puddler got $17. I do not mean to denigrate either the skill of or the health hazards to puddlers—in Sheffield, England, they could expect to die by age 31, and the life expectancy in the United States was probably little better—but common laborers also were working in a hazardous industry.

cause. They will go it alone, as individuals; they downright refuse to unite, and no amount of rhetoric matters.

These considerations bring us to a seeming conundrum: Why has it so often been the skilled workers who have taken the lead in organizing trade unions? I think this enigma can be dissolved. Many commentators have been misled by their attachment to the phrase "occupational ladder." By and large, this metaphor is false; a happier term would be "occupational tree." Just as it is nearly impossible to move from noncommissioned to commissioned rank in the army, so was it nearly impossible to move from a blue-collar to a managerial job. Imagine a tree with the branches inclined upward from the trunk; call the lowest branch I, the next highest II, etc. On each branch call the lowest job (nearest the trunk) A, the next highest B, etc. Promotion along any branch is largely automatic and depends on seniority (unless you grossly offend your superiors). But to move from I-Z to II-A is a dreadful task; you will probably need a patron on branch II to drop a rope and pull you up. How does this schema apply to the formation of trade unions? The workers at point Z are the most skilled workers on that limb. They can no longer hope to advance as individuals; they expect to live out their lives at point Z, and none will get ahead unless point Z moves upward. So they form a craft union, which is concerned solely with the position of point Z. They do not aim to lift the entire branch, but only to tilt its end upward. This may force the rest of the branch downward; sometimes, however, (see Chapters 20, 26), skilled workers may make common cause with unskilled to improve working conditions in a whole industry.

Although the impact of the Civil War on the South was in time moderated, the four years of battle had lasting consequences in the North that can fairly be called revolutionary. The inflated prices of wartime, added to the swelling market for foodstuffs, uniforms, and munitions represented by the Union military purchases, resulted in giant pools of liquid capital. These funds could be multiplied further by the growing number of commercial banks. Aggressive capitalists, with their enlarged resources, were not long to push railroads across the Mississippi and over the plains to the Pacific. While bankers supplied the funds for these ventures, new iron and steel mills produced the rails and locomotives and freight cars. Other entrepreneurs seized on the discovery of petroleum to start refineries for producing kerosene for lamps. As for tobacco, whiskey, wheat, sugar—processors of these farm products reached toward monopoly and gained huge profits. But the men who grew those raw materials, the farmers, were the most numerous group of victims of the total process. Prices of agricultural crops, especially the great staples of wheat and cotton, fell steadily from 1865 to 1896. Many farmers were ground down against the anvil of their fixed debts. The squeeze was aggravated by the monetary and banking policies of the federal government.

Business interests were the guiding force in the national capital, in state governments, at city halls. This interlacing of commerce with politics was particularly glaring during some of the violent labor strikes that rocked the period. In response, trade unions in many industries were likely to begin with the most skilled craft. It would hardly exaggerate to say that capitalists, including thousands of small owners, got ahead rapidly at the expense of other segments of the society.

SOME NOTABLE EVENTS

1864 George M. Pullman builds first sleeping car for railroads.

1865 Union Stockyards in Chicago open, Dec. 25.

1866 National Labor Union organized, Aug. 20.

1868 George Westinghouse patents air brake for railroads.

1869 First transcontinental railroad: Union Pacific and Central Pacific connect near Ogden, Utah, May 10.
Black Friday on New York Stock Exchange, Sept. 24.

1870 Standard Oil founded, Jan. 10.

1871 Chicago fire causes losses estimated at $196 million.

1873 Slaughterhouse Cases.
Jay Cooke & Company closes, Sept. 1 (Document 17-2).

1874 National Grange issues Declaration of Purpose, Feb. 4.

1875 Resumption of specie payments, Jan. 14; (see mid-Chapter 18).
Bessemer steel making at Pittsburgh initiated by Andrew Carnegie.

1876 Telephone patented by Alexander Graham Bell.
Munn v. *Illinois* asserts state power to regulate railroads for the public interest.

1877 Railroad strikes paralyze area from Baltimore to St. Louis.

1878 Knights of Labor adopt constitution.
F. W. Woolworth opens his first successful 5 & 10.
Bland-Allison Act, Feb. 28; vetoed by Hayes.

1880 U.S. census: 50,155,783 (28.2% urban).
Incandescent light patented by Thomas Alva Edison.

1886 Haymarket Square riots in Chicago.
American Federation of Labor is founded.

1887 Daimler develops first functioning automobile.

1890 Ocala Demands of the farmers' protest movements, December.

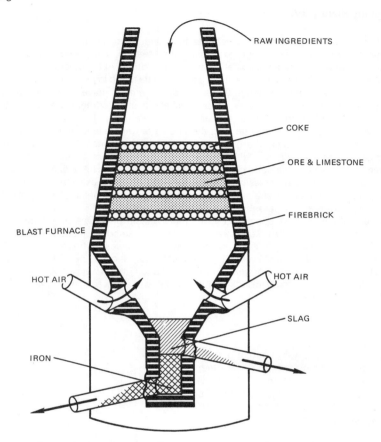

RAW INGREDIENTS

COKE

ORE & LIMESTONE

FIREBRICK

BLAST FURNACE

HOT AIR

HOT AIR

SLAG

IRON

To make steel it is necessary first to convert iron ore to solid, or pig, iron. This is done in the blast furnace. Iron ore, limestone, and coke (a coal product, almost pure carbon) are placed in the furnace, and a blast of hot compressed air is forced through the mixture. This ignites the coke. The heat then melts the iron which slowly trickles down to the bottom of the furnace. But iron ore is not pure iron; it is necessary to rid it of foreign matter. The hot furnace does this by burning the impurities, and forcing them to unite with the oxygen in the compressed air. They thus become oxides, which are lighter than the molten iron, and float on top of it in the form of slag. The slag is skimmed off, to be used for a number of purposes, before the iron is discharged from the bottom of the furnace. The whole process takes from three to six hours, and a modern furnace will produce 500–1200 tons of pig iron and 200–500 tons of slag each day.

Pig iron has a 3–4 per cent content of carbon, which makes it brittle and inflexible. Steel-making is the process of removing this carbon, as well as certain other impurities, most commonly sulphur and phosphorus. In the open hearth furnace, a mixture of gas and air is forced over the pig iron and burned. At a temperature of 1800° C the iron will melt, and the carbon will "burn." When a substance "burns" it combines with oxygen, and becomes an oxide; oxides of the impurities found in pig iron are light, and will float on the iron, which has now become steel. They can then be skimmed off, just as the slag was skimmed off the pig iron, before the steel is discharged from the furnace.

Ways to Study History XVII

Trace a family. Quite apart from the schools that stem from the theories of Sigmund Freud, psychologists for decades have sought to analyze child-rearing, interplay of heredity with environment, effective modes of schooling, social control of individuals. At the other extreme of the range of levels of abstraction, genealogists have spent a zillion years trying to prove that a certain person had seventeen eminent ancestors. Although the latter approach might have its occasional uses, nearly always it is just antiquarianism or, worse, pride. Most efforts at melodramatic psychohistory, such as a recent biography of Senator Charles Sumner, have been equally childish.

But solid reasons exist for pondering the course of generations. In perusing the economic history of North America, I think of a good friend of mine. His grandfather was a Canadian farmer north of Toronto. His father left home at 15 and went to Providence, Rhode Island, where he took work as a machinist. When the automobile boom started he was prepared; he became president of a parts plant. My friend went to a progressive college, then shifted to a business education in graduate school. After founding a successful company he became chairman of the Management Department of a large state university. His daughter is a pure intellectual.

Similar patterns can be uncovered in the more distant past. One of my favorite books was edited by F. O. Matthiessen, *The James Family* (1947). The American founder was a poor boy who became one of the richest men in the land: fast freight companies, railroads, land speculation; the son made no money whatever and wrote religious tracts; two grandsons became a great psychologist and a great novelist. To me another gem is Aubrey C. Land, *The Dulanys of Maryland* (1955), which does as much as a book could do to show how political power and wealth were used to escalate each other in colonial America.

Document 17-1

About a decade after the war ended, a growing number of blacks emigrated from the Deep South to such states as Kansas. Frederick Douglass, while asserting the full right of Negroes to live wherever they chose, in 1879 questioned some qualities of this movement.

It does not appear that the friends of freedom should spend either time or talent in furtherance of this exodus as a desirable measure, either for the North or the South. If the people of this country cannot be protected in every state of the Union, the government of the United States is shorn of its rightful dignity and power, the late rebellion has triumphed, the sovereignty of the nation is an empty name, and the power and authority in individual states is greater than the power and authority of the United States. . . .

The colored people of the South, just beginning to accumulate a little property, and to lay the foundation of family, should not be in haste to sell that little and be off to the banks of the Mississippi. The habit of roaming from place to place in pursuit of better conditions of existence is never a good one. A man should never leave his home for a new one till he has earnestly endeavored to make his immediate surroundings accord with his wishes. The time and energy expended in wandering from place to place, if employed in making him a comfortable home where he is, will, in nine cases out of ten, prove the best investment. No people ever did much for themselves or for the world without the sense and inspiration of native land, of a fixed home, of familiar neighborhood, and common associations. The fact of being to the manor born has an elevating power upon the mind and heart of a man. It is a more cheerful thing to be able to say, I was born here and know all the people, than to say, I am a stranger here and know none of the people.

It cannot be doubted that, in so far as this exodus tends to promote restlessness in the colored people of the South, to unsettle their feeling of home, and to sacrifice positive advantages where they are or fancied ones in Kansas or elsewhere, it is an evil. . . .

Document 17-2

As the Civil War financier Jay Cooke learned to his detriment, it was perilous to allow your personal fortune to become entangled in the financing of a railroad. The winning gambit was to use somebody else's money, whether federal funds that you borrowed or grants given outright by a local government or receipts from selling bonds to outside investors. This description was given in a speech in San Francisco as early as 1873.

For many years it has not been the American fashion for the owners of railroads to put their own money into their construction. If it had been it would have insured a more conservative and businesslike use of that species of property. The favorite plan has been to get grants of land, and loans of credit from the General Government; guarantees of interest from the State governments; subscriptions and donations from counties, cities and individuals; and upon the credit of all this, issue all bonds that can be put upon the market; make a close estimate as to how much less the road can be built for than the sum of these assets; form a ring . . . for the purpose of constructing the road, dividing the bonds that are left; owning the lands, owning and operating the road until the first mortgage becomes due and graciously allowing the Government to pay principal and interest upon the loan of her credit, while "every tie in the road is the grave of a small stockholder." Under this plan the only men in the community who are absolutely certain not to contribute any money are those who own and control it when it is finished. The method requires a certain kind of genius, political influence, and power of manipulation, and furnished one clew to the reason why railroads "interfere in politics." The personal profit upon this enterprise is not a profit upon capital investment, but the result of brain work—administrative talent they call it—in a particular direction.

Document 17-3

This payroll from the carding room of a cotton mill in Holyoke, Massachusetts, is interesting in several respects. The list of names (portions omitted) shows that the so-called New Immigration from southern and eastern Europe had begun to flood New England towns by 1889, the date of the ledger, that supervisory personnel and craftsmen were commonly of northern European stock, that a large discrepancy existed between pay of skilled and unskilled. All employees worked ten hours a day; most earned less than a dime an hour. This is considerably below the earnings of the average worker in the nation's industries, who is reported to have gotten $486 in 1890.

Names	Total Hours	Price	Amounts
Overseer			
J. W. Doran	60	40	24.00
		. . .	
Grinders			
J. Danforth	60	15	9.00
G. Meinay	60	15	9.00
J. Manning	60	15	9.00
F. Downie	60	15	9.00
M. Morrison	60	15	9.00
Geo Pray	60	15	9.00

Names	Total Hours	Price	Amounts
Railways and Drawing			
J. Laternak	*60*	*7*	*4.20*
P. Yourka	*60*	*8*	*4.80*
J. Lapoint	*60*	*7*	*4.20*
A. Garcoa	*60*	*7*	*4.20*
M. Wodjikoski	*60*	*7*	*4.20*
N. Ash	*60*	*7*	*4.20*
D. Chomerni	*60*	*7*	*4.20*

Document 17-4

Modern retailing took its origins in the decades after the Civil War. The spate of goods emerging from farm and factory was screaming to be sold, with the result that new institutions were devised. Urbanites got the department store, Macy's in New York and Marshall Field in Chicago. Rustics got mail-order merchandising as symbolized by the Sears Roebuck catalog. Indispensable to these drives was advertising. Earlier merchants had posted simple notices in the newspapers, but they had not known the hard-sell except by word of mouth. Now it appeared in print, and spearheading the innovation were patent-medicine producers. This ad is a manifestation of do-it-yourself, the American way. It also reveals a lack of historical knowledge among those who speak of the "new" drug usage.

ERRORS OF YOUTH

Sufferers from
Nervous Debility,
Youthful Indiscretions,
Lost Manhood,

BE YOUR OWN PHYSICIAN

. . . Perfectly pure ingredients must be used.

Cocain (from Erythroxlon coca) 1 drachm.
Jerubebin 1-2 drachm.
Hypophosphite quinia, 1-2 drachm.
Geisemin, 8 grains
Ext. igratiac amarac (alcoholic), 2 grains
Ext. Septandra, 2 scruples
Glycerin, q.s.
    Mix

. . . by remitting us $3 in post office money order, or registered letter, a securely sealed package in its pure state will be sent by return mail from our private laboratory. . . .

The Politics and Foreign Relations of a World Power

Half of this chapter will state some reasons for regarding the United States already by 1850 as a world power. But the point in contention might well be exposed here, before we observe the jousts between the national parties. The argument that economic self-interest had little to do with American policy abroad in the waning years of the century has usually had a corollary: that suddenly in 1898, as from the brow of Jove, the United States appeared on a global stage as a lusty infant. Indeed, a recent book with the subtitle *The Emergence of America as a Great Power* advances just this theme. It would be hard to miss the mark by more. Allowing for personal preferences in terminology, the argument below will resemble that given above opening Chapter 9. The United States was a recognized power as soon as it voted for independence on 2 July, 1776. (How can anybody doubt it who has read the correspondence of Vergennes at the time?) It was a world power by the Oregon Treaty of 1846. Only a great power could have forced France out of Mexico at a time when the United States had just finished the Civil War. In the years from

1850 to 1892 the United States had a confrontation on alien shores with every other strong nation in the world—and never came off second-best.

Without much distortion, federal politics in the postwar era could be summarized in one word: stalemate. However, the topic needs more explication than one word. The quadrennial (mock?) battles between the national parties were not all of politics. An informed study of politics at the state level in New York shows that the issues that swayed voters were not those great problems of monetary policy or the tariff or anti-monopoly. They were purification of elections and the stifling of alcoholic beverages (see Document 17-4). Most jurisdictions before about 1890 had no secret vote (the Australian ballot); the polls were still conducted by openly declaring your choices. The virtuous Protestant citizens, and for once they were right, thought this procedure abetted corruption. They also thought that liquor was evil. The extremists wanted prohibition; that is, illegalization of all alcoholic drink. Way back in 1851 Maine had taken the lead in banning the sale of liquor; twelve states did the same in the next four years. This mania for sanctifying your neighbors swept the nation. But to a great degree it was sham. As hooch was suppressed, patent medicines thrived, and some were highly alcoholic. One nostrum vender was informed by the Commissioner of Internal Revenue in 1883: ". . . to draw the line nicely, and fix definitely where the medicine may end and the alcoholic beverage begin, is a task which has often perplexed and still greatly perplexes revenue officers, and especially where a preparation contains so large a proportion of alcohol as yours does." One especially popular brew, Peruna, was 28 per cent alcohol; at least one Peruna alcoholic was reported to be a respected member of the Women's Christian Temperance Union. As one aspect of their high-powered merchandising, manufacturers put their swill in ornate bottles; you could drink out of a bust of George Washington or a log cabin or an Indian maid. Few of these bottles remain; one researcher speculates that people destroyed them so that they could buy new, full, replacements without having their neighbors see the incriminating relics. On such foolishness as this did the fate of office-seekers depend.

The emergence of new, often local or regional, issues caused a fragmentation of national politics that seemed as severe as that which preceded the Civil War. The Prohibition (of liquor) party put forward a presidential candidate for the first time in 1872. Four years later the Greenback party had its maiden run for the office. Greenbackers were often farmers, and in the Old Northwest they often belonged to the Patrons of Husbandry. One consequence was the so-called Granger laws, enacted by states to set maximum prices that could be charged by such companies as railroads and grain elevators. The fracas brought one major and enduring benefit: it produced a decision by the United States Supreme Court as incisive as any that tribunal has ever handed down. A recurrent problem in American history has been to fix the role of the federal judiciary in the national polity. That question was faced squarely by Chief Justice Morrison R. Waite in *Munn v. Illinois* (1876). His opinion has been crystallized in a phrase—judicial restraint. At issue was a statute that placed a ceiling on rates levied by grain elevators. One firm protested that the regulation took away its property without due process of law and thus violated the Fourteenth Amendment. The Chief Justice replied in quiet and unpretentious terms:

> . . . When one becomes a member of society, he necessarily parts with some rights or privileges which, as an individual not affected by his relations to others, he might retain. . . .
>
> Common carriers exercise a sort of public office, and have duties to perform in which the public is interested. . . . Enough has already been said to show that, when private property is devoted to a public use, it is subject to public regulation. . . .
>
> We know that this is a power which may be abused; but that is no argument against its existence. For protection against abuses by legislatures the people must resort to the polls, not to the courts. . . .

Bravo! But, at the time, inspirations were few, tensions were many.

Every area had its localized causes of unrest. Southern whites had to grapple with the failure of their lost cause, their war for sectional independence, their struggle to sustain slavery and injustice. The effort, not easy, has not ended; as a boy in Memphis I was nurtured on horror stories of Sherman's soldiers stealing chickens and ripping up featherbeds (Why so many decades of preoccupation with cheap cotton ticking?). A fine essay that tries to differentiate "the Southern character" from that of other white Americans gives four differentiae. Of the four, two originated with the Civil War. One is a visceral sense of what it feels like to be poor; prior to the conflict, a typical Southron was not impoverished below his counterpart in the North. Another was personal knowledge of what it means to lose a war.* In addition to the economic and social and psychological strains of the postwar years, secessionists had to put up with legal stresses. Thousands were forced to endure oaths of loyalty to the United States. They had to meet the accusation that the Confederacy was a bastard, illegitimate from its conception. This matter became explicit in the highest court, *Texas* v. *White* (1869). During the war the state government had owned some federal bonds. It sold them to raise funds to pay for Confederate supplies. After the war, the Reconstruction government brought suit against the buyers on the grounds that the secessionist government was not sanctioned and the sale had been therefore illegal. The Chief Justice agreed, pointing out that as rebels during the war, Texans had claimed no interest to participate in Washington's Congress, nor in its courts. In his words: "All admit that, during this condition of civil war, the rights of

---

*It is trite, but important, to mention that several million Americans in all reaches of the land have had some insight into the meaning of being conquered. Some forms of education are much more costly than others.

the State as a member, and of her people as citizens of the Union, were suspended. The government and the citizens of the State, refusing to recognize their constitutional obligations, assumed the character of enemies, and incurred the consequences of rebellion." Here is the authoritative doctrine on secession. The wartime regime in Texas had no legal authority to sell the bonds or to do any act whatever; it had no constitutional validity.

Southern blacks also had legal problems. The Civil Rights Act of 1875 had seemed to prohibit inns, public conveyances, and places of public amusement from discriminating against Negroes. Some believed that the law meant what it seemed to say. But when the issue emerged from the Supreme Court, the decision was that the Thirteenth Amendment had dealt exclusively with slavery: "Mere discriminations on account of race or color were not regarded as badges of slavery." As to the Fourteenth Amendment, it merely banned "state action of a particular character. . . . Individual invasion of individual rights is not the subject-matter of the amendment." The sole dissenter from this sophistry came from Kentucky, Justice John Marshall Harlan, who will merit further mention below (Chapter 29). He expostulated that the ruling rested "on grounds entirely too narrow and artificial." *Munn* v. *Illinois* had determined that institutions charged with a public function were subject to public regulation. Congress had, legitimately, imposed rules.

> The supreme law of the land has decreed that no authority shall be exercised in this country upon the basis of discrimination, in respect of civil rights, against freemen and citizens because of their race, color or previous condition of servitude. To that decree—for the due enforcement of which, by appropriate legislation, Congress has been invested with express power—every one must bow, whatever may have been, or whatever now are, his individual views as to the wisdom or policy, either of the recent changes in the fundamental law, or of the legislation which has been enacted to give them effect.

Or take another regional manifestation of prejudice. On the Pacific slope, the worst explosions were against Chinese immigrants. But before going forward, it may be best to retrace some steps. A theory of prejudice has already been advanced in foregoing chapters with the argument that nearly everybody fears an alien whom he perceives as different from himself in ways that are, to him, significant. To a white, some peculiarities of a Chinese were as immediately obvious as the distinctions of the Negro. Probably in his hostility to Asians, the typical Easterner was just as bad as the Westerners. But since few Chinese ever got to the East, the tension can properly be regarded as sectional. Like some other American racial prejudices, it also was tinged with class antagonism through labor competition. For some years after the Civil War, the federal government legalized the importation of labor on contract. The result was an anachronism—indentured workers a century after their day was done. For the nation as a whole, this measure had little effect. But under its provisions, Chinese were brought into the Far West, in gangs, virtually in bound servitude. By about 1880, at least one fifth of the wage earners in California were Chinese. And in plain fact, they did work for less pay than whites. In addition to this rational grievance, true-born Americans had irrational ones; during the long depression after 1873 they were unemployed, idle, desperate, anxious to find somebody they could kick in the ribs. One book explores the complexities of this ethnic encounter, with concentrated regard to the white trade unions of California. As the author points out, the Europeans transplanted to the New World have been confronted by three nonwhite groups: the aboriginal Indians, the conscripted blacks, and Asians. The record of those who deemed themselves civilized was, to speak kindly, nauseating.

> Central to each transaction has been a totally one-sided preponderance of power, exerted for the exploitation of nonwhites by the dominant white society. In each case (but especially in the two that began with systems of enforced labor), white workingmen have played a crucial, yet ambivalent, role. They have been both exploited and exploiters. On the one hand, thrown into competition with nonwhites as enslaved or "cheap" labor, they suffered economically; on the other hand, they benefited [through relatively higher status] by that very exploitation which was compelling the nonwhites to work for low wages or for nothing. Ideologically they were drawn in opposite directions. Racial identification cut at right angles to class consciousness.

The clash against most of the Indian cultures was more acute yet, and the resulting oppression was more horrendous (Document 18-3). But we today must try to confront this situation honestly; what would we have done? Without implying anything about "progress," about advanced or retrograde societies, it must be said that many tribes were still in the Stone Age; they were hunting and fishing societies or migratory agriculturalists. Even now many whites who are generally decent in their outlook find it hard to understand that some Indians want to be fundamentally different and resent the notion that white mannerisms are superior—if indeed they are. Among the Saks and Fox in Iowa, for instance, conventional modes of education are a failure; when children are called on in class, they stolidly refuse to compete with each other. In spite of such evidence, the federal government in Canada is trying to wipe out the treaty rights of Indians. Its justification is that Indians should be treated just like everybody else; they say they want to end discrimination. And in the United States, public policy can be worse than hypocritical, it can be genocidal (Document 18-3).

Social tensions were aggravated by the faultlines in the economy. As an example, we might return to a theme that has recurred often in these chapters—the medium of exchange; that is, money and banking. The subject really is not particularly complicated, but many persons simply turn off their minds when they hear "foreign exchange rates." They need not. The situation

FIGURE 18-1. *Cartoons and the American Character*

One of the brightest channels into the study of American history is lit by the cartoonists. Perhaps the United States has not produced an individual who could rank with Honore Daumier, but it has had several draftsman who provide illumination along with their wit. This is especially true in political and diplomatic history. Counting by generation, the country has held Art Young, Bill Mauldin, Herblock, Jules Feiffer.

Other spheres of interest have attracted genius. Who can forget the gibes at national character or the rakish displays of whimsy printed in *The New Yorker*? A more sardonic tone has typified the cartoons on economic and social questions—and in general they have taken the side of the underdog, striking out at the Establishment. But the downtrodden have taken their share of the abuse. This visual attack against Chinese immigrants appeared in *The San Francisco Illustrated Wasp*, 8 a century ago was similar to the one that developed after President Nixon announced in August, 1971, that a fixed amount of gold would no longer be paid for any dollar in United States paper money. At the beginning of 1873 the Treasury would redeem existing greenbacks in either gold or silver. Then came the "Crime of '73," when Congress dropped all silver coins from the emissions by the mint. Until this time a dollar could be exchanged for 412.5 grains of silver, 90 per cent pure. Now the value of silver was no longer guaranteed by the federal government. The legal (at the Treasury) ratio of gold to silver had been 1:16; now the value of the baser metal fell. By 1876 a dollar's worth of silver would buy only 90 cents' worth of gold. In technical terms, there was a premium on gold for international transactions, but the ramifications run farther. Suppose that a British exporter made a sale in the United States. He might be paid in American greenbacks. He would then use the paper money to buy gold, and ship the gold to England where he would spend it to buy pounds sterling. But because he had to pay a premium in New York to buy the gold, his income in British funds was lessened. These disparities functioned as a supplementary tariff, just as an increase in American continental freight rates would have done. Thus, for much of manufacturing, the monetary fluctuations of the times had a mixed effect: reduced prices for their goods on one hand; elevated tariffs on the other. But too much should not be made of the tariff influence. For industrialists by and large, the trend that overwhelmed all others was falling costs of production coupled with vanishing receipts per unit through reduced prices. Some years ago I wrote a book about this era entitled *Age of Excess*; now I will label it the era of cheap wares, with the proviso that many of the cheapies were also goodies. The quality of goods in general clearly did not decline, and countless Americans became the first people ever to enjoy so elegant a variety of consumables.

This phenomenon leads us partway toward unravelling an apparent tangle. Several social and economic grumbles have been recounted, but in the political sphere, the historian of a republic such as the United States ordinarily would expect that its more able citizens will enter national politics. But, until 1890, they did not. It is hard to imagine a less potent bunch than the presidents of that period. To validate this statement, an easy battery of tests can be run.

December, 1877. A fine study by Alexander Saxton, *The Indispensable Immigrant: Labor and the Anti-Chinese Movement in California* (1971) reminds us that agitation against Asians was a continuation of a racist impulse that had existed in America from its origins. Saxton also underscores the most extreme form of that racism. Having stated that Easterners carried the cancer to California with them, he states:

Their responses were largely shaped by previous responses to Indians, to immigrants, and especially to Negroes and Negro slaves. The numerous expulsions of Chinese from mine camps and the anti-Chinese ordinances written into the codes of local mining districts duplicated actions already taken against blacks.

For example, the Center for American Civilization, Brandeis University, had a gallery of the nation's chief executives. Most of the early ones there have a lean and hungry look, although John Adams, Andrew Johnson, and Grant had some tendency to be portly. But they were nothing like the mast-fed 300-pounders who succeeded them. But looking at more objective evidence in *The Congressional Record,* we learn that almost no laws of consequence were enacted for a decade after 1877. This conclusion will not be universally conceded. Some historians have eulogized Cleveland and Theodore Roosevelt as "virile Anglo-Saxons," whatever that might mean; others have written of the Civil Service Act of 1883 as a milestone on the road to human liberty. The two presidents will be discussed below; the statute needs a brusque rebuttal. It is certainly true that unleashed ferocity of a public official against his subordinates should be put in harness, but the measure in question had another effect in giving all the lesser bureaucrats the power to stamp on the faces of ordinary citizens. Nor did the evil end there. In specific school districts in several cities, employment of a teacher continued to be open to covert bribery, and the post of court probate officer in New York County is much coveted; it is not always raffled at a low price. But the ordinary customs officer probably was no longer subject to a party excise under the Civil Service Act. Since the political machines could no longer tax their placemen, they had to raise campaign funds by other methods. The obvious resource was the fat cats. Can't you hear a senator, aspiring to the presidency, implying to a businessman: "I will introduce a bill that would save you $3,000,000 in taxes next year, if you will contribute liberally to my race for re-election."

To date, so far as I know, satisfactory hypotheses that might apply to American political history in all periods do not exist. Conjectures about interest groups are doubtless helpful, as are some remarks about sectional differences and about ethnic variations. But no hard-and-fast conjuncture of social or economic pressures with political behavior can be assumed. Perhaps the Latin maxim should be revised to read "give them bread or circuses." Certainly the federal elections of the late nineteenth century offer hints that millions of citizens knew how to vote against their own well-being. But, in this political madhouse, a few patterns can be seen. A list of presidents reveals the states that the professionals regarded as crucial, the swing vote:

1876	Hayes—Ohio
1880	Garfield—Ohio
1881	Arthur—New York
1884	Cleveland—New York
1888	Harrison—Indiana
1892	Cleveland again—New York

So for twenty years three states contributed—might a poker player say "threw in"—every chief executive. Physically the presidents had much weight, politically they had little. No color; a drab bunch. Their meager distinctions tell the story: one fathered an illegitimate child, another got assassinated. Such deeds do not ease the turmoils of a nation.

These gloomy reflections are a help in understanding how brilliantly the Founding Fathers had carried out their aims. They wanted a government of checks and balances, and they created it. During the Civil War the president had refused to execute writs issued by the Supreme Court. After the war, Congress impeached the president. Later yet, a president, Cleveland, repeatedly vetoed the measures of Congress. However, he did not have as many opportunities as he might have wished, for Congress did not send him many measures. Pursuing our argument beyond the District of Columbia and into the electoral districts, the sagacity of James Madison in the Tenth Federalist Paper becomes pungent. In a republic so large and so diversified, he declared, no tyranny can exist because no majority can be formed. He was almost right. For three decades, it was virtually impossible to weld an electoral, or a congressional, majority. Few Americans have occasion to realize how different their federal government is from the parliamentary modes of other republics. In Canada the bills put forward by the cabinet are binding on every party M.P. If a member chooses not to support a party measure, he is expelled from the caucus. In distinction, Congress knew very little party solidarity. Votes were more likely to split regionally than along factional lines. One illustration can be given from 1893, when an amendment was offered to provide for unlimited coinage of silver with the old ratio to gold of 1:16. The nine Atlantic states from Maine to Pennsylvania had 99 representatives, 45 Democrats and 54 Republicans. The vote was 98 Nays, one Aye. Conversely the representatives of the eight states from Colorado to the Pacific were nine Republicans, a Populist, and seven Democrats. They voted 13 to 4 in favor of the amendment. Party lines meant little. The Democratic president who wanted to defeat the measure had to rely mainly on Republican votes.

But if we want to find men who could think incisively about civic problems, we should look not to the White House but to Congress, particularly to the Senate. Nelson M. Aldrich of Rhode Island, who became the father-in-law of John D. Rockefeller, Jr., was in my judgment a scoundrel, but he knew precisely how to use import duties to promote the causes that he wanted to promote. Even slicker was Orville Platt of Connecticut. Once he was back home mending his political fences. He drove his buggy past a field where a farmer was working, and stopped for a chat. A herd of sheep came along a cross-road. Said the farmer, "Them sheep been shorn." Said Platt, " 'Pears so. At least on this side." The anecdote shows only that he was canny; he was also wise. In one brief speech on the Senate floor in 1890, he acutely predicted more than two decades of judicial interpretation. Under debate was the Sherman Anti-Trust Act. Platt said that as submitted it applied to virtually all of the nation's business, and was unconstitutional because it wiped out state rights under the federal system. It could properly apply only to interstate "transportation." Five years later the Supreme Court accepted Platt's doctrine (discussed below, Chapter 20). His lucidity carried beyond; he also anticipated the Court's ruling in the Standard Oil Case of 1911 (Chapter 21). The course of his reasoning must concern us here, because it was crucial not only to domestic federal policy but to foreign relations as well. Platt talked about "eight representative woolen establishments" in his state that together employed 2,000 men. Even in the relatively prosperous year 1887, they had jointly taken a loss of $50,000. He went on: "They are running their business at a loss; they are making articles to which this bill refers; and this bill says that if those eight men should combine to get a fair, living profit upon their manufacture, that contract, that agreement is against public policy, unlawful and void." This theory he decried as "utterly unreasonable" and "immoral."

The problem posed must be seen from various perspectives. One surely is the cupidity of business, as Adam Smith had explained more than a century earlier: "People of the same trade seldom meet together, even for merriment and diversion, but the conversation ends in a conspiracy against the public, or in some contrivance to raise prices." On this matter, time and space have changed nothing; the Glasgow of then was the Gary, Indiana, of now.* But the public's angle of vision is not the only one; think of the poor manufacturer. The crucial lubrication in promoting worldwide competition for many commodities was provided by railroads (early Chapter 17) and also by steamships on rivers, canals, and oceans. For reasons already discussed, the supply of goods in the United States was growing more rapidly than demand, which was restricted by the inequalities of income distribution. Several labels have been used to summarize this condition; reputable scholars have chosen to call it unconsumption, but my own favorite appellation is excess capacity. Whatever the tag, businessmen sweated with the burden as if they were starred in the myth of Sisyphus, hopelessly rolling a rock uphill.

Thus we swerve toward a consideration of American diplomacy. However, it seems desirable to grasp at that topic before the difficulties of excess capacity became real. Chronologies become tangled, but we will not twist events too far in saying that the first nation to be put down was the United Kingdom. This suppression obviously had been going onward since the origins of British America. We have caught glimpses: the rancor by the Puritan fathers during the Commonwealth in England, obstructionism against royal governors, the War for Independence, the semi-farcical War of 1812 that nonetheless beat down British naval power on the Great Lakes, the struggle for predominance in Texas and Mexico and Oregon. By 1850 the American thrust was reaching farther. In that year, by the Clayton-Bulwer Treaty, it reached Central America. Space cannot be found here for the morass of maneuvers

---

*It may seem strange to those historians who believe that the "benefits of hindsight" are indispensable to their trade, but I will make a simple assertion: the best interpretations of the circumstances being described were those that issued from eye-witnesses.

FIGURE 18-2. *Alexander Gardner, The Overland Stage for Denver*

After the Civil War, the practice of having a staff artist with a transcontinental exploring or survey party was commonly revamped; the sketch or painting was replaced by the photograph. The accompanying picture was taken by Alexander Gardner, and was part of the first large-scale effort at a photographic rendition of the mystical terrain that lay beyond civilization. Americans had only hazy ideas of what the West was like; most still do. Those with proper skepticism might well look at a painting of the High Country by some noodle-head and scoff "Pure romanticism." But Gardner's photographs have a graininess and a calm that can turn bleak. They *feel* authentic and thus impart conviction. In the medium of the stereographs, Americans found a new technique through which they could learn about their country.

Born in Paisley, Scotland in 1821, Gardner came to the United States as a youth to help build a Utopian colony in Iowa. Within a decade he was back in New York. During the Civil War he worked out of Washington as a military photographer for that eminent entrepreneur Matthew B. Brady. In the autumn of 1867 Gardner moved westward with the extension of the Kansas Pacific Railroad, intended to link St. Louis to the Union Pacific. Along the way he took his flat, dead-pan photographs. Although their emotionality is not apparent at once, they are highly revealing.

This one, of a United States Overland Stage leaving Hays City, Kansas for Denver, recalls several major themes in American history. It suggests the barrenness at the time of that country, "289 miles west of Missouri River." It shows how primitive transportation was before roadbed was laid and rails placed. The military guard on top of the stagecoach reflects the still much present Indian antagonists. Finally, and you may need a magnifying glass to detect this, all of the soldiers are black. Evidence produced in the last few years suggests that blacks played a large role in subduing the Great Plains. One study tells of the significance numerically—and in other respects—of the "Negro Cowboy." Certainly the black as soldier was no longer new; when the Civil War ended, almost 200,000 were in Union armies.

about the Mosquito Coast and such like, but the quarrel about an isthmian canal was vital. Nobody yet could be exact as to the route that would be most advantageous. So the game was to leave all doors open. Hostilities between Great Britain and the United States became so great that the secretary of state said a "collision will become inevitable if great prudence is not exercised on both sides." However, in the negotiations he shot from the hip:

> There is not one of these five Central American states that would not annex themselves to us tomorrow, if they could, and if it is any secret worth knowing you are welcome to it—*Some of them have offered and asked to be annexed to the United States already.*

Note the context. America had recently fought a bloody war against Mexico. Her Congress was torn with anger about slavery, anger soon to be fended off by the Compromise of 1850. Even so, her diplomats felt able to bluster against the strongest naval power on the Atlantic. The diplomats, as so often, resorted to a stall. The two powers agreed that neither would "occupy" or "exercise dominion" over any part of Central America. Nobody knew what it meant, so the Senate gave its consent.

When the Civil War started, the Foreign Minister of the United Kingdom saw a chance to whittle down a rival. He wanted secession to win. In pursuit of that policy, the British government permitted shipyards there to build warships for the Confederacy. But its gauge of the balance of power was squinty. Large elements of its own working class resisted the pro-Southern policy. Also the British authorities were pitted against two of the toughest-minded statesmen the United States has produced, the president and Charles Francis Adams. Lincoln was adamant that any construction of vessels for the Confederacy was a belligerent act against the Union. British shipbuilders sought to sidestep this assertion by an evasion. The bottoms were constructed in the United Kingdom, but they picked up their armaments elsewhere; therefore, so it was contended, they were not warships at all. Adams, the Minister at St. James's, was not put off. These Confederate commerce raiders built in Britain captured or disabled more than 250 American merchant ships. The most notorious of the raiders was the *Alabama*. Adams kept his son and secretary, Henry (Chapter 19), working overtime to copy documents attesting to the nature of the *Alabama*. At last the evidence was delivered to the Queen's Advocate. Meanwhile that gentleman had gone insane. For five days the documents were unnoticed. Then the strain became worse when a shipyard began to build the so-called rams. These ironclad steam warships were designed for the obvious purpose of blasting through the blockade being maintained by Yankee wooden hulls. Fortunately at just this time in the summer of 1863, Union armies triumphed at Gettysburg and Vicksburg. The English Foreign Minister had second thoughts about the wisdom of his course. At last, on September 3, he ordered that the rams be detained. The order was secret, and Minister Adams knew nothing of it. Two days later he wrote a formal note: "I trust I need not express how profound is my regret at the conclusion to which her Majesty's Government have arrived. . . . It would be superfluous in me to point out to your Lordship that this is war." This matter usually called the *Alabama* claims dragged along for years after the war. At last the British government took the unusual, almost unique, step of making a public expression of regret for having allowed the ship to leave its waters. An arbitration commission finally in 1872 awarded the United States damages of $15,500,000.

The France of Napoleon III was confronted over the same issue. In 1864 he had to back down, even though he had tried hard to keep his conspiracy secret. The vessels intended for the Confederacy were sold to other buyers, and none reached the South in time to count for anything in the War. Even more humiliating to France was the course of events in Mexico. The invasion of that country began in 1861 as a Franco-Anglo-Spanish venture, with the normal justification that the expedition was meant only to collect just debts owed to Europe. The latter two nations soon withdrew, leaving Napoleon to pursue the project on his own. His armies conquered the country, and he installed an Austrian archduke as the emperor of Mexico. Here was a direct challenge to the Monroe Doctrine. The thrust never had a prayer of success, but the Union could not thwart it until the Civil War had ended. No American was furtive about what would happen then. One Bostonian wrote to his sister: "I mean to go to Mexico and fight the French after this war is done. It . . . would certainly be good fun to cut off those little red-legged sinners, who have been swelling about their fighting and victory." By January, 1864, the New York *Herald* was sneering:

> As for Mexico, we will, at the close of the rebellion, if the French have not left there before, send fifty thousand Northern and fifty thousand Southern troops, forming together a grand army to drive the invaders into the Gulf. That is the way we shall tolerate a French monarchy in Mexico.

In the spring of 1867, Napoleon withdrew his armed forces from the "arch-dupe" on the Mexican throne. That worthy died before a firing squad. There would be no francophile monarchy in North America.

The United States also got the best of Russia, although only with the exploration of Alaskan oil fields a century later did the dimensions of that triumph begin to emerge. By 1867 the Russians had controlled Alaska for more than two centuries. Apart from a rather modest fur trade, they had found nothing there to interest them. They had tried to exploit some mineral properties, but by 1854 that effort had died. Trade gains fell badly, the Russian-American Company declined steadily, and at last collapsed. The Czarist government was in serious fiscal troubles. And there was the glaring outward push of the United States. Already by 1860, according to a paraphrase memorandum to the Russian court: "They have taken California, Oregon, and sooner or later they will get Alaska. It is inevitable. It cannot be prevented; and it would be better to yield with good grace and cede the territory." So they did. The treaty of purchase in 1867 set a price of $7.2 million—for a domain that would become the most extended state in the Union. A story holds that Secretary of State Seward was so eager to conclude the deal that he, in the middle of the night, tossed in a whist hand, called some aides, and signed the documents at 4 in the morning.

Step by step the United States was building a Pacific empire (ah, those 300 million potential customers in China). In the year it acquired Alaska it also occupied Midway. This island, 1,134 miles west of Hawaii, would prove to be a handy coaling station in the age of the steamship. The Yankees, partly by muscle, partly by tact and charm, secured entry into major ports of Japan (Document 18-2). Perhaps the slickest operation of them all was in China. In 1858–1860, Britain and France had twice used armed might there, once to secure concessions, then to get them ratified. America took no part in these adventures and paid no bills. But after the Europeans had made their points, the United States pointed out that because of a most-favored-nation clause in a treaty with China, Americans were entitled to all concessions that had been made to anybody else. Anybody who has studied American foreign policy, especially since the Monroe Doctrine, will wonder at the contention that the Yankees were "innocents," ripe for exploitation; most often they were the exploiters of other major powers.

Relations with Germany were less decisive. But the blur should not detain us unduly, because the country at issue, Samoa, was not at all central to American purposes. Probably today the typical reader of these pages could not go to a globe and locate those islands to within a thousand miles. American intercourse with the archipelago reached back as far as 1838. But Germany acquired a privileged position there. Then in 1872 the United States negotiated a treaty giving it exclusive rights to a naval station at Pago Pago. This gain was upset when the Senate refused to ratify the treaty—a frequent recurrence to which we will return soon. A muddle ensued that lasted for twenty-seven years. In 1878 the United States gained a naval station—not exclusive—at Pago Pago. Germany began to push harder for privileges. Britons were in the scramble for land grants, trade concessions; one politician said of a leading seaport, "I never saw so good a place as this Apia; you can be in a new conspiracy every day." The situation was so edgy that the United Kingdom and Germany allowed their envoys in Washington to explore a resolution. Germany suggested that the commercially dominant nation in Samoa, herself, should control the islands. Britain, for a price to be paid elsewhere, endorsed the scheme. The United States spoke firmly for the autonomy of the archipelago, so the meeting broke up without issue. In these maneuvers, none of the powers cared a whit about the Samoans.

The next year, 1888, the Germans declared war against Samoa and deposed the king. America strengthened its fleet in adjacent waters—she had three warships there, Germany three, England one. Then the Almighty intervened with a hurricane—the British ship survived, but the other six all went under. One American newspaper revived the old doctrine of special providences: "Men and nations must bow before the decrees of nature. . . . Surely the awful devastation wrought in the harbor of Apia makes our recent quarrel with Germany appear petty and unnatural." As Chancellor, Bismarck acted reasonably. Secretary of State Blaine, often a sword-rattler, became a dove. Everybody liked everybody, except the Samoans. The outcome was a three-power protectorate over the archipelago. It did not work out. At last after the Spanish-American War it was abandoned; Germany took the two largest islands, and the United States took the others.

After this survey of American policies abroad, a few generalizations seem proper. First, virtually around the world, in regard to a wide range of conflicts, the United States had either won over or beaten off nations already great plus some destined to become so:

United Kingdom
France
Germany
Russia
Japan
China

We should abandon the illusion that the expansionist republic suddenly became a world power at the very end of the century. Second, the nation's negotiators were still negotiating, and they were careful not to lean too hard. America's aims were proportioned to her strength. In China she wanted what Britain and France got, but no more. In Samoa, she was willing to split the spoils with Germany. She did not try to seize Alaska, she bought it. In Japan her agent was most polite. The time of American belief in her omnipotence had not quite arrived. Third, the nation's objectives abroad were related to her domestic situation. Although it may seem silly to us to think that we can understand diplomacy merely by reading the formal communications between governments, a whole generation of diplomatic historians worked on that assumption. You went to the archives of a half-dozen foreign offices, you made (often inaccurate) copies or translations of the documents, and—presto—truth. No sense can be made of the doctrines advanced by American officials without realizing two salient facts about the internal situation in the nation: that many businessmen, including farmers, were harassed by a belief that additional markets for their products had to be found overseas; and that Americans, including missionaries, had an inflated sense of their own power and righteousness.

Finally, and this reflects on all the preceding assertions, the chief difficulty of the United States in dealing with other nations was to get agreement at home. Part of the trouble here arose from clashes within the economy or within the society, but much came from the political institutions.

Only tremulously can we refer to "the" foreign policy of the United States. The president may be launched on one course, the State Department on another, the Navy embarked on a third, the War Department on a fourth, a foreign ministry on a tack of its own. Normally the president can come close to working his will, but often not. In the nineteenth century, Congress, particularly the Senate, often blocked him. We have seen how it failed to act on a treaty with Samoa. In 1867 Secretary Seward obtained a treaty with Denmark to buy the future Virgin Islands for $7.5 million. It died in the Senate. President Grant in 1870 submitted a treaty annexing Santo Domingo to the United States. In spite of his assertion that the agreement was "an adherence to the Monroe Doctrine," the Senate voted it down. For all that, even though the nation did buy Alaska, the purchase continued to be known as "Seward's folly."

American politics at the national level from 1865 to 1890 was a stalemate. The presidency switched often from one party to the other. Only Grant served two consecutive terms. The chief executive, usually a Republican, was likely to be confronted by at least one house of Congress controlled by the other party. Even within his own ranks he could not sway the members of Congress. No significant federal laws were enacted except a series of Civil Rights Acts ostensibly to benefit freedmen, and even they had little effect for seventy years. Some changes were effected at the state level: regulation of rates for railroads and grain elevators, reform of elections, temperance measures for alcoholic beverages. Probably the most influential agency of government in the nation was the Supreme Court, which handed down some of the weightiest decisions in its history. But even though the customary political processes were proving impotent to resolve the internal problems of the United States, a federal government that seemed helpless on domestic matters was exerting a powerful thrust outward from American shores. In the four decades after 1846 the our eagle had clawed at the interests of the United Kingdom, Mexico, France, Germany, Russia, Japan, and China. In all those contests, the worst result for the United States was a draw.

SOME NOTABLE EVENTS

1850 Clayton-Bulwer Treaty, April 19.
1850–
  1854 Taiping Rebellion in China.
1852–
  1870 Napoleon III is emperor of France.
1853 Gadsden Purchase from Mexico, Dec. 30.
1853–
  1856 Crimean War between Russia and English-Turkish allies.

1854 Commodore M. C. Perry secures from Japan the first treaty of friendship she signed with any Western nation, March 31.
  Marcy-Elgin Treaty with Canada, June 5; first treaty signed by U.S. providing reciprocity in tariff concessions.
  Ostend Manifesto, Oct. 18, tries to assert U.S. interests in Cuba.

1855 Newfoundland given virtual
self-government.

1857 Japan signs with U.S. her first
commercial treaty with any
Western power, July 29.

1857–
1858 Sepoy Rebellion in India against
British.

1858 Treaty of Tientsin with China, June
18; Britain and France force
trade concessions.

1860 Garibaldi's Red Shirts conquer
Naples and Sicily, which are
annexed to Sardinia-Piedmont,
initiating Italian unification.

1861 Kingdom of Italy proclaimed, a
united nationalist regime.
Russian serfs emancipated by
Alexander II.

1862–
1890 Bismarck is chancellor of Prussia;
proceeds with German
unification, expansion.

1863–
1867 Maximilian is emperor of Mexico.

1864 International Red Cross founded.

1865–
1866 Atlantic Ocean is first spanned by
cables, laid by Cyrus W. Field.

1866–
1867 U.S. pressure helps to force
French troops out of Mexico and
to topple Maximilian's puppet
government.

1866–
1870 Fenian Irish-independence raids
from U.S. into Canada opposed
by U.S. Army.

1867 Dominion of Canada formed by
British North America Act,
July 1.
Second Reform Bill in Great Britain
further widens the suffrage.
U.S. buys Alaska for $7.2 million
from Russia.

1868 Ten Years' War in Cuba begins; first
of rebellions against Spain.

1869 Suez Canal opens, dominated by
Britain.

1870 Franco-Prussian War won by
Bismarck, who annexes two
French provinces.

1871 Tweed Ring overthrown in New
York City; turnover in urban
political machinery.
Treaty of Washington settles
Alabama claims, May 8.
German Empire formed under
Wilhelm I.
Third Republic of France replaces
Louis Napoleon's Empire; it
lasts until 1940.

1872 Crédit Mobilier exposed
(congressional railroad subsidies
bought with kickbacks).
Prohibition party for first time puts
up presidential candidate.

1873 Silver demonitized by Coinage Act.

1875 Spain apologizes and pays indemnity
for *Virginius* seizure.

1876 Greenback party for first time puts
up presidential candidate.

1877–
1878 Russians win war against Turkey.

1878 Serbia, Rumania, and Montenegro
become independent by Treaty
of Berlin.
Bland-Allison Act, Feb. 28
Democrats win Congress for first
time in twenty years.

1882 First Chinese Exclusion Act to block
immigration.

1883 Pendleton Act (federal civil service).
Germany, Austria, Italy form Triple
Alliance, eventual preliminary
lineup of World War I.

1884 Berlin Conference on African
colonies.

1885–
1886 British seize Burma.

1887 Interstate Commerce Act.

1888 Australian (secret) ballot introduced
in Louisville; first use in U.S.

1889 U.S., Britain, Germany agree to
condominium over Samoa,
June 14.

1890 Sherman Anti-Trust Act against
monopolies.
Sherman Silver Purchase Act.
McKinley Tariff Act.

1891–
1892 Chile humiliated in *Baltimore*
dispute with U.S. and its
"gunboat diplomacy."

Ways to Study History XVIII

Take a fresh look. Several exciting schema have been advanced in the last twenty-five years for understanding particular facets of American history. Perhaps none was more needed or more overdue than the new conceptualizations about foreign policy leading to the Spanish-American War. For decades the fashion was to emphasize the ambitions of public officials and the dreams of missionaries—the White Man's Burden revisited. Anybody who questioned whether the search for markets abroad was also involved—well, he was written off as a dirty Marxist. Thus skeptical lines of thought were vulgarized into some absurd theory that all businessmen were conspirators, which was of course ridiculous: ha, ha. The simple fact is that all segments of the labor force have special interests, whether employers, employees, or college professors, and each is sensitive to its own interests. The formulation of diplomacy is often a very complex matter, and I doubt if anybody today would want to deny that Protestant ministers had a hand in Washington in the late nineteenth century, but so did other groups.

Three scholars deserve notice for their contributions to this topic since 1955. In that year Norman Graebner demonstrated that perhaps the policy-makers of the ante-bellum years are best perceived in terms other than "continentalism"; what they wanted was not more agricultural land but three ports on the Pacific aimed at the markets of China. This thread ran unbroken for the next fifty years, as Charles S. Campbell showed in *Special Business Interests and the Open Door Policy* (1951). A painful strike at the traditionalist view was administered by Walter LaFeber in *The New Empire* (1963). By his showing, such diverse forces as politicians and financiers and industrialists and trade unions saw their problem as a glut of domestic markets and they saw their saviors as foreign buyers. Even LaFeber does not push this analysis far enough; he says little about farmers. My suspicion is that producers of staple crops such as cotton and wheat saw their own difficulties in the terms just stated. This further extension was made by William Appleman Williams with considerable detail in *The Roots of the Modern American Empire* (1969).

Document 18-1

President Grover Cleveland in 1889 was presented with a bill that appropriated $10,000 to provide seeds to farmers in a drought-stricken area of Texas. He vetoed it. The message below brings up two significant trends. One is the growing ideology of *laissez faire,* the notion that governments should not meddle with the economy. But this doctrine was applied selectively.

Although federal agencies were giving considerable aid to railroads, to the merchant marine, to manufacturers through protective tariffs, Cleveland here denies an extension of aid to farmers. Thus his words also mirror a pronounced shift in the balance of power within the country, away from agriculture and toward the commercial-industrial interests.

. . . *I can find no warrant for such an appropriation in the Constitution, and I do not believe that the power and duty of the General Government ought to be extended to the relief of individual suffering which is in no manner properly related to the public service or benefit. A prevalent tendency to disregard the limited mission of this power and duty should, I think, be steadfastly resisted, to the end that the lesson should be constantly enforced that though the people support the Government the Government should not support the people.*

The friendliness and charity of our countrymen can always be relied upon to relieve their fellow-citizens in misfortune. This has been repeatedly and quite lately demonstrated. Federal aid in such cases encourages the expectation of paternal care on the part of the Government and weakens the sturdiness of our national character, while it prevents the indulgence among our people of that kindly sentiment which strengthens the bonds of a common brotherhood.

It is within my personal knowledge that individual aid has to some extent already been extended to the sufferers mentioned in this bill. . . .

Document 18-2

Commodore Matthew B. Perry in 1854 secured a treaty of friendship with Japan, but it was little more than a covenant for shipwrecked seamen, the traditional "wood and water treaty." The true breakthrough was effected by an American consul general in 1858, who secured a sweeping commercial agreement. In his phrasing, "The pleasure I feel in having made this treaty is enhanced by the reflection that there has been no show of coercion, nor was menace in the least used by me to obtain it. There was no American man-of-war within one thousand miles of me for months before and after the negotiations. I told the Japanese at the outset that my mission was a friendly one; that I was not authorized to use any threats; that all I wished was that they would listen to the truth that I would lay before them." The following statement by the prime minister of Japan confirms this version—and contains sobering adumbrations (see Chapter 28).

When our power and national standing have come to be recognized, we should take the lead in punishing the nation which may act contrary to the principle of international interests; and in so doing, we should join hands with the nations whose principles may be found identical with those of our country. An alliance thus formed should also be directed towards protecting harmless but powerless nations. . . . Our national prestige and position thus ensured, the nations of the world will come to look to our Emperor as the Great Ruler of all the nations, and they will come to follow our policy and submit themselves to our judgment. . . . now is the opportune moment offered us by the changed condition of the world to throw off the traditional policy three centuries old, and make a united national effort to seize the opportunity for realizing the great destiny awaiting our country, as stated above. For this purpose, speedy permission is respectfully and humbly solicited for opening intercourse with foreign countries.

Document 18-3

The Commissioner of Indian Affairs in 1871–1872 was an educated man, a scholar. But he shared the bias of most of his contemporaries. Few Americans at that time realized or admitted that the constant pressure of the advancing frontier and the repeated failure of the government to honor its treaties made the Indian uprisings nearly inevitable. By 1890 all of the western tribes had been herded onto reservations, but the process was not as quick and easy as this document predicts.

It belongs not to a sanguine, but to a sober view of the situation, that three years will see the alternative of war eliminated from the Indian question, and the most powerful and hostile bands of to-day thrown in entire helplessness on the mercy of the Government. Indeed, the progress of two years more, if not of another summer, on the Northern Pacific Railroad will of itself completely solve the great Sioux problem, and leave the ninety thousand Indians ranging between the two transcontinental lines as incapable of resisting the Government as are the Indians of New York or Massachusetts. . . .

No one will rejoice more heartily than the present Commissioner when the Indians of this country cease to be in a position to dictate, in any form or degree, to the Government; when, in fact, the last hostile tribe becomes reduced to the condition of suppliants for charity. This is, indeed, the only hope of salvation for the aborigines of the continent. If they stand up against the progress of civilization and industry, they must be relentlessly crushed. The westward course of population is neither to be denied nor delayed for the sake of all the Indians that ever called this country their home. . . . And it is because the present system allows the freest extension of settlement and industry possible under the circumstances, while affording space and time for humane endeavors to rescue the Indian tribes from a position altogether barbarous and incompatible with civilization and social progress, that this system must be approved by all enlightened citizens. . . .

Society and Ways to Understand It

While most Americans were revelling in the country's increasing power in the international arena, more thoughtful observers began to be disturbed by the divisions and tensions within the nation. Henry George, anticipating a concept made famous by the great historian Frederick Jackson Turner, blamed the fissures in part upon the rapid disappearance of the frontier. "The general intelligence, the general comfort, the active invention, the power of adaptation and assimilation, the free, independent spirit, the energy and hopefulness that have marked our people, are not causes, but results—they have sprung from unfenced land. . . . The great fact which has been so potent is ceasing to be. The public domain is almost gone—a very few years will end its influence, already rapidly failing." The increasingly mixed ethnic nature of the country worried others. In 1880 6.5 million of the 50 million Americans were immigrants, most of whom chose to live in the rapidly growing cities. (Twenty cities reported populations of more than 100,000 in that year.) Although many hoped that eventually the melting pot would eliminate the immigrants' diverse cultures, in the meantime a substantial part of the population either could not or would not abide by American values (discussed below). Another 6.5 million people were black. More than 1,500 of them were to be lynched in the next ten years. Political corruption, the coagulating power of certain big businesses, rural and urban poverty, the impersonality of big cities—all these could be perceived as either the causes or symptoms of a growing malaise. Even a man who presumably had everything going for him could feel this illness (Document 19-1).

Although many of the pre-war reform movements continued in the seventies and eighties, the moral fervor and the optimism which had characterized them earlier had evaporated. Few people could any longer believe in the imminent perfectibility of American life, and certainly not in theoretical utopia. The practical, the concrete, and above all, the personal, reigned. Religion continued to be important, and its stress was laid even more restrictedly upon personal salvation. The bonds between sanctity and philosophy had atrophied, and the churches only attempted to influence the most private aspects of morality. Slavery no longer existed to prick the ministerial conscience, and abolition had been the only important political issue on which religious opinion had spoken.

A (possibly apocryphal) story about Dwight Moody, the most popular revival preacher of the last part of the century, illustrates the depths to which revealed religion had fallen. A lady approached Moody after one of his sermons, saying that she loved his preaching but was not sure whether she agreed with his theology. "My theology?" he supposedly queried, "I didn't know I had one." Indeed the glutinous soothing syrup which Moody dispensed bore no relation to Jonathan Edwards' chill Calvinism, and not much to the sturdy self-reliance of Charles Grandison Finney. (See early Chapter 14 on revivalistic religion.) And where Finney fought for abolition, Moody's social doctrines reflected the prejudices and interests of his audience, drawn from the business middle class. A national magazine could say of him in 1896, "He is the enemy of sectionalism and all hostility of class to class. His mission is to arouse the conscience and awaken the spiritual side of men, to make them patient, long suffering, diligent."

Another form of personal religion became prominent in the latter part of the century. The Church of Christ, Scientist, founded in 1879, maintained that physical health (and general harmonious well-being) could be achieved by a proper spiritual attitude and alignment with the forces of good. Its adherents believed that the physical world didn't really exist, that it was just a reflection of mental realities. This belief recognizes the importance of psychosomatic ailments, but the growth of Christian Science as an organized credo must be credited to the personality of its founder, Mary Baker Eddy. Of a strictly Calvinist New England family, Mrs. Eddy was a chronic invalid most of her life, and during her middle years both poor and unhappy. From her childhood she seems to have been searching for a sense of harmony, as well as for fame and attention. After a series of mystical experiences, many of her physical symptoms evaporated, and she set about forging a systematized creed of spiritual control over health. Her greatest talent seems to have been as a teacher. One former student affirmed the "Spiritual or emotional exaltation which she was able to impart in her classroom; a feeling so strong that it was like the birth of a new understanding and seemed to open to them a new heaven and a new earth." Everyone who knew her, even those with whom she quarreled, agreed that her very presence implied that something exciting was going to happen. By 1889 Mrs. Eddy had personally taught more than 600 pupils, who then spread across the country disseminating her message. Although, given the miserable state of medical practice at the time, Christian Science probably made a real contribution to the health of many people, Mary Baker Eddy's religion stressed the individual over the group as much as that of Dwight Moody.

Religious opinion was silent about poverty, about exploitation of labor, about cut-throat competition, about racism. But it shouted loudly about the evils of liquor and any deviation from a unworkably rigid standard of sexual morality. The churches, and such non-sectarian groups as the Women's Christian Temperance Union, were adamant on these questions. In accordance with the prevailing belief that any vexing problem could be legislated out of existence, they worked hard for strict censorship and the prohibition of alcohol, and against the legalization of prostitution or divorce.* No play could depart from the strict rules of romantic sentimentality, or portray a woman who was not pure without showing her retribution immediately and obviously. The guidelines for printed literature were not so tightly drawn, but they were growing increasingly restrictive. Chicago maintained one police officer whose sole duty was to go about the city ferreting out "obscene" works of art. His test was simple: if a painting or sculpture cost more than $50, it was unquestionably not pornographic.

Although the more assiduous guardians of other people's morals would not have consciously adhered to the policeman's standard, hard cash was fast becoming the only viable standard by which to gauge right and wrong. The immensely popular Horatio Alger books of the era illustrate this tendency. Typically, a poor boy would do a minor sort of good deed, or show character in a trivial way. Unbeknownst to him, a rich man was benefitted, or observed him, and the virtuous lad would be rewarded out of all proportion to his deserts with eventual great wealth, or the boss's daughter. Virtue was plainly not a substantial enough reward for itself. McGuffey's Readers, of which 100 million copies were sold between 1850 and 1900, promulgated the same idea. A chimney sweep found himself in the fireplace in a lady's bedroom. He spies

---

*Belief in the efficacy of the law was not confined to "moral" questions. During these years the Indiana legislature decreed, by fiat, the value of pi (3.1416) to be four.

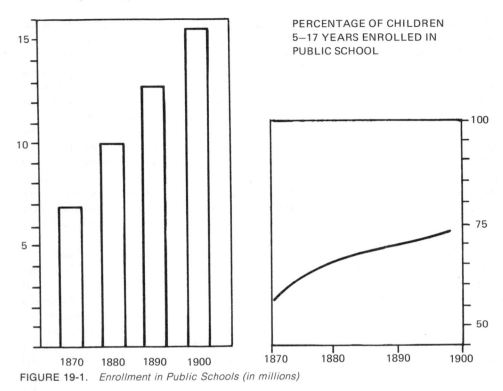

PERCENTAGE OF CHILDREN
5–17 YEARS ENROLLED IN
PUBLIC SCHOOL

FIGURE 19-1. *Enrollment in Public Schools (in millions)*

a "fine gold watch." Although he wants to take it, his conscience forbids him. The next day the lady summons him, and rewards his honesty by adopting him. Disproportionate punishments could result from petty misdeeds as well: when a small boy snitches a piece of cake his mother threatens him with everlasting Hell, because "no liar can enter the kingdom of Heaven."

Americans wanted to believe that virtue would bring wealth; they also wanted to believe that the rich were good. A Philadelphia minister presented a talk on this theme more than 6,000 times, becoming rich himself. "Ninety-eight out of one hundred of the rich men of America are honest. That is why they are rich. That is why they are trusted with money. That is why they carry on great enterprises and find plenty of people to work with them. It is because they are honest men." Although this theme was self-deceptive in many ways, it carried a socially useful corollary. To become rich was a man's first duty, but his money brought the responsibility to use it unselfishly. The old doctrine of the stewardship of wealth had never entirely died, and the self-help lecturers were helping to revitalize it. When they preached for "success" they also exhorted their businessman listeners to behave in an honorable manner, to spend their money for the good of the community, and to treat their employees justly. While this advice was often ignored, it did help to alleviate the harshness of a relentless pursuit of profit (see late Chapter 17 on labor conditions).

Many Americans would have agreed that "to make money honestly is to preach the gospel," and that the desire for wealth was utterly normal, if not always entirely benign. But Henry George told them that thirst for money stemmed from fear of poverty. "And thus the sting of want and the fear of want make men admire above all things the possession of riches, and to become wealthy is to become respected, and admired, and influential. . . . Men instinctively admire virtue and truth, but the sting of want and the fear of want make them even more strongly admire the rich and sympathize with the fortunate." Perhaps the same fear made them despise the urban poor, who were often marked with the stigmata of foreignness as well as that of poverty.

Middle America feared the great cities, which they believed to be the breeding grounds for all manner of vices and corruptions. In some respects the country was correct in thinking the cities unwholesome. In 1870 the infant mortality rate in New York was 65 per cent higher than it had been in 1810. Polluted water made typhoid fever endemic in some cities; old tenement houses bred disease-carrying rats. But the squalor of the slums was often credited to their inhabitants' moral turpitude. Small-towners and the urban middle class feared that the cities would destroy democracy and morality. They believed political corruption was an exclusively urban phenomenon, and that the immigrants—ignorant, anarchic, "wet"—were to blame.

With a few exceptions, scholars have not paid much attention to the effects of population densities. The psychology of individualism, which was essential in frontier areas, became irrelevant or harmful in thickly settled cities. It might be permissible to throw your garbage out the door in Barrio Morcelo, Puerto Rico, but the same expedient does only damage in Spanish Harlem. If the population density of parts of Manhattan was ubiquitous in all parts of New York City, the 200 million people of the United States could be placed in three of the five boroughs of that one urban incorporation. Bombay and Calcutta were never so jammed together. What is more appalling, districts of New York were almost surely more crowded seventy years ago than they are now. The idea of the pure country and dirty city was stimulated by racism and ethnic intolerance. Although this antipathy was expressed most strongly against blacks, the new—and even the old—immigrants felt its sting. Asked "You don't call . . . an Italian a white man?" a western construction boss replied, "No, sir, an Italian is a Dago." In Minnesota and the Dakotas there were self-segregated Swedish districts and Norwegian districts; the Anglo-Saxon merchants who fattened off them despised both nationalities impartially. We have seen (early Chapter 18) how the Chinese were mistreated in California; in 1883 Congress suspended Chinese immigration for ten years.

The United States has been called a melting pot. It seems to me that this image is misleading. Scattered ethnic enclaves endure to this day, mostly in rural areas, such as the Amish. Others which have now disintegrated managed to preserve their cultural distinctness for generations after their founders came to America. But this conservatism was much easier to sustain in the isolation of a relatively self-sufficient rural village than in a diverse city, and by the end of the nineteenth century almost all new immigrants were living in an urban environment. Even in the city a few ethnic groups managed to create a stable neighborhood in which their culture could be passed along almost intact. The distinction between an ethnic neighborhood and a slum is crucial. In an ethnic neighborhood those individuals who can afford better housing than is available will often refrain from moving out. Instead, they might buy the tenement in which they live and renovate it. A slum offers no human advantages to balance its physical decrepitude; an ethnic neighborhood does. In the North End of Boston the Italian immigrants who came in the late nineteenth century found a slum and created an ethnic neighborhood; it has been stable for generations. Although its residents have certainly adapted to the United States, they have also preserved much of the culture that accompanied their ancestors. But this experience was far from common. Much more frequently only a few trivial parts of European tradition persisted into the third generation. The first generation would be unable to become "American," and would not try. Although proud of their children's greater adaptability, the first generation would nonetheless attempt to bring them up in accordance with tradition. But the second generation was often ashamed of their parent's "foreignness," embarrassed to be unable to quite escape the chains of the past, and determined that their children would do so. The third generation thus became completely homogenized. A few words of the Old Country language, a taste for a few unusual foods, were all that remained to them out of a complex tradition. Thus the immigrants were "melted," in the sense that their ethnicity was broken down, but the traits that they brought to this country never went into the pot to influence others. America chose to discard them, and few Americans regretted their loss.

Jane Addams, the founder of Hull-House, was one of the few. She recognized the merits in the Old Country traditions which she saw in the ethnic neighborhoods of Chicago. But as a well-to-do, educated young woman, she was horrified by the congested, filthy conditions there. On a trip to Europe she had seen a settlement house in London, and in 1890 began the first such facility in the United States. The residents of Hull-House provided a varied assortment of services to the sweatshop district in which they lived, and to the city as a whole. They offered hot lunches to factory workers, sponsored courses in cooking and hygiene as well as a University Extension, provided a gymnasium, an assortment of social and debating clubs, concerts, and art exhibits. They got the state to pass a law for the safety inspection of factories—and one of them became the first inspector. They fought against child labor and for compulsory schooling and better sanitation facilities.

The women of Hull-House were a remarkably effective group, who were often able to get what they wanted by guile when persuasion would not suffice. Most of them came from the same background as Jane Addams— prosperous families in midsized towns in Middle America who had been able to give their daughters a much better education than was at all common for women at that time. At college the girls had wanted to make the world a better place, to be publicly useful at a time when the private utility of marriage and motherhood was the only respectable avenue open to female talent. There is reason to believe that Jane Addams was desperately unhappy for a while before she began her experiment at Hull-House. With enough money to travel, to do almost anything she might choose, she could find no occupation to engross her capabilities. Her contemporaries often found themselves in the same quandary; some of them seized on the alternative of settlement work with fervor.

With varying degrees of ambivalence, Jane Addams' fellow-workers shared her respect for the virtues of the immigrants; they were powerless to halt the rush to exchange those virtues for American traits. The only people whose values today are substantially different from those of the rest of the country are neither immigrant nor more than marginally urban. Despite efforts to assimilate them for more than 300 years, many Indians still cling to a distinctively Indian cluster of attitudes—and this despite the total destruction of the economic system out of which those attitudes had arisen.

In a sense it is pointless to speak of "the Indian." The warlike Iroquois did not much resemble peaceful agriculturists of the Southwest; the settled fishing people of the Northwest differed from the nomadic hunters of the plains. But all the Indian peoples shared two qualities which they refused to abandon and to which the rest of the country has not been able to accommodate itself. First, they disapproved of Western European economic competition and regarded niggardliness as a disgrace second only (in some tribes) to cravenness. In the hunting economy that dominated many tribes, generosity was essential to the survival of the group. Not every hunter could be lucky all the time, and any possession could be quickly replaced from the surrounding environment. Furthermore, in many tribes the animals and the land belonged to everyone; an individual only "owned" something when he had caught it or made it. It was then his pride to be able to give it away.

The second belief which the Indians shared was even more un-American than their unwillingness to accumulate and consume. Each group felt a sacred relationship between themselves and a particular piece of land. Even the buffalo-hunting plainsmen, who seemed like aimless nomads to white eyes, considered specific places to be their own, by religious right. In recent years a group of Indians in the Southwest has been carrying on a running skirmish with the Forest Service over their right to such a place. The officials say that this area, a mountain side which contains a remarkably beautiful lake, should be turned over to multiple uses—cattle grazing permits should be issued, and hikers and fishermen should be allowed in. The Indians reply that this lake and the land around it is sacred to them, that life began there. Their religion involves reaffirmation of man's unity with the earth and the sky, and certain rites are performed by the lake. Aside from participants in these, no one should enter this area at all.

A Nez Percé chief reminded his son (to become Chief Joseph) of the ties between the people and the land:

> Always remember that your father never sold the country. You must stop your ears whenever you are asked to sign a treaty selling your home. A few years more, and the white man will be all around you. They have their eyes on this land. My son, never forget my dying words. This country holds your father's body. Never sell the bones of your father and your mother.

Joseph buried his father in the Wallowa Valley in northeastern Oregon, saying at the time, "I love that land more than all the rest of the world." Nonetheless, he could not keep it. After being given 1,200 acres of reservation land in "exchange" for their million acre valley, Chief Joseph's band eventually attempted to flee to Canada, were caught after a retreat of extreme hardship, and shipped off to the Indian Territory (Oklahoma).

Another group of Indians became a cause célèbre in 1879. The Poncas, a small band from Nebraska, had been sent to the Indian Territory, where many of them died and all were living in extremely unwholesome conditions. About 30 returned to their old home, because the last son of their chief had begged to be buried by the Niobrara. They were bringing his body home. The Indian agent in Oklahoma called for their forcible return, since they had left the reservation without permission. In a court decision which gave the Indians the right, as individuals, to the protection of the courts under the Fourteenth Amendment, they were permitted to stay in Nebraska, but lost all treaty rights.

This case and others like it, aroused a good deal of sympathy for Indians and anger at the machinations of the "Indian Ring" in Washington. But much of the sympathy came about for the wrong reasons, and many of the measures proposed by those who considered themselves the Indians' best friends have only made things worse. "Crooked Indian Agents" aroused much ire. There probably never were very many of those, but it seemed to assuage the consciences of people who had stolen a continent from its owners to rant at those who deprived them of a few cattle or bolts of cloth. Eastern supporters of Indians cherished a romantic, sentimental view of Indian life. *Hiawatha* was required reading, and an extremely sentimental contemporary novel about an Indian princess, *Ramona,* became a best-seller. At the same time, most well-meaning Americans believed that the only way for the Indians to survive

FIGURE 19-2. *Charles M. Russell, An Indian Old Man*

This drawing by Charles Marion Russell symbolizes both the final destruction of the old Indian way of life, and the desperate efforts made by some groups to stay off reservations, to preserve their freedom. Chief Joseph of the Nez Percé led his people on a desolate 1,300 mile trek towards the sanctuary of the Canadian border, to be slowed by cold and starvation, and finally captured before he crossed it. Sitting Bull did manage to escape to Canada, and stayed for several years. When we consider the love which Indians had for their own land, such flight indicates that liberty was valued yet more. But even life itself was not secure under reservation bonds. On December 29, 1890, the 7th Cavalry (George Armstrong Custer's old outfit) murdered hundreds of Sioux at Wounded Knee on the Pine Ridge Reservation in South Dakota. When terrified women tried to save their children by running into nearby gullies, they were pursued and cut down. The figure in this drawing might well have been a survivor of this massacre, a man whose way of life has been destroyed, and who is forced to walk alone.

Russell (1864–1926) went to Montana at the age of sixteen, and worked there as a cowboy. Entirely self-taught, he amused himself and his friends by sketching the life around him, and thought he was a pretty sharp trader when an Eastern dude paid $100 for two paintings. Although he supported himself as an artist from the time he was thirty, he never lost his feeling for the open spaces and a cowboy's life. Like Frederick Remington (Figure 17-2), much of the power of Russell's art derives from his precise observation and empathy with his subject matter.

was to become like white Americans as quickly as possible. They failed to see that even if this would work for more than a tiny minority of individuals, it would mean the extinction of the groups *as Indians*. They worked to have tribal reservations broken up and assigned to individuals in severalty, a move that was disastrous for several reasons. First, individually owned land can be sold; much of it quickly passed into white hands. Second, individual owner-ship contradicts both qualities of Indianness discussed above. To prosper under this system, a man must learn to be personally acquisitive. Almost to live at all he must abandon the idea of a sacred relationship to a specific place. This the Indians have steadfastly refused to do.

Indians wanted to remain in their ancestral homelands; white men wanted to move whenever they could turn a profit. Even the profit was not always necessary. For some families the lure of opportunities farther west became a goal in itself, and they needed no specific spur to make them move. Hamlin Garland's family moved from Ohio to Wisconsin, to Iowa, and then to the Dakotas. When he returned to the Midwest after six years in Boston, and found them living quite pitifully on the high plains in a sod dugout, he declared, "I clearly perceived that our Song of Emigration had been, in effect, the hymn of fugitives." In some areas land prices rose so rapidly that farmers could turn a tidy profit by staying just ahead of the main line of settlement— clearing a tract, selling it in a year or two, moving west, and repeating the process. But even when it was profitable, the effect of this process on the minds of the people and the quality of life was lamentable.* (See Document 17-1.) Newness, bigness, growth were all, ripeness nothing. Even the churches defined prosperity in terms of change—a new building, more members. The hoopla of town boosterism replaced a feeling of community, while informal village rituals began to yield to formal social organizations—lodges, church "circles," clubs. Nostalgia for uptorn roots fostered the growth of genealogical, patriotic, and historical societies.

Climatic differences complicated the hazards of mobility. Farming methods which worked in Illinois were disastrous in western Nebraska—or anywhere west of the 100th meridian. (This line cuts Kansas, Nebraska, and the Dakotas almost in half. West of it, annual rainfall is less than twenty inches.) Unfortunately, by the time the Homestead Act was passed in 1863 most of the wetter land, which could be cultivated by methods and tools familiar to the midwestern farmer, had been taken up. To farm the Western wheat lands successfully a man needed much more land than 160 acres, and he needed a heavy capital investment in machinery (Figure 29-3). Aside from the ever present spectre of drought, residents of the trans-Mississippi West had to

---

*This same mobility, and its ill-effects, can be seen in many modern suburbs. All houses must be substantially the same, to facilitate resale. Everyone expects to move in a few years time, so they neither make real friends nor are especially concerned about the good of the community.

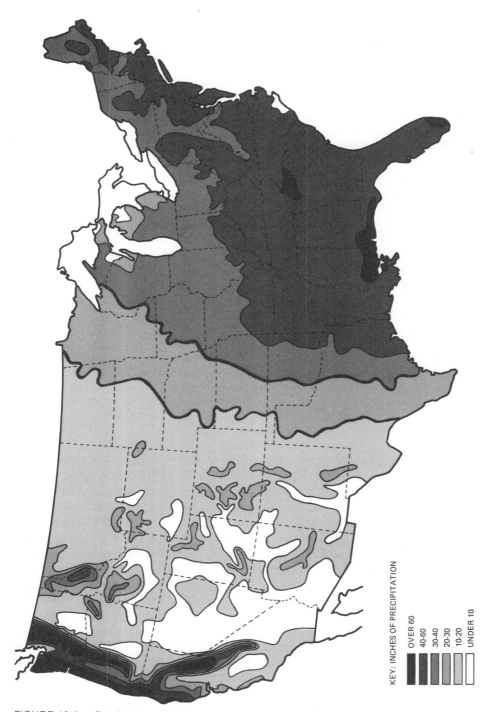

KEY: INCHES OF PRECIPITATION

OVER 60
40-60
30-40
20-30
10-20
UNDER 10

FIGURE 19-3. *Rainfall Belts*

face periodic invasion by grasshoppers. From 1874 to 1877 they came every year when the crops were half-grown, eating everything—growing plants, cloth, hoe handles. Land values tumbled as the disheartened returned east. One man sold 80 acres, a span of mules, a wagon, and a cow for $225. Human misery was intense among those who could not leave. A Norwegian immigrant woman wrote home in February of 1877, "This fall we got 124 bushels of wheat, 224 bushels of oats, and 11 bushels of barley. This is all the locusts left us. They took all the corn, all the potatoes, and all the vegetables we had planted. We did get enough for our needs this year, but we were not able to pay off any of our debts."

Why did they come? In part, out of sheer optimism. The Myth of the Garden—the nearly nonexistent infinite-ideal frontier of the family farm (Chapter 14)—had become too deeply imbedded in the American consciousness to be easily refuted by a few facts. Going West had meant increased opportunities for so long that it was hard to believe that it might have come to mean destitution. But town promoters and land speculators, the railroads in particular, did all they could to encourage the credulous to move west. Many Easterners were wary of "The Great American Desert"; speculators countered with the dictum, "rain follows the plow." One wrote of western Kansas,

> Just in the same proportion as the country has been opened up to cultivation the rainless limit has receded. We are not yet prepared to believe that it will during this generation recede beyond the western limits of this state. But we believe that the entire state will some time be settled. We are satisfied that the rainless belt has retreated before the march of civilization and that wherever civilization has pressed hardest there the limit is farthest west.

By 1890 these advertisements, and the pioneering urges of the American people, had done their work. The Census Bureau declared that there was no longer a line of settlement, a frontier. Henceforward opportunity was to be restricted to the place where it had always been greatest, the city. The Myth of the Garden and of the rugged family farmer had also been sadly shaken.* The increasing dependence of farmers upon machinery, Eastern capital, and a sophisticated transportation network, along with the inhospitality of much of the West to agriculture,—all this combined had nearly toppled it. But a new Myth was arising, one which could persist indefinitely because it did not require the reinforcement of personal experience. The Cowboy became the new American Adam. Actually the era of cattle drives and cowtowns was very short. By the mid-eighties railroads and barbed wire had ended it. And the ritual violence which is an indispensable part of the Myth was more a part of mining frontier than cattle frontier. But just at the time that the cowboy was

---

*It has not entirely fallen even yet. Observe the concern of politicians and other commentators over "preserving the family farm."

becoming nothing other than an unglamorous farm laborer, dime novels were establishing the Cowboy as the ultimate American Hero.

He was free, he was strong, and he would brook no challenges to his unrestrained individuality. He lived by a simple code of honor, was quick to resent any affronts to his dignity, to punish his insulter with his trusty Colt. His best friend was his horse; no man, and especially no woman, could order him about. This combination of traits was to become extraordinarily appealing to the American people. While the nation still believed in the cult of individualism, its exercise had become impossible for all but a very few—the very rich and the resigned poor. Practically everyone had to cooperate, to constantly compromise their desires. Most people, in the pursuit of success or even stability, had to compromise on honor and dignity as well. In an age when "morality" was fast becoming synonymous with abstention from sex and liquor, standards of behavior in almost every other aspect of life were cloudy. But the Cowboy was free. He carried everything he needed to earn his living within himself, and he did not want to "make money," so he could meet with his fellows as equals, and judge them on the basis of a few uncomplicated personal traits. Their money and power were simply not relevant.

This myth eventually came to be soothing even to the real victims of the westering urge—the small farmers. Their lives had long been pictured as the quintessence of bucolic joy. They might have few urban sophistications, but they possessed great security, ample food, and a kindly joviality that more than made up for it. Hamlin Garland, who came of such folk, was much upbraided when he helped to puncture this pleasant fiction. His writing portrayed small farmers as people living with the insecurities of great poverty, brutalized by boring, endless labor, and quenched by loneliness and a narrow society. Garland's people, particularily his women, are permitted a brief adolescent interlude of hope and joy, and then spend their lives struggling through an unremitting round of hard work that never gets them anything but more of it. Garland's portrayal was probably too unrelievedly harsh to be accurate, and its realism is marred by sentimentality. But undoubtably many rural people (East as well as West, South as well as North) did live lives as sullen and hopeless as those he describes. His work served as a useful antidote to the doses of optimism with which Americans had been periodically injected.

Indeed, it was not at all unusual for American writers of this era to project a feeling of depression about the state of America, as a glance at the work of a few of them will show. Henry Adams, writing about the upper classes of society, was similarily pessimistic in his one novel, *Democracy*. He despaired not over the circumstances of people's lives, but over their moral and esthetic insensibility. Mrs. Lightfoot Lee, young and charming widow, is bored by New York and Boston, and goes to Washington in the hope that the nation's political center will possess vitality. From the first the banality of the city's formal social functions horrifies her. Everything to do with political life seems ugly and meaningless. But then she meets Senator Silas Ratcliffe, an immensely powerful man. The possibility of sharing that power as his wife appeals to her, even though Ratcliffe does not share her views on certain ethical niceties. As governor of Illinois during the Civil War, Ratcliffe had feared that the "peace party" would carry the state, and that disunion would follow. He accordingly held back the Chicago vote until the returns from the southern part of the state were in, and made sure that the Union majority in the northern counties was sufficient to carry the state. This situation poses a neat moral dilemma, but Ratcliffe's action appalls Mrs. Lee, and Henry Adams. I doubt that his great-grandfather or grandfather would have been especially shocked. From henceforward Adams contrasts the corruption of Ratcliffe and other exponents of democracy with the virtues of Carrington, another arche-typal "Southern Cavalier." It is he who finally breaks up Madeleine Lee's intended marriage to Ratcliffe by revealing that the man had accepted a bribe, but as an admirable model Carrington is no more appealing than the Senator. Possessing the capacity for fine moral judgments, he chose to pose on the sidelines and make them, disdainfully, like Adams himself. *Democracy*'s chief failing as a novel lies in this attribute of the author's: he was seldom willing to let characters reveal their nature by actions, but was constantly assessing them from afar, playing the aloof observing author.

Henry James' work does not fail in this respect, but his novel *The Bostonians* resembles *Democracy* in several ways. Both books satirize honored features of American life. Adams chose democratic institutions, James philan-thropy, particularily feminine philanthropy. Both contain a Southern hero, although James' is much more realistically drawn. Most importantly, both stress the mechanically ugly, the greedily heartless nature of America. The country has no grace—it hasn't the time. It has no beauty—money that might go for beauty is squandered on display. Both James and Adams drew their inferences from an examination of the urban monied class, and concluded regretfully that it wasn't as leisured or as cultured as its opposite number in Europe. This was doubtless true, but to judge "America" without even glancing at ninety per cent of its citizens is acting on frail evidence.

James found the feminist movement in America ridiculous; he believed its proponents to be cold-hearted and self-seeking. Certainly the ones he portrayed were both. He didn't think that they could possibly be sincerely working for the good of other women, since to him feminine happiness lay in the traditional roles of wife and motherhood. However, in *The Bostonians* he indicates that this activity is likely to be unsatisfactory as well. Perhaps he believed that no contentment was possible in a society as warped as the American.

William Dean Howells, editor of *Harper's* and for thirty years the dean of American fiction, agreed with James that male-female relations were likely to be unsatisfactory. He ascribed many of their pitfalls to unrealistic expecta-tions and adolescently romantic misconceptions. In *A Modern Instance* the heroine, Marcia Gaylord, is maniacally delighted when Bartley Hubbard asks her to marry him. Having decided to be in love with him, she has deluded herself into believing that he is a worthwhile man. Her father knows differently, but would not dream of interfering with his daughter's choice. Because of an imagined infidelity, she shortly afterward breaks with Bartley as violently as she had clung to him. Perfection or filthiness, passion or hate, are the only choices Marcia thinks are possible. Soon Bartley decides to leave for Boston, upon which Marcia decides to become passionate again, and they marry. Over the next few years Bartley's morals, flimsy enough to start with, steadily decay. Although his worthlessness is apparent enough to everyone else, Marcia steadfastly ignores it. She cannot allow herself to recognize that she might have made a mistake. Bartley's heedlessness and Marcia's hot temper have made for repeated scenes between them, which, while not lessening her jealous devotion, have cooled his slight affection. Finally he deserts her. Her response is to refuse to believe it. She insists to herself and to others that he is coming back to her. Eventually she rids herself of deluded passion by substituting neurotic hatred, but her feelings for Bartley remain the most important thing in her life, and aside from her child, the only thing. Howells scorned the sentimental romanticism which American women delighted in, but he was able to sympathize with those whose lives were ruined by it. Marcia, who could have been a simple, gentle woman, was destroyed by her belief that romantic love atoned for a multitude of evils, and by her refusal to face any reality which contradicted her faith.

Mark Twain viewed female sentimentality with a much harsher eye than Howells'. In the *Adventures of Huckleberry Finn* it is linked with an underlying rapacious cruelty. The women of the Grangerford family moon over a dead daughter, whose specialty had been crayon drawings which sentimentalized death. They are interrupted in this pursuit by the need to round up the menfolks to go shoot members of another family with whom they are feuding. A small Missouri town reveres an old lady for her piety—but she sells a slave "down the river" because the price was too good to pass up.

Women's cruelty was often the more vivid because of the contrast with their view of themselves as creatures both gentle and genteel, but men were vicious too. Shootings, lynchings, tar-and-featherings are almost daily occurences. Men attacked each other to defend their honor, to protect their property, or simply to break the monotony. The sleepy surface of life often cracked, and revealed violent impulses that were usually acted upon. When no excuse for hurting another person appeared, animals provided a handy substitute. Huck speaks of the residents of a small Arkansas town, "There couldn't anything wake them up all over, and make them happy all over, like a dog-fight—unless it might be putting turpentine on a stray dog and setting fire to him, or tying a tin pan to his tail and see him run himself to death."

Only Huck and the escaped slave, Jim, feel no need to go berserk. They are not bored, because they are able to enjoy the simple physical things around

Addison Gallery of American Art, Phillips Andover Academy, Andover, Mass.

FIGURE 19-4. *Winslow Homer,* Eight Bells

    Winslow Homer (1836–1910) was a graphic artist throughout his adult life. During the Civil War he was an illustrator for *Harper's Weekly,* limited to drawings that could be turned into wood-cuts. He was an ardent fisherman and hunter, and many of his paintings depict the outdoors of New England and Canada. The Caribbean, especially the Bahamas, provided the subjects for many works of his later years. In these final efforts Homer revealed, more than any earlier American artist, the potentials of water colors as a medium. The plastic vigor of his water colors from the tropics also marks a departure from the stoic majesty of such canvasses as the one shown here, *Eight Bells* (1886).

    Homer never stayed away from the ocean for long. Born in Boston, he later made his them—the ripples on the water, the sound of the wind, the taste of catfish and pone. Real life is more important to them than defense of a stylized code of honor or their self-importance. But this "reality" does not exist for others, and Huck and Jim are only able to have it when they are isolated from the rapacity of the rest of the human world. And the world won't let them alone. It sees Jim as its rightful prey because he is a slave, and Huck because he is a boy, whom adults can justly hound and mold. But even if they were not particularily vulnerable, their very apartness, their willingness to ignore the scrabbling and the self-puffing which consume everyone else would make them dangerous. Their society flaunts individualism, but cannot tolerate actual differentness. Significantly, at the end of the book Huck cuts for the hills, hoping to find some peace in a place where people are not. But even this sanctuary can be at best short lived.

When *The Adventures of Huckleberry Finn* appeared in 1885 it was widely criticized for its lack of gentility. Although it was not blemished by the demon sex, its characters were considered too coarse, and its language too vulgar, for it to properly fulfill the main function of literature, to uplift and to inspire. It is then no wonder that the following year the nation's foremost painter, Thomas Eakins, created a scandal by requesting a male model to remove his loincloth in an art class which included women students. Although in the preceding 10 years Eakins had helped turn the Pennsylvania Academy of Fine Arts into a source of serious artistic discipline, prudery easily overcame beauty, and forced his resignation (Ways to Study History XIX).

Although most Americans' artistic imagination stopped at advertising calendars and samplers extolling home sweet home, great changes were being made in the visual arts. The possibilities of the portrait were expanding. Some painters were departing from the stiff, "posed" portrait to show people in activity—boxers boxing, housewives cleaning. Albert Pynkham Ryder was experimenting with new techniques of color and line, and creating pictures whose symbolic meanings were more important than their representational ones. Winslow Homer, although not as profound an artist as Eakins or Ryder, was enraptured by the raw beauty of the Maine coast, and was painting landscapes that bore little relation to the manicured romances, derivatives of

---

permanent home on the coast of Maine. The whaling industry was in its dying years when he was an adolescent, but seafaring and the fisheries continued to loom large in the port towns of the northern Atlantic coast. Homer's appreciation of the workaday tensions between man and the sea both diminished and exalted the human dimension; individuals have no character in this painting except as they cope with the elements. He exulted in the external world: "The Sun will not rise or set without my notice, and thanks."

His verbal statement of his aims approximates that of Bingham in the preceding generation (Figure 13-6): "When I have selected the thing carefully, I paint it exactly as it appears." He did not, but the slant of his bias was clear.

FIGURE 19-5. *Albert P. Ryder,* White Horse Grazing

Albert Pinkham Ryder (1847–1917) may well have been the first major American painter to break with the Gospel of Work. Undoubtedly he brooded over each canvas, and he toiled over it—often too much. He never did master the craft of painting; his thickly caked pigments were so badly mixed that already many of his works have darkened and deteriorated. Also, although he differed from Thomas Eakins in that he became a financial success in his middle years, the two were the same in not caring about money. (See "Ways to Study History XIX" and Figure 19-6.)

Ryder was born in the erstwhile whaling center of New Bedford, but he spent his adult life in virtual solitude in a congested Manhattan. Here he helped to invent the life style of the bohemian. He the Barbizon School, which had heretofore been the standard product of American landscape painting.

In architecture, Henry Hobson Richardson was proving it possible to be both a creative and a financial success. Fascinated by the Romanesque style, he did buildings of massive red sandstone, with heavy piers and rounded arches. Trinity Church in Boston is a typical and felicitous example of his style. Although some of his buildings are drab, and others chaotic, the best are both graceful and integrated. One of his finest was the Marshall Field wholesale store in Chicago. Although much of the wall space consisted of windows, grouped in fluidly rhythmic patterns, the heavy sandstone and granite supporting piers bespoke solidity, while their seven-story sweep pointed upwards.

Richardson's Chicago store was a great success, both artistically and publicly, but skyrocketing urban land costs were making the large masonry building obsolete. The same high costs were forcing buildings to become taller, but as a masonry structure grew higher it required more and more massive supporting pillars at ground level. These in turn took up expensive space, and reduced the amount of window space which could be used for display purposes. Steel skeleton construction posed no such dilemma. Combined with the recently developed mechanical elevator, it imposed no practical limits on height, and since the external walls were a mere shell against the elements, bearing no weight, they could consist almost entirely of glass wherever that seemed desirable (Figure 29-4). But until Louis Sullivan attacked the problem, no architect perceived the artistic possibilities of this type of structure, probably because most architects were degenerates, content to apply the styles of past "periods" to new construction. Since the tall office building had no direct progenitor, they could only try to disguise it. Its increasingly elongated proportions made that increasingly difficult. Sullivan saw no reason for the disguise; he was fascinated by the possibilities for beautiful innovation provided by skeletal steel. In the Monadnock Building in St. Louis he provided an almost unbroken wall of glass at ground level for display (others had attempted to ape the heavy piers of masonry construction) and emphasized the structure's height by graceful vertical pillars, another new idea.

The Monadnock Building was acclaimed, but much of Sullivan's work

lived in a garret. His floors were littered with garbage, old newspapers, unwashed dishes. Amid the squalid rubble an alert visitor might detect a check for $500 which he had neglected to deposit. The division of artist from philistine was becoming visible. How unlike Charles Bulfinch, the great Boston architect of a century earlier, whose home provided a meeting-place for great merchants (Figure 12-2).

Ryder's canvas. *White Horse Grazing* cannot be precisely dated because he often worked at a single conception for a decade or more; the year 1885 should be close. Perhaps the best label for his vision would be mystic. Records show that he was capable of prolonged and close observation of the external world, but his paintings seem to be a controlled fling outward from internal passions.

was too innovative to have a broad appeal. Few people were yet able to escape the honeyed trap of the traditional, or able to see beauty except in terms of adornment. Nonetheless, American architecture seemed on the verge of a breakthrough to new forms. But in 1893 the Columbian Exposition set it back. This World's Fair drew more than 27 million visitors, more than any before. Its attractions ranged from prize livestock to a 150-ton cannon to a map of New York State made of pickles. The "White City" in which the Fair was housed enthralled visitors as much as its contents; the buildings had been designed as an integrated whole in the Greek Revival style (Chapter 12). Except for Sullivan's Transportation Building, none had any merit. The Exposition grounds were dazzling, but inane. Sullivan recognized the damage the Fair had done: "Thus architecture died in the land of the free and the home of the brave—in a land declaring its democracy, inventiveness, unique daring, enterprise and progress." Soon no one with any pretensions to gentility would consent to live in a house undecorated with pillars and portico, and business-men who could afford it were having their commercial structures embellished the same way. The incongruities and inconveniences of this design made no dent in its fashionableness for years.

In 1883 Matthew Arnold, esteemed English poet and critic, wrote a short analytic essay on the United States, in which he said that the country was not "interesting." His two criteria were beauty and distinction. He said that America lacked beauty because of the absence of the patina of antiquity, the layered look of history. No one cherished any particular patch of ground, and consequently everything was ragged at the edges. Its citizens were hardly ever distinguished, because the cult of the "average man" dominated the popular imagination. To be different was not to be honored. The frenzy over the Columbian Exposition illustrates some of the reasons for this phenomenon. Despite boosterism, Americans did not trust themselves to develop their experience into its own artistic expression. Imitation of the European was safer. Public indifference and contempt drove most American artists into exile—either physically or mentally. Their isolation from American life then made their work less telling than it might have become.

In the 1850's only Herman Melville publicly despaired at the human future. By the 1890's no thoughtful person remained optimistic. Modern man, capable of enduring without believing, had arisen in those fifty years. So many successes had turned out to be failures. The ambitions of continental-ism had been achieved, the folk with a manifest destiny had reached the Pacific, but now Henry George and Frederick Jackson Turner warned them that the old game had ended. The economy seemed deranged, in spite of the massive inflow of Europeans who contributed so much to the material growth of the nation. Unfortunately, as it seemed to the old-stock Americans, those very immigrants brought antipathetic folkways. Perhaps the best summary to this chapter is a book by Michael Lesy, a documentary dramatization of life during a farming depression in a town in Jackson County, Wisconsin. News stories of 1885 to 1900 from the local newspaper, plus artfully juxtaposed photographs, comprise *Wisconsin Death Trip*. The title is apt. Elsewhere I have called attention to the prominence of suicide in the works of great American writers of this period (Document 19-1), and Lesy's book fleshes out the literary evidence with the stark stare of documentary images. Rural life was not happy. Our great-grandfathers were not exuberant men. Through their ears and into their minds, while they were thrashing about desperately, they were listening to a daily litany of disaster.

SOME NOTABLE EVENTS

1865 Yale opens first fine arts department in any U.S. college
Mendel unveils his laws of heredity.

1868 University of California chartered.

1869 Wyoming grants the first women's suffrage in the U.S.

1870 The Vatican adopts the dogma of Papal infallibility.
Graduate work organized at Harvard and Yale.

1872 *Scientific Monthly* founded.

1874 Women's Christian Temperance Union founded.

1876 Thomas Eakins begins teaching anatomy at the Pennsylvania Academy of Fine Arts
Dr. Felix Adler founds the Society for Ethical Culture.
Johns Hopkins founded as a purely graduate school.
American Library Association formed.

1877 Thomas Edison patents the phonograph.

1878 Church of Christ, Scientist, formed.

1879 Henry George, *Progress and Poverty*.

1880 Salvation Army begins in the U.S.

1881 Wharton School of Finance and Economy founded.
National Red Cross founded.

1882 Chinese immigration suspended for 10 years (Chinese Exclusion Act).

1883 New York *World* under Pulitzer launches "yellow journalism" in U.S.

1885 Mark Twain, *The Adventures of Huckleberry Finn*.
William Dean Howells, *The Rise of Silas Lapham*.
Henry James, *The Bostonians*.

1887 Edward Bellamy, *Looking Backward*.

1889 Hull-House founded.

1890 Congress adopts its first international copyright law.
William James, *Principles of Psychology*.

1891 Cal Tech and the University of Chicago founded.

Ways to Study History XIX

Pore over portraits. Several years ago I devised an exercise for a graduate seminar in American biography and autobiography. Having picked a dozen slides, mainly in color, I projected them for the class. The students were told that each subject was an American, that each picture had been made by an American, and the date of creation of each. The assignment was then to write an imaginary biography of the subject up to the time the portrait was made. What traits of character are shown by his face, his stance, his expression? What social class did he represent? Where in the nation did he live? What typical experiences had he had? This assignment was frankly experimental, but the results were surprisingly rewarding; many students produced sagas that were highly inventive and also historically precise.

You might want to try the game with this depiction of *Mrs. Edith Mahon* by Thomas Eakins (Figure 19-6). The painter lived in Philadelphia, 1844–1916. His works are truly a gallery of his countrymen: opera singers, clerics, pugilists, men rowing on the Schuylkill. He also did a haunting Crucifixion. His effort was always to depict the thing as it was, while giving to the canvas a vividity that seemed to reach into nature. It says much about the esthetic standards of the late nineteenth century that he was never a success; the finest collection of his works is in the Philadelphia Museum of Art where it was lodged gratis by his widow.

Eakins' methods were painfully painstaking. If ever a man was infected by the Gospel of Work, it was he (yes, it even invaded art). The better to depict the human body, he studied anatomy and went to autopsies. He profited from photography. Planning to paint a carriage drawn by four horses, he worked with a photographer on countless rapid-action shots of the event. Then he made a small statuette of each horse. Then he began to paint. Never intended for public view, the other products were mere preliminaries.

Document 19-1

Walt Whitman stopped writing in 1873, and for more than twenty years afterwards American poetry did not exist in any serious sense. Edwin Arlington Robinson (1869–1935) began a new era with his first volume of verse, published in 1897. Notice the simplicity of the language, and the ease, the naturalness, of the expression in this poem. Robinson was one of the first Americans to realize that language need not be flowery to be "poetical." Also, he seems to have recognized what the psychologists now call "free-floating anxiety," an anguish which has no discernable cause.

> *Richard Cory*
> *Whenever Richard Cory went down town,*
> *We people on the pavement looked at him:*
> *He was a gentleman from sole to crown,*
> *Clean favored, and imperially slim.*
>
> *And he was always quietly arrayed,*
> *And he was always human when he talked;*
> *But still he fluttered pulses when he said,*
> *"Good-morning," and he glittered when he walked.*
>
> *And he was rich—yes, richer than a king—*
> *And admirably schooled in every grace:*
> *In fine, we thought that he was everything*
> *To make us wish that we were in his place.*

FIGURE19-6. *Thomas Eakins*, Mrs. Edith Mahon *(Ways to Study History XIX)*

So on we worked, and waited for the light,
And went without the meat, and cursed the bread;
And Richard Cory, one calm summer night,
Went home and put a bullet through his head.

Document 19-2

One of the leading American novelists for forty years, William Dean Howells also encouraged the development of younger writers. When Stephen Crane interviewed him for the New York Times in 1894 Crane's career had hardly begun, and Howells' reputation was very high. Here Howells discusses the function of the novel and the novelist.

I believe that every novel should have an intention. A man should mean something when he writes. Ah, this writing merely to amuse people—why, it seems to me altogether vulgar. A man may as well blacken his face and go out and dance on the street for pennies. The author is a sort of trained bear, if you accept certain standards. If literary men are to be the public fools, let us at any rate have it clearly understood, so that those of us who feel differently can take measures. But, on the other hand, a novel should never preach and berate and storm. It does no good. . . .

It is the business of the novel to picture the daily life in the most exact terms possible, with an absolute and clear sense of proportion. That is the important matter—the proportion. As a usual thing, I think, people have absolutely no sense of proportion. Their noses are tight against life, you see. They perceive mountains where there are no mountains, but frequently a great peak appears no larger than a rat trap. An artist sees a dog down the street—well, his eye instantly relates the dog to its surroundings. The dog is proportioned to the buildings and the trees whereas, many people can conceive of that dog's tail resting upon a hill top. . . .

[The novel] is a perspective made for the benefit of people who have no true use of their eyes. The novel, in its real meaning, adjusts the proportion. It preserves the balances. It is in this way that lessons are to be taught and reforms to be won. When people are introduced to each other they will see the resemblances, and won't want to fight so badly.

Document 19-3

Although Mark Twain had little in common with Henry Adams and claimed he was unable to read Henry James, he shared their ironic distrust of human nature and the democratic process. "Purchasing Civic Virtue" illustrates his pessimism.

Every man is a master and also a servant, a vassal. There is always someone who looks up to him and admires and envies him; there is always someone to whom he looks up and whom he admires and envies. This is his nature; this is his character; and it is unchangeable, indestructable; therefore republics and democracies are not for such as he; they cannot satisfy the requirements of his nature. . . .

At first we granted deserved pensions, righteously and with a clean and honorable motive, to the disabled soldiers of the Civil War. The clean motive began and ended there. We have made many and amazing additions to the pension list but with a motive which dishonors the uniform and the Congresses which have voted the additions, the sole purpose back of the additions being the purchase of votes. . . . We have the two Roman conditions: stupendous wealth with its inevitable corruptions and moral blight, and the corn and oil pensions—that is to say, vote bribes, which have taken away the pride of thousands of tempted men and turned them into willing alms receivers and unashamed.

The Great Faultline, 1893–1898

This is a good point for some blunt assertions. With the possible exception of the years 1786–1788, the worst peacetime crisis in American history began with the financial panic of 1893 and culminated in the Spanish-American War. This remark may well be resented by many, especially by students and by blacks; these groups can with justification speak of the nuclear weapons, the threat of mass annihilation, the continuing oppression of blacks, the palpable insanity of the war in Viet Nam, the defects of the educational system, the lack of good jobs for young people—of any jobs. These grievances will be confronted below. But my initial statement should stand. In the closing years of the last century, American voters and American institutions were faced with several showdowns. They did not deal wisely with a single one of them. The price for those failures is still being paid, and the end is yet to come.

Before laying out some specifics, more assertions. Due in large part to the maldistribution of income, the economy was in a worse condition than ever before. Dislocations in the business world aggravated the ruptures in society. We have looked at some of the earlier race riots (early Chapter 15) and we will look at some that have occurred since World War II (Chapters 29 and 30); be it noted here that white-black tensions were as violent in the 1890s as at any other time. Complementing the racial strife were clashes of worker with employer. Talk of actual revolution was common, and middle-class folk valued the Army and the National Guard as weapons to suppress insurrection. The social and economic conflicts boiled over into politics. Probably elections have never been more corrupt, more violent, dirtier. The judiciary has never been more prejudiced. And all this seething mass spilled over the nation's borders and called itself a foreign policy. The consequence was a major break in American diplomacy. An unhappy land sought solace in grasping for commitments abroad that inflicted injustice on millions of others while grossly wasting American output; productive capacity that might have gone to improve sanitation in cities, to cite one example, went into battleships. But then, given the configuration of the American spirit at the time, was it not inevitable that wealth would be poured into swords not plowshares? Lament it as we may, the country's policy-makers had come to see military expenditures as the handiest solution for the glutted state of the economy that had been developing since as early as 1873. Businessmen and politicians seldom look for any answer which, even though it might promise to be lasting, is for the moment difficult; they want a quick way out of the box. They seldom look beyond the next balance sheet, the next election.

But it will not do to exaggerate the abruptness of the changes. The underlying difficulties of the economy had originated decades earlier, but they had grown worse. More important, people had become more aware of them. In addition to the ugliness of the Haymarket outburst, other eruptions had burst out. One focus of discontent was the favoritism by governments. A great commentator on the events of the period, Henry Demarest Lloyd, remarked: "The Standard has done everything with the Pennsylvania legislature, except refine it." The five railroads from the East Coast to Chicago were a glaring case of excess carrying capacity, and Standard Oil had also used this circumstance to get huge concessions in the freight rates charged to it; the so-called rebates. Here was another focus of animosity—the railroads. Thousands of farmers and other shippers were convinced they were being cheated; if you were unfortunately located in a spot that was served by only one trunkline, you might pay twice as much as a competitor paid to ship his product twice as far. That could mean your death. To quote Lloyd again: "The movement of the railroad trains of this country is literally the circulation of its blood." (See Document 20-1.)

The truth of that remark was underscored by strikes. Beginning in 1876, the span of one year saw eight important walk-outs; the next summer the series culminated in a tie-up of lines from the Atlantic to St. Louis. Railroads, burdened with gigantic fixed costs, could not tolerate such disruptions. So the

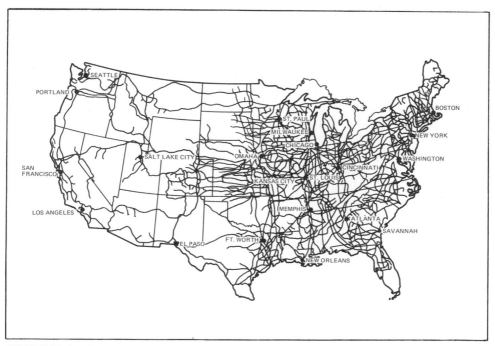

FIGURE 20-1.   *Railroads in the U.S., 1890*

companies felt compelled to wipe out all unions. Simply to report that would be far too facile, for they also worked toward quite detailed tactics for achieving the aim. A show-piece here is the Burlington strike of 1888. Establishment of the Interstate Commerce Commission in 1887—partly at the behest of some major railroads—had not instituted any machinery that could stop a strike by the Brotherhood of Engineers and by the Firemen, the two strongest unions. About 2,000 men hit the bricks. The strike lasted nearly ten months. Union sympathizers were convicted of planting dynamite to blow up track. Federal circuit courts issued injunctions to halt the walkout. Most crucial, strikebreakers could be hired. One company executive put it thus: "The result has demonstrated the fact that an abundance of labor will break up any strike, no matter how strong the striking party may be. We can easily get two thousand engineers if we need them." While goods were redundant, so were workers. This condition existed throughout the country.

Other examples will shortly be given, but they should not obscure the general situation. You will read of the Homestead strike, of the pardon of the Haymarket defendants. These episodes contributed to the existing malaise. But a couple of celebrated events do not create a ubiquitous state of mind. Thousands of shoot-outs, many of them in obscure mining towns or at lonely junction points, were built into a gestalt pattern that some psychologists would call "free-floating anxiety," or a general state of mental depression. Even they did not know what they were afraid of, but they were very afraid (See Document 19-1).

The Homestead strike of 1892 illustrates several major developments. Carnegie's decision five years earlier to convert this giant mill from production of rails to structural steel reflects the growth of cities, the origins of the skyscraper, rising land values. The strike shows the invention of techniques for smashing a trade union. In 1889 a contract was signed, to last for three years, covering the 4,000 workers at Homestead; at that time the Amalgamated Association of Iron and Steel Workers had more than 20,000 members in the nation. With a large fraction of its organization composed of skilled workers, it was one of the strongest unions in the country. The contract with Carnegie gave widely differential treatment to the assorted occupations. Due to the shortage of skilled workers and the growing glut of unskilled immigrants, the hourly rate for common labor was 14 cents while other employees got as much as $14 a day. A newspaper reported on a "sober and thrifty" Welsh immigrant in Homestead whose family lived in "a large, handsome cottage in the Queen Anne style, gaily painted," with a parlor organ, electric lights, upholstered furniture, and deep carpets.

As the expiration date of the collective-bargaining agreement drew near, a board wall topped by barbed wire was built around the mill. At regular intervals, three inch portholes were cut. At this point some of the conflicts within the entrepreneurial class become manifest. Carnegie was in Scotland; the top executive on the spot was Henry Clay Frick. The two agreed that the union had to be destroyed. But it seems that Carnegie wanted to close down the plant and wait the opposition out. Frick chose a different course, and it says a good deal about the period to note that it was the hard-nosed antagonist who had his way. He locked out 800 men, prompting a strike by the entire labor force. He hired 300 armed guards from the Pinkerton detective bureau. When they arrived at Homestead, an all-day battle ensued. Ten strikers and three Pinkertons were killed. The governor of the state sent 8,000 militia to the town. But the walkout dragged along for more than three months, because the company had trouble getting skilled recruits to act as strikebreakers. At last production resumed with 2,000 workers, of whom only 400 had been employees before the strike. The union at Homestead had been crushed.

Another noteworthy product of labor strife was the decision by Governor John Peter Altgeld of Illinois to pardon the surviving defendants in the Haymarket case. Had he been prudent, he could probably have taken this action without arousing great controversy; since the trial six years earlier, hundreds of citizens had circulated petitions for amnesty. The common argument was that the men had expiated their guilt. But Altgeld did not take this ground. Far from conciliatory, he charged that the men had been unjustly convicted. His message pulsated with indignation at the conduct of the trial. He insisted that the jury had been deliberately packed, its members biased, the judge prejudiced, and the verdict founded on a rule of law that was ridiculous. That these rebukes should come from a prominent statesman was remarkable, but even more extraordinary was the reaction to the pardon. Almost the entire press responded with frenzy. They shouted apoplectically that Altgeld was not a Democrat at all but an outright anarchist. The republic was losing its nerve.

Psychic stress was exacerbated by the state of the economy. At the beginning of 1893 a large railroad went into bankruptcy—it had short-term debts of $18.5 million and liquid assets of about $100,000. Banks started to crumble:

January—April	28 suspended payment	
May	54	"	"
June	128	"	"

Worried foreigners began to unload their American securities and pull their capital home. It flowed out in gold. Drains on the treasury's gold stocks were more acute because of the Sherman Silver Purchase Act of 1890, which masqueraded as an effort to more than double the volume of silver bought and coined by the treasury. (With the expansion of silver mining in the West, the price of that metal had fallen: $1.15 an ounce at the passage of the Bland-Allison Act in 1878; in 1890 it was only 94 cents.)

The monetary stringency was felt especially keenly by farmers. In consequence, the small farmers, especially of the Midwest and South, began to focus their needs politically through a newly strengthened third party, the Populists (see Document 20-2). In 1892 they put forward some novel demands. Again, as in the reaction to the Haymarket pardon, the response to their audacity was extreme, even though the proposals were reasonable enough. One plank of their platform called for government ownership and operation of railroads, telephones, telegraphs. Acceptance of this policy would have saved the nation a lot of grief from that day to this. Another plank was the so-called subtreasury plan, under which a farmer who deposited his crop with a federal agency could get from the government up to 80 per cent of the cash value of the collateral. This is in essence the procedure later adopted under the New Deal, with rhetoric calling it the "ever-normal granary" and with bureaus called the Agricultural Adjustment Administration, the AAA. In the 1890s when it made considerable sense, it was not adopted; in the 1930s when it made little sense, it was picked up as a desperate panacea (Chapter 26).

In the presidential election of 1892, the People's party tallied more than a million votes in the nation. The most interesting area to study here is the South, which Vann Woodward and others have shown to be the fulcrum of Populist strength (see Ways to Study History XX). Faced with a new challenge to their traditional voting strength the national Democratic Party felt cornered. If they espoused free coinage of silver in order to win the Mountain states and the prairies, they would lose the conservatives whom they needed to win the East. But the Atlantic seaboard would not suffice, they must have the South

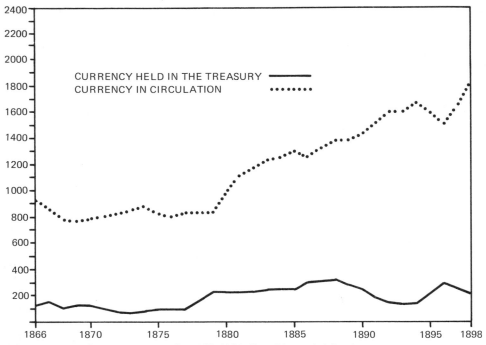

FIGURE 20-2. *Currency in the U.S., 1866–1898, (in millions of dollars)*

also. As it turned out, the Populist vote in the latter region was limited to 362,000. To achieve this outcome, the Democrats held off their challengers mostly with physical coercion. Look at Georgia, where in October of 1892 the Populist candidate for governor lost by a 2-1 margin, and a month later the party's nominee for president was credited with less than 20 per cent of the votes and ran third behind the Republican. The landed classes in Georgia feared that their entire system was toppling. Hadn't that rabblerouser, Representative Tom Watson, been telling both whites and blacks: "You are made to hate each other because upon that hatred is rested the keystone of this arch of financial despotism which enslaves you both"? Fear begets repression, and in the campaign an estimated fifteen blacks were killed by Democrats. The Democratic governor was heard to say "Watson ought to be killed and it ought to have been done long ago." In one county the Democratic chairman sent around to planters a flyer, "It is absolutely necessary that you should bring to bear the power which your situation gives over tenants, laborers and croppers." Negro field hands were carted to the polls packed like sardines, and voted like sardines. Voters were paid off in cash while the whiskey flowed from barrels. Impostors were brought into the state across the Savannah River to stuff ballot-boxes with fake votes. In Watson's congressional district, around Augusta, the vote was about twice the number of legal voters. While it was not the first time in American history that an election had been rigged, and it was not to be the last, this instance was extreme. White Populists began to get the impression that the power structure would never permit them to unite with blacks in order to gain power. This impression was hammered home by later elections. At length, in despair, the radical whites reverted to reaction, by returning to the old convention of white solidarity to stamp on the blacks. It was an atavistic spasm, and Tom Watson joined in.

Another effort at unified opposition among disinherited groups was launched among railroad workers. The kingpin was Eugene Debs, and the organization was the American Railway Union (ARU). Its structure, unprecedented on the railroads, was advanced for any portion of trade unionism in the United States. The technical term would be industrial unionism; that is, a single agency to bargain for all employees of companies turning out a given line of products, whether rubber or steel or automobiles or whatever. In the contrasting system, craft unionism, the workers are subdivided by skill or trade, so that one employer might deal with a dozen or more separate unions. This latter scheme had been habitual with the railroad Brotherhoods, and to some skilled workers it had brought benefits. For the semiskilled it had failed miserably. The task, as Debs saw it, was to weld together these disparate groups so they could bargain collectively. His venture had only two assets: the talents of a handful of organizers, and the grievances of legions of railway hands. It had no traditions, no structure, no experience, no money, and it faced the combined opposition of dozens of the strongest corporations in the world.

This hostile power proved overwhelming, and in the Pullman boycott we can watch it work. The initial successes of the ARU had been amazing. In a year it organized 150,000 men and became the largest union in the nation. In a strike against the Great Northern, the best managed of all large American railroads, it won nearly all of its demands. Then it encountered the collaborative enmity of a phalanx of companies. The union, to aid strikers against the company that made and operated Pullman sleeping cars, decreed a boycott against the cars. To speak gently, this move was not wise, and Debs did what he could to prevent it. The union would not move any train hauling Pullmans, and the railroads would not cease attaching Pullmans to trains. From Chicago westward, the blood of a nation stopped circulating. Now the massed power came into play. The twenty-four railways centering or terminating in Chicago were joined into the General Managers Association. These companies together had

a capital of 818×10^7
41,000 miles of track
221,000 employees

That monolithic (for the moment) Goliath would be a match for any David. But next the parasites began to bleed their host.

The ARU had appealed to other unions for help. Most answers were evasive. Only one promised full help. The national officers of most of the Brotherhoods worked against the strike. On one railroad where 400 Locomotive Engineers joined the strike, the president of the order denounced their action as a violation of his union's rules, and proclaimed that unemployed engineers could legitimately take the jobs of their "brothers." The head of the Conductors said that he had "neither authority nor inclination" to help the ARU. Later he explained that any industrial union like the ARU had to be opposed by a craft union like his own, "no matter what the conditions at Pullman were."* Debs' reply to this hostility was bitter: "Every concession the railway companies have ever made, has been wrung from them by the power of organized effort." He was right. In this instance the union, supported by many civic leaders, had asked that the original dispute be submitted to arbitration. A spokesman for the company answered that there was "nothing to arbitrate" (The spokesman was not George M. Pullman; he was on vacation. It was uncanny how the corporate autocrats managed to become unavailable when a strike was imminent.).

In spite of these handicaps—the combined opposition of the Pullman Company, two dozen railroads, virtually every commercial newspaper and magazine—for the first ten days of the boycott the union seemed on the road to victory. Subsequently Debs claimed that the railroads were hanging on the ropes: "Their immediate resources were exhausted, their properties were paralyzed, and they were unable to operate their trains." Then came the cruncher; the federal government, instead of being the referee, became a giant pugilist in the opposition corner. From this round forward, the tactics used were a series of low blows. They were ostentiously dirty, and designedly so. Since President Cleveland at the time had his hands full with a tariff bill in Congress, federal policy was made largely by the attorney general of the United States. But he needed deputies on the spot in Chicago; his solution was to appoint as special federal attorney to handle the situation the same man who was counsel to a large railroad involved in the boycott. The attorney general made no bones about his objective: "I feel that the true way of dealing with the matter is by a force which is overwhelming and prevents any attempt at resistance." His reasoning went thus. (1) Any national railroad strike was

---

*These conditions need not be detailed here; a few specifics will suffice. In less than a year beginning in July, 1893, the number of employees fell from 5,500 to 3,300. Dividends were actually increased, while payrolls declined 38 per cent. Rents in the company-owned houses were not reduced. Perhaps worst of all was the omnipresence of that would-be dictator, Mr. Pullman. One resident explained: "We are born in a Pullman house, fed from the Pullman shop, taught in the Pullman school, catechized in the Pullman church, and when we die we shall be buried in the Pullman cemetery and go to the Pullman hell."

automatically illegal.* (2) The causes of the strike in the town of Pullman were not relevant to the legality of the boycott. (3) Local and state officials could not be trusted to police the dispute. The second point may be conceded. The first may be technically accurate on the basis of the precedents then existing, but it was not a constructive approach to the problem. The third was simply absurd; in retrospect we must shake our heads sadly and say that Altgeld's image stemming from the Haymarket pardon had come home to haunt him.

However deceitful, the third postulate was needed for the attorney general's full program. First his agent procured from two federal judges an injunction against the boycott on several grounds, including interference with the mails and obstruction of interstate commerce. Its terms were amazingly sweeping; it forbade any person to do or say anything to promote the walkout. Next, ironically on Independence Day, the president rushed onward to a tragic climax by sending the United States army into Chicago. This act brought heated protests from Governor Altgeld, who pointed out, correctly, that the president could under the express words of the Constitution send federal troops into a state only to remedy certain evils and by certain procedures. The stipulated evils were not present. Nor were the proper procedures followed: "local self-government is a fundamental principle of our Constitution. Each community shall govern itself so long as it can and is ready and able to enforce the law." The response from the White House was haughty:

> While I am still persuaded that I have neither transcended my authority nor duty in the emergency that confronts us, it seems to me that in this hour of danger and public distress, discussion may well give way to active efforts on the part of all in authority to restore obedience to law and to protect life and property.

The strike was dead. The union was destroyed. Debs went to jail for contempt of court. But the episode cannot be abandoned without more analysis; it raised issues that have persisted to the present. One preacher made this contribution to the discussion: "the Anarchist is a savage in a civilized country who is trying to turn civilization into barbarism." How often has it happened in American history that the propertied classes and their pensioners, such as college administrators, have blockaded all the water taps through which justice might flow and then denounced anybody who tried to tap the water main as a saboteur?

Then, too, Altgeld was speaking sound doctrine when he called for the widest possible application of Jefferson's dictum that the government is best

---

*In no way do I intend to minimize the gravity of similar situations; recent strikes by postal employees and sanitation workers have reminded us that some functions are indispensable. But if the right to strike is to be denied, another mechanism to insure equity must be substituted. I doubt if compulsory arbitration is the answer. Why not tie the wages of essential civil servants to those of carpenters and steelworkers?

that governs least. Supporters of the New Deal and its successors have hailed every growth in federal power as an advance of human welfare (Chapter 26). Today, when the bureaucracy in Washington and elsewhere has reached an appalling stage of rampaging elephantiasis, we can have a keener appreciation of Altgeld's protests. We can see better why as much control as possible should be returned to the neighborhoods. And of course we can now see better how the matter touches on the division of power among the branches of government. For decades many liberal historians wrote as if the "great presidents" were synonymous with "the strong presidents," and wrote scornfully about weak executives like Harding (Chapter 24). Events have reminded us that a president can be too strong; it is more than ever true that absolute power corrupts absolutely. Finally, it might be remarked here that we hear the phrase "law-and-order" so often linked that we unfortunately think as if it were all one word. This is by no means so. Many Americans have always been ready, when they feared for the maintenance of order, to forego the rule of law. Thus we get arrests without warrants, detention without trials, suppression by the authorities of peaceable public meetings. Observing in a few months the Great Northern strike, the Pullman boycott, a farflung coal strike, one periodical lamented: "It is probably safe to say that in no civilized country in this century, not actually in the throes of war or open insurrection, has society been so disorganized as it was in the United States during the first half of 1894; never was human life held so cheap; never did constituted authorities appear so incompetent to enforce respect for the law." To this the republic had fallen.

As this passage suggests, the influence of government can also be too weak in respect to certain issues. For instance, Grover Cleveland had been re-installed in the White House after making powerful pleas for tariff reduction. But he was balked by Congress. The Wilson-Gorman bill aimed to reduce import duties from an average of 49 per cent of value to 30 per cent. The measure was passed by a large majority of representatives. But the Senate adopted more than 600 amendments. After months of haggling and log-rolling and back-scratching, the bill became law without Cleveland's signature; the defection of eight Democratic senators who voted for their constituencies (oh, those sugar states such as Louisiana and Maryland) rather than with their party proved to be the margin. The recurrent gold crises also highlighted the limitations of federal power. Cleveland simply did not have tools with which he could block the steady drainage of gold out of the country; as fears heightened abroad that the United States might leave the gold standard, investors in Europe sold their American securities and brought their capital home. Pressure against the gold standard was intense, and the only way that Cleveland could fend off a departure from "sound money" and "fiscal honesty" was to borrow from private agencies frequent injections of gold. This policy depended on the cooperation of investment bankers, and they dictated the terms of the loans. In simple fact, the most powerful man in the nation was not the president but rather the private banker J. P. Morgan, who could reach large supplies of capital (Chapter 21).

Other impediments to remedial actions by the federal government were interposed by the courts. The class bias of the Supreme Court was blatant. Perhaps its holdings in the various cases arising from the Pullman boycott can be justified by existing precedents. But the same argument cannot be made for three other decisions. One involved the meaning of the Sherman Anti-Trust Act of 1890. The constitutional basis of this statute was the power of Congress over interstate commerce. But ruled the Court: "Commerce succeeds to manufacture, and is not a part of it." Even if we concede that the defendant, a sugar refiner, was a manufacturer, it does not follow at all from the quoted edict that manufacture is not a part of interstate commerce. The next major decision was, if possible, worse. A tax of 2 per cent on personal and corporate incomes of more than $4,000 had been imposed by the Wilson-Gorman Act. A petitioner appealed that the tax violated the constitutional provision that all "direct taxes" had to be apportioned among the states according to population, and also that it breached the requirement "all duties, imports, and excises shall be uniform throughout the United States." A lawyer for the appellant warned that validation of the statute would lead to graver abuses until the nation would see "finally a provision that only the twenty people who have the greatest estates should bear the whole taxation, and after that communism, anarchy, and then, the ever following despotism." Outside the judicial chambers the rhetoric was equally florid, and equally irrelevant. As the proposition was put by the leading law journal in the East, it was the job of the Supreme Court to deliver "a crushing defeat of the pet schemes of the scum of Europe." After some legal complications, plus appeals to protect "thousands of widows and orphans" from an unjust exaction, a bare majority of the Court voted to disallow the income-tax clause.

A third judgment was as abhorrent as the second. An appeal came to the Supreme Court against a state law requiring separate coaches on railroads for blacks and whites. The statute did not violate the Fourteenth Amendment, ruled the Court, if the coaches were equal in quality. Only one justice dissented, and he composed a model of concision: "Our Constitution is color-blind." To this subject we will return (Chapter 29).*

In the field of diplomacy, American policy had been founded on a careful assessment of means against ends. It had studied the balance of power, and then sought precise and limited goals. Now it became grandiose. In

---

*A comment, to be expanded below, seems appropriate. Here was a blanket endorsement by the highest bench of the "separate but equal" doctrine. When it was rejected by a successor Court in 1954, that body most unwisely ventured on elaborate non-judicial exhortations. It might have simply reiterated, "Our Constitution is color-blind."

seeking to use braggadocio to win the reputation of being a world power, the nation's power became more unstable.

Hawaii gives an introduction to this theme. Americans in the China trade had become involved there before the eighteenth century ended, especially to buy sandalwood that they carried to the Asian mainland. American officials made several efforts at closer relations with the archipelago: a treaty of intended annexation in 1854, a reciprocity treaty (mutual reduction or elimination of tariffs) in 1855. But these efforts were blocked by opposition within the United States. Then recurrent crises hit the islands' biggest industry—sugar growing. The first reciprocity agreement between the two governments, made in 1875, was renewed until the McKinley Tariff Act of 1890. This statute pulled a cute trick: not only would domestic planters get a bounty of 2 cents a pound, but henceforth all foreign sugar would enter duty-free. To sugar planters in Hawaii, many of them transplanted Americans, the measure was disastrous to their market position. The revolution they organized in 1894 won without bloodshed, and it won with the aid of the United States. Several strands of influence can be seen. The influence of paleface planters was undoubtedly vital; they wanted to become a territory of the republic in order to regain their markets for sugar. They had the support of the American envoy, who proclaimed that "the Hawaiian pear is now fully ripe, and this is the golden hour for the United States to pluck it." The merger was encouraged by new strategic-mercantile concepts that were current; in 1890 Alfred T. Mahan had published the most compelling work in this vein. His book was entitled *The Influence of Sea Power upon History, 1660–1783,* but its message to contemporaries was urgent: it argued that no nation could succeed in the worldwide struggle for markets unless it had ports around the globe, plus a strong navy. The latter objective was advanced when, from 1890 to 1892, Congress voted funds for four warships. For a few years, however, the Hawaiian annexationist movement was stalled. Its most effective opponent was Grover Cleveland, returned to the White House in 1893. At that time a treaty to annex Hawaii was pending in the Senate. But it had not been ratified. The new president withdrew it, saying: "The mission of our nation is to build up and make a greater country out of what we have, instead of annexing islands." This should not be taken to mean that Cleveland was cautious in the assertion of American power; far from it.

A telltale episode is known as the Venezuelan boundary dispute. Although Great Britain way back in 1814 had taken over a portion of Guiana from the Dutch, the limits of its sovereignty there had not been settled. Many persons believed that the contested area held rich mineral deposits. Also the multiplication of Irish and German immigrants within the United States brought a growth of anglophobia. The American government, engaged since 1887 in trying to resolve the Venezuelan boundary with Great Britain, decided in 1895 to force the issue toward arbitration. It had a rapacious terrier to do the job; the man who had been attorney general during the Pullman boycott had moved up to the Department of State, and his message to England read in part as follows:

> Today the United States is practically sovereign on this continent, and its fiat is law upon the subjects to which it confines its interposition. Why? It is not because of the pure friendship or good will felt for it. It is not simply by reason of its high character as a civilized state, nor because wisdom, justice, and equity are the invariable characteristics of the dealings of the United States. It is because, in addition to all other grounds, its infinite resources combined with its isolated position render it master of the situation, and practically invulnerable as against any or all other powers.

Although this statement was so self-righteous and domineering as to be intolerable, Great Britain had to tolerate it, because it was true. During the entire life of the Monroe Doctrine, no American diplomat had claimed that it required arbitration of every dispute in Latin America that involved a European country. The expansive doctrine revealed a changing temper in the United States toward its relations abroad. Cleveland himself called the obstreperous communique "the best thing of the kind that I have ever read."

Responsible British officials were almost as irresponsible as the Americans. More than four months passed before they replied at all. The answer came by mail, not by cable. It was a peremptory rejection. The president got Congressional approval to name a commission to fix the boundary. Then the United States should employ "every means in its power" to maintain that line. To the hazard of war was added the threat of renewed financial panic; British investors hastily pulled their capital away from Wall Street, while bankers and brokers denounced Grover Cleveland for his impetuosity. But the fall in the stock market lasted less than a day; American investors took up the slack that Europeans had created. Just as there was no acceleration of the depression, there was no war. Great Britain was in no condition to fight the United States. She did not have one strong ally in the entire world. Her relations with France over African territory were so strained that they would verge on war by 1898. Germany had built up a steel industry that greatly enhanced its capacity for naval construction and other munitions. England initiated friendly talks, and in the event the Venezuelan border was indeed arbitrated. American assertiveness had its way.

These thrusts and counterthrusts, plus others, comprised the field of force for the election of 1896. From the formal opening of the campaign, remarkable events ensued. Normally a president controls the national convention of his party. Exceptions, some of them marginal, can be noted: John Adams in 1800, the other Adams in 1828, John Tyler in 1844, Lyndon Johnson in 1968. But the repudiation of Grover Cleveland by the Democratic nominating conclave in 1896 was unmistakable. Although he had allies, the preeminence of Governor Altgeld at the meeting in Chicago was clear. On point after point, the platform was a decisive rejection of the administration. Whereas the president had been struggling to sustain the "single monetary standard" of gold, his party now declared for the conversion into coin of all silver presented at the mint, with a ratio to gold of 16 to 1. It denounced the Supreme Court's judgment on the income tax in tones as stern as those that Lincoln had used about the Dred Scott case. It condemned "government by injunction" in the Pullman boycott. The document declared that "as labor creates the wealth of the country, we demand the passage of such laws as may be necessary to protect it in all its rights." In the perspective of time, these planks were surely more significant than the nomination for the presidency of a ninny named William Jennings Bryan. In spite of the contrary pretensions of some historians, Bryan was a nobody who would never become a somebody. Listen to him talk at the convention in Chicago:

> You come to us and tell us that the great cities are in favor of the gold standard; we reply that the great cities rest upon our broad and fertile prairies. Burn down your cities and leave our farms, and your cities will spring up again as if by magic; but destroy our farms and the grass will grow in the streets of every city in the country.

He did not see how the cities had been superseding rural areas for decades. In his boyhood he learned little, and in his adage he forgot most of that.* Even though he managed to secure the Populist nomination also, even though he would be put forward two more times by the Democrats, he did not fool all of his contemporaries; after that famous Cross of Gold oration in Chicago, Altgeld turned to his friend Clarence Darrow: "I have been thinking over Bryan's speech. What did he say anyhow?" Bryan lived in Lincoln, Nebraska. Readers who have never seen the River Platte should still enjoy the pungency of the comment that he was like that stream: an inch deep, and a mile wide at the mouth.

The Republican was no bargain either. William McKinley was the dreary sort who drones along about the virtues of God and motherhood. After he sponsored the tariff act of 1890 he was beaten for re-election to the House of Representatives. But he soon recovered to serve two terms as governor of Ohio. As against Bryan, he had advantages: brains and money. The first belonged to Mark Hanna, an industrialist who was notorious for buying votes at the polls in Cleveland. Hanna also saw to the money. Standard Oil and J. P. Morgan gave $250,000 each. Hanna and James J. Hill were seen daily in a buggy going from one corporate office to the next in Manhattan. Republican campaign funds mounted to at least $3.5 million; one estimate from a sympathizer put

---

*But note his role in forestalling war as Wilson's secretary of state, Document 22-1.

the total at twice that. The Chicago office alone spent almost $2 million, of which 75 per cent came from New York; at last the "usury states" were sending back part of the booty. The G.O.P. distributed five throw-aways for each voter, 100 million of them. Publicity was not the only Republican tactic. Altgeld, admittedly no impartial witness, claimed later that they stole 100,000 votes in his state. Our evidence is spotty as to the amount of economic coercion that some corporations exerted on their employees, but clearly there was some: a contract with a shipyard in Wilmington, Delaware, provided for cancellation if the Democrats won the election.

They didn't. The major consequences, ironically, were not those expected. Most Americans thought that the crucial contest in the campaign was whether the federal government, by re-instituting the unlimited coinage of silver, would boost the level of prices. Inflation did come, but the remonitization of silver had nothing to with it, and neither did the switch from Democratic to Republican control in Washington; it came with an enlarged supply of gold from the Rand fields in South Africa and the Klondike strikes. The chief results of 1896 lay in two other directions. One was the emergence of the Republicans as a (semi-) permanent majority in the nation. In a presidential tally of 14 million, McKinley's plurality topped 700,000. His party did not lose a single county in New England. He swept the East. Bryan won the South, and the silver-mining states, and most of the prairies, but that was all and it was not enough. Excepting the unusual circumstances of 1912 and 1916, the Republicans would not lose another federal poll until the New Deal (Chapters 22, 26).

It is not clear whether the second major shift was due to the political flopover at the capital. Perhaps the changes in America would have brought it anyway, no matter which party had held power.* But the import of the switch can hardly be doubted. The United States altered drastically its stance toward foreign relations. In an earlier period America's world power had been born and consolidated because it had been careful not to make commitments that exceeded its resources. Insofar as possible, for instance, it hid (not always gratefully) behind the British navy. To summarize the transformation in a different way, American foreign policy since 1789 had meant a careful measuring of aims against means. One recent writer has characterized the transition as going from realism to romanticism. Thus on the one hand we have President Jefferson averring that New Orleans must not become the possession of a strong European nation; on the other, President Wilson declaring that we must make the world safe for democracy. The former objective could be attained, and was. The latter was not, and could not have been.

It was Cuba (ninety miles from home) that galvanized the growing

---

*Granting a few honorable exceptions, questions of this rank have not been studied astutely. In 1961 a historian-politician said to me about a pure historian: "He thinks it still matters who is president." The proposition is worth some thought.

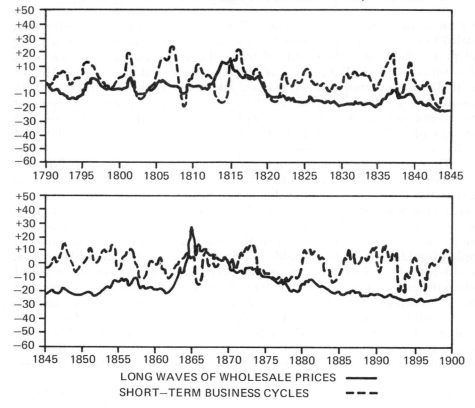

FIGURE 20-3. *Secular Business Trends vs. Short-run Cycles*

Statistics is commonly said to have begun with the English economist W. Stanley Jevons a century ago. The emerging techniques can be remarkably useful, but many historians are still ignoring them or making a muddle of them. The applications of statistics can deal with a range of problems that goes far beyond economic history: Did immigration influence voting patterns? Did religious affiliations affect the kinds of books that were popular? A person can go a long way by knowing a little about correlations and linear regressions. Several superb books exist, but I do not know of any 25-page introduction that surpasses the first chapter of H. T. Epstein, *Elementary Biophysics* (1963).

The above chart illustrates one way that statistics can be helpful in separating elements that in reality are entangled. The great man in initiating this type of analysis of the American economic story was the late Wesley Clair Mitchell; among his successors the biggest name is Simon Kuznets. The above chart is an effort to distinguish the secular trends (long waves in prices) from the shorter run business cycles that usually last seven to ten years. In actuality the two phenomena are going on simultaneously, but, by refined manipulations, scholars have made at least approximate differentiation.

In seeking to understand the political history of the last third of the nineteenth century, a crucial consideration is the effect of the constantly falling level of prices on farmers who were also debtors. Some of the implications for other interest groups have been discussed above in Chapter 17.

American jingoism. After Cubans rebelled against Spanish rule in 1868, President Grant wanted to sustain the insurgents. He was held back. But in the next three decades the restraints weakened. Also an innovation by the German government—the payment of a bounty on exports of beet sugar—drove Cuba's cane sugar planters to desperation. The main market for Caribbean cane sugar had always been Britain; now Germany with its beet sugar became a strong competitor for the British market, and the price in London of unrefined cane sugar fell 50 percent. Revolution in Cuba began in February, 1895. Intrigue became elaborate within the United States. A Florida senator secured the appointment of his son as agent for Cuban insurrectionist bonds in England. Senator Henry Cabot Lodge of Massachusetts raved against Spanish "butcheries" and, quite properly, denounced the occupying army for herding Cuban civilians into concentration camps. Not so properly, he emphasized that a free island "would mean a great market to the United States; it would mean an opportunity for American capital." The atmosphere in Washington became fervid. But within the Democratic ranks, resistance remained strong. One party leader wrote in his diary, "The jingoism in the air is a curious thing, and unaccountable, except on account of the unrest of our people, and the willingness to turn from domestic to foreign affairs, always making greatest allowance for political maneuvering, and the ridiculousness of conducting foreign affairs by such town meetings as the Senate and House have become." When Congress resolved that the Cuban rebels should be recognized as belligerents, the president still refused to take that step.

The balance between the contending forces was tilted by the 1896 election, which added to the strength of the party that held the highest concentration of expansionists. That McKinley became president was also a change, but not a vital one. He would do whatever he thought was popular; Joseph G. Cannon commented that McKinley kept his ear so close to the ground that he got it full of grasshoppers. The crucial factors in rallying militaristic sentiment were a few politicians, missionaries, and commercial periodicals. The press fabricated a vogue in favor of the late Emperor Napoleon, of all people. Clerics explained that we must free the world from paganism; seemingly this slop played a large role in McKinley's behavior (Document 20-3). All this registered deep on a widespread sense of anxiety and depression. Just read Theodore Roosevelt writing to his friend Senator Lodge during the Venezuela boundary dispute: "Let the fight come if it must. I don't care whether our sea coast cities are bombarded or not; we would take Canada." Probably the strongest wind to fan the flames came from part of the urban press. As cities grew, circulation of newspapers grew with population. Some dailies had outgrown the staid mold of the past; they sent special correspondents to Cuba to telegraph regular stories about Cuban babies being bayonetted by Spanish villains. They instituted red headlines. All of this paraphernalia was put to lurid use when the American battleship *Maine* exploded and sank in Havana harbor, 15 February, 1898. Two hundred fifty sailors were killed. Why the ship was there is irrelevant here. Why the explosion occurred is not definitely known and never will be. What was determinative was the American reaction, which can be illustrated from the front page of the Kansas City *Star*:

HE SAW THE TORPEDO

MAIMED SEAMAN'S STORY

Senator Lodge thought that, apart from the businessmen of Boston, the voters of his state were nearly unanimous for war. As a correspondent wrote to him, "I have not met a man . . . in the aristocratic upper crust in which you and I are imbedded, who considers that we have any justifiable cause for war. Below that crust . . . the wish for war is *almost* universal." Theodore Roosevelt, Assistant Secretary of the Navy, wrote to a New York banker: "We here in Washington have grown to feel that almost every man connected with the big business interests of the country is anxious to court any infamy if only peace can be obtained and the business situation be not disturbed." The city editor of a Manhattan newspaper wrote to the president: "Big corporations here now believe we will have war. Believe all would welcome it as a relief to suspense." This seems plausible. Standard Oil and other giants wanted to expand their exports, and Asia seemed the most promising goal. Some executives thought that hostilities would conduce to this end. Most religious sects were expansionist. Doubtless many Americans were outraged by Spanish brutalities in Cuba. By the end of March, 1898, the French ambassador was reporting home, "A sort of bellicose fury has seized the American nation." Perhaps it would be too glib to say that McKinley lacked the courage to stand up to pressure; his conception of politics in a republic was that the majority of the moment should not only have its way but also that its inclinations should not be questioned. He wrote a message to Congress asking authority to use American might to restore peace and stable government in Cuba. It did not call for Cuban independence. Not daring to make this demand publicly for fear it would offend conservative senators in his own party, he presented it privately to Spain. Spain refused. By now the president was out of control on Capitol Hill. After some tangles in Congress, a war resolution was passed on 25 April. A Republican congressman tried to summarize the development: ". . . possibly the president could have worked the business out without a war, but the current was too strong, the demagogues too numerous, and the fall elections too near."

Once the United States was at war against Spain, the scope of its operations grew at once. A fleet was sent immediately to the Philippines where it destroyed ten moribund Spanish vessels. Not one American life was lost, no American ship was seriously damaged. The acquisitive atmosphere of wartime facilitated the annexation of Hawaii. Again there were delays because the president was timorous, but at last he committed himself: "We need Hawaii just as much and a good deal more than we did California. It is manifest destiny." A joint resolution annexing Hawaii and making it a Territory passed through Congess. By that time the largest expeditionary force in American history put out to sea for Cuba—17,000 men. It was badly commanded; a sane general does not land his troops in an open roadstead and send them ashore in heavy surf. Fortunately the Spanish leaders were none too efficient either, but their soldiers were brave and some battles were bitter. More than one historian has been bemused by the sentence of Secretary of State John Hay: "It has been a splendid little war." It did not seem so to the men on the battlefields. In the words of Theodore Roosevelt after the famous charge up San Juan Hill, "Tell the President for Heaven's sake to send us every regiment and above all every battery possible. We have won so far at a heavy cost, but the Spaniards fight very hard and charging these intrenchments against modern rifles is terrible. . . . We *must* have help—thousands of men, batteries, and *food* and ammunition." Colonel Roosevelt may have been a coward morally, but he was not a physical coward, and he knew the odds.

The cause of Spain was of course hopeless. But she was not conquered on land anywhere in the Caribbean. Obliteration of her fleet there forced her to yield. The war was ended by a treaty concluded at Paris on 10 December, 1898. Spain gave up all title to Cuba, and ceded to the United States both Puerto Rico and the Philippines.

In the middle five years of the last decade of the nineteenth century, any interpretation of the United States as "the land of consensus" would have met with scorn. Millions of Americans feared that the nation would be torn by its second civil war within forty years. But this time it would not be North versus South. The conflicts could not be pigeonholed so neatly. It was black against white, employers against wage earners, farmers against Wall Street, Italians or Poles against Anglo-Saxons, Protestants against Catholics, gentiles against Jews. The contradictions within the nation were revealed in a setting of financial panic, devastating depression, race riots, labor strife, the culmination of the long struggle over the currency. The depression can be seen now to have been caused chiefly by the lopsided and self-destructive structure of personal incomes. But the years of hard times did not bring adjustments; the distribution of rewards was as unjust and as unworkable in 1903 as in 1893, in spite of attempts to enact a federal income tax and other corrective laws. The shedding of red blood did not improve black-white relations. Only the monetary situation found a corrective. Even that did not come from the wisdom in Washington. It came from gold strikes in South Africa, Alaska, the Klondike. The manifold frustrations of countless citizens primed them for the release that "a splendid little war" might bring.

SOME NOTABLE EVENTS

1890 Sherman Anti-Trust Act, 2 July.
Sherman Silver Purchase Act, 14 July.
McKinley Tariff Act.
Pension Act.
Ocala Demands issued in Florida by farmers' organizations, December.
Arthur Thayer Mahan, *The Influence of Sea Power upon History.*

1892 Homestead strike, June 28–mid-October.
People's party (Populists) gets more than 1,000,000 votes.

1893 Financial panic begins in January; becomes severe depression.
U.S. begins to appoint "ambassadors," 1 March.
Columbian Exposition in Chicago, May–October.
American Railway Union organized, 20 June.
Altgeld pardons Haymarket defendants, 26 June.
Repeal of the Silver Purchase Act, 1 November.
More than 600 financial institutions have gone bankrupt in the year.

1894 ARU strikes against Great Northern, 13 April–1 May.
ARU boycotts Pullman cars, 26 June–19 July.
House of Representatives opposes the annexation of Hawaii.

1895 *U.S.* v. *E. C. Knight Company*, 20 January, decision limiting Sherman Anti-Trust Act.
Gold outflows from Treasury in January total $43 million—a record.
Pollock v. *Farmers' Loan and Trust Company*, 8 April.
National Association of Manufacturers formed.
In re Debs, 27 May, conviction as outgrowth of Pullman strike.
U.S. intervenes in Venezuela boundary dispute, July.

1896 Presidential vote is 14 million; McKinley's plurality is 700,000.
Senate resolves in favor of recognizing Cuban rebels as belligerents, 28 February.

1897 Exports rise; economy begins to revive.
European powers seize territory in China.

1898 De Lome letter published, 9 February; public outcry against Spanish ambassador.
Maine sunk at Havana, 15 February.
McKinley submits his war message, 11 April.
Congress resolves for independence of Cuba, 20 April.
Congress resolves for annexation of Hawaii, 7 July.
Paris Peace Treaty with Spain, 10 December.

Ways to Study History XX

Let your sympathies flow. No scholar would question the ability of C. Vann Woodward to be patient; he did a study of the Wormley Conference of 1877 that rests on a sweeping exploration of the sources and that catches hold of a vast panorama of American economics and politics. Woodward has advanced some interpretations that seem to me, perhaps even in a few instances to him, mistaken. But besides his industry he has shown wide range and acute imagination (an oft-misunderstood word the definition of which will be probed in Chapter 27).

Admirable though these qualities are, they are not the key to Woodward's greatness as a historian. He was born and reared in Georgia, and he has not forgotten the agonies and the joys of poor farmers, whether white or black, in the South. This empathy was palpable in his doctoral dissertation and first book, *Tom Watson* (1938). The biography is not flamboyant, but in it the human passions surge and roar. Where the author is describing a young congressman risking his career by orating that all poor Georgians regardless of color must stick together, every reader can perceive his exultation in his hero. But he does not gloss over Watson's evils. As the aging senator becomes a bigot spewing hatred against blacks and Jews and Catholics, we realize Woodward's horror. In this reversal, the author seems to imply, lies an enigma that I cannot fully comprehend. If we could understand it, we might approach the core of the Southern contradictions as they have worked out over time.

The most ambitious effort to return to this problem, among Woodward's subsequent works, was *Origins of the New South, 1877–1913* (1951). Here again are diligence in research—and the same old sympathy. No study trying to cope with so broad a theme can be called definitive, but this one will survive as a monument, and every future student will have to pay homage to it.

Document 20-1

Henry Demarest Lloyd (1847–1903) published his "Story of a Great Monopoly" in 1881. Readers may be surprised to learn that the early power and prosperity of Standard Oil stemmed from its marketing of kerosene as an illuminant. Gasoline, before the automobile, was virtually a waste product called "stove naphtha."

Kerosene has become, by its cheapness, the people's light the world over. In the United States we used 220,000,000 gallons of petroleum last year. It has come into such demand abroad that our exports of it increased from 79,458,888 gallons in 1868, to 417,648,544 in 1879. It goes all over Europe, and to the far East. The Oriental demand for it is increasing faster than any other. . . . Very few of the forty millions of people in the United States who burn kerosene know that its production, manufacture, and export, its price at home and abroad, have been controlled for years by a single corporation, the Standard Oil Company. The company began in a partnership, in the early years of the civil war, between Samuel Andrews and John Rockefeller in Cleveland. Rockefeller had been a bookkeeper in some interior town in Ohio, and had afterwards made a few thousand dollars by keeping a flour store in Cleveland. Andrews had been a day laborer in refineries, and so poor that his wife took in sewing. . . .

The contract is in print by which the Pennsylvania Railroad agreed with the Standard, under the name of the South Improvement Company, to double the freights on oil to everybody, but to repay the Standard one dollar for every barrel of oil it shipped, and one dollar for every barrel any of its competitors shipped. . . . Ostensibly this contract was given up, in deference to the whirlwind of indignation it excited. But Rockefeller, the manager of the Standard, was a man who could learn from defeat. He made no more tell-tale contracts that could be printed. . . .

Document 20-2

William A. Peffer, member of the United States
Senate from Kansas, became a leading Populist.
This exposition appeared in his *The Farmer's
Side* (1891).

The American farmer of to-day is altogether a different sort of man from his ancestor of fifty
or a hundred years ago. A great many men and women now living remember when farmers were
largely manufacturers; that is to say, they made a great many implements for their own use. Every
farmer had an assortment of tools with which he made wooden implements, as forks and rakes,
handles for his hoes and plows, spokes for his wagon, and various other implements made wholly
of wood. Then the farmer produced flax and hemp and wool and cotton. These fibers were
prepared upon the farm; they were spun into yarn, woven into cloth, made into garments, and
worn at home. . . .

Coming from that time to the present, we find that everything nearly has been changed. All
over the West particularly the farmer thrashes his wheat all at one time, he disposes of it all at
one time, and in a great many instances the straw is wasted. He sells his hogs, and buys bacon
and pork; he sells his cattle, and buys fresh beef and canned beef or corned beef, as the case
may be; he sells his fruit, and buys it back in cans. . . .

Besides all this, and what seems stranger than anything else, whereas in the earlier time
the American home was a free home, unincumbered, not one case in a thousand where a home
was mortgaged to secure the payment of borrowed money, and whereas but a small amount of
money was then needed for actual use in conducting the business of farming, there was always
enough of it among the farmers to supply the demand, now, when at least ten times as much is
needed, there is little or none to be obtained, nearly half the farms are mortgaged for as much as
they are worth, and interest rates are exorbitant. . . .

Document 20-3

On 21 November, 1899, a delegation from the
General Missionary Committee of the Methodist
Episcopal Church came to see President McKinley. One delegate reported that McKinley spoke
to the group as follows.

Gentlemen, just a moment. I have something I would like to say. And first, just a word with
you, esteemed Bishops. Last winter Congress increased the army by several regiments, but
provided no chaplains for them. Now I believe in army chaplains. . . . But some time ago I
appointed a Methodist chaplain, who came to me with letters and recommendations from half a
dozen presiding elders, doctors of divinity, etc., as well as members of Congress and senators,
and recently they have had to court-martial him for various misconduct, and I suppose we shall
have to cashier him—greatly to my regret as a brother Methodist. . . .

Hold a moment longer! Not quite yet, gentlemen! Before you go I would like to say just a
word about the Philippine business. I have been criticised a good deal about the Philippines, but
don't deserve it. The truth is I didn't want the Philippines, and when they came to us, as a gift
from the gods, I did not know what to do with them. When the Spanish war broke out Dewey was
at Hongkong, and I ordered him to go to Manila and to capture or destroy the Spanish fleet, and
he had to; because, if defeated, he had no place to refit on that side of the globe, and if the Dons
were victorious they would likely cross the Pacific and ravage our Oregon and California coasts.
And so he had to destroy the Spanish fleet, and did it! But that was as far as I thought then.

When next I realized that the Philippines had dropped into our laps I confess I did not
know what to do with them. I sought counsel from all sides—Democrats as well as

Republicans—but, got little help. I thought first we would take only Manila; then Luzon; then other islands perhaps also. I walked the floor of the White House night after night until midnight; and I am not ashamed to tell you, gentlemen, that I went down on my knees and prayed Almighty God for light and guidance more than one night. And one night late it came to me this way—I don't know how it was, but it came: (1) That we could not give them back to Spain—that would be cowardly and dishonorable; (2) that we could not turn them over to France or Germany—our commercial rivals in the Orient—that would be bad business and discreditable; (3) that we could not leave them to themselves—they were unfit for self-government—and they would soon have anarchy and misrule over there worse than Spain's was; and (4) that there was nothing for us to do but to take them all, and to educate the Filipinos, and uplift and civilize and Christianize them, and by God's grace do the very best we could by them, as our fellow-men for whom Christ also died. And then I went to bed, and went to sleep, and slept soundly, and the next morning I sent for the chief engineer of the War Department (our mapmaker) and I told him to put the Philippines on the map of the United States, and there they are, and there they will stay while I am President! . . .

Don't go yet, please! Just a word more, friends; there's no hurry! . . . And before we part I just want to say to you, whatever men may think about me, or not think, I am a Methodist, and nothing but a Methodist—a Christian, and nothing but a Christian. When I was a little child my dear old mother used to take me to Methodist prayer meeting and class meeting. When I grew older I early joined the Methodist Church and Sunday school, and then became a Sunday school teacher, and afterward a Sunday school superintendent, and member of the Epworth League. . . . And by the blessing of heaven, I mean to live and die, please God, in the faith of my mother!

FIGURE E. *William Sidney Mount,* The Banjo Player

A native of Long Island, William Sidney Mount lived from 1807 to 1868. He got some formal training at the National Institute of Design, but illness drove him back to his rural habitat, fortunately for his art and for posterity. The son of a prosperous inkeeper, Mount delighted in music and in a cool draught of beer. His approach to art was to hang loose; his work seems easy and relaxed. He opined, "I never paint on a picture unless I feel in the right spirit." The tone of his art is expansive, the palette is founded on grays and browns, but accented by exhilarations that burst from an unerring sense of the texture of light at different hours of the day. Toward the end of his life he believed that Rembrandt was giving him personal messages about how to cope with the mysteries of optics.

His outlook was relentlessly democratic. "Paint pictures that will take with the public—never paint for the few." Mount's ebullience extended to his subjects as well as to technique; Walt Whitman applauded him for his portrayal of a black man who had won a goose at a raffle. This specific Negro, so Whitman said, was an individual American and not an insipid stereotype. The plaudit was deserved. Of all outstanding writers in the United States, Whitman, Emily Dickinson, and Mark Twain seem closest to Mount in a fervor to record the nobilities of everyday life.

FIGURE F. *John Singer Sargent,* Robert Louis Stevenson

Robert Louis Stevenson (1850–94) is remembered as the author of *Treasure Island* with its pegleg Long John Silver. But that and *A Child's Garden of Verses* are only two of his many works on which Americans doted for generations. The Scottish writer can epitomize for us the idolatry that the United States lavished on British culture toward the end of the nineteenth century. Self-esteeming Americans preferred British writers to their countrymen, British painters to their compatriots.

Thus it is fitting that this portrait of Stevenson was done by John Singer Sargent (1856–1925). Begotten by a Philadelphia doctor who had retired to Europe, Sargent was born in the citadel of Renaissance painting—Florence. His archetypes were the portraits done centuries earlier by Frans Hals and Velásquez. He painted people, for fees running as high as $5,000. He delighted in his work, but we must wonder if he respected it. Stevenson, who sat for this picture in 1884, called Sargent "a person with a kind of exhibition manner and English accent. . . ." The painter himself called portraiture "a pimp's profession." When a subject asked prior to his first sitting if Sargent did not want to chat with him a while to find out what sort of man he was, the reply was doubtless languid: "No, I paint what I see." If Bingham or Eakins (Figure 13-6; Figure 19-6) used those words, we could guess what he meant. But Sargent went on: "But I don't dig beneath the surface for things that don't appear before my eyes." When a female subject objected to the way he painted her mouth, he suggested that the feature should be omitted altogether. Another woman complained of the way he had depicted her nose. He hastily replied that she could easily fix "a little thing like that" after she got home.

His mastery of surface texture was supreme, and for that his age respected him and paid him well. To drop the subject there should speak volumes about the age of John Singer Sargent. The protagonists of his paintings are exposed only to the degree that is socially useful to them.

Courtesy of the Suffolk Museum & Carriage
House at Stony Brook, L.I. Melville Collection.

FIGURE E. *William Sidney Mount,* The Banjo Player

Courtesy of The Taft Museum, Cincinnati, Ohio

FIGURE F. *John Singer Sargent,* Robert Louis Stevenson   (above)

FIGURE G. *Rafael Tufino,* Fiesta Poster   (right)

III FIESTA DE LA MUSICA PUERTORRIQUEÑA

TEATRO TAPIA
NOV. 1968

INSTITUTO DE CULTURA PUERTORRIQUEÑA

To Vicky and Ray with love, to free persons like you are.

Courtesy of the photographer

FIGURE H. *Henry Linschitz,* Maine Tidepool

FIGURE G. *Rafael Tufino,* Fiesta Poster

When critics think of posters as a legitimate form of modern art, they are likely to think first of the playbills of the Frenchman Henri Toulouse-Lautrec (1864–1901). Perhaps the highest that this genre has reached in the contemporary United States is the best of the sleeves (jackets) for LP records. Advertising posters for movies, to cite one example, are invariably sensationalistic and have no visual grip at all.

This defect does not characterize all countries. Several nations in Latin America have raised what might be called public—non-easel—art to a range far above what Americans have reached. Again the immediate images are the murals of Mexico. In spite of the exciting work in this mode that has been done by men like Ben Shahn (Figure 26-3), perhaps the two greatest murals existing in the United States were created by Diego Rivera (Detroit Institute of Arts) and Jose C. Orozco (Dartmouth University).

Puerto Rico shows a far different face from the mainland. Although the island had no tradition in the visual arts to compare with that of Mexico, it has become since World War II a breeding ground for graphic innovation. This creativity rests heavily upon institutional sponsors, whether the government of the Commonwealth or private organizations; either might print a thousand copies of a billboard to entice customers to come to an outdoor film or to eat fresh fruit. Although Rafael Tufino, one of whose advertisements is shown here, approaches middle age, his productivity does not dwindle. Besides dozens of silkscreens for public display, he has done lithographs for sale to tourists (some of which mock tourists) as well as a mural for the Hilton hotel in Mayaguez, the third largest city in Puerto Rico.

The island may or may not be a part of the United States, so this illustration may or may not belong here. Puerto Ricans are exempt from United States income taxes, but they are subject to conscription into the American army. Officially the island is an *Estado Libre Asociado*—the only one.

FIGURE H. *Henry Linschitz,* Maine Tidepool

Probably most observers would agree that photography with its offshoots is the most significant new form of art to emerge in the last 150 years. Much of this book (especially its "Ways to Study History") has tried to show new angles of vision, new windows through which we can peer into the past. Now here is a question that might allow us to be another type of Peeping Tom: Which artistic media have been embraced most passionately at specific times and places in the American past? For alert Americans at the beginning of World War II, literature would have held the first rank. Perhaps many of the problems of universities in the United States derive from their continuing emphasis on the written word, while their students have been shifting focus to other (and equally legitimate) types of expression. The regnant mode of the last two decades has surely been music; in a popularity race of the 1960's the Beatles would have beaten Ralph Ellison if they were walking. Second only to music would be the movies.

But the arrival of motion pictures, first silent and then with sound, is not the only innovation in photography in the twentieth century. Consider this illustration, which was not meant to be printed on a page at all; it was intended for projection in color onto a screen. The resultant luminosity can only be called overpowering. Equally remarkable, this image was captured by an amateur photographer, Henry Linschitz, whose interests reveal the interpenetration of occupations that typifies the best products of the contemporary world. He worked at Los Alamos during World War II, and he has since taught at universities and done research in physical chemistry and biophysics. How did such a person come to have so much delight in the abstractions supplied by rocks, by sea, by living creatures? In his professional world, he has a special concern with photobiology, the manifold responses of living things to light. In his private world, he is married to artist Suzanne Hodes (Figure 14-2). This color slide of a tidepool on Monhegan Island, Maine, was taken from a height of approximately two feet.

PART V

How Successes Can Be Frustrating
1898–1929

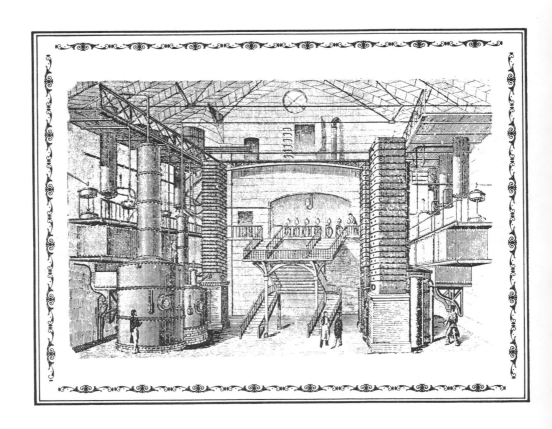

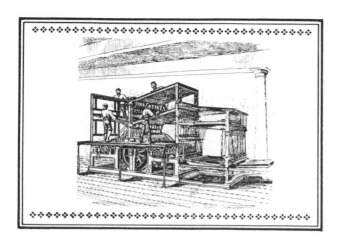

The Economy Surges—and the Fog Descends, 1898–1907

Both among the populace and in the Senate, the treaty ending the Spanish-American War provoked debate. A startling switch had occurred since the war began. Prior to that, many businessmen had been extremely cautious; they were skittish when mention was made of armed conflict. Commercial interests become jittery at any uncertainty, and wartime by definition is a period of dislocation and risk. Contrariwise, the self-proclaimed libertarians had joined the clamor to oust the Spaniards from Cuba; in Chicago, for instance, Altgeld and Lloyd and Darrow were noisy agitators in the cause. But with the appearance of the treaty, the two factions in a sense exchanged positions. Some industrialists could see no reason why, having endured the trials of war, the nation should not keep advantages to be gained by legal dominion over foreign markets. Conversely, advocates of the war now found that they did not want to taste some of its fruits. Their reasons varied. For most, the particular sticking point was the clause providing for acquisition of the

Philippines (Document 20-3). Some arguments used were perilously close to racism: that brown-skinned peoples could not learn the democratic way of life (Document 21-1). Altgeld on the other hand denounced these skeptics who claimed that "this people or that people are incapable of self-government."* Darrow told a mass meeting that he would not swap "the republic of Jefferson" for "the empire of McKinley." He demanded that the president "take away his lawless crew, remove his Christian cannon from those far-off shores. . . ."

The appeals to Christian forbearance and the Declaration of Independence did not prevail. The forces that vanquished them can be reviewed. Religious spokesmen were almost unanimous; of all denominations that declared themselves, only Quakers and Unitarians fought against imperialism. Politicians great and small flew the ensigns of rampant nationalism. It would be extreme to regard these appeals as mere stalking horses for material greed. But the desires of Americans for added sales in foreign markets were as weighty as the other pressures put together. Albert J. Beveridge, blunt for a man campaigning successfully in 1898 for a seat in the United States Senate, explained: "American factories are making more than the American people can use; American soil is producing more than they can consume. Fate has written our policy for us; the trade of the world must and shall be ours." After the war John Jacob Astor, great landowner and railroad pirate, came back from Europe with predictions of huge orders there for American electrical products and machinery. President McKinley a year later tried his own summary: "We want to send the products of our farms, our factories, and our mines into every market of the world; make the foreign peoples familiar with our products; and the way to do that is to make them familiar with our flag." Americans wanted to sew up not only foreign markets for our products but also sources of the raw materials to fabricate them. Thus Mexico was invaded by crews prospecting for crude oil. Mammoth forests in Canada were bought for woodpulp. Since the Mesabi fields in Minnesota were tied up by competitors, Bethlehem Steel looked for iron ore in Chile as well as in Cuba. Prognoses by businessmen are often faulty. Probably the main significance of overseas areas for the United States in the next three decades was not as markets, nor as providers of raw materials, but as outlets for American funds.

It is opportune to glance at the history of capital markets in this period. To do so sagely, we must backtrack fifty years. In the decade before the Civil War, the center of security flotations had migrated from State Street in Boston to Wall Street. The reason is easy to grasp: a slow rate of population growth in Boston went parallel to a slow pace of capital accumulation, and did not have

---

*Illinois citizens had reason to doubt this argument; trickery was open at the 1896 election in Chicago. Corruption among politicians there would rival any practitioners in Manila. The late John F. Kennedy repeated an appropriate joke about meetings of the Chicago common council at this time: You could empty the room by shouting: "Alderman, your saloon is on fire."

the resources to finance a majority of the long-distance railroads. But this relocation of investment banking had not brought about a change in the function. Only a narrow range of securities were traded publicly: federal and state bonds, railroad bonds often guaranteed by some civic authority—that was about it. The lack of quickly available liquid capital became critical. At the beginning of the century, most investments had been commercial, and involved consumer goods which could be quickly converted into cash. But by century's end, fixed costs could be preponderant in a steel mill or an oil refinery, while many companies continued to be owned by a family or by a limited number of partners. These sunk investments had to be made fluid or convertible into other forms of capital. One attempt at a solution after the financial panic of 1893 was the expansion to an "outside" market on securities not officially up for public trade, i.e., a streetcurb market around the New York Stock Exchange. During the four years of the depression, the number of issues traded thus rose from about 30 to 200 or more. But this quasi-underground technique was not adequate. More creative was the device of issuing a wider variety of security or stock certificates, and of linking that innovation with the amalgamating of several former competitors to form a larger corporation that would be better known. Often an operation of this type hinged on an independent promoter who might weld an agreement among several erstwhile competitors and then issue several kinds of securities. (Bonds would have first claim on all earnings, with an interest rate of 6 per cent or so; preferred stocks were not a legal liability on the owner, but hopefully they would yield 7 or 8 per cent dividends; common stocks might not get anything at all, but often they were expected to earn 12 per cent.) Frequently these shenanigans brought grief to those who bought stock, or even bonds, even though the promoters usually came out well ahead.

The central purposes of these maneuvers merit repetition. First, to form by mergers some larger companies that would therefore have broader reputations. Second, to appeal to more investors by issuing different classes of securities, some offering a secure income, others hinting at higher incomes for persons willing to take risks. The whole idea was that this variety of issues could attract investors for a greater totality of liquid capital, and although neither material assets nor earning power had been increased, this produced more capital than could be drawn by the more limited range of issues beforehand. This scheme was greatly advanced during the depression of 1893 when preferred stocks of the industrial concerns did better than those of the railroads. Of the latter, one (Northern Pacific) had to scale down its capital values,* while the other that was most actively traded (the Wabash) paid no dividends. Turning to the largest industrials, only two preferreds failed to pay dividends, and one of the two (General Electric) did so to conserve its cash, not because it was losing money. Such new giants as American Tobacco and U.S. Rubber paid dividends throughout the depression. The public standing of

---

*The great theorist on this resolution was Thorstein Veblen, about whom see Chapter 25.

Sewing Machine

The sewing machine works by interlocking two threads. The needle's eye holds one, and the other is held in a bobbin under the throat plate, and passed through the upper thread by means of a shuttle. Both threads must be kept under a constant tension. Also required is the presser foot, which holds the fabric firmly against the throat plate, and the feed dog, which moves the fabric along under the stationary needle, one stitch at a time.

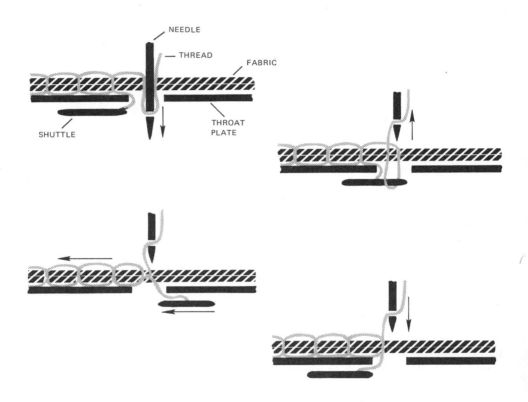

(1) The stitch begins when the needle pierces the fabric, and passes below the throat plate.
(2) The needle rises, leaving a loop of thread on the underside of the fabric. The shuttle passes through this loop.
(3) The feed dog (not shown in the diagram) moves the fabric forward one stitch length. During this process the needle remains stationary, and the shuttle returns to its original position. Since both threads are under tension, this pulls the slack loop taut.
(4) The mechanism is ready to begin another stitch.

This invention certainly eased the burden of the domestic seamstress. More importantly, it revolutionized the clothing industry. When all tailoring had to be done by hand, every garment was made-to-measure. Ready-to-wear clothing would have to be almost as expensive as custom tailored, and consequently there was no market for it. Except for a few expensive men's suits, all clothing was made in the home, consuming great amounts of the housewife's time. Thus only the rich, who could pay a seamstress to make their garments, could afford to have more than a very few.

securities in industrials was much enhanced in 1898 when the Morgan partners underwrote offerings by a steel merger. Again we must be sure not to exaggerate: Morgan too could make mistakes. In 1902 he promoted the International Mercantile Marine, which merged the two largest American transatlantic steamship companies with two British firms. He advanced $11 million in cash, and formed a syndicate to raise another $50 million cash. He got skunked, and so did investors. The latter took a combined package of commons and preferreds at $100, thinking that they could sell the common at $35 and the preferred at $85. It did not happen. Even Morgan had to wait years before he could recoup his stake; when he got out, he probably lost at least a million dollars.

Now some further oddities appeared. Just at the moment when a broader market for securities in industrial corporations became visible, that addition to liquidity paled in importance beside a new phenomenon that deserves to be explained. The chief innovation that was occurring at the turn of the century was the emergence of the giant corporation. Change was organizational more than it was technological (Chapter 23). However, paradoxically, the firms that were expanding most quickly and reorganizing most dynamically were likely to be following a timeworn strategy that had been stated explicitly by Carnegie: Put all your eggs in one basket, and watch that basket. In today's language, such firms were the opposite of diversified conglomerates. The businessman of 1900 was not the general entrepreneur of fifty or a hundred years earlier. He was a specialist. And although it is important to ask why this was true, I cannot give an answer that seems convincing—only guesses that seem plausible.

One scholar has presented a list of the fifty largest industrial firms in 1909. Only thirteen of them produced goods aimed at the ultimate consumers, you or me, and these produced tobacco, or meat, or whiskey, or petroleum products, or tires, or sewing machines.* The other thirty-seven corporations had few customers because each made semi-finished commodities; they produced structural steel for sale to big contractors, or locomotives for sale to railroads, and so on. In technical lingo, they turned out producers' goods. Thus in several senses they were not participants in the "distribution revolution" that was so critical to the period'. They were not shooting *directly* at a mass market, and such businesses would tend to stress specialized trade relationships rather than broad or diverse ones. The picture is further confused. Many of the big mergers at the end of the century were initiated by industrialists, not by investment bankers.

Furthermore, a whole new element was emerging. Advertising was

---

*Here we have the problem of categories again. Most sewing machines were probably being sold to housewives, but many were going to the garment districts because the manufacture of ready-made garments had already become significant.

nothing novel, but display advertising was. National circulation magazines first began to depend on display ads late in the century. Then another step was taken: institutional advertising. We have already pointed to the "catalytic phrases" as an indicator of the emotional climate of a given generation("God"; "Liberty"; above all, "Land"; see early Chapter 11). One easily remembered index of the business climate of an era is to identify the tallest building on Manhattan Island. When the 47-story Singer Building was completed in 1908, it was twice as tall as any other structure in the United States. Its suzerainty was short-lived. It was surpassed in 1912 by the Woolworth Building, 60 stories, 792 feet. Singer's product was oriented to both consumer and producer; Woolworth's only to consumer. Then the latter was overtaken by the Chrysler Building after the war. Again the matter of scale is crucial. With no intention of making a play on words, it might be said that Woolworth dealt in units that were measured in nickels and dimes, Chrysler in hundreds of dollars. But Chrysler turned out to be too specialized to own the highest building. It in turn was outranked in 1931 by the Empire State, 1,472 feet. It has housed as many as 25,000 companies, ranging from magazine publishers to real-estate developers to clothing distributors.

This reversal is crucial, but not easy to explain. We might call it the faint beginnings of the diversified conglomerate firms. Several facets can be distinguished. First, even while J. P. Morgan was financing corporations on an unprecedented scale, he was losing his monopoly in this realm. Second, investment banking as a specialty was destined to decline, as more companies became able to reinvest their profits and thus became independent of all external capital. Third, the substitution effect must be considered. Some new organizations began to turn in a massive way into research and development. Over the next few decades the result was an extension of alternatives. It became almost meaningless to talk about "steel"; what kind of steel? You could not talk about transportation in terms of trains: trucks and new forms of water transportation had also to be considered.

These developments were so multifoliate and varied that it is hard to look at them systematically. Looking at only one contingent in a brigade, consider how the partners in Standard Oil took their winnings in several directions. One went to Florida, where he developed Key West, built railroads and hotels, got the main street in Miami named for him. Another helped to found the Amalgamated Copper Company, which was in a growth market with the expansion of telephone communications. Others muscled their way into American Tobacco. Perhaps most important of all, the Rockefellers had their own bank in New York, and competed with Morgan for contracts in the launching of big-time ventures. Then there was that dastardly combination of the bankers, the Kuhn, Loeb group with Edward H. Harriman. Harriman almost defies belief. At the beginning he was a stock speculator. Out of one operation, which involved issuing $75 million in additional securities while spending only $18 million on improvements, he and his associates took a profit of $23

FIGURE 21-1. *Frank Lloyd Wright, F.C. Robie House*

Economic booms can do wonders for domestic architecture, as the newly rich seek to make manifest their wealth. In doing so they may not only chagrin their neighbors but also provide themselves with uncomfortable housing, as at Hyde Park. But under proper tutelage from an architect, they can enrich the community as well as their family. More than any American designer since Samuel McIntire (Figure 10-4), Frank Lloyd Wright knew how to create homes for the wealthy.

The urban home shown here was done for F.C. Robie. When finished in 1908, it was just off the campus of the University of Chicago on the city's south side. It can be taken as the archetype of Wright's "Prairie House": low horizontals, sweeping eaves, as much interflow of interior with exterior as the climate and setting will permit. The first floor is one huge room, with dining area in the rear divided from the living room by a giant brick fireplace. One's eyes move naturally around both sides of the fireplace and through an aperture between the chimneys. To look through the continuous banks of windows onto the sweeping porch is like looking from a stateroom onto the deck of a ship.

Wright's incredible life began in 1868 and lasted nearly a century. Besides houses, he created the Guggenheim Art Museum in New York, office buildings, research centers, the first church of cast concrete, a night club, a mile-high structure for the Chicago World's Fair of 1933 that was never erected, and the Imperial Hotel in Tokyo. He was responsible for dwellings that could be built in the 1930's for $6,000, including his fee. He stooped to designing individual pieces of furniture to fit in specific places in specific rooms. His offhand remark was, "In a work of art, there are no trivial details."

million. Before he was finished he had direction of 25,000 miles of track with 70,000 employees—Union Pacific, Central Pacific, Southern Pacific. He did not fudge on expenditures to improve the physical facilities of his roads: where other lines needed a locomotive to move each ten cars or less, he used one for every 35 or 40. His ambition was boundless. Joining with his trans-Mississippi railroads, he controlled 35,000 miles of steamship routes on the Pacific. He began manipulations to get railroads in Manchuria and Siberia. Presumably if these had succeeded, he would next have sought oceanic lines on the Atlantic. What inspires awe is his ability to find lieutenants who were so expert in carrying out his intentions. His railroad empire was divided into seven systems, on a geographical basis, and thus got seven possible solutions to a problem. It could choose the best. A few examples must suffice here. It proved possible to reduce the volume of correspondence by more than 30 per cent. Many routine reports could be done away with. (The problem of intra-office memoranda will be perused in Chapter 28; every employee of a public university must sometimes hope that a shortage of paper will save us.) Harriman like James J. Hill realized that you can't make money hauling empties. So the 75,000 freight cars in the empire were pooled. Ton-mile and passenger-mile figures were studied closely. Within two years the passage of empty freights on the system had been cut by 54,000,000 car-miles. But for all these efficiencies, Harriman never reached his purpose of an around-the-world transportation system using both land and water; world politics had frustrated his aim until he died in 1910.

At this juncture it would be easy to leave a false impression. The glitter of the mighty can bemuse us. So can the miseries of the humble. But a crucial fact is the presence of a chance to get ahead. An adolescent immigrant from Italy has left us his memoirs. His first job was on a gang that was digging a sewer in Brooklyn. The padrone said that if the men did not work for him, police would come and put them in jail. But one day the immigrant went off to Newark and got "work on the street." That was better, until it stopped. He went back to Brooklyn where he met a bootblack "and learned the business."

> We had said that when we had saved $1000 each we would go back to Italy and buy a farm, but now that the time is coming we are so busy and making so much money that we think we will stay. . . . There are plenty of rich Italians here, men who a few years ago had nothing and now have so much money that they could not count all their dollars in a week.

Several times these pages have discussed the consequences of cuts in transportation costs. The implications of these changes for the location of certain industries might now be discussed. In spite of numerous exceptions, a principle can be stated: Usually a prosperous firm was so situated as to minimize its freight charges. For instance, the factor of cheaper labor will go far to explain the migration of cotton-textile manufacturing from New England

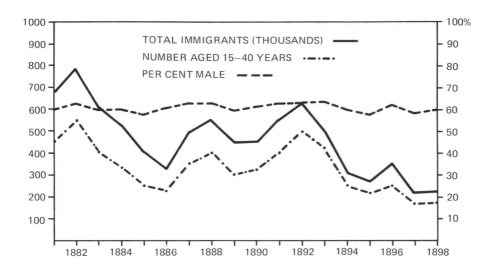

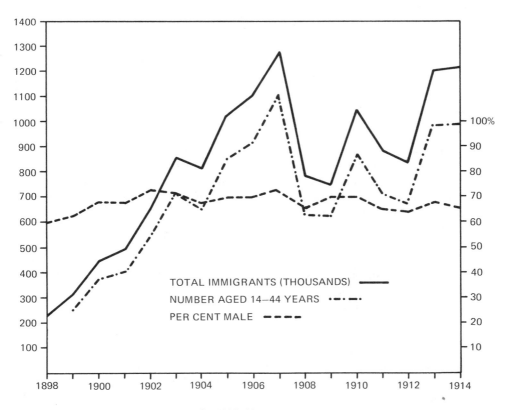

FIGURE 21-2. *Immigration in the U.S., 1899–1914*

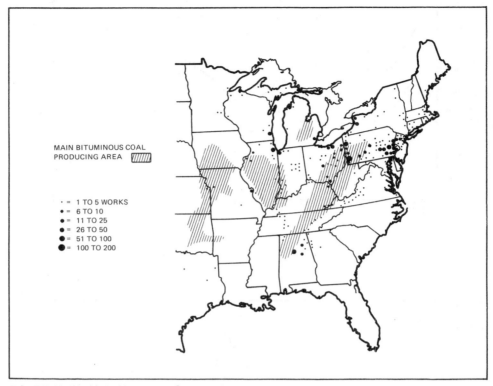

FIGURE 21-3. *Main Bituminous Coal-producing Areas*

to the Southern Appalachians, but this differential will not account for the transfer of the center of shoe manufacturing from Lynn, Massachusetts to St. Louis. In both these manufactories, the charge per ton of shipping the raw material is not much different from the charge of shipping the finished product, but the shoe industry found a Midwestern location would place it closer both to its raw materials and to a focal point in its market. The circumstance is otherwise when a large part of the weight or bulk of the raw material is lost in processing it. Obviously an oil well must be located where the deposits are. But a marked shift occurred in the placement of refineries. The first primary locus was in Cleveland, partly because it was near the fields, partly because Rockefeller and his partners lived there. When they realized that most of their sales were overseas, they bought or built refineries along the Eastern seaboard. The location of iron and steel mills shows graphically the determinants of a processor of weight-losing minerals. A treaty had drawn an international boundary from Lake Superior to the Lake of the Woods. Under it, the Mesabi iron range in Minnesota proved to lie in the United States. The Sault Sainte Marie Canal, joining Lakes Superior and Huron, made it feasible to move Mesabi ore to the southern shores of the Great Lakes where it could be fused with coal from the Alleghenies. For decades the Soo Canal moved more tonnage than any other canal in the world, including Suez and Panama. From it sprang the $50-million mill of U.S. Steel at Gary, Indiana, plus several other mills along the shores of the Lakes.

The spurt in the economy produced its own kind of politics. While the emperors of antiquity held the masses in check with the reliable combination of bread and circuses, in the early years of this century, that ancient formula was split two ways. For most of the urban poor, the power structures of local neighborhoods produced the bread, while national politics offered the circuses. At the time, enough people were still in want that bread came first, so it belongs first here. The stream of immigrants needed special help. A million a year were arriving. The great majority were young and hearty, but many lacked money, lacked skills that could be sold in America, could not even speak English. The opportunity to rise in society was there, surely, but it cost the newcomers both sweat and years. Employers deliberately pitted them against one another. Policemen did not like them, especially when a cop was of a different nationality. They had trouble finding a job. So they were at odds with each other, with their bosses, with the police and the courts. Every immigrant was desperate for a friend, any friend. The lucky ones found help from three types of people: their fellow countrymen, social workers, and political bosses. Some studies have been made of urban social groups, but the one to pay most attention to mutual help among immigrants has to do with the Chinese.* Historical works make reference to burial societies among Negroes and among immigrant groups, but not much is really known yet about these institutions that must have touched the hearts of many displaced persons. For that matter, few historians have heeded how appropriate the phrase "displaced person" is, not just for immigrants from Greece or Poland but also for migrants who had never crossed a national boundary. A boy from Mississippi who wound up in Detroit was almost sure to feel that he did not belong there at all. Moving on to social workers, some of them served a very useful function. So far as I know, the most remarkable battalion of women in American history lived at Hull-House, Chicago in the early years of this century. But then, we have already had an introduction to these ladies (early Chapter 19).

The foregoing leaves the third group of patrons of the poor. These benefactors were the professional politicians, scornfully called in some circles "the old-line pols." It is rash to scorn them. One reason is that they were so numerous. A qualified English observer tried to take a frequency count for his country compared to the United States. The population ratio was about 1:2. However, England had only 4,000 men whose chief trade was politics, whereas in America the estimate was 500,000. The same commentator remarked that in politics as in war, organization is everything, and these professionals formed into phalanxes. They were likable; they liked others in

---

*Today, in Calgary and probably elsewhere, it is a justified boast of leaders in Chinatown that "our people do not go on welfare." The community takes care of its parishioners. In this respect, but with critical distinctions, the relation might be compared to slavery in the United States.

return; and they wanted to help their neighbors. We should not romanticize them; they were thieves. But they stole in a relatively gentle way, and they gave back part of their gains. The fixers flourished in a day when the phrase "social welfare" did not even show in the lexicons of most governments in the United States; the typical well-to-do citizen thought the whole notion was immoral because it would encourage indolence and alcoholism. For voluminous information about sub-national governments in the United States, the journalist Lincoln Steffens had no peer. Philosophizing about political bosses he had known, he found that, by and large, they were a good bunch. But he distinguished this group of "principals," men who could think and act for themselves, from the "heelers" who could do nothing but take orders (for illustrations of how a heeler worked, see Document 21-4). It can be noted in passing that this last distinction has been a common belief among Americans. Steffens' contemporary Clarence Darrow, when approving jurors in a criminal trial that involved strikers, would always take a corporation president in preference to a shop foreman, because he thought the former would have more independence of mind to follow the evidence. Or one could reach all the way back to the words of the Essex Result (1778): "all the members of the state are qualified to make the election, unless they have not sufficient discretion, or are so situated as to have no wills of their own." Two further statements about junior governments and their politics seem valid. First, they had little power beyond the maintenance of public peace, and even there the strains in the society were often too severe for them to cope. Municipalities were the frail creatures of the states, with only delegated powers that could be suspended or removed at the whim of the senior government; a major struggle of the period was the effort to get Home Rule for the metropolis. The status of the states was better, but not by much. They could and did pass a few types of humanitarian legislation: factory-inspection, minimum wages and maximum hours, laws to benefit female and child workers, but the limits on their accomplishments were stringent. Note for instance that at least a dozen states elected as governor a man of considerable ability and broad views. Altgeld may be taken as representative of these executives. In retrospect, his achievements seem almost entirely negative. He could veto evil bills. He could pardon prisoners who had been falsely convicted. He could try to restrict injustice, but he could do little to promote equity. Part of the defect lay in his own ideas of public authority: even when the depression of 1893 was at its worst, he would not endorse the idea of public works to relieve unemployment. The fight for livelihood was up to the individual, while the state could only stand by and wait for the hard times to go away.

Second, the "great issues" being debated in Washington were seldom the issues that swayed the average voter. Congressmen and presidents argued about the tariff, about revision of the National Banking Act, sometimes about conservation of natural resources. The common man worried about whether the ward boss would help him to get a job with the streetcar company or would provide him with a free turkey for Thanksgiving or would wangle his son out of jail. National politics and precinct politics were related to each other, but the relationship was not simple or direct. But while seeking to particularize and to make concrete, we should not go too far in atomizing the electoral scene. A careful study of state politics has parceled out two areas of concern where a candidate, if he were to succeed at the state level, had to find a workable straddle: election reform, and alcoholic beverages (Chapter 18 opening). These two reforms, if they deserve that name, tended to merge because the clamor for both of them came generally from the same group—white Anglo-Saxon native-born Protestant rural voters.

Anybody today knows that the cities are not Utopias. But the countryside did not and does not deserve that rank either. No convincing picture has been made to show that bucolics have been more upright that urbanites. The bias against city folk, however, was persistent, and often it oozed forth from racial prejudice. Describing his colleagues in the New York legislature in 1885, Theodore Roosevelt sermonized that the worst of them were from cities. A few from that locale were educated and ethical, "but the bulk are very low indeed. They are usually foreigners of little or no education, with exceedingly misty ideas as to morality, and possessed of an ignorance so profound that it could only be called comic, were it not for the fact that it has at times such serious effects on our laws." But the evidence of similar abuses among other segments of the electorate is strong. Adams County, Ohio was a farming district. Nearly everybody was native-born Protestant white. The county seat was the only one in the state with neither railroad nor telegraph, so it could not easily be polluted by outsiders. Most people were poor. After the Civil War the two parties were evenly balanced. One of the few commodities that these rural folks had to sell was their votes, so they did. The system persisted, openly, for decades. Under a law saying that anybody convicted of selling his vote should be disfranchised for five years, prosecutions were started after the 1910 election. One name in four was stricken from the registration lists. To a woman who is hungry, virtue seems trifling; to a man who is poor, so does honor. The condition was summarized by a rhymester:

> Many people sold their vote
> For to buy an overcoat,
> Or to buy a sack of flour,
> Thinking it a prosperous hour.

But Theodore Roosevelt, exposed to these exposures of the social roots of scandalous politics, could write that neither "capital" nor "labor" but the individual must bear the guilt for crooked government.

Roosevelt will do as a symbol for the epoch of national politics that we are now reviewing, since he was president virtually throughout its duration. He shouted and waved his arms, but his feet never moved. Some historians still refer sweepingly to "The Progressive Era." But the federal government in this period did little. There were crying abuses of federal legislation in the

By permission of Edward Steichen

FIGURE 21-4. *Edward Steichen, J. Pierpont Morgan*

import duties and in the National Banking Act. Laws in both realms were highly discriminatory against the agricultural sector of the nation. Because the men who raised staple crops such as cotton or wheat perennially had an export surplus, no tariff could possibly protect their market, so it could not raise the price of the items they were selling. But it could raise the price of the manufactured goods they were buying, and it did. In this regard, matters had not changed much since the times of John C. Calhoun. The "hard money" monetary statutes, as has been noted, also were unfavorable to rural areas. But Roosevelt never thought it opportune to review the laws in either of these fields of policy. His concern was not with justice but with the retention and expansion of office. He came to high power due to his birth, due to his courage in warfare, due to his frenetic energy, due to his speechifying loquacity. He never understood that huge numbers of Americans were being treated wrongly by the federal government. His analytic mind might have been as dense and amorphous as potato chowder, but he had cunning; he gave to voters a few dreams in which they could get lost. As Roosevelt expanded, the fog grew denser, with himself revolving in the fog; he became a master of cant. One of his closest advisers is known to have said to him, "What I most admire about you, Theodore, is your discovery of the Ten Commandments."

Henry Adams observed that Roosevelt was "pure act." Steffens charitably wrote that "Roosevelt's lies were unconscious" and further noted the president's "old rule": "Never to deny anything unless it is true." The most caustic evaluation of all contemporaries might be the one made by Mark Twain

---

This photograph of the domineering investment banker must rank as one of the greatest portraits ever done. It reflects not only the advances in materials but also the expanding conceptions of what could be done with camera and film (see Figure 18-2). Perhaps Morgan never realized how devastatingly he had been pictured by photographer Edward Steichen. Seventy years after this print was made, many viewers see the subject as holding in his left hand a dagger, whereas the actual object is merely the burnished arm of a chair. Morever the dagger appears to be a bowie knife that a sadist might use to butcher his enemies; it is not a subtle stiletto. The characterization calls to mind a frontier mode of fighting duels; the officials gave to each combatant a bowie knife and locked them together in a room. Then they waited until one knocked on the door to come out.

Morgan was an aggrandizer. He could be polite when that seemed the shrewd tactic to improve his opportunities, but his impulses were the reverse. He was the fulcrum around which grew the biggest American organizations of his time. Occasionally he miscalculated, as with the International Mercantile Marine; but usually not, witness United States Steel and International Harvester. Living in an age when access to liquid capital was vital, he was born floating in it and quickly learned how to make more flow into his pond. His father was an investment banker in London; J. P. was born in the insurance capital, Hartford; he was educated genteely in Boston and at the University of Göttingen. Yet he was coarse and ruthless. As an aging man he took his mistress on his yacht to the fashionable resorts of the Atlantic. He was a stalwart of the Episcopal Church and expressed concern that his immortal soul should ascend to Heaven.

His dominant urge was not to create but to control. He owned perhaps the finest private art collection in existence. Some of his manuscript collections were housed in a rare book museum which eventually became a magnet for scholars. But other collections seem to have been guarded like dragon hoards, such as the fossil horse collection in the Museum of Natural History to which a famous scholar of evolution was recently denied access, apparently through some restrictive intention of the long-dead financier. Even in the grave, his grasp stayed firm.

to Andrew Carnegie: "Mr. Roosevelt is the Tom Sawyer of the political world of the twentieth century; always showing off; always hunting for a chance to show off; in his frenzied imagination the Great Republic is a vast Barnum circus with him for a clown and the whole world for audience." Another perceptive contemporary philosophized: "Americans have no political ideas; they follow leaders who attract them or who know how to manage them. The kind of political leaders they like are human circuses."

Confronted with the perplexities of anti-trust enforcement, the chief executive went from one foot to the other, much in the fashion of the other President Roosevelt a generation later (Chapter 26). The Northern Pacific Case shows one extreme, and to explain it the facts must be pared down a bit, without distorting the problem or its resolution. Two railroad magnates, Harriman and James J. Hill, wanted the same railroad to give their other lines an entry into Chicago. Their struggle drove the market value of stock in the desired company up 1,000 per cent. The stock exchange became so unsettled that Morgan stepped in. His answer was to form a holding company, Northern Securities, in which Hill and Harriman had representation. At this stage, Roosevelt decided that the federal government should act in accord with the anti-trust laws. The attorney general brought suit under the Sherman Act. The next parry was for Morgan to pay a social call to the White House, where he reportedly said to the president, "If we have done anything wrong, send your man to my man and they can fix it up." Finally, on 14 March, 1904, the Supreme Court ordered the dissolution of the holding company by a vote of 5 to 4. This episode posed a problem vividly, for the two best judges on the Court disagreed. Harlan wrote the decision for dissolution of the trust. But Holmes dissented, with the acid comment that Harlan's interpretation of the Sherman Act "would make eternal the *bellum omnium contra omnes* [Hobbes' "war of all against all"] and disintegrate society so far as it could into individual atoms." Holmes was quite possibly right, but his wisdom did not prevent the president from being annoyed at what seemed to him the treachery of his protegé, whom he had recently named to the Court. Roosevelt, in plain truth, did not want to have the problem posed vividly.

For a vignette of the president standing on his other foot in regard to the nascent trusts, the Tennessee Coal & Iron episode in 1907 provides one. Whereas in the Northern Securities incident the catalyst had been an excessive demand on the exchange for a specific stock, the difficulty here was an absence of demand. A large brokerage firm had made sizeable loans against the collateral of Tennessee Coal & Iron stock. The brokers needed cash, and they could not market the securities. So a proposal was made that U.S. Steel should buy the stock in question, giving in exchange its own bonds that could be sold on the open market. But would the federal government intervene again on the grounds that the effective merger of two large competitors violated the Sherman Anti-Trust Act? The head of U.S. Steel went to Washington to find out. Roosevelt did not object, and so J. P. Morgan's choice firm got control of another billion tons of coal and 600 million tons of iron ore.

From this muddled thinking, little good could come. To make a fast summation, we might note that the Roosevelt administration, with nearly eight years of power, proffered 44 indictments under the Anti-Trust Act. The Taft government, which lasted only four years, brought 65. Obviously the difference in quantity should not be regarded as decisive. But a glance at the impact of specific allegations confirms the impression given by the numbers. One indictment under President Taft was against the imperialistic Du Ponts (Chapter 23). Another was against U.S. Steel for its purchase of the Tennessee Coal & Iron stock. It says a good deal about the rank of William Howard Taft as chief executive (Chapter 22) that he did not know about this charge before the general public could read it in the newspapers; even then, he did not anticipate that his predecessor and sponsor, Roosevelt, would resent the charge. Or look at the Elkins Act (1903). Supposedly the law aimed to stop rebates and other discriminations by common carriers. Allegedly the rebates had been of great benefit to Standard Oil (Document 20-1), but Rockefeller denied it (Document 21-2). The new law decreed that any departure by a railroad from its published rates was self-evident proof of discrimination; moreover, the man who accepted a rebate was just as guilty as the company that paid it. But notice—one draftsman of the statute was an attorney for the Pennsylvania Railroad. Would it not be logical for a carrier to try to use federal power to avoid being victimized by giant shippers such as steel and petroleum producers? It often happened in this period that an economic interest would try to fight off a competing group by recourse to public favors.

Another feature of the Roosevelt administration was the importance, previously substantial and now growing, of ethnic politics. This theme can be illustrated by reference to two minority groups, blacks and Jews. To consider blacks first, their political power had waned markedly since Reconstruction. The ordinary white at best was indifferent to their plight in the polity; odds were that he was hostile to their participation in civic affairs. Ninety per cent of all Negroes were still south of the Mason-Dixon Line, where they were systematically disfranchised between Reconstruction and 1910. Techniques and results varied from state to state, but a couple of examples can be cited. Louisiana achieved the following reduction in voter registration:

	White	Black	Total
Registered 1 Jan. 1897	164,088	130,344	294,432
Registered 17 March 1900, new constitution	123,437	5,320	130,757

(Parenthetically note that many of the novel requirements hit at poor whites as well as blacks. One cute device was to make the suffrage dependent upon payment of a poll tax. This trick might be carried further by making the tax payable in the spring when cash is notoriously scarce among farmers. It could be extended further yet by requiring the farmer to produce the receipt for his poll tax at the autumn election, in a country where people were not addicted to elaborate filing systems.)

But a migration of blacks to Northern cities had begun, although it was far short of the dimensions it would attain later, and in some key districts the black vote might be important. So Roosevelt made gestures to win it. Since the death of Frederick Douglass in 1895, the most prominent Negro leader in the country had been Booker T. Washington, president of Tuskegee Institute in Alabama. The president shared a meal with him at the White House. It would be wrong to label this action as flamboyant and hollow; it infuriated the racist extremists, so to them Roosevelt's courtesy was not without meaning. But this positive motion should be seen in context—of the Brownsville outrage for instance. This Texas town was not receptive to three companies of black infantrymen who were transferred to its environs in 1906. The first two weeks saw several outbreaks between civilians and soldiers. At last some men shot up Brownsville and killed a white resident. They were never identified. However, an Army investigator concluded that their Army buddies must know who the culprits were. When nobody came forward to identify them, the president ordered every man in the three companies discharged without honor. Among these (approximately) 450 men were six winners of the Congressional Medal of Honor. A fortnight later Roosevelt informed a friend that because the case was "of vital concern to the whole country, I will not for one moment consider the political effect." Self-deception was becoming the mood of public life.

Another index is Roosevelt's manipulation of the Jewish vote as the waves of immigrants from Russia and Poland rolled into the Eastern cities. In 1903 Congress had established the Department of Commerce and Labor. Three years later the president needed a dramatic move to draw Jewish votes in a New York election, so he named a Jew (significantly, chief executive of the giant department store of R. H. Macy) to head the newly formed department and thus gave him control over immigration. Soon after, a large dinner was held at which the president explained how he had made his choice. The story has it that Roosevelt contended that he had sought only to find the best man for the job, without regard to any other consideration. Certainly he had not thought about the candidate's race or religion or political party. This high-mindedness, he said, could be confirmed by the master of ceremonies. The gentleman in question, himself Jewish, was the top man at the banking firm of Kuhn, Loeb; unfortunately for Roosevelt, he was also deaf. He replied, "Dot's right, Mr. President, you came to me and said 'Chake, who is der best Jew I can appoint Secretary of Commerce?'"

Another segment of the population that deserves notice is the industrial labor force. As already noted, this category is too broad for effective analysis. Some occupations, particularly locomotive engineers, building trades, and the printing trades, were doing quite well. But semiskilled and unskilled workers, whether digging ditches or employed in large factories, had a rough time. The branches of government causing the most trouble for strikers were the police and the courts. In many jurisdictions the favorite indictment for use in labor disputes was the charge of conspiracy; by this sleight of hand, an act that was legal if committed by one man became illegal if committed by several. We cannot examine here the deeds of courts in all the major cities, but representative decisions can be cited. Although exceptions can be found, it is broadly true that the Supreme Court after 1900 seemed to reverse the line of doctrine that it had endorsed earlier in regard to legislative power over working conditions. In 1898 it had upheld a Utah statute fixing a maximum work-day of eight hours in mines. But in *Lochner* v. *New York* (1905) by some elaborate sophistries the Court disallowed a law that banned bakers from working more than ten hours; since the public interest, read the decision, was in no way affected by this topic, the regulation was unconstitutional. The reactionary trend did not stop there. New York also passed a statute pertaining only to women and minors which decreed that they could not work at night nor could they work more than ten hours a day. The Court's judgment said:

> So I think, in this case, that we should say, as an adult female is in no sense a ward of the state, that she is not to be made the special object of the exercise of the paternal power of the state and that the restriction, here imposed upon her privilege to labor, violates the constitutional guarantees.

Does equality for women necessarily imply identical treatment? And what of the children?

In two fields of legislation the Roosevelt terms brought advances: protection of the consumer by inspection of foodstuffs and drugs, and protection of posterity by reducing the exploitation of natural resources. An approach toward the first objective was made by the Meat Inspection Act and the Pure Food and Drug Act of 1906. The federal inspector of meat might be notoriously lax or even corrupt in performing his duty, and the legal sale of patent medicines is greater now than in 1905. But no president should be condemned on the ground that he did not find an instant solution to a complicated problem. The same caution should be used in evaluating the efforts made early in this century to preserve natural resources. The alertness of a Boston bookseller to his environment in 1851 (Document 14-2) should not suggest that many Americans had even begun to grasp the concept of ecology. For this reason the accomplishments of the early twentieth century seem meritorious. There had always been powerful Americans who were devoted to nature; one might think of Presidents Jefferson and John Quincy Adams. But to the typical citizen the landscape conveyed little beyond the hope for a quick fortune. Greed was not quashed by the Roosevelt administrations; it was impeded. Under one law, three million acres in the West were irrigated in four years. More than 2,500 water-power sites were reserved from private development (on the spurious ground that they were to be federal ranger stations). Roosevelt's term of office saw the creation of five national parks, which doubled the number that had existed when he became president.

It remains to say some words about foreign relations. Diplomacy in Europe can best be left for the following chapter on American involvement in

World War I, so the present discussion can be limited to policy toward Latin America, especially the Caribbean, and toward the Far East. Some common fallacies should be rejected at the start. (1) Some circles have relied on the terms "interventionist" and "isolationist." To most historians using these words, the former has applied to the good guys, the latter to the bad. But neither term has much meaning, if any. What kind of intervention, where, when? What kind of isolation, from whom, how? (2) Until the late nineteenth century the United States did avoid committing itself militarily—and to a great extent diplomatically—in the quarrels of Europe (Washington's "Great Rule" steadily adhered to). But American attachments to the European economies were continuous and every effort was made to increase them. (3) In the Pacific and in Latin America, United States involvement was recurrent, and it was political as well as commercial. "Isolationism" was always quite selective.

United States commitments in the Caribbean ensued from the practice of some Latin American nations of forfeiting on their bonds held in Europe. When Venezuela did so, Britain, Germany, and Italy tried to force her to honor her obligations by attempting to impose a blockade on all her ports. The contestants were willing in principle to arbitrate. With Roosevelt taking an active part in the negotiations, this decision was reached. He said later that a refusal by Germany would have led him to intervene with armed force. Historians for years believed that his claim was typical braggadocio, but a recent study proves that he not only made the threat but backed it up by sending a naval squadron toward the area. So far, so good; the Monroe Doctrine has been upheld. But the president's next foray to enforce those tenets was less fortunate. It must be understood in the light of British policy: England had posed to the United States an alternative. Either you must let us curb those Latino countries that commit offenses against our citizens, or you must curb them. Roosevelt chose the latter course. In his 1904 message to Congress he proclaimed:

> Chronic wrongdoing, or an impotence which results in a general loosening of the ties of civilized society, may in America, as elsewhere, ultimately require intervention by some civilized nation, and in the Western Hemisphere the adherence of the United States to the Monroe Doctrine may force the United States, however reluctantly, in flagrant cases of such wrongdoing or impotence, to the exercise of an international police power.

James Monroe and John Quincy Adams had sought to prevent European meddling in the Americas; now the Roosevelt Corollary virtually reversed the policy to justify American meddling.

British goals in the Far East lured the United States into that area also. Not that this nation needed much tempting; its businessmen and to a lesser extent its public officials had been hungry in the Pacific for more than a century. But with the Open Door Notes of 1899 and 1900, the federal policy toward China carried hints of retaliation. The industrial countries of Europe along with Japan were, like buzzards, plucking flesh from China. These formal Open Door Notes responded by stating two American aims: to preserve the territorial integrity of the nation, and to secure there equal commercial treatment for citizens of all foreign governments. A test came in 1905. For three years Great Britain had been publicly allied with Japan. When that country made a surprise attack on Manchuria in 1904, the British hoped to see Russia thrust back into Asia. Then Russia could be used as a counterweight to the German push westward. Confronted by these complicated moves and counter-moves, Roosevelt's initial hope was that hostilities in the Far East would continue until both combatants collapsed; then his country would not face "either a yellow peril or a Slav peril." Later he realized that he might be able to use both of the belligerents to preserve the Open Door in China, so he began maneuvers pointed toward a negotiated peace. Russia was on the verge of popular revolution; Japan was financially threadbare. The two nations met at Portsmouth, New Hampshire in 1905. Due partly to Roosevelt's pressure on Russia, Japan came out ahead. One of her gains was a protectorate over Korea, which would have considerable consequences for the future.

In the interval between the two Open Door Notes, the Boxer Rebellion against all foreigners broke out in northern China. The United States joined with other major powers in sending troops to suppress the outbreak; some of the invaders did not exhibit the finest behavior. Several features of American policy toward China deserve mention. One premise was that production of goods in the United States was so efficient that no European company could compete in the Far East; as *The Times* (London) commented irritably: "Even protectionist organs are for free trade in China, where freedom is for the benefit of American manufacturers." Further, basic flaws in Roosevelt's approach to foreign relations erupted. He had parcelled out the entire earth into "barbarous" distinguished from "civilized" countries. Within this dichotomy, he regarded Australia as more important than India. China he thought had no potential whatever, so he organized a conference where Japan and Russia agreed to a peace for China without any Chinese voice at all. To block Russian expansion in Asia, he agreed to the Japanese holding the dominant influence in Manchuria while the British and Americans were granted prime rights in the Yangtze valley. Going beyond the concession of a Japanese protectorate over Korea, he agreed to let Japan have "suzerainty over" that nation. The other chief provision of the Taft-Katsura Agreement (29 July, 1905; never submitted to the Senate because it was not a treaty) bound the United States for the time being to accept the goals of the Anglo-Japanese alliance. But what sort of aims were behind American policy?

The new American commitments in the Far East led to arguments that the United States needed a greatly enlarged navy. Chief agitators for this program were the president, Admiral Mahan, and such senators as Beveridge and Lodge. Having secured from a reluctant Congress the battleships that he wanted, Roosevelt sent the fleet in 1907 on an around-the-world cruise. This move has been praised as a brilliant stroke for overawing the Japanese, but it still seems like a strange tactic. However one regards it, it proceeded from a false postulate. Having started from the exaggeration that the United States could dominate the western Pacific, Roosevelt had moved to the exaggeration that Japan was a present menace in the eastern Pacific. If so, then why put his fleet in her waters where it could be attacked treacherously? The answer probably lies in a bluster that he had made in 1903: "America's geographical position in the Pacific is such as to insure our peaceful dominion of its waters."

In spite of the costly lessons of World War II, this illusion would persist for decades.

The prolonged depression from 1865 to 1896 had convinced capitalists that they must eliminate competition in order to maintain the prices of their products at a profitable level. In many industries this thrust toward monopoly—together with friendly governments plus advancing technology that lowered costs of production and distribution—did indeed bring profits. It also gave millions of Americans the highest standard of living that the world had ever known. Further, it brought businessmen into numerous and often shifting alliances with the politicians who maneuvered at the summits of governments. These developments had diverse results for different groups of ordinary people. The fortunes of many skilled workers and petty entrepreneurs shot forward dramatically. Politically, some groups of New Immigrants, especially Jews and Italians, gained influence far more quickly than the Irish had done two generations earlier. Other groups, notably blacks and poor Southern whites, actually lost political power that they had previously held. The decade from the Spanish-American War to the financial panic of 1907 can now be seen as a false prosperity. It did little to improve the status of the common man, and its aimless rhetoric befogged the reasons for his misery. Meanwhile the federal authorities energetically pursued the goal of overseas expansion.

SOME NOTABLE EVENTS

1897–

1914 Exports of capital from U.S. exceed imports in every year.

1898 Union Pacific Railroad falls under domination of Edward H. Harriman.

1899 International Paper formed.

1901 U.S. Steel formed; first billion dollar corporation.

Hay-Pauncefote Treaty with Britain for isthmian canal in Central America.

1902 DuPont Corporation acquired by new (du Pont) management.

Newlands Act for land reclamation, 17 June.

1903 Ford Motor Company opens its first plant.

Hay-Herrán Treaty with Colombia is signed for canal rights, but they refuse to ratify.

Panama rebels against Colombia, enabling U.S. to secure canal rights.

Department of Commerce and Labor established.

Elkins Act, mainly against railroad rebates.

1904 Supreme Court orders dissolution of Northern Securities Company.

1905 *Lochner* v. *New York*; Supreme Court rules against state labor regulations.

1906 Harvey Firestone begins to make pneumatic tires.

Hepburn Act gives Interstate Commerce Commission the power to set reasonable rates.

Pure Food and Drug Act.

Brownsville, Texas race riot, 13 August.

1907 Financial panic begins, 13 March.

Moyer-Haywood-Pettibone case in Idaho.

1908 Eugene Debs leads Red Special campaign of Socialist party.

Henry Ford begins to sell the Model T.

1910 Speaker Joseph G. Cannon loses his dictatorial powers in the House.

Ways to Study History XXI

Join a team? This maxim should be ignored, or reversed. Since World War II, research grants have become available from foundations, often awarded in a lump sum to a university on condition that a group of the faculty will dream up some "trail-blazing project." They seldom do. The late Justice Oliver Wendell Holmes, Jr. once wrote that being a judge meant to sail by yourself through the Arctic ice. The same metaphor can be applied to the study of the past. A historian walks into his office or the library, closes a door, and tries to learn what really happened. If lucky, he comes close to success. If he feels depressed when alone, he should not try.

Two eminent men can be seen as illustration. Allan Nevins published about as many important works as any American historian of his generation. For quality of output as well as quantity, he inspires awe. But on some ventures he was thwarted by his research assistants. Thus, he published a multi-volume study of Henry Ford and his motor company. But be wary. The text carries a photographic copy of a contract with the caption: "Tires, at four for $26." The contract was really for wheels; surely Nevins knew a wheel from a tire, but did he check his collaborators' work?

A study of a specific company has commonly been called a work in business history. Probably no practitioner in this specialty has done better work than George Sweet Gibb: first a book about a silverware manufacturer (1946), then an analysis of a textile-machinery builder (1950). Next, judged by the superlative standards of his earlier publications, he came a cropper. He was co-author of one volume (1956) in the mammoth history of the Standard Oil Company (New Jersey). These particular pages of print might give you the impression that the corners of several rugs had never been lifted. Some important issues seem to have been left to slip away between the responsibilities of the team members.

Collaborations can work, but they are treacherous.

Document 21-1

The author of these remarks, Carl Schurz, had been a United States senator and a secretary of the interior. Perhaps more important are two other facts: he was himself an immigrant from Germany, and his warnings were a convocation address at the University of Chicago.

. . . *It is an incontestable and very significant fact that the British, the best colonizers in history, have, indeed, established in tropical regions governments, and rather absolute ones, but they have never succeeded in establishing there democratic commonwealths of the Anglo-Saxon type, like those in America or Australia.*

The scheme of Americanizing our "new possessions" in that sense is therefore absolutely hopeless. The immutable forces of nature are against it. Whatever we may do for their improvement, the people of the Spanish Antilles will remain in overwhelming numerical predominance, Spanish creoles and negroes, and the people of the Philippines, Filipinos, Malays, Tagals, and so on,—some of them quite clever in their way, but the vast majority utterly alien to us, not only in origin and language, but in habits, traditions, ways of thinking, principles, ambitions,—in short, in most things that are of the greatest importance in human intercourse and especially in political cooperation. And under the influences of their tropical climate they will prove incapable of becoming assimilated to the Anglo-Saxon. They would, therefore, remain in the population of this republic a hopelessly heterogeneous element,—in some respects more hopeless even than the colored people now living among us. . . .

No, we cannot expect that the Porto Ricans, the Cubans, and the Filipinos will maintain orderly governments in Anglo-Saxon fashion. . . .

Document 21-2

Having retired from active participation in Standard Oil in 1897, John D. Rockefeller nonetheless was a witness before a federal commission investigating the problem of trusts. He denied that they had secured unfair rebates from railroads. Rather, so he said, their growth ensued from advantages over other firms which were to the benefit of society.

It is too late to argue about advantages of industrial combinations. They are a necessity. And if Americans are to have the privilege of extending their business in all the States of the Union, and into foreign countries as well, they are a necessity on a large scale, and require the agency of more than one corporation. Their chief advantages are:

(1) Command of necessary capital.

(2) Extension of limitations of business.

(3) Increase of number of persons interested in the business.

(4) Economy in the business.

(5) Improvements and economies which are derived from knowledge of many interested persons of wide experience.

(6) Power to give the public improved products at less prices and still make a profit for stockholders.

(7) Permanent work and good wages for laborers.

I speak from my experience in business with which I have been intimately connected for about 40 years. Our first combination was a partnership and afterwards a corporation in Ohio. That was sufficient for a local refining business. But dependent solely upon local business we should have failed years ago. We were forced to extend our markets and to seek for export trade. This latter made the seaboard cities a necessary place of business, and we soon discovered that manufacturing for export could be more economically carried on at the seaboard, hence refineries at Brooklyn, at Bayonne, at Philadelphia, and necessary corporations in New York, New Jersey, and Pennsylvania. . . .

Document 21-3

It is ironic that Carnegie, who was about to spread his largesse around the world, was heedless of the welfare of his city when he made his fortune. Beatrice Webb, an outstanding English social scientist, visited his factory in Pittsburgh in 1898, and recorded these observations in her diary after a young executive had shown her about.

We were told both by our young man and afterwards by Frick, that they never hesitated to tear up and demolish any of the plant if they thought a new plant would pay handsomely on the new capital to be expended. The value of the old plant was simply written off. It is said that Carnegie's Works replace all their plant every three years. It is, I think, to this lavish generosity towards their brainworkers and stimulus to their co-operative energies combined with this extravagant expenditure on improvements, that the Carnegie business owes its rapid and phenominal success. . . .

Towards Labour they have acted for the last six years in a niggardly and oppressive fashion. They have abolished Trade Unionism throughout all their works—steel, coke, and mines and railways. . . . These 30 or 40 eager young men, who run the concern, have their whole energies absorbed in money making; they have as the ideal before them the lives of Mr. Carnegie and Mr. Frick—men who directly they have made their pile, leave Pittsburg and, to use the words of our young guide, "entertain finely in Paris and London." Not a member of the firm has any connection with the Federal, State or Municipal Government. It is only another aspect of this kind of Capitalism, that the State of Pennsylvania and the city of Pittsburg are so abjectly corrupt that State and City have become bye-words, even among American politicians. . . .

Document 21-4

When George Washington Plunkett, age 82, died in 1924 he was rich and renowned. He had run a business as a harbor contractor in New York, but his real trade was politics; he was leader of an assembly district for Tammany Hall. His revelations in a set of interviews published in 1905 are an instructive and amusing account of how the system worked.

There's an honest graft, and I'm an example of how it works. I might sum up the whole thing by sayin': "I seen my opportunities and I took 'em."

Just let me explain by examples. My party's in power in the city, and it's goin' to undertake a lot of public improvements. Well, I'm tipped off, say, that they're going to lay out a new park at a certain place.

I see my opportunity and I take it. I go to that place and I buy up all the land I can in the neighborhood. Then the board of this or that makes its plan public, and there is a rush to get my land, which nobody cared particular for before. . . .

What tells in holding your grip on your district is to go right down among the poor families and help them in the different ways they need help. I've got a regular system for this. If there's a fire in Ninth, Tenth, or Eleventh Avenue, for example, any hour of the day or night, I'm usually there with some of my election district captains as soon as the fire engines. If a family is burned out I don't ask whether they are Republicans or Democrats, and I don't refer them to the Charity Organization Society, which would investigate their case in a month or two and decide they were worthy of help about the time they were dead of starvation. I just get quarters for them, buy clothes for them if their clothes were burned up, and fix them up till they get things runnin' again. . . .

How to Get into a War

World War I had been in train for more than two and a half years before the United States was a belligerent. Its origins must be sought abroad. The outbreak of hostilities arose from a wide range of pressures, and some of them should be appraised. Apparent in the issue were changes in military technology, struggles for colonies and markets, rising clamors of nationalism, shifts in the balance of power in Europe. To begin with the last category, all of the major governments except Russia were roughly equal in the efficiency of their administration in mobilizing the resources of the nation. Nor were their rates of population growth widely disparate. What did change dramatically was their relative capacities to produce certain vital industrial goods. Drastically increased possibilities for destruction accompanied this explosive productivity in all the industrial nations.

The weight of this development toward destructiveness shifted enormously because of alterations in the techniques of warfare. Modern weaponry

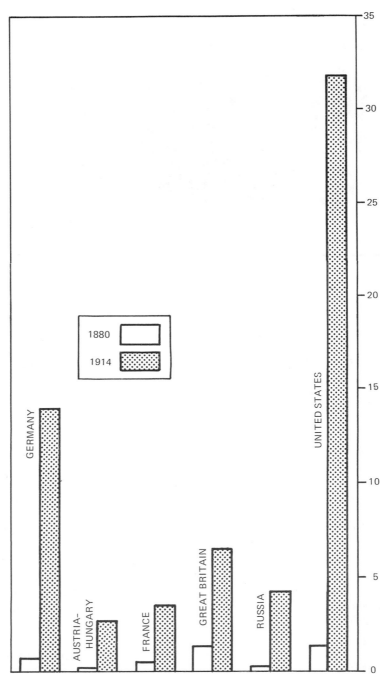

FIGURE 22-1. *International Steel Production, 1800–1914 (millions of tons)*

could consume metal at a pace that was beyond the imagination at the time of the Civil War. Relative strength on the oceans had also shifted. Until about the Crimean War (1854–1856) ships of the line were wooden. They took a long time to build, and they lasted some sixty years. England's accumulation of such vessels was so great that nobody felt like competing for control of the seas. But then came the steel hull, coupled with great strides in naval artillery. One British battleship completed in 1888 could have destroyed the entire fleet of ironclads launched in Britain prior to that decade. Fear of a drastic imbalance in sea power versus Germany prompted a British "naval scare" and a construction program that initiated eight battleships. But their guns still used gunpowder—an explosive so shattering that the weapons had very short lives. This meant that target practice had to be severely restricted. Even prior to the completion of these vessels, another design for big guns using cordite instead of gunpowder was originated. This in turn brought a new type of battleship, and so on. Now that Great Britain no longer had the "stock" of wooden warships, its advantages were reduced to two: (a) a stock of trained naval personnel, and (b) freedom from conscription into the army thus leaving more manpower available for industrial production. But as soon as another country could spare power from its land forces, it could bid for control of the seas. Beginning in 1898, Germany did just that.

One element in the indispensability of naval power was the fact that no nation was self-sufficient in military matériel. Consider nitrate. It supplied the nitrogen essential to all explosives, and nearly all nitrates came from Chile. While Britain dominated the Atlantic, she could cut off the German supply. But in 1910 a scientist at the Kaiser Wilhelm Institute in Berlin (one of the few governmental research establishments in the world at that time) devised a method to capture free nitrogen from the atmosphere. Goodby Chile, goodby English navy. As suggested, cordite had already been invented as an "improvement." Gunpowder consists of sulphur and charcoal (the fuels) plus nitropotassium (the charge, oxidizing element, explosive component). Cordite is the single molecule of nitrocellulose that holds both fuel and oxidizing agent. The latter is far more powerful; the direction of its blast can also be better controlled. By this time a good deal of brain power was at work on implements of aggression. One destructive weapon led to another. Submarines were horribly vulnerable (partly because their hulls were as thin as eggshells) to the better gunnery at longer range of surface vessels. So torpedoes were fabricated that would go farther. Nations were making other types of preparations for conflict. Great Britain's Chancellor of the Exchequer in 1909 created domestic turbulence by asking an increase in the budget of £15 million. Five years later, Germany imposed a military levy of a billion marks, a ghastly burden on a country with the resources that she had then. She cashed in nearly all of her foreign assets. She finished widening the Kiel Canal from that city to Wilhelmshaven, so that her large warships could move from the North Sea to the Baltic without becoming too vulnerable to attack. In the midst of this hurly-burly of preparedness, the French had exhausted most of their possible responses. They had no more able-bodied men who had previously been exempt from the army draft and thus could not expand their forces by the device of eliminating exempt categories. The best expedient they could find was to extend the term of each conscript from two years to three.

The precipitant in this seething pot was the Russo-German rivalry in the Balkans and the Middle East. Germany, as her power grew, had become increasingly resentful that she had been blocked out of the colonization of non-industrial countries, by the United States in Latin America, by other European powers in Africa and Asia. Next she tried to push eastward; a memorable symbol was the Berlin to Baghdad Railroad. This thrust collided with Russian ambitions to expand southward toward the Black Sea and the Bosporus. A violent clash (the Balkan War) began in October 1912; the victors were Serbia, Greece, Albania, and Bulgaria, who triumphed over Austria-Hungary. The latter was the one firm European ally of Germany—which had now miscalculated Habsburg power. In the prelude to World War I (as later in the antecedents of World War II), Germany's ambitions waxed greater than her energies. The moves eastward might well have succeeded if she had limited herself to this expansion on land; instead she had wasted much of her force by trying simultaneously to challenge British suzerainty of the oceans.

Roosevelt was also thinking about naval power, and he showed that he would go to any lengths to get it. The acquisition of the Panama Canal proved that the United States could bully a tiny country in Central America, but everyone knew that anyway. It also showed that we could bully Great Britain, which, facing the German threat, desperately needed to find a friend somewhere. For the present, the background must be stripped down severely. Policy-makers could not agree on the best route for a transisthmian ditch: Nicaragua or the Panama isthmus in Colombia. The situation was further complicated because a treaty of 1850 (Chapter 17) pledged that neither America nor Britain would seek "exclusive control" over a Caribbean ditch. To some minds the matter became urgent during the Spanish-American War; a new battleship at San Francisco took 68 days to go the 13,000 miles to Key West through the Straits of Magellan. Now a peculiar sort of circular logic seeped into minds in Washington: the nation required a Central American canal so that it could move ships more quickly, and it required a two-ocean navy to protect the canal. So the United States procured from England a new agreement that wiped out the 1850 treaty.

The remaining task was to secure a right-of-way. Long since, a French firm had started a canal across the Isthmus of Panama (part of Colombia) but had scrapped the project. It was willing to sell out to the United States; unfortunately, however, its rights were due to expire soon. Thereafter Colombia would be free to seize the physical property and lease it to the highest bidder. In America, Congress pressed the president to get the required real estate, in either of the two desired countries. Roosevelt's emissaries negotiated a treaty with the Colombian government for the Panama route, but the Colombian senate rejected it. Fulminating against the "contemptuous little creatures" trying to thwart his aim, Roosevelt sent a warship to Colombia. It arrived on 2 November, 1903. Two days later, a thousand Panamanians rebelled against Colombia. American forces would not let Colombian troops attack the rebels. In another two days, the American president had recognized the independent republic of Panama. So the canal was built, completed in 1914 a few days after the war began in Europe. Roosevelt offered interpretations of his behavior that look incompatible. He declared that "every action" of his administrations had been "in accordance with the highest, finest, and nicest standards of public governmental ethics." But he also said publicly, "I took the canal zone and let Congress debate, and while the debate goes on the canal does also." Take your choice.

Meanwhile the United States was having its domestic-foreign irritations. That Roosevelt had taken a generally pro-Japan stance at the Portsmouth Conference (late in Chapter 21) does not imply that he took a similar position at home. He had been mainly interested in expanding American business interests in the Orient (as we shall see below), not in favoring Orientals. Meanwhile, Asian immigrants to the United States had aroused hatred for decades. Early in this century the bias manifested itself in discrimination against Japanese children in schools, especially by California. The demand was strong: Keep them out of the country altogether. In 1908 the two nations reached an agreement. The United States conceded that Japanese formerly resident in this country plus close relatives of Japanese currently resident here, should receive entry permits. In return, Japan agreed to discourage emigration of unskilled laborers. This so-called Gentlemen's Agreement would later be an influence on the events of World War II and on the climate of opinion in which that conflict took place.

From the financial panic of 1907 until the outbreak of European war in 1914, American policy in fiscal, foreign, and political affairs was made in a consciousness that the economy was very shaky. Depression was sometimes relieved; ebbs and flows did occur. But depression was endemic along with the basic maldistribution of income. The responses of the federal government, whether under Roosevelt or Taft or Wilson, were anemic. Details need not be explored, but some matters should be mentioned. Whereas Roosevelt had refused to touch the problem of tariff rates, his hand-picked successor plunged in with a call for reduction of import duties. Already Taft was breaking the rules of American politics. The prudent president sends his advance agents to Capitol Hill before he makes any public commitments. They count heads, make deals, swap votes on this for votes on that. Instead, Taft called a special session of Congress for the sole purpose of revising the tariff. When the Payne bill was submitted to the House, the chief executive admitted that its rates were not as low as he had wished, but claimed that they were "substantial reductions." At this stage he should have been wary. The worst was yet to come. Guided by Nelson Aldrich of Rhode Island (son-in-law of the elder Rockefeller), the Senate voted more than 800 amendments. Duties were sharply raised on several iron and steel products, lumber, textiles. The Payne bill had included an inheritance-tax clause; it disappeared.

Now Taft's afflictions multiplied quickly. The final version of the Payne-Aldrich Act brought only a small reduction over-all, and it was regarded as prejudicial to the Midwest. Strong sectional antagonism to the administration emerged. It was aggravated when he bungled the questions of conservation and finally fired a popular administrator from Pennsylvania. These missteps killed any pretense of unity in the Republican Party. The president's fulcrum in the House of Representatives had long been the Speaker, whose power over legislation a decade earlier had been overwhelming. In a sense, his voice had been more decisive than the president's when a bill was being considered. The chief executive could veto a measure, but his veto could be overturned by a two-thirds vote. When the Speaker obstructed a bill, appeal was nearly impossible. Each proposal was required to have a special rule to reach the floor of the House. The Rules Committee had five members. The Speaker was a member, and he appointed two others from his own party and two from the opposition. If he turned thumbs down on a proposal, it was dead. But in 1910 the outraged Midwestern insurgents upset the whole system. They joined with delighted Democrats to decree that in future the Rules Committee should be elected by the whole House. The Speaker has continued to be highly influential, but not the autocrat that he was at the end of the nineteenth century; his power now comes from seniority, from his effect on patronage, from, occasionally, respect.

These formal enactments both reflected and exacerbated the convulsions in the American party system. Wilson's election as president in 1912 and his re-election in 1916 should not be seen as an index of the growing strength of the Democrats. On the contrary, they had lost ground. To a noticeable degree, the Socialists gained where the Democrats lost. Over the years only two avowedly Socialist members of Congress were elected: one a German from Milwaukee, the other a Jew from the lower east side of New York City. But no sweeping interpretation should be based on these scraps of evidence. Much of the Socialist support came from the prairies and the plains: the most popular Party periodicals were published in Kansas and Missouri, while the highest percentage of a state vote that the Socialists ever captured occurred in Oklahoma. These radical encroachments served to shake up the other parties. Already in 1897 Judge Holmes, then on the Supreme Judicial Court of Massachusetts, was writing: "When socialism first began to be talked about, the comfortable classes of the community were a good deal frightened." By 1905 President Roosevelt was alarmed; he thought the growth of socialist beliefs and votes were "far more ominous that any populist or similar movements in the past." These ejaculations were not a formula to either

Democrats or Republicans telling them what adjustments they should make to hold the electorate. A goodly amount of political skirmishing—which had little effect on the economy—can merely be summarized. Roosevelt had a falling out with Taft, partly because of ideology, but mainly because he felt personally affronted. When Taft dismissed Gifford Pinchot from the federal conservation program, Roosevelt felt that his ideas as well as his appointee were being abused.

Meanwhile, the difficulties of trying to expand American business interests in the Far East caused further friction between Roosevelt and Taft on the diplomatic scene. Attempts to draw American capital into land ventures in Asia had been building up over a number of years, and during his presidency, Roosevelt had himself especially tried to promote railroad building. When J. P. Morgan was considering pulling out of a syndicate that had been formed for this purpose, Roosevelt wrote to him: "I cannot expect you or any of our big business men to go into what they think will be to their disadvantage." However, he went on, if the reason for Morgan's projected withdrawal was his fear that the government of the United States might not support him, he should be assured that the administration will "do all that in its power lies to see that you suffer no wrong whatsoever from the Chinese or any other power in this matter." Speaking personally, "My interest of course is simply the interest of seeing American commercial interests prosper in the Orient." Taft worked from this latter assumption too, and tried to use government pressures to further the cause of American private capital in China. Obstructed by a secret agreement between Japan and Russia, the United States failed in Manchuria. By the time in 1910 that American defeat was apparent to most sensible people, Roosevelt was telling Taft that the drive had been doomed from the start. The United States could not have much economic strength in the Far East unless it had military power there. But American voters would never consent to stationing large-scale land forces in Asia. The Open Door, he warned, was empty words if a military power such as Japan chose to ignore it.*

Even after it became obvious that prominent financiers had lost interest, the president and his highest advisers persisted. A shift of stance came with Taft's successor, Wilson. As early as 1902 when he was president of Princeton, Wilson had stated that the United States should "command the economic fortunes of the world." Five years later he said: "Concessions obtained by financiers must be safeguarded by ministers of state, even if the sovereignty of unwilling nations be outraged in the process. Colonies must be obtained or planted, in order that no useful corner of the world may be overlooked or left unused." His subsequent demand at the conference at Versailles for "self-

---

*As late as 1945, no responsible person that I knew in Military Intelligence in Washington would have challenged this postulate: This nation must not commit large armies on the land mass of Asia. The disasters that have followed from the abandonment of this policy, first in Korea and later in Viet Nam, are obvious to anybody who can see. But then, some can't: *Miro, miro, y no ve.*

determination of nations" should be interpreted in the shadow of this attitude. When he entered the White House in 1913, he was expecting "many sharp struggles for foreign trade." He declared then that nothing concerned him more "than the fullest development of the trade of this country and its righteous conquest of foreign markets." Some commentators have written that President Wilson repudiated dollar diplomacy, that his foreign policies were not swayed by the requests of gluttonous lobbyists. The evidence against this view is stubborn. When nationals of the major powers joined together in 1913 to propose the Six Power Loan to China, Wilson refused to accede to a request that he as president should ask American bankers to join the group. But Secretary of State Bryan was forthright about the reasons for the refusal: the Americans would "not have a controlling voice" in the syndicate. The same worthy made a revealing remark on the first day of the National Council of Foreign Trade in Washington in May, 1914, just before World War I began in Europe. The president, he said, had stressed the intention of his administration to "open the doors of all the weaker countries to an invasion of American capital and enterprise." He said too: "My Department is your department; the ambassadors, the ministers, and the consuls are all yours. It is their business to look after your interests and to guard your rights."

These declarations of federal policy make no sense unless they are seen in the context of domestic problems. Let us attempt a quick summation of the dilemma at home. Chiefly because of a hopelessly lopsided distribution of personal incomes, purchasing power was not adequate to buy the goods and services that the economy could produce.* A large part of the maldistribution of income could be attributed, in turn, to the agglutinated formation in the preceding fifty years of a small number of near-monopolies that could usually dictate their own terms at the bargaining table. In the presidential campaign of 1912, the four prominent candidates stood for four different approaches to this situation. President Taft initiated several prosecutions against unpopular trusts, but his total career suggests that he had no desire to alter the fundamental contours of American society. Roosevelt, running for the Progressive Party, repeatedly declared that giant business was here to stay, that the sole course for the federal government to provide justice to the common man was to regulate Standard Oil and similar firms; however, during his nearly eight years in the White House he did not accomplish, or even attempt, significant regulation. Wilson too was emphatic: he wanted to bust them up, to dissolve them into smaller units that would truly compete with each other. Debs, in urging that the only solution was confiscation and public operation,

---

*At the end of World War II, some economists were quite agitated over the relative merits of "underconsumption" and "overproduction" theories of the Great Depression. The dispute seems pointless. What seems central to me is two propositions: An indispensable element in causing the economic collapse was the faulty distribution of incomes. The major cure for the collapse was to give purchasing power to people who would spend it.

was caustic: "Competition was natural enough at one time, but do you think you are competing today? Many of you think you are competing. Against whom? Against Rockefeller? About as I would if I had a wheelbarrow and competed with the Santa Fe from here to Kansas City."

Faced with these alternatives, a plurality (not an impressive one) chose Wilson. Now he had not to talk but to act. He didn't; he went on talking. Much space has been wasted in pseudo-learned tomes on the Federal Trade Commission Act and the Clayton Act, both passed late in 1914. A retrospective view can be cruelly unfair, but now it seems clear that these two laws have changed little in the ways that businessmen behave. The former claimed that it would outlaw "unfair trade practices." A clause in the latter announced that the capacities of employees should not be "an article of commerce." What happened? Although historically the courts have played the leading role in emasculating the Federal Trade Commission, it should be recorded that Wilson started the process by packing it with wealthy conservatives. Perhaps it was never meant to do much; at any rate it never has. The Clayton Act has meant less. When it was acclaimed at its passage as "the Magna Carta of labor" by the president of the American Federation of Labor, he was being an ass, as he frequently was. Promptly upon enactment of this folderol, President Wilson announced that his campaign platform had now been duly passed because the administration had effected the reorganization of the economy.

To be fair to Wilson, two earlier laws must be considered. They did have conseqences. The Underwood-Simmons Tariff Act of 1913 was the first significant reduction in import duties since 1857. Two possible benefits may be suggested here, and they both stem from the same postulate: A sound mechanism for keeping the peace is to treat people more equitably. The new import duties were more kindly to rural areas in the United States at a time when that was probably desirable. And they were more conducive to fair exchanges in international trade at a time when that was probably desirable. The other law, the Federal Reserve Act, is still the law of the land (although, as will be seen in Document 26-1, its operations have been considerably changed). Propellants toward this innovation were many. Defects in the National Banking Act have been, if not scrutinized, at least noted, as have institutional changes in the economy. But when the bias of American politicians was for "whoa" rather than for motion, a new statute could be carried only by urgent needs. The financial panic of 1907 and the unending depression that followed it provided considerable acceleration. Simultaneously, the bankers of New York City seemed to be losing ground to competitors in outlying parts of the country. So the lobbyists came to Washington.

Except for temporary perversions in a few states, Americans have always believed that banks—even the central bank—should be privately owned and privately run (although today several other federal agencies swing considerable weight at the Reserve). (On the basic functions of central

FOR PRESIDENT

M.Baci
1920

EUGENE V. DEBS

FIGURE 22-2. *Campaign Poster for Eugene V. Debs*

The following judgment is sure to be challenged by most American historians, but I will make the assertion nonetheless: Eugene Debs was the most significant politician in the United States in this century. Obviously my statement also requires some definition of a "significant politician": (1) He banking, see Document 26-1.) Thus when the Federal Reserve System was founded in 1913, its charter provided that it should be owned and managed by the private banks that belonged to it, called the "member banks." Twelve Federal Reserve Banks were established, and their location shows vividly where the financial centers of the nation were situated at the time, as shown in Figure 22-3. A map of this kind, if read with an awareness of other developments, can be worth volumes. Note for instance that San Francisco was regarded as the linchpin of a huge area that runs from the eastern border of Utah to the coast; Los Angeles didn't count for shucks. Most of the vast area presided over by Dallas had few people, but production of crude oil had already become vital to the national economy. The Southeast, notoriously outside the national economy at the time, got two Federal Reserve Banks because of its place in the international setting. Why did little old Pennsylvania and New York each get a Bank of its own? Any decent explanation of the sites for these Banks must be tortuous. The reasons of course involved business, but they also involved politics. For instance, five Banks were placed west of the Mississippi, which was quite disproportionate to population and to economic significance, but each state west of the Mississippi had two Senators.

So the trans-Mississippi sections and the Southeast got their Federal Reserve Banks, and they were better off in regard to credit facilities than they had been under the National Banking Act, but they still did not get equitable treatment from the monetary system. When the number of banks failing outright or suspending gold payments rose steeply after 1920, most of these in default were in rural areas of the South and Midwest, not in the East. The

---

must have a clear impact on ordinary voters' expectations from the government. (2) He must help to alter the fundamental structure of the political system.

Debs was born in 1855 in Terre Haute, Indiana, and regarded that town as his home all his life. But he did not really live there. After the American Railway Union was crushed during the Pullman strike (see Chapter 20), he made his living as a travelling lecturer for various radical periodicals almost until he died in 1926. His speeches do not now read well. To modern ears his rhetoric often seems purple, and he seems to repeat the same old exhortations. But his contemporaries did not find him trivial or irrelevant. There is no intention here to load the argument by stating that he was five times the Socialist candidate for President or by pointing out that in 1912 he received one vote for every four received by a Republican incumbent; after all, Bryan was nominated three times and got more votes than Debs ever did. What is vital is that Bryan did not force his opponents into altering their sales pitches, while Debs did.

In one sense this campaign poster is phony: in 1920 Debs was not wearing a bow tie because he was in the Federal prison at Atlanta, Georgia, having been convicted for anti-war agitation under the Sedition Act of 1918. Perhaps the flavor of his thought and the impression he made on others will be conveyed by two brief quotations, both from his internment at Atlanta. To one reporter, Debs commented on the Russian Revolution: "All along the track of the ages, wherever a government has been overthrown by force and violence, that government had been maintained by force and violence." After a visit to Debs, Lincoln Steffens wrote to his sister: "He's a Man—"

FIGURE 22-3. *Location of the Federal Reserve Banks, 1913*

causes for the concentration of these banking calamities in certain districts cannot be blamed entirely on the new monetary arrangements, but they surely played a big part. The mechanics of the Federal Reserve System need not be dissected in detail. (But see Document 26-1.) The Act created three different categories of member banks depending on size, and stipulated a certain ratio of "reserves" to assets for each. Later amendments altered the arithmetic ratio, but it was the definition of "reserves" that caused endless trouble. For the law allowed cities in smaller places to count as a portion of their reserves the deposits that they carried in banks in larger cities. The latter banks could then count the same money as part of their reserves. As will be seen below, many agricultural regions were in chronic financial difficulties after 1919. When farmers were unable to meet their notes on time, their banks would draw home their deposits from New York or Boston. This unwise set of regulations governing "reserves" thus spread instability through the whole monetary mechanism of the country. The disruption was serious from 1920 forward; it would become disastrous after 1929 (Chapter 26).

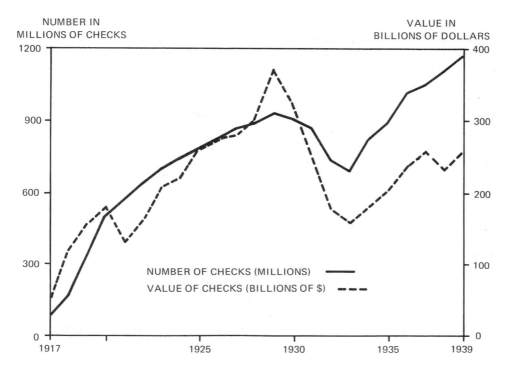

NUMBER IN
MILLIONS OF CHECKS

VALUE IN
BILLIONS OF DOLLARS

NUMBER OF CHECKS (MILLIONS) ——
VALUE OF CHECKS (BILLIONS OF $) ‑ ‑ ‑

FIGURE 22-4. *The Federal Reserve System and the American Economy*

This graph should make immediately visible a few major changes in the condition of the United States from 1917 to 1939. It shows the great increase in the volume of commercial bank deposits and the concomitant use of checks as money; in modern America about 90 per cent of all purchases are being made with checks.

But breaks in the trend should be noted, some chronological, others regional. The chart shows a temporal interruption, in sharp declines from 1929. After 1935 the number of checks being cleared was greater than ever before, while their accumulated value was greatly depressed; more checks were being written for smaller sums. At the depths of the depression, Americans in several areas devised again, as in colonial times, devices for doing business without money—or checks, because they did not have bank accounts. They resorted to "due bills," which might today be called I.O.U.'s. A friend who was then a young man in Montana reports that these pledges of faith would sometimes be endorsed a dozen times from one holder to another, although they did not have as security even a commerical deposit in a bank.

If the diplomacy of the Wilson administration was shaped by what it took to be the material interests of the nation (not just of business but of farmers and wage earners, so too was it shaped by the "missionary impulses" of its sponsors, particularly the president. Wilson's ambitions to mold the entire globe in his own image knew no limits of either space or time; he wanted to enact his own conceptions of morality into a universal code of behavior. The implications of this attitude for foreign policy glared forth in his actions toward Mexico, which had been ruled for decades by a corrupt tyrant. But the dictator had been ousted by a liberal in 1911, who in turn was murdered by his chief general two years later. At this point Wilson broke an American tradition that stretched back to the founding fathers. The United States had always recognized as the *de jure* government of a foreign land any faction, however unsavory, that held *de facto* control of the territory. Not Wilson: he was too high-minded. Denouncing the ruling group in Mexico as "a government of butchers," he withheld recognition. Next he started plots that were founded in fantasies. Another revolution took place. The president of the United States did not approve of the new leader in Mexico, so he schemed to replace him by an unscrupulous general. It turned out that the general, unable to defeat the constitutional forces of the incumbent president unless he got tangible American support, began making raids across the Rio Grande to provoke American intervention in Mexico. He got his wish. Earlier, in April 1914, Wilson had sent American naval forces to occupy Vera Cruz to retaliate for the arrest there of American sailors. Now he sent more than 6,000 soldiers into Mexico as a punitive expedition. When an armed clash came with Mexican troops, Wilson drew up a message to Congress. Fortunately, before he delivered it to capitol hill he learned that he had his facts wrong.

However, the president did haul Great Britain, a very reluctant Britain, into supporting his opposition to the Mexican dictator of 1913–1914. Wilson assured the English that he would "teach the South American republics to elect good men." The lesson did not stick.

But Great Britain could not afford to let the Americans down in the Western Hemisphere, because she desperately needed the United States as a counterweight to Germany. World War I began in a few frantic days at the beginning of August, 1914. A jab by one government brought an immediate parry by another, and the fracas was on. It was not a flurry of fists or even the popping of rifles or thrusts of boyonets; it was the drifting of poison gas and the boom of artillery launching thousand-pound shells and the spreading of the miasma of hate. Contemporaries could vaguely predict how horrible their future would be. On the day that Great Britain declared war, the Foreign Minister, Sir Edward Grey, stood in his office in the evening looking out the window. He was addicted to a stable, gentle world. Lover of wild birds and of fishing, he revered the civilized amenities of a country gentleman. His reaction to these dread circumstances was a lament: "The lamps are going out all over Europe; we shall not see them lit again in our lifetime."

What course should the United States follow in such troubled seas? Events refined this general problem into more specific ones. The administration's early response to the European declarations of war showed a level-headed attitude. A significant statement to the press came from Secretary Bryan on 15 August. France had approached Morgan's banking house to ask it to float a war loan in the United States. The firm wanted to know if American authorities would approve the venture. Bryan, having first expounded his arguments to Wilson (Document 22-1) stated: ". . . in the judgment of this Government loans by American bankers to any foreign nation which is at war is inconsistent with the true spirit of neutrality." The president in addressing the Senate on 19 August sketched the reasons for avoiding partiality: "The people of the United States are drawn from many nations, and chiefly from the nations now at war. It is natural and inevitable that there should be the utmost variety of sympathy and desire among them with regard to the issues and circumstances of the conflict. Some will wish one nation, others another, to succeed in the momentous struggle. It will be easy to excite passion and difficult to allay it. . . . The United States must be neutral in fact as well as in name during these days that are to try men's souls. . . ."

Had the administration held to these precepts, the United States might never have become a combatant at all. The reasons for its failure to do so should be inspected. Some historians have argued that the president did not realize the policies that were being advanced because, at the very time the war was starting in Europe, his wife was dying in Washington. If tenable, this argument seems tangential. His speech to the Senate quoted above is not incoherent. Besides, presidents are paid not to be distracted: lesser men do their jobs while they are being sued for divorce, their children are entering mental hospitals, the boss is threatening to fire them. Three other forces that prompted Wilson to alter his policies quickly seem to deserve more extended examination: (1) the condition of the American economy, (2) his own Anglophilism which was shared (or exceeded) by many of his close advisers, (3) extreme legalism, which had been a dominant characteristic in the English colonies from the beginning. (See mid-Chapter 1.)

An obvious extension of Bryan's announced discouragement of war loans would be to place a complete or partial embargo on foreign trade, to ban shipments either to the entire world or just to Europe. But such a move might be disastrous in domestic politics. Wilon had come to the White House as a minority president, and his prospects did not look bright. Worse, the economy had been bobbing down but never far up since 1907; the recession deepened at the turn of 1913–1914.* Most efforts that have been made to justify Wilson's hostility to an embargo seem fragile—that German submarines menaced American lives as well as property (prohibit persons as well as goods), that

---

*Tidiness would require that this sentence be substantiated by quantitative data. None have been compiled. The reliable statisticians do not make even annual estimates of Gross National Product before World War I. But the qualitative evidence is quite strong.

German submarines were a worse danger than British blockades (an embargo would halt both threats), and so on. The imposition of an embargo was not pursued for cold politico-economic reasons. The president's chief adviser, Colonel Edward M. House, wrote to him on 22 July, 1915: "If it came to the last analysis, and we placed an embargo upon munitions of war and foodstuffs to please the cotton men, our whole industrial and agricultural machinery would cry out against it."

So the stand toward war loans that Bryan had announced was quickly reversed. It is questionable whether the president understood finance sufficiently to recognize that policy was taking an about-face. Events proceeded thus: A vice-president of a New York bank wrote to the counsellor of the State Department saying that if temporary credits were not granted to the Allies, the "buying power of these foreign purchasers will go to Australia, Canada, Argentina, and elsewhere. . . . If we allow these purchases to go elsewhere we will have neglected our foreign trade at the time of our greatest need and greatest opportunity." In sending these arguments forward to Wilson, the bureaucrat found ways to imply that they were original with him. The president's reply was a superlative piece of gibberish, in a conversation on 23 August, 1914:

> There is a decided difference between an issue of government bonds, which are sold in open market to investors, and an arrangement for easy exchange in meeting debts incurred in trade between a government and American merchants. The sale of bonds draws gold from the American people. The purchasers of bonds are loaning their savings to the belligerent government, and are, in fact, financing the war. The acceptance of Treasury notes or other evidences of debt in payment for articles purchased in this country is merely a means of facilitating trade by a system of credits which will avoid the clumsy and inpracticable method of cash payments.

What was that "difference" again?

Within a few months the Morgan firm (the elder J. P. had died; the house was now headed by J. P., Jr.) became the procurement agents in the United States for both British military branches, to receive a commission of 2 per cent on all purchases. Soon after the company got a similar contract from the French government. Under these agreements, it seems that the younger Morgan made greater profits during World War I than his father had made in a lifetime. After the war, a partner in the bank observed: "Our firm had never for one moment been neutral; we didn't know how to be. From the very start we did everything we could to contribute to the cause of the Allies." From the mouth of J. P., Jr., in 1936: "In spite of President Wilson's urging impartiality 'even in thought' we found it quite impossible to be impartial as between right and wrong. . . . We agreed that we should do all that was lawfully in our power to help the Allies win the war as soon as possible."

It must be admitted that the interpretation set forth here would be disputed by many students, and some of them have written volumes whereas this account is only a couple of pages. But the observations of informed contemporaries cannot be blinked off, and although one is entitled to ask whether the contemporaries being cited here were either representative or perceptive, I think they were. A joint Anglo-French loan was floated in the autumn of 1915 for a half billion dollars. James J. Hill had a comment: "One who looks only at the plain facts will see that the grant of this credit for the purpose stated is far less an accommodation to the countries that ask it than an act of necessity for the United States." Letters back to the Foreign Office from the British ambassador in Washington point in the same direction. On 21 November, 1915: "The brutal facts are that this country has been saved by the war and by our war demand from a great economical crisis; that in normal times Great Britain and her colonies take forty per cent of the total export trade of the United States. We have therefore the claims of their best customer and at the present moment our orders here are absolutely essential to their commercial prosperity." Again, on 13 August, 1916, "The reason why there has been no embargo on arms and ammunition is not sympathy with us, but the sense that the prosperity of the country on which the administration depends for its existence would be imperilled by such a measure."

Admittedly, in Wilson's mind the issue of an embargo was garbled with the other two determinants of policy: his pro-English bias, and his legalisms. The Anglophilia of the president and his coteries can be seen from both sides. Its negative aspect was a hostility to traits not English. A popular (derogatory) term among them was "hyphenated Americans"; that is, Italian-Americans, Irish-Americans, and so forth. Our ambassador to England, Walter Hines Page, lashed out, "We Americans have got to . . . hang our Irish agitators and shoot our hyphenates and bring up our children with revererence for English history and in the awe of English literature." President Wilson, indicting the critics of the Versailles Treaty after the war, proclaimed, "Hyphens are the knives that are being stuck into this document." On the positive side, most major actors in American foreign policy nearly all thought that England was beautiful.

While there is always a risk of being tedious by racking up a series of quotations, it still seems proper to attempt to capture the tone in which our diplomats communicated with each other. Right after the European War started, the British ambassador called on Wilson, and then reported to Sir Edward Grey: "The President said in the most solemn way that if that [the German] cause succeeds in the present struggle the United States would have to give up its present ideals and devote all its energies to defence, which would mean the end of its present system of Government. . . . I said, 'You and Grey are fed on the same food and I think you understand.' There were tears in his eyes, and I am sure we can, at the right moment, depend on an understanding heart here." Wilson's pro-British sentiments were not new, nor could they be called clandestine. The parliamentary system, so he had written, might well be superior to "congressional government." He had made it clear that in his opinion immigrants from the British Isles were distinctly superior to the riffraff pouring in from eastern and southern Europe. Part of the tragedy is that he had no confidantes who dissented from these opinions. Probably the most prejudiced of his informants was his ambassador in London. The English navy followed its ancient practice of detaining and seizing American exports. The United States followed its ancient practice of insisting: "Free ships make free goods," and drafted some strong protests to Whitehall. On one occasion when the American ambassador had delivered such a protest to Grey at the Foreign Office, he added: "I have now read the despatch, but I do not agree with it; let us conside how it should be answered!" More heartrending yet was his reaction when the State Department instructed him to present at the Foreign Office a comprehensive list of complaints against British violation of the carrying trade of neutrals. His own protest was not against English outrages but against the American note; he wrote home to the State Department (21 October, 1915) that it contained "not a courteous word, not a friendly phrase, nor a kindly turn in it, not an allusion even to old acquaintance, to say nothing of an old friendship . . . there is nothing in its tone to show that it came from an American to an Englishman." Colonel House, while not so hopelessly lopsided, was far from impartial. While in London in January 1916 he said to the American envoy there, "The United States would like Great Britain to do those things which would enable the United States to help Great Britain win the war." A prelude to the next phase of this analysis seems advisable.

Sir Edward Grey does not enjoy a high standing in the ranks of foreign ministers. But the reasons to deprecate him are obscure: he got what he wanted. In his own retrospective sentences:

> Blockade of Germany was essential to the victory of the Allies, but the ill-will of the United States meant their certain defeat. After Paris had been saved by the Battle of the Marne, the Allies could do no more than hold their own against Germany; sometimes they did not even do that. Germany and Austria were self-supporting in the huge supply of munitions. The Allies soon became dependent for an adequate supply on the United States. . . . The object of diplomacy, therefore, was to secure the maximum of blockade that could be enforced without a rupture with the United States.

Grey's diagnosis was right, and he used it to the advantage of his country. The two themes illustrated above may not have caused the United States to enter the war had it not been for a third consideration: the compulsive legalism of the president and most of his aides. It is questionable that "international law" ever means much in a crisis. But what is worse, in the instance at hand, is that Wilson and his corrupted little courtiers in Washington did not act in a judicious fashion. This conclusion can be approached by looking at their handling of three crucial issues:

1. the British treatment of American commerce on the Atlantic
2. the American treatment of armed British merchant ships
3. Germany's use of submarines

Before starting a slightly more detailed discussion of these three issues, another matter can be disposed of quickly. Germany never protested the American sale of armaments to the Allies, although such sales definitely angered the people of Germany. It was common practice then, and still is, for a neutral to sell contraband to a combatant.

From the beginning of the war, the royal navy was pitiless in its encroachments on neutral rights on the Atlantic. It might halt an American ship, search it, seize goods, sometimes escape into a British port under guard. The State Department made repeated protests. It also made indiscreet concessions, as when Secretary Bryan in December, 1914, admitted that a belligerent could legitimately justify its behavior not only by "rules of international law" but by "self-preservation." Given that argument, a nation can validate anything. But at times the Allied high-handedness went so far as to disturb the tranquillity in Washington, where the worst rankling came in the summer of 1916. The Allies began to open and search U.S. mails on the high seas. As the State Department notified the English and French: "To submit to a lawless practice of this character would open the door to repeated violations of international law by the belligerent powers." Even more provocative to the president was publication by the British of a blacklist of hundreds of American persons and companies who, because they had allegedly been trading with the enemy, were declared off-limits to all Commonwealth subjects. After this, Wilson informed Colonel House: "I am seriously considering asking Congress to authorize me to prohibit loans and restrict exportations to the Allies." Would to Providence he had, but he did not.

The disposition of the administration toward the combatants also appeared in its policy toward armed British merchant vessels. The Allied arming of merchant men was made even more questionable because some of the ships found it advantageous to fly the United States flag in order to sink German U-boats. Here was a field (or a sea) on which international law collapsed. A common earlier belief held that a merchantman could be armed for "defensive" purposes although not for offensive ones. However, the hull of a submarine was so fragile that any weapon could be offensive—including depth charges. Germany held that all precedents were irrelevant. A major problem for Washington was whether these armed Allied merchant vessels should be allowed to enter American ports. They had been classified early in the war by the State Department as peaceful ships. But were they? No doubt can exist that the weaponry was a benefit to Allied merchantmen.

	Total Attacked	Sunk by Torpedo	Sunk by Gunfire	Escaped
Defensively armed	310	62	12	236
Unarmed	302	30	205	67

A single incident will expose a further part of the picture. On 19 August, 1915, the German submarine U-27 had stopped a British freighter and given the crew ample time to debark. Then U-27 began bombarding the English vessel to sink it. Another merchantman approached flying an American flag. Permitted to draw near by an unsuspecting submarine, she sank U-27. Wilson posed the problem clearly: "The matter of armed merchantmen is not so simple. . . . It is hardly fair to ask Submarine commanders to give warning by summons if, when they approach as near as they must for that purpose they are to be fired upon." However, this view was expressed privately; publicly the government did not do anything that restrained Allied abuses. Occasionally an armed vessel was allowed into an American port only on condition that its guns be removed, but, as with the blockade and other infractions of neutral rights, the general problem was never solved.

To my mind, the preceding two issues have been badly neglected by many analysts of the period, who seem to have an *idée fixe* about Germany's submarine warfare. The Kaiser managed to have the worst of two worlds. He was so faltering, due in large part to his fear of alienating the Unted States, that he did not use submarines for a quick knock-out. On the other hand he used them enough that he did alienate the United States. He was first on one foot, then on the other. At the beginning of the war he did not have enough U-boats to do serious damage to his enemies. He built more. Sometimes he authorized their use; the episodes that had the deepest impact on American attitudes are listed in Some Notable Events at the end of this chapter. But for us today, perhaps three generalizations should be proffered. Human beings try to cope with the innovations of the present in terms of old precedents, which often do not apply. Second, as shown in Figure 22-5, by the time the United States entered the war in the spring of 1917, Germany had built its submarine fleet to the point where it could hack out a great toll. Had it not been for American production of Victory ships, the Allied tonnage would have fallen drastically, perhaps fatally. Third, Wilson's personal opinions were crucial. On 20 May, 1915 after the *Lusitania* sinking, he stated: "Each Government should understand that the rights which we claim from it have no connection which we can recognize with what we claim from the other, but that we must insist on our rights from each without regard to what the other does or does not do." A mountainous difficulty was that he was disposed to insist much more strongly to the one side than to the other.

The president sacrificed almost his last inch of side-step when the *Sussex* was sunk in March, 1916. Americans were on board, but not one was killed. Nonetheless, Wilson dispatched an ultimatum saying that if Germany did not abandon its methods of submarine warfare, he would sever diplomatic relations. Germany, for the moment, said it would not sink merchant vessels without warning, but reserved its right to resume unrestricted submarine warfare if the British continued their blockade. When this crisis had been passed, for the moment, the president complained to his secretary of the navy: "I can't keep the country out of war. They talk of me as though I were a god. Any little German lieutenant can put us into the war at any time by some calculated outrage." A chief executive who turns over the foreign policy of his

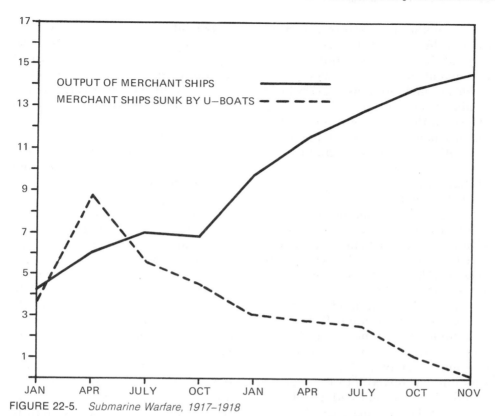

FIGURE 22-5. *Submarine Warfare, 1917–1918*

country to any little lieutenant serving another government has gone too far.

Determined efforts were made in Congress to impede the course of the administration. Consider now only two proposals. Each of them was blocked by the Wilson team using a combination of patronage, disingenuousness, and outright deception. As early as January, 1915, a bill was introduced to ban shipments of munitions from the United States. Insiders, including the president and the British ambassador, thought a stiff fight might be needed to stop its passage since Americans were so upset by violations of neutral commerce. Just at the climax of a struggle in Congress, a U-boat sank Britain's liner *Lusitania*, killing Americans and thus reversing the object of domestic hatred. England had lucked out, due to German ineptitude. By late summer the State Department evolved its final bit of double-think on this question. The new secretary of state (Bryan had resigned in a disagreement with the president during the *Lusitania* crisis) proceeded from the true assertion that the United States had never maintained in peacetime a large military force. He went on with balderdash: "The United States has always depended upon the right and power to purchase arms and ammunition from neutral nations in case of foreign attack. This right, which it claims for itself, it can not deny to others."

543

Another proposal in Congress was more moderate: it can be designated as a mild attempt to keep the federal government out of trouble. The Gore-McLemore Resolution warned against Americans travelling on armed belligerent ships. Unfortunately the measure was windy and clumsy. To defeat it the administration used every technique at hand. Wilson's forces argued that a submarine could not take adequate precautions for the passengers and crew of prizes; therefore they must cease completely to attack merchant vessels. A famous memorandum composed by the State Department at this time conveniently omitted a paragraph from Chief Justice Marshall's decision in the *Nereide* case on the status of the armed merchantman: "She is an open and declared belligerent; claiming all the rights, and subject to all the dangers of the belligerent character."

American relations with Germany remained more or less static for nearly a year; in fact, at times the president seemed to be turning against the Allies. (See early Chapter 24 for Wilson's "peace and social justice" campaign of 1916.) Meanwhile, however, Germany had been expanding her submarine fleet. She decided to try to smash her opponents quickly. On 31 January, 1917, she announced that any vessel, even if unarmed and neutral, that ventured into a forbidden zone around the British Isles and France, would be subject to attack without warning. Wilson had forced his own hand by his previous ultimatum at the time of the *Sussex* episode, and he referred to that sad event when he went before Congress on 3 February to explain his termination of diplomatic relations. His story held two false statements: the *Sussex* did not sink but was towed into Boulogne, and no Americans were killed. Within the month the president had asked for authority to arm United States merchant vessels. When a small group of senators opposed him, Wilson spitefully referred to them as a "little group of willful men, representing no opinion but their own. . . ." He won; the country lost. On that day the issue was decided; with armed American merchant ships venturing into the prohibited zone, an explosive incident was bound to happen. The declaration of war by Congress on 6 April was an anti-climax.

Since no gain could accrue from using these pages to scrutinize the battles and campaigns of American engagements in Europe, the tale can be finished quickly. A few generalizations may be hazarded. First, American entry was essential to Allied victory. Without it the Allies would have gotten nothing better than a draw, and they might well have lost—and we know that German terms of peace were still harsh. Second, a part of the results is recorded in the statistics of fatalities (in millions of men): Germany 1.8, Russia 1.7, France 1.385, Austria-Hungary 1.2, Great Britain .947, United States .106. But these figures hardly begin to show the damage that was done. Distrust became endemic, not only distrust of others but lack of confidence in one's own powers to influence destiny, the revival of an almost seventeenth-century belief that life is preordained. Winston Churchill phrased it thus in 1929:

Events passed very largely outside the scope of conscious choice. Governments and individuals conformed to the rhythm of the tragedy, and swayed and staggered forward in helpless violence, slaughtering and squandering on ever-increasing scales, till injuries were wrought to the structure of human society which a century will not efface, and which may conceivably prove fatal to the present civilization.

But beyond all this was the experience of a new kind of emptiness for the individuals surviving. Boys who were growing up in the years around 1930 can tell you that the damage and the grief did not all go instantly, mercifully, to the grave. They can speak, if only with the intuition of children's hearts, of one-legged men careening about on crutches. They can remember ex-soldiers who were as lethargic as some tuberculars—but with a difference. The *vieux soldat,* as he sat in an arm chair on his lawn, wrapped in blankets even on a warm day, had vague and indifferent eyes. He had been subjected to poison gas. Although he got a small pension, was life on these terms worth much?

Looking first at the European combatants in World War I, we can see that the origins of the conflict were many. They varied from one nation to another. Desire for national glory was a mighty force, as was the desire for colonies that would be subservient economically. A major role was played by improvements in military, particularly naval, technology: substitution of cordite for gunpowder, new methods for securing nitrates, the submarine, heavier artillery, poison gas, to a lesser extent the airplane. But the entry of the United States can be seen in less complex terms. Immediately before and during the early years of the war, the federal government was preoccupied with domestic worries—an economy that continued to be soft, reform of the tariff and of banking laws. When Europe went to war in August 1914, the Wilson administration for a brief time struggled to keep the country neutral. But as Americans became increasingly aware that the prosperity of their economy was dependent on war orders from the Allies, their neutrality steadily melted away. This trend could draw on two persistent pools of energy. Numerous Americans with power in their hands felt that they were partners in the British heritage; they and the English had shared a cultural communion, breaking the same loaf and drinking the same wine. Second, from the time of the first English planters in the New World, Americans had been demented by legalisms. So the United States furnished aid that was indispensable to Allied victory. As we contemplate the ghastly price paid for triumph, it seems that the game was not worth the candle.

SOME NOTABLE EVENTS

1908 Germany lays down four all-big-gun battleships. When Britain responds by starting eight *Dreadnoghts* in 1909, the naval war is on.
Root-Takahira Agreement, 30 Nov.

1909 Payne-Aldrich Tariff.

1910 Germany learns how to fix free nitrogen from the air.

1911 Canadian Parliament refuses to ratify a reciprocity agreement with U.S. about import duties.
Standard Oil and *American Tobacco* decisions by Supreme Court.

1912 Roosevelt gives his "New Nationalism" speech, 21 Feb.
Titanic wrecked on maiden voyage and sinks; 1517 lost, 14–15 April.
Progressive Party issues its platform, 5 Aug.
The Balkan War begins, Oct.

1913 Taft vetoes literacy test for immigrants, 14 Feb.
Wilson is first president since John Adams to make personal appearance before Congress; he asks for tariff reduction.
Underwood-Simmons Tariff also contains income-tax clause.
Pujo Committee issues report on money and banking.
Federal Trade Commission Act, 10 Sept.
Clayton Act.
Federal Reserve Act, 23 Dec.

1914 Wilson orders Marines to occupy Vera Cruz, Mexico.
Austrian archduke is assassinated in Serbia.
World War I begins, 30 July–4 Aug.
Wilson appeals for American neutrality, 19 Aug.

1915 U.S. approves "commercial credits" to Allies, March.
Submarine sinks the *Falaba*; one American drowned, 28 March.
Another U-boat sinks *Lusitania*, 128 Americans killed, 7 May.
U-boat sinks *Arabic*, 19 Aug.
British vessel flying American flag sinks U-27, 19 Aug.
Lansing's *modus vivendi*, Dec.

1916 Jones bill promises independence to Philippines in five years, 4 Feb.
Gore-McLemore Resolution, March.
U-boat sinks the *Sussex*, 24 March; Wilson's ultimatum to Germany.
Rural credits law, 17 July.
Keating-Owen child labor act, 8 Aug.
Federal workmen's compensation law, 19 Aug.
Adamson Act decrees eight-hour day on railroads, 3 Sept.

1917 Wilson's "peace without victory" speech, 22 Jan.
Wilson appeals to Congress for a declaration of war, 2 April.
Congress declares war, 6 April.

1918 Wilson presents Fourteen Points to Congress, 8 Jan.
By May, U.S. has a half million soldiers in France.
Espionage Act, 16 May.
Wilson announces Four Points in speech at Mount Vernon, 4 July.
By November, U.S. had nearly 5 million men under arms, of whom 1,390,000 saw combat service (for fatalities, see Figure 30-1).
Democrats lose both houses of Congress, 5 Nov.
Armistice ends hostilities, 11 Nov.

1919 Versailles Treaty between Allies and Germany, which signs on June 28.
Wilson has a stroke, 2 Oct.

1919–
1920 Versailles Treaty fails of ratification by the Senate.

Ways to Study History XXII

Ransack the archives. Often a scholar is too hasty in concluding that because he holds in his hands a primary source, therefore he has evidence appropriate to his purposes. Repeatedly, in working in the papers of William Jennings Bryan when he was secretary of state, I would find a draft of a memorandum to the president. Fortunately the Wilson Papers were in the same repository, the Library of Congress, and they contained the message that the president had received from Bryan. When the draft was compared to the actual message, the two sometimes diverged widely. The former shows the way that Bryan's mind worked; the latter shows a part of the information, true or false, on which Wilson based a particular decision.

W. Stull Holt has succinctly indicated an additional difficulty that might arise in dealing with documents from either governmental or business files. Both types of institution have developed cryptography to a high state. In the process of either encoding or decoding, a meaning may be altered. As anybody who has dealt with Western Union will know, a message can also be scrambled while it is on the wires.

Holt's article is entitled: "What Wilson Sent and What House Received: Or Scholars Need to Check Carefully," *American Historical Review* (1959–1960). On 29 October, 1918, Colonel Edward M. House was in London as the president's personal envoy. The war was nearing an end. A text written on Wilson's typewriter states: ". . . too much success or security on the part of the Allies will make a genuine peace settlement exceedingly difficult, if not impossible." The cable received by House from the president reads: ". . . too much severity on the part of the Allies will make a genuine peace settlement exceedingly difficult if not impossible." Not only are the nuances shifted, but the two versions look in different directions. Which one is relevant depends on what question the historian is asking.

Document 22-1

The only phase of his career when William Jennings Bryan showed signs of distinction came while he was secretary of state. The reasoning behind his opposition to any loans to belligerents can hardly be faulted. In this memorandum to the president, dated 10 August, 1914, he explained it (see above Chapter 22 on American response to outbreak of war).

First: Money is the worst of all contrabands because it commands everything else. The question of making loans contraband by international agreement has been discussed, but no action has been taken. I know of nothing that would do more to prevent war than an international agreement that neutral nations would not grant loans to belligerents. While such an agreement would be of great advantage, could we not by our example hasten the reaching of such an agreement? We are the one great nation which is not involved and our refusal to loan to any belligerent would naturally tend to hasten a conclusion of the war. We are responsible for the use of our influence through example and as we cannot tell what we can do until we try, the only way of testing our influence is to set the example and test its effect. This is the fundamental reason in support of the suggestion submitted.

Second: There is a special and local reason, it seems to me, why this course would be advisable. . . . If we approved of a loan to France we could not, of course, object to a loan to Great Britain, Germany, Russia, Austria or to any other country, and if loans were made to these countries our citizens would be divided into groups, each group loaning money to the country which it favors and this money could not be furnished without expressions of sympathy. These expressions of sympathy are disturbing enough when they do not rest upon pecuniary interests—they would be still more disturbing if each group was pecuniarily interested in the success of the nation to whom its members had loaned money. . . .

Electricity, Autos, and Chemicals

In much writing about the United States from the day of the Armistice until the Black Tuesday in October, 1929, when the stock market entered upon its long descent—in those unfortunate depictions, the decade was The Golden Twenties, an age of "Fords, flappers, and fanatics." By these accounts, the rich young Americans went to Paris to have fun, and rich old Americans went to their broker in Pasadena to study the word from Wall Street on the ticker. Both of these groups existed, but the average American had no experience of either way of life. Men of my father's generation, whether executives or factory hands, did not even take a week's vacation in the summer. The typical standard of living was rising, but in 1929 it was still far below what most of us have known in our lifetimes. Obviously gross differentials exist in the United States today; they existed also fifty years ago. Thus one task in this chapter is to identify the segments of American society who were eating chicken and those who gnawed the bones.

Breaking down the whole into its parts is much easier for the years after World War I than for any earlier period because we have more accurate measurements. Having said so much, we must admit that formidable difficulties remain. The best to be hoped for is fairly reliable estimates. Informed guesses for Gross National Product (GNP) on an annual basis (not to mention monthly) can be made for the period since 1919. However, zealous and honorable economists will doubtless continue to argue about many questions pertaining to our past. One question is familiar to all: How much did the cost of living change? This query, fundamental as it is to many collective-bargaining contracts and social-welfare schemes, subsumes a host of lesser questions. Thus it cannot be answered with precision and will always be subject to some dispute. However, to shift focus again, we must insist that some estimates are better than others. The effort here is to offer the best we have.

Let us sample the juice we can squeeze from the pulp available. Adjusting all figures to the 1929 level of prices, Gross National Product climbed from $74.2 billion in 1919 to $104.4 in 1929. Further adjusting for the growth in population, GNP per capita went from $710 to $857 over the same span. So in the latter regard the rate of development is not exactly booming—say, a bit less than 2 per cent a year. What is startling is the stability of the price level. Estimates vary, but existing indices peg wholesale prices at the end of the decade with only a difference of 1 or 2 points from where they had been at its beginning, with minor fluctuations in the interim. Probably this outcome resulted from identifiable forces. Over-all growth tended to push prices upward, but two major groups of influences worked as offsets. More details on each will be offered below, but generalizations might be given now. Three clusters of industries must be regarded as sick: farming, (particularly of such staples as cotton and wheat), coal mining, and textile manufacturing. None of these industries was dying in a nationwide sense. Man must have food, but the traditional base of American agriculture was withering. Man must have heat, but coal was being displaced by hydroelectric power, natural gas, fuel oil. He must have clothing, but New England mills were overpowered by Southern producers and by foreign suppliers. Prices were also thrust downward by gigantic increases in output per man-hour in several boom industries, of which the three most important form the title of this chapter. Failing of an imaginative and constructive solution to these downward pressures on prices—hence on profits—Americans turned to the same old solution. They looked for markets abroad. But they wanted to keep the home markets for themselves, so they tried to block out imports. Therefore foreigners had no U.S. dollars to buy American goods. The wily Yankee had a solution to that conundrum. He loaned to foreigners the U.S. funds with which to buy American products. A fine way indeed to manage an economy.

Repeatedly in this chapter it will be necessary to look back at developments on the home front during the war. For instance, in spite of the absence

- ☐ CRUDE MATERIALS
- ▨ CRUDE FOOD
- ▥ MANUFACTURED FOOD
- ▨ SEMI-MANUFACTURES
- ▧ FINISHED MANUFACTURES

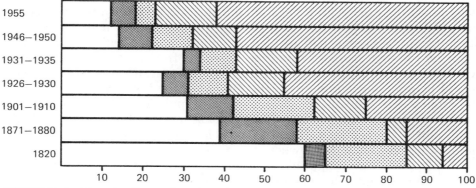

FIGURE 23-1 *Changing Exports from the U.S., 1820-1955*

in the armed forces of about 5 million men in 1917–1918, GNP increased about 15 per cent. Here an index of physical output becomes helpful. For agriculture it barely changed, but for mining and manufacturing the increase came close to 40 per cent, and for transportation it slightly exceeded that mark. Due to the stable production from farms while demand for their output soared, prices paid to them had risen rapidly during the war. But for the husbandman the depression started in 1919, not a decade later. The total value of farm products was $21.4 billion in 1919, down to $11.8 billion by the time of the financial panic. This decline did not result in any shortage of foodstuffs or textile fibers for the American or foreign consumer; on the contrary, surpluses were increased. When a farmer gets less per unit for his crop, his instinct is to produce more units. The decline was in prices:

	Cotton, lb.	Corn, bushel	Wheat, bushel
1919	35.3¢	$1.51	$2.16
1929	16.7¢	.79	1.03
1932	6.5¢	.31	.38

These figures cast immediate doubt on some scholarly interpretations. One author has asked what happened after World War I to LaFollette's Progressive movement in its attempt to sell its reform program in the rural heartland (mid-Chapter 24). His answer is: Nothing. This should not surprise anybody who glances at the above table. When a South Carolina redneck sees the price of cotton fall by half, when a corn-and-hog farmer in Illinois sees the price of corn fall by half,* he gets discouraged about optimistic reform programs.

An individual farmer could do nothing to bolster the sagging prices. The fundamental dilemma of the producers of staples was that they had to sell on a world market, so that the price at which they could export their surplus also determined the price within the United States. Reductions in freight charges, not only by railroads within each country but by improvements in merchant shipping on the oceans, had enabled previously isolated regions to hurl their crops into foreign markets—from the American frontier, from Russia, India, Australia, Argentina, Canada, Mexico. Over the next fifty years three factors would help to alleviate the problem. One was brutal but effective: eliminate the farmer (see mid-Chapter 26 on New Deal policies). The trend has been strong and accelerating to reduce employment in agriculture, particularly the small units—sharecroppers, hired hands. This has made it easier for the large holders and corporate landowners to combine and win political favors; the Farm Bloc in Congress appeared as a cohesive unit after World War I. As will be seen (mid-Chapter 26), one of its chief efforts was to free prices within the United States from their dependence on world prices. Third, mechanization has virtually supplanted manpower in turning out produce from the land (Figure 29-3).**

Before we analyze the problems of the mines, let us pause for a short story about a miner who found some options to exploitation—an English immigrant of extraordinary ingenuity. In the first two decades of the century he worked in Bitumen, Pennsylvania (lovely name that: "coal tar")—one mine, one store. The employee, with five children, could never get out of debt at the store. For fourteen years of steady labor he drew no cash whatever. Each month he got a "statement" showing the residue of his debt. He kept every statement. At length, knowing of a treaty in force between his native country and the United States requiring that any immigrant from the one nation to the other had to be paid in "coin of the realm," he contacted the British embassy in Washington. The upshot was that the coal company was forced to pay the

---

*As a sidelight, consider the   11-to-1 ratio. A good farmer would sell pork on the hoof when a hundredweight brought 11 times as much as he could get for a bushel of corn; when values altered beyond that crucial point, he sold corn.

**The possibilities of modern technology can carry this process to extremes that boggle the mind. It can even cancel out weather, for those willing to invest in one firm's product—a portable trailer about 20′ × 6′ × 6′ which contains horizontal trays at 1′ intervals. On Monday you plant oats in the bottom tray; on Tuesday in the next up, and so on. By Sunday you can harvest the bottom tray. This vehicle can grow enough fodder for about three dozen cows.

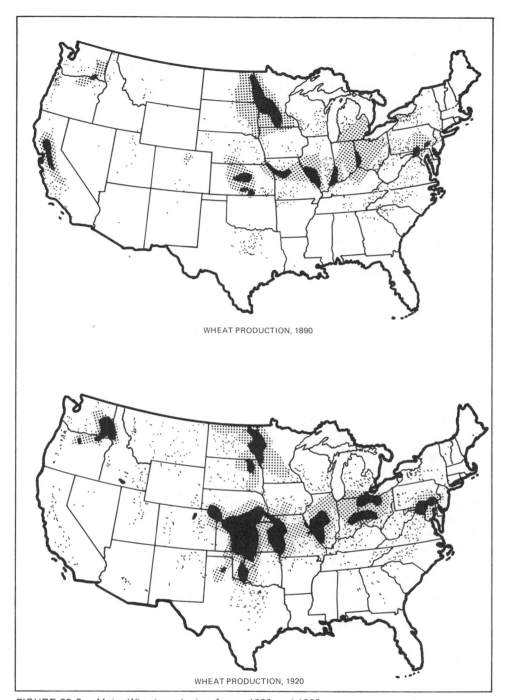

WHEAT PRODUCTION, 1890

WHEAT PRODUCTION, 1920

FIGURE 23-2. *Major Wheat-producing Areas, 1890 and 1920*

553

miner his fourteen years in back earnings. To retaliate, the company store brought suit against him to pay his overdue bills. He had gone home to England. Moral: The working class could find a multiplicity of ways to hit back at their employers.

The problem of the coal mining industry can be stated quickly; the production of all mineral fuels declined some 30 per cent from 1920 to 1929, due in considerable measure to improvements in the efficiency of industrial processes that had used coal by the thousands of carloads.

Before the decline and prior to World War I coal miners as a group had two shields against exploitation. One was their combination into a union which had influence in many but not all coal fields; at the end of this chapter we will see how it was almost destroyed by 1933. The other form of self-protection was personal mobility. One study for a portion of the industry—anthracite—concludes with a model. Of 200 mine workers (aged 20 years) in 1865, half had died of natural causes by 1902. Another fifteen had died from occupational injuries. Three had become foremen in mines; a few had risen higher in the industry. A handful had become lawyers or politicians or started small businesses. Some had left the region in northeastern Pennsylvania to work in steel or construction or on the railroads. But these types of fluidity were notably reduced after the return of peace in 1918. As coal output slumped, both vertical and horizontal mobility fell with it.

The case of cotton manufacturing was different: The industry migrated. In the basement of Baker Library at the Harvard Business School, any investigator can find large wooden crates holding the office records of defunct textile firms. The bulk of these archives were donated by New England companies some fifty years ago as they went bankrupt; for several segments of the economy the depression began before 1929. To watch the textile industry move southward is to witness a balance of advantages that shifted slowly, then like an avalanche. New England had the benefits of priority. It had established plant, abundant capital, a skilled labor force. Before the Civil War these assets were enhanced because the South had an impervious obstacle to manufacturing: current studies make clear that a plantation was a better investment than a factory. But after the Civil War the balance had begun to tilt. Northern factories were elderly and inefficient. Now it was Northern capital that could find more profitable outlets. Changes in machinery reduced the significance of skilled labor. A Southern industrialist—once beyond the risky and uncertain point where he could get his plant into operation—would have several advantages. He could save transportation costs from being located near his source of raw materials. An almost unlimited supply of cheap labor was available. His worst obstacle would be raising liquid capital in an area that had been eroded by war. So the clamor for "the New South" became a crusade; towns pawned their futures to buy the machines for a new mill. Ironically, the machine-builders of the North sought to save themselves by selling out their customers at home; in payment for their products they accepted stock in

Southern companies. By World War I the migration to the Southern uplands, the Appalachian towns from Virginia to Georgia, was firmly established. Massachusetts cities such as Lowell and Lawrence and Fall River were doomed before 1929. The next year the national president of the Textile Workers could say, "There is, perhaps, more destitution and misery and degradation in the mill towns of New England today . . . than anywhere else in the United States." By this time the North was competing against the South on the worst possible terms. It too could offer cheap labor, and did.

Before this chapter proceeds to the boom industries of the era, it should make clear that not everything was black or white. Two clusters of the economy that were teetering back and forth were steel and railroads. These industries can be made analogous in other ways, both historical and analytical. Each was old in that it was operating in large part with equipment that had been in use for decades. In this respect, each resembled the textile mills of New England; they used ancient equipment because they had stodgy and ignorant executives. Carnegie never made a similar mistake. Bankers had moved into these two fields of finance exactly because they were already established; railroad bonds or stock in U.S. Steel could be sold to the ordinary investor. It was a defect that J. P. Morgan did not know much about the production of steel; the irremediable fault was that he did not place the direction of the company into the hands of men who did understand how to plan future operations, how to coordinate activities, how to check on results. A clear index might be seen in salaries of tycoons in these two industries, which have for a long time been much lower than the earnings of leaders in the boom industries to be examined in a moment. Perhaps it's true that you get what you pay for.

Another similarity with the moribund textile trade was the fact that neither rails nor steel could come to settled terms with its labor force. Two examples from each industry must suffice here. During the war, all railroads had been brought by federal law under the jurisdiction of the United States Railroad Administration, which was to provide an integrated network. After the Armistice, the Brotherhoods countered with a proposal for nationalizing the railroads called the Plumb Plan. It had three basic objectives: (a) the road must give adequate service to users, (b) previous owners of the combined lines should get adequate compensation, (c) charges must not exceed the amount needed to meet the first two aims. This plan was affirmed by members of the Brotherhoods, although many of their leaders opposed it. The A.F.L. also supported it, although president Samuel Gompers did not like it.

To get a clear focus we must look backwards and forwards. In retrospect, we can say that American railroads should have been a unified venture from their beginning in 1830, financed and controlled by the federal government. Apart from a little detachment of promoter-speculators, everyone involved would have benefited from this scheme: investors, workers, maybe even managers. Government-operated national railways were common in Europe. Many American railroads before World War I were sustained by the involuntary donations of bondholders, as arranged through reorganization of capital structures. Since that time they have offered constantly declining services at the continued expense of various levels of government by means of tax levies and public subsidies. In 1919, however, the Plumb Plan did not stand a chance of a fair hearing. National politics would stamp it out in 1920 and 1924, but it was still an influence on the course of those presidential elections. By the latter bout at the polls, the dramatic strike of 1922 had been staged by railroad shopmen. (A "shopman" was anybody not part of the operating crew that rode on the train; he was not unionized; see Chapter 20.) The walkout was provoked by a reduction in wages. The successful effort to stifle the upheaval was greatly aided by a federal judge's injunction, which was almost a duplicate of the one issued against the Pullman boycott. Some railways felt that they had to make concessions, at least on paper. The best-known agreement was the union-management plan on the Baltimore & Ohio, by which the employees agreed to improve efficiency if management would share with them the gains from this. No scholar yet has proven whether management kept its part of the bargain, but every traveller knows whether or not efficiency on the railroads has been improved.

I am not the sort to count lines of space on the front pages of 187 influential newspapers in order to reach a conclusion, and nobody has done the job for me, but it seems likely that the Great Steel Strike of 1919 attracted more attention than any labor conflict since the Pullman boycott. After the Homestead strike of 1892, trade unions had been in tatters in the steel industry. For most occupations, wages during the war had barely kept pace with the cost of living. Steelworkers had a grievance that was not shared by employees in most other industries: they worked twelve hours a day every day—84 hours a week, at a time when the typical work week was 8 hours a day only 6 days a week. Toward the end of the war the A.F.L. began a movement to organize the industry. This attempt was obstructed because fully twenty-five of its member unions claimed jurisdiction over some craft or other in the mills. A decision was made to use a joint organizing committee; after the workers had joined up, they could be parcelled out among the constituent groups. The true director of the organizing committee turned out to be an anarcho-syndicalist from Chicago, who had been preaching industrial unionism for more than a decade. The employers and the press did not really need this excuse for their raucous clamor against the Great Steel Strike as "bolshevist"; they used the same epithet against the Plumb Plan. Beginning on 22 September, 1919, the strike at its peak involved an estimated 376,000 men. They did not have the resources to win. Within four months the walkout was over, and many of its leaders were blacklisted. But the movement was not a complete failure because it rallied opinion, especially in the Protestant churches, against the working conditions in steel mills. Before the decade ended, the companies had felt constrained to institute the eight-hour day.

The Great Steel Strike provides the scenery for a fine short story by Thomas Bell. The union shutdown, which was never strong in the Pittsburgh area, centered in South Chicago and the adjacent Indiana cities that rim Lake Michigan. The narrative centers on a Hungarian immigrant in Gary, Indiana. He speaks only a few words of English, and he neither knows nor cares about trade unions. When other workers shut down the plant, he stays home. One night he wanders down to the picket lines just to see if anything is going on. A riot occurs; a policeman is hit in the head with a club, and he dies. The inoffensive Hungarian is seized, tried, convicted of manslaughter, and spends fifteen years in an Indiana prison. Then another inmate makes a death-bed confession to the pertinent act of violence. Our Hungarian friend is compensated $1,000 for each year he had served unjustly. He takes his "savings," returns to his native district in Hungary, and instantaneously becomes the biggest landowner in the whole region. The title of Bell's story: "The Man Who Made Good in America."

Vast numbers of Americans were having an easier time making good. Four groups of industries can be singled out as the paths to spectacular success after World War I: construction, electric power and its spin-offs, automobiles, industrial chemicals. The next several pages will scrutinize each of these in turn and point out some links among them. Historically, by any of the customary categories the building of homes, warehouses, factories, churches, and other stationary structures had always been the most productive segment of the economy in terms of value of product. This continued to be true. As would happen again after World War II, huge demand for housing had built up during the hostilities that ended in 1918. The portion of national income that is attributable directly to construction doubled between 1919 and 1926, and began to sag slowly from this peak. As will be seen shortly, other boom industries also had topped out before 1929 and started to decline. This construction upsurge was tied to the prosperity of the other new industries that required factories and office buildings and warehouses. It was linked equally to the growth of urban sprawl. To choose four suburbs scattered across the country: growth in population in Queens County (New York) was 100 per cent in the decade; in Grosse Point (Detroit) 700 per cent; in Shaker Heights (Cleveland) 1,000 per cent; in Beverly Hills (Los Angeles) 2,500 per cent.

This outthrust from compacted cities was obviously spurred by growing use of cars. But of the three new conglomerations of growth industries, the first to have a heavy impact was electric power. Again, advance warnings seem timely as we search for terms by which to classify this kind of growth. We may doubt that the word "generator" is appropriate; can it really be applied to any

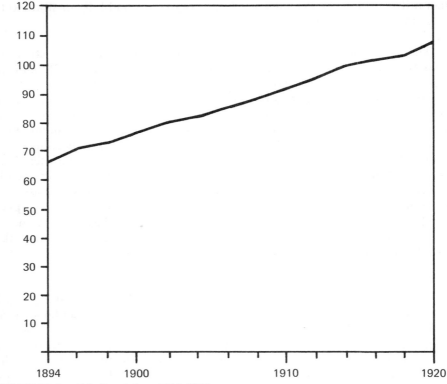

FIGURE 23-3. *U.S. Population, 1894–1920*

source of energy? Second, the phrase "natural resources" can likewise be misleading, since its meaning depends on the ability of human beings at a given time and place to harness and control nature. As understanding of electricity improved, it became possible to transform other types of potential power, especially coal and water, into kinetic current and to transmit it over unprecedented distances. Also the power could be divided into tiny units and sent around to individual motors; the vertical factory with power distributed by means of leather belting could be replaced by the one-story horizontal plant stretching over acres of land. The import of these possibilities for population densities is apparent. Relevant to the same topic is the first giant application of electricity apart from fabrication and lighting—the electric streetcar. From about 1890 to 1910 the construction of trolley lines took the place that had been held by railroads; it spearheaded the expansion of the nation's economy, reaching a peak of $2.5 billion from 1900 to 1909. Without this source of cheap rapid transportation, the spread of cities could not have happened as it did. Another stimulant to the same result was the growth of telephones; the purchase of equipment for expansion of systems doubled from 1900 to 1910, and doubled again in the next decade.

Novel uses spawned markets, so that production of electric energy by central stations rose about twenty times from 1902, the year of our first reliable statistics, to 1929, while many factories were not resorting to central stations at all but had their own generators.* As late as 1907 only 7 per cent of the nation's dwellings had electric current, and that figure soared beyond two thirds by 1930. But long before radio was carrying canned diversions into homes, the motion picture had passed beyond spectator sports as a form of public entertainment. By one reliable account, movies in the decade after 1920 were the fourth largest industry in the nation; attendance at the flicks may have passed attendance at church, and the vice cost about the same as the virtue. Before 1900 Thomas Alva Edison had produced a workable movie camera, and the first commercial show had been exhibited in Manhattan. As early as 1908 at least 8,000 movie houses existed, a number which would nearly double by 1929, and which would begin shrinking rapidly after the advent of television.

Radio was the only electric device to capture the middle-class household before the Great Crash. Refrigerators, washers, dryers, dish washers, toasters, blenders, shavers, hair curlers, knives, stereos—that panoply of appliances that now clutter every proper domicile—were not seen until the depression, and most of them only after World War II. This reflection highlights the rapid expansion of radio. We first have figures for annual sales for 1922. Covering the span from that year to 1929, sales rose 14 times, to reach nearly $1 billion. As a technical innovation broadcasting had been possible as early as 1907. But its exploitation posed several organizational problems: to manufacture sets, build a marketing network, produce programs, establish stations to magnify them in many localities. A serious attack on these obstacles began with the foundation of Radio Corporation of America (1919) which set up the National Broadcasting Co. in 1926. The next year the Columbia Broadcasting System was formed. Understandably the stations were dominated in the early years by reports of real events: the uproarious Democratic national convention of 1924 was heard by multitudes, and the voice of sportscaster Graham McNamee may have been the best-known in the land. But with the networks, patrons were blessed by studio programming featuring Barney Google and Rudy Vallee.

Until 1926, when Henry Ford was persuaded to scrap the Model T for the Model A, his plants achieved wonders of output and profitability. The history of Ford is to a great extent the history of the Model T (as Volkswagen

---

*Each of the developments discussed here was of course crucial to others. We could write a formula: electricity + streets + construction + streetcars + autos + radios = suburbs. Understanding would benefit by juggling the elements in this formula, and several other influences could be inserted.

The Four Stroke Engine

The gasoline engine converts thermal power, created by burning gasoline within the cylinder (thus *internal* combustion engine) to mechanical power, transmitted by the turning crankshaft. To do this requires four distinct operations.

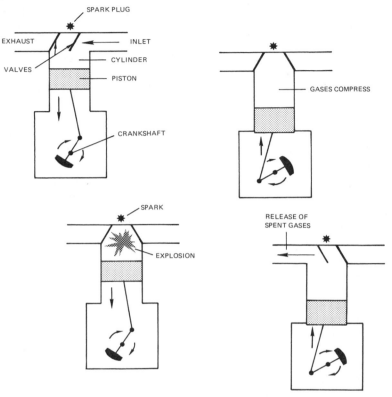

(1) The piston (which must be tightly sealed within the cylinder) is pulled down, drawing a mixture of vaporized gasoline and air through the intake valve into the combustion chamber. The gasoline has been previously changed from a liquid to a vaporous state, thereby mixing it with air, in the carburetor.

(2) The piston is pushed up, compressing the gasoline-and-air mixture to seven or eight times its previous density. It is now almost ready to be exploded by the spark plug.

(3) The intake and outlet valves are closed, the spark plug ignited and the pressure of the exploding gases then forces the piston down, thus turning the crankshaft and providing power as well as momentum for phase four and repeated phases one and two.

(4) The outlet or exhaust valve opens, and the piston rises to expel the spent gases. It is now ready to repeat phase one.

Several other points must be made. First, an inefficient piston (one that does not fit snugly in the cylinder, for example) delivers less power per cycle than a properly operating one. Second, since a piston delivers power during only one of its four strokes, a one-cylinder engine tends to run unevenly: the crankshaft is constantly accelerating and decelerating. This problem is overcome by using several pistons, timed to perform different strokes at any given moment. Third, while gasoline is by far the most common fuel used in the internal combustion engine, almost any substance which will vaporize and ignite at a spark will do—even hair tonic.

for many years was the Beetle). Ford was employed as an engineer at Detroit Edison while he was developing his car. When he started the Ford Motor Company in 1903, he had not yet arrived at his great insight. But three years later he had it, and he persuaded his few associates: he would build an automobile that was sturdy, hence needed few repairs, simple, hence easy to repair, durable, hence depreciation to the buyer would be low, cheap, hence the number of consumers could be broadened, standardized, hence he could, for instance, paint every car black, and unchanging, hence he did not need to re-tool his factories every year. The formula was brilliant. In 1908, when the first Model T was marketed, he sold 10,000. By 1914 the sales reached a quarter of a million; perhaps equally important with his production procedures was Ford's achievement of an efficient set of agencies for merchandising his product. In 1923 the company hit a peak by moving well over two million new vehicles.

The consequences of this expansion should be seen from more than one angle. Original cash investment was $28,500, all from Detroit investors. A lawyer put up $5,000, a coal dealer $2,500. Within a decade both men were millionaires. Or we can look at the situation from the standpoint of employees. In 1914 Ford announced a minimum wage of $5 a day for all production workers. This spectacular change has been derided by many radicals in the last fifty years who have claimed that it brought to the company better workers and that the assembly lines offset the increase in hourly rates by hastening the speed-up (Chapter 26). It was not regarded as a fraud by laborers at the time; they clustered at the Ford employment gates. Most important of all, we must see it in the terms of the typical American. For a portion of the labor force—employees in factories, coal mining, and transportation—these are the number of months that they had to work to earn enough to buy a basic Model T touring car at the factory:

1909	22.2 months
1914	10.8
1919	6.0
1923	3.0

This ratio is about the same now as it was fifty years ago; improvements in the real earnings of workingmen cannot be sought in the realm of automobile prices. The question of whether cars are better now than they were then depends on many dubious elements in the definition of quality. But the impact on society is much easier to elucidate. Railroads and later subways, in their effect on urban growth, were centripetal forces; everybody wanted to live near the station. Trolley lines acted as threads, in that families wanted to live along the line but trolley stops were frequent. The automobile was the true centrifugal influence, hurling suburbs out in many directions. Cars also altered such cultural patterns as courtship practices. Gone forever were the days when

FIGURE 23-4. *Ford Motor Company Assembly Line*   Courtesy of the Ford Motor Company

When the Ford Motor Company started marketing its Model T in 1908, the head of the operation had already determined on the formula that would serve him well for twenty years (see the adjoining pages on Ford's career). Boiled down into theoretical terms, Henry Ford's package depended on the aphorism from Adam Smith that specialization of labor is a function of the size of the market (see the opening of Chapter 3). But Ford's shrewdness reversed the equation: The size of the market depends on the specialization of labor. In retrospect his idea seems simple—Don't bring the man to the job, bring the job to the man. Many revolutionary ideas seem simple after somebody else has had them; compare James Watts' improvements on the steam engine ("How Did It Work?" 2).

It is generally acknowledged that Ford's first assembly line was opened in August, 1913, in his new factory in the Detroit suburb of Highland Park. At that time the assemblage of a Model T chassis took twelve and a half hours of labor. Then the maxim was applied of delivering the work to the worker. In half a year, a chassis was being assembled in one hour and thirty-three minutes. When Ford announced in 1914 that his company would pay a basic wage of $5 a day, he was counting on a reduction of this magnitude in his labor costs. It must be noted that, for every 12 employees who were fabricating automobiles, the company had one man devising tools that would help to make cars cheaper and better.

How did the innovator get the idea for the assembly line? If Ford read Adam Smith, he didn't let on. A common anecdote, of doubtful authenticity, has him watching the carcasses move through a packing plant in Chicago, watching the throats get slashed at one station, the giblets removed at another, the skin peeled off. Packing houses were analysts, breaking their material into components; by contrast, auto assembly factories were synthesizers.

a fellow could only take his girlfriend to the church social or go with her to the kitchen, under her mother's suspicious eyes, to make taffy. The new modes are impossible to quantify, but the qualitative evidence is memorable. A juvenile-court judge in Indiana called the car a "house of prostitution on wheels." Another in Denver told of girls who carried contraceptives around in their compacts.

The third new sheaf of growth industries that began to flare out before 1929 can be cast under the general rubric of industrial chemicals. Again we can indicate the trends by talking about one company, DuPont. As with the big car makers, the interaction of technology with organization must be grasped. Giant corporations in this century have followed one of three strategies for growth. (1) Railroads, steel, and tobacco (processors of metals and of farm products) have shown little or no imagination. They have merely ridden a rising market, selling the same products to a growing number of customers. (2) Some companies have reached out overseas for additional raw materials (oil companies) or customers (auto manufacturers). (3) A few firms diversified into new types of goods made by novel methods to reach new types of customer. Most innovations have come here. The outstanding example has been chemicals. Before outlining the story of how DuPont was coerced by its own problems into instituting a "decentralized" table of organization, it should be observed that almost at the same time three other giants were being forced into similar conclusions: General Motors by its desire for foreign markets, beginning in 1920, Jersey Standard by its quest for foreign supplies, starting 1925, Sears by its decision to establish retail stores, starting 1929.

DuPont had been founded in 1802 to make gunpowder. In 1913 explosives still constituted 97 per cent of its sales. Many other species of chemicals could find markets. Synthetic plastics (in the form of bakelite) had been known since 1869; potash was needed for fertilizers; German dyes were excluded from the American market during World War I, and so on. Technical possibilities did exist. By war's end DuPont had a huge staff: its payrolls went from 5,300 in the autumn of 1914 to more than 85,000 four years later. Obviously the market for its only product was due to fall drastically. It decided to diversify into five other lines—dyestuffs and allied organic chemicals, vegetable oils, paints and varnishes (including lacquers for car bodies), water-soluble chemicals, cellulose-derived synthetics. The immediate result was disaster. For the new products, increased sales meant greater losses. Men who knew only explosives were making decisions about pyroxylin. Men accustomed to reaching a handful of large buyers were incompetent to reach millions of customers for pocket combs. As early as 1919 a committee recommended ways to drastically re-structure the company, but the chief executive resisted. As the postwar recession became more severe, DuPont losses kited. The profits still being made on explosives were not enough to cover deficits on the other products; the firm showed a net loss for the first six months of 1921. At last the company adopted the decentralized or multi-divisional structure. Here are the two chief recommendations made by the subcommittee on reorganization: It made no sense to put all engineers in one category, all salesmen in another, etc., since it is related effort which should be coordinated, and not "like things." Thus those concerned with lacquers should be in one division, with dyes in another. Second, each division should be under the command of one man with full say, subject only to the proviso that if he failed he would be fired. These semi-autonomous divisions would be coordinated by the Executive Committee of the entire firm, which would allocate resources for expansion on the basis of recent performance plus anticipations of future prospects. It would also order the firings of division managers.

Before we look at the great stock market crash of 1929—certainly a significant subject—we must be sure it does not blind us to other basic influences. Plunging security prices may trigger a depression, but they cannot by themselves cause one. Behind them lie several kinds of inequities in the distribution of income, which we have already examined and will again. But first it seems worth while to say a bit about how far federal policies helped to further injustice and to bring about the shortage of consumer purchasing power. The actions of Congress and the federal executive branch can be left until Chapter 24, but the rulings of federal courts and officials that subverted most attempts at trade unionism should not lurk in the shadows unseen. World War I saw the mushrooming of so-called "employee representation plans," which might more properly be termed company unions. This development was spurred by a requirement that employers doing war production should bargain collectively with their workers. Although the company union was a fake, large companies found it a neat piece of flummery. Some 400,000 people were smothered in the device in 1919, nearly 1.5 million by 1926. The extent to which federal officials meant to be impartial about the labor market was shown by their administration of the adjunct rule that exempted workers in "essential industries" from military conscription. When munitions employees at Bridgeport, Connecticut went on strike, President Wilson ordered them restored to the draft rolls unless they returned to work.

Here it must suffice to look at three Supreme Court decisions. *Hitchman Coal & Coke Co.* v. *Mitchell* (1917) began a decade earlier. The coal fields unionized by the Mine Workers were gravely threatened by the competition in consumer markets from non-union companies in Kentucky and West Virginia. Therefore the union sent organizers to the Hitchman mine. No employee was signed to membership, but they did sign pledges to join up as soon as a majority of the workers had similarly decided to do so. The firm then extorted from its employees a yellow-dog contract, promising not to join any union. A federal district judge issued a temporary restraining order against the UMW. Four and a half years later, in December, 1912, he had issued a "perpetual" injunction against any efforts to organize the Hitchman mine. His grounds were three: The UMW was a common-law conspiracy. It violated the Sherman Anti-Trust Act. It was inducing breach of contract. On appeal, a federal circuit court threw out the first two grounds and reversed the third, holding that a worker was free to join the union (although at the risk of losing his job). Thus the breach-of-contract issue came plunk before the Supreme Court. There the decision of the circuit court was reversed. The ruling held that efforts by the UMW to induce "concerted breaches of the contracts" were "unlawful and malicious." In a dissent written by Brandeis, three justices held that since the purpose sought—collective bargaining—was legal, the union's actions could only be illegal if its methods were outside the law, and they were not. (Brandeis had a reverse corollary that was far from friendly to unionism. In *Dorchy* v. *Kansas*, 1926, he held that "a strike may be illegal because of its purpose." Only in California was a strike legal without regard to purpose.)

Within the confines of judicial thinking fifty years ago, only one rejoinder to this line of argument could possibly be effective. It was the reply "judicial restraint," which Justice Holmes elegantly restated in *Truax* v. *Corrigan* (1921). An Arizona law of 1913 had sought to restrict issuance of injunctions against peaceful picketing. Chief Justice Taft wrote the decision that struck down the statute as violating both the due-process and the equal-protection clauses of the 14th Amendment. Even Holmes, for all his eloquence, for all the veneration of judicial restraint, for all the mouthy worship of state rights, could not win his colleagues. He might win us:

> There is nothing I more deprecate than the use of the Fourteenth Amendment beyond the absolute compulsion of its words to prevent the making of social experiments that an important part of the community desires in the insulated chambers afforded by the several States.

This view seemed to him imperative even though "the experiment may seem futile or even noxious to me." His opinion, be it recalled, was in dissent.

Let us sum up backgrounds to the Great Crash: major portions of America were not able to bargain in ways that might have bolstered their purchasing power: farmers were strafed by competition from other countries, coal miners by other sources of energy, New England textile companies by the South, industrial workers by federal and state governments. These groups were the bottom of the pyramid. At the apex were the owners of America, whose flamboyancy was most gaudy on the New York Stock Exchange.

A lopsided impression must be avoided here. One reads many references to chauffeurs or bootblacks who were speculators on Wall Street. Good estimates are that about 7 per cent of the population were buying shares. This is not a negligible proportion, being perhaps 30 per cent of the heads of families. But most of them had slender assets and were mere dabblers. Further, a large portion of their purchases (and of all purchases) were bought on margin; that is, on credit. Further, the margin could go as high as 90 per cent of the selling price of the stocks. Further, a large part of these margin allowances came from call loans—grants of credit by stock brokers that could be cancelled on notice. One huge corporation had accumulated such a reserve of undistributed profits (General Motors) that it had a billion dollars in call loans in New York. Right here is a window into the financial turmoil. Employees of big corporations did not have the bargaining leverage that could have given them the incomes needed to buy the commodities that flowed from the big corporations. Neither did stockholders, for the board of directors would not pay out the profits that investors should have gotten. The company would not spend the money to build new factories or new machinery, because it could not use profitably the physical capital that it already owned.

Obviously there was no real dilemma here: More than one handle could be seen that would set the wheels turning smoothly. But the tycoons were too stupid or too greedy to seize any of them. So the available funds that were not being spent for useful purposes spilled into speculation. Real estate in Florida was reputed to be a hot item; one Miami newspaper in 1924 printed more inches of advertising than any paper had ever printed in a year, and the next summer another Miami sheet ran 504 pages, the largest single issue anywhere up to that time. But that land boom smashed, and the popular destination for money became Wall Street. Many Americans simply were not intelligent enough to use their surplus funds in productive ways. Speculation is easy, since the price of any limited commodity will rise as long as long as increasing numbers of fools want to buy it. Here are some figures at opening time on the New York Stock Exchange on 3 March, 1928, with the price given first and the annual dividend stated last, both in dollars:

American Can	77	2
General Electric	$128^{3}/_{4}$	5
General Motors	$139^{3}/_{4}$	5
R.C.A.	$94^{1}/_{2}$	0
Woolworth	$180^{3}/_{4}$	5

Unless special factors intervene (for instance, a high growth rate, as in uranium mining at one time or in photocopy equipment recently), you are wise to unload a common stock when its selling price goes beyond ten times dividends. For all its charming Ivy League graduates and for all its numerous confidence men, the market had gone far out of line. So it crashed.

Thursday, 24 October, 1929 came to be known as Black Thursday. Nearly 13 million shares were sold that day on the New York Stock Exchange, which suffered the widest drop in its history. General Electric, going above 400 a few weeks earlier, opened at 315 and closed at 283. R.C.A. went down during the day from $68^{3}/_{4}$ to $44^{1}/_{2}$. These numbers only afford a tardy index to what had been happening for a long time. The economy had been vulnerable for the entire decade. A postwar slump had been overcome by booms in construction and auto sales. A slump in 1924 was offset by construction and electrical appliances. A rather severe sag in 1927, due in appreciable measure to the drop in car sales as Ford made his change-over from the Model T, was survived. Perhaps the main element that kept the American economy at least in convalescence before 1929 was its insane symbiosis with the outside world, to be discussed in Chapter 24.

As has been emphasized above, perhaps to a fault, the Great Depression was largely a result of the lopsided distribution of incomes. Persons with savings, unable to perceive a commodity that they could reasonably hope to sell to consumers at a profit, turned instead to the stock exchanges and to other types of speculative ventures. Their blunders were compounded by large corporations who, unwilling to invest their undistributed earnings in their own lines of product, went so far as to deposit them in Wall Street banks which then used their cash surpluses for call loans. Prices of common stocks especially rose to absurd heights, and when the Great Crash came in 1929 its repercussions were both widespread and deep. Although few predicted the disaster, it was predictable. Since the end of World War I, three gigantic segments of the economy—agriculture, coal mining, and textile manufacturing—had been depressed. In addition, major industries had been sustained only by lending to foreigners the American dollars that could then be used to buy American goods; this "subsidize the foreigner" policy applied particularly in Germany and Latin America. However, while some economic sectors were clearly obsolescent, others were having a lusty adolescence. To the Census Bureau, construction continued to be the leading industrial group. But the new energy-source of electricity was more vital. Generators, transformers, high-tension wires, the telephone, the radio, these formed a whole complex of tangible investments. The internal-combustion engine gave us the automobile. Ford dominated the manufacture of cars just as DuPont seized the lead in producing industrial chemicals, from consumer goods such as rayon to producers' goods such as lacquers and solvents. So the decade after 1919 saw millions of Americans live in misery while others thrived beyond their dreams. Conversely, during the Great Depression many almost starved, but others benefited from hard times.

SOME NOTABLE EVENTS

1895   Giant hydroelectric generator installed at Niagara Falls, N.Y.

1896   Telephones in U.S. number one for 175 people; by 1914, one for 10.

1903   Ford Motor Company founded.

1906   Harvey Firestone's factory in Akron takes order for 2,000 sets of pneumatic tires.

1908   Ford markets the first Model T.

1909   Ford builds his first branch assembly plant in Kansas City.

1910   U.S. census: 92,407,000 (47% urban).

1913   U.S. steel production is 31 million tons.

1914   Electric trolleys are running over 40,000 miles of track.

1914–
  1931   Rayon output rose 69 times.

1914   Sales of Model T reach a quarter of a million.

1917   DuPont buys 27.6% of available stock in General Motors.

   Hitchman Coal & Coke Co. v. *Mitchell*

1919   Great Steel Strike begins, 22 Sept.; called off 8 Jan., 1920.

   Plumb Plan for nationalization of railroads is advanced.

   6.7 million passenger cars in use.

   Daily air-mail service from New York to Chicago starts.

   Radio Corporation of America organized.

1920   U.S. census: 106,466,000 (50% urban).

   Transportation Act of 1920 (Esch-Cummins Act) approved, 28 Feb.

   KDKA in Pittsburgh is first radio station to broadcast regularly.

   GM, incorporated in 1908, moves toward decentralized structure.

1921   *Truax* v. *Corrigan*

1922   Annual sales of radios are $60 million; hit $843 million in 1929.

   Baltimore & Ohio Plan ends shopmen's strike on railroads, 15 Sept.

1923   Lacquers introduced to U.S. markets.

   Chrysler begins to produce cars.

1925   Standard Oil (N.J.) begins to change to decentralized structure.

   Florida land boom tops out; collapses in 1926.

1926   National Broadcasting Corporation organized as first major network.

1928   First full-length all-sound movie is released.

   Real earnings of employed wage earners are 32% higher than in 1914.

1929   Sears, Roebuck begins to change to decentralized structure.

   23.1 million passenger cars in use.

Ways to Study History XXIII

Generalize, and then qualify. A promising project can be virtually destroyed if it works with categories that are too broad (see "Ways to Study History X"). It can also be made unbearable for readers if it refuses to conceptualize at all. The latter defect is glaring in *A History of American Life*, edited by Arthur M. Schlesinger, Sr. and Dixon Ryan Fox (1927–1948). Several scholars think that this series set the study of social history back by a full generation. Most of the books came as close to crude empiricism as the historian can get; they were sequences of unrelated facts. They can still be used as reference volumes to learn specific details, but they attempt few interpretations. Anybody who tries to read one from beginning to end is likely to find it tedious.

Scholarly work since World War II has tended to be much more analytical than its ancestors. Moreover, often the analytic framework is stated explicitly. Thomas C. Cochran's *Railroad Leaders, 1845–1890: The Business Mind in Action* (1953) proceeded from the sociological concept of social role. That is, he assumed that the job made the man, not vice versa. What obligations did a railroad executive have? Who defined his duties? What sanctions were applied to ensure compliance? But Cochran's exposition, including 300 pages of extracts from 100,000 letters written by 61 men, makes clear the limits of deviation from the standardized formula.

Alfred D. Chandler's *Strategy and Structure* (1962) expounds the reorganization of four giant corporations—General Motors, DuPont, Standard Oil (New Jersey), and Sears, Roebuck. Each firm adopted a "decentralized" form and thus they were similar. But each came to this innovation for its own reasons, in response to a different set of pressures, with a different group of personnel, dividing their powers in various ways.

Document 23-1

The problem of second-hand, or fifth-hand, goods confronts many industries. Some used products are handled by a scorned fringe of the retailers; to buy discarded jewelry or guitars you must go to a pawnshop. But most residences that are sold by respectable real-estate agencies (they scorn pawnshops) have already been occupied. Similarly the emergence of a used-car market early came to plague the automobile manufacturers. Soon after World War I the Ford Motor Company decided that this end of the dealership should yield to the agency a gross profit of 20 per cent over the cost of purchase of the old vehicle. But when the general sales committee of GM discussed the issue in 1925, they reached a different verdict.

1. Is it definitely established that the used car is the "dealer's own problem" and that it will be an increasingly important part of automobile retailing?

After considerable discussion, the following points were generally agreed upon:

The sale of new cars depends largely upon the used-car situation. This is especially true in the high-priced classes, where 80 per cent of the new-car sales involve trade-ins—in some instances it being necessary to sell two used cars in order to move one new car.

It was unanimously agreed that the future volume of sales on new cars would depend largely upon the efficient selling and servicing of used cars. It is, therefore, necessary for the manufacturer to take an interest in the sale of used cars. . . .

3. Should the dealer who is fortunately situated so that the volume of new-car business is naturally larger than the average, in proportion to capital employed and necessary operating expense and who therefore may enjoy abnormally high profit, be encouraged to allow more liberal prices for used cars taken in trade? . . . It was generally agreed that the Ford policy, whereby the dealer is required to make money on the used-car end, is unsound, at least as applied to our business. . . .

Domestic and Foreign Politics of Self-Deceit, 1916–1928

If a historian means to reject highly popular interpretations, honesty suggests that he should do so at once and bluntly. If it were permissible to determine truth by taking public-opinion polls, a large number of recent commentators would tell you that the great presidents of the twentieth century have been Theodore Roosevelt, Wilson, Franklin Roosevelt, and Kennedy. But while public opinion might grant public office, it does not always look at facts. Staring at the record, it might seem that the three most suitable presidents have been Harding, Coolidge, and Eisenhower. Not that these Republican worthies deserve any high praise. Corruption in high office was perhaps as bad in the Harding administration as it has ever been (but why are folks in such a hurry to forget Major General Harry H. Vaughan of the Truman years, or Eisenhower's crony Sherman Adams?). Coolidge was noted for his genius at sleeping. Eisenhower won note for his ability to garble a sentence. It will be hard to find positive gains that we can credit to any incumbent of the White House in this century. But if almost any action by the chief executive is almost certain to be mistaken, it is best if they do nothing. The man who sits on his hands and does nothing will not help us much, but neither will he provoke much trouble..The three presidents from the GOP who seem to merit a dab of praise accomplished little, but they did not fall into temptations that might have destroyed massive segments of mankind. Two other caveats might be recorded here, one having to do with political party, the other with sectionalism. The word has been bandied about that the Democrats were the "liberals," whatever that may mean. The party did hold prominent members who fought hard for social legislation, such as Alfred E. Smith and Robert Wagner in New York. But the thundering voice in its council came from two groups of reactionaries—the white South and the urban bosses. Republicanism had its own troglodytes; it also had George W. Norris in Nebraska, Robert M. LaFollette (and later his son) in Wisconsin, Fiorello LaGuardia in New York. The struggles of these three men will be discussed below; for the moment let us note that their constituencies also have bearing on the question of regionalism. Two, besides being Republican, were also Midwestern. It is easy to put together a long list of politicians in the heartland who succeeded in their pursuits by fighting in identifiable ways for some form of social justice.

Backtracking again, Wilson's campaign for re-election in 1916 is an illuminating sequence. A cynic would see it, with some reason, as an opportunistic sell-out to reform. The president was running scared. Put in the coarsest sense, he was trying to buy votes. But being a Southern gentleman who had also been president of an Ivy League university, he could not send his bagman down to the polling place as Mark Hanna had done for the Republicans twenty years earlier. He bought, not a vote, but a bloc of voters. His handicaps were great. Personally, he inclined to be frosty. The war was a dilemma to him. Should he be for "preparedness" or against it? Whichaway did the votes lie? What ethnic groups would swing the decision in key areas? For that matter, who could point to the key areas? He backed and filled, hitched and hauled.

Mileage posts can be mapped. The appointment of Louis D. Brandeis to the Supreme Court is worth analysis, coming at the beginning of the campaign on 28 January, 1916. It was fiercely resisted by anti-Semites. Portions, only portions, of big business opposed it because Brandeis had bad-mouthed the "monopolies" and stood as the Louis if not the David of the little man. But men on State Street in Boston had long been hiring him as a shrewd attorney in a railroad reorganization. They could not see a millionaire committing tyrannicide. Jews favored the nomination; so did most voters who held to the standard of fair play. The nomination was confirmed by the Senate. But for us the crucial consideration is this: What motivates a presidential aspirant? For Wilson, later acts serve as a floodlight, with the president backstaging all others. In 1914 and 1915 he had blocked a bill for loans to farmers. Suddenly he became a fervent advocate. We can ask why—but the bill passed.

Next came a splurge on statutes for the kiddies in the cities, for workers on ships and trains. As the election drew closer, the tempo of administration-sponsored legislation was stepped up. A child-labor bill, having languished for six months in the Senate, became law on 1 September after strong pressure from the White House (only to be invalidated by the Supreme Court in *Hammer* v. *Dagenhart*). Two days later the president signed the Adamson Act that decreed an eight-hour day on the railroads; for months the country had been threatened by a nationwide strike, until at last Wilson prevailed over determined opposition by rail executives. Three days after that the Senate agreed to the Revenue Act of 1916. Under the 16th Amendment (1913), Congress had levied a 2 per cent tax on personal incomes above $4,000. The House had doubled this basic levy in 1916; now the Senate added a further surcharge of 13 per cent on incomes over $20,000. The final measure also imposed new taxes on corporations and raised the imposition on inheritances. These steps toward social equity, coming right before a presidential election, show how crude political maneuvers can work for humanitarianism.

But probably the main ingredient in the campaign of 1916 was Wilson's shuffling on international affairs. Early in the year he was gallant for "preparedness." Alleging that constitutional provisions made it impossible to bring the National Guard in the several states under full federal control, the administration asked for a new reserve force to be called the Continental Army. The president also asserted that the United States needed "incomparably the greatest navy in the world." He went on a great tour of the Midwest to muster support for this line. However, he kept his ribs covered. When the Continental Army failed to win congressional favor, Wilson withdrew the proposal and permitted the secretary of war to resign. Years later the victim wrote: "I once heard a description which as nearly fits the case of President Wilson as any other I know. In describing someone it was said, 'He was a man of high ideals but no principles.'"

During the summer Wilson stopped being strong for preparedness and became strong for peace. The catalyst was the Democratic national convention in June. The governor of New York was the keynote speaker. He mentioned that in a number of instances his country had refused to be provoked into war. His audience demanded specifics. He gave some. Unexpectedly, the gathering started to betray strong feelings. It began to chant when informed of each crisis: "What did we do? What did we do?" The keynoter would roar back, "We didn't go to war, we didn't go to war!" On the following day the permanent chairman of the convention gave all the credit, falsely, to the president: "Without orphaning a single American child, without widowing a single American mother, without firing a single gun or shedding a drop of blood, he wrung from the most militant spirit that ever brooded over a battlefield the concession of American demands and American rights." Woodrow Wilson heard the message.

He put together peace with social justice. That was his campaign. By the end of September he was proclaiming that the Republicans meant to involve the nation in war both in Europe and in Mexico. Democratic campaigners were waving the slogan, "He kept us out of war." They were greatly aided by the loudmouth bellicosity of such prominent opponents as Theodore Roosevelt and by the shilly-shallies of the Republican nominee, Charles Evans Hughes, former Republican governor of New York and soon to be Chief Justice of the United States. Again, we have good reason to abandon a common, almost traditional, interpretation of this campaign. With high melodrama it has Hughes going to sleep thinking he had won, but waking up to learn that he lost due to an unexpected reverse in California. This depiction goes way too far. After all, people in a lot of other states voted against the Republicans. The answer may lie in such Democratic plugs as this one on the eve of the election:

The Lesson is Plain:
If You Want WAR, vote for HUGHES!
If You Want Peace with Honor
VOTE FOR WILSON

"Iffy history" is nearly always treacherous, but this conjecture may be offered: If a plebescite had been taken on American entry into World War I, the declaration of war would have been rejected decidedly in the vast realm between the mountains, from the Appalachians to the Rockies, from Pittsburgh to Denver. Wilson's policy would probably have been rejected in the Far West as well. It might have won on the Atlantic coast, but I am not convinced even of that. Wilson was re-elected. So—he helped take us, not out of war, but into it.

While Wilson's tactics in 1916 may seem canny, he followed a course in 1918 that must be called puerile. With the war still on but apparently nearing its close, the president decided to issue his October Appeal. His new wife (m. December, 1915) advised against: "I would not send it out. It is not a dignified thing to do." Right she was. He asked flat-out for a Democratic majority in Congress; the implication was that a denial would be a lack of confidence in him personally. Contrary to his long-standing hallucination, American politics is not a parliamentary system. He got a bloody nose.* In the House the Republicans ended with a 47 vote majority, having gained 25 seats. Their margin in the Senate was only two; they had won five seats.

The president chose to ignore these warnings. Within less than three weeks after Armistice Day the personnel of the commission to the Paris Peace Conference was announced. Chief delegate was the chief executive. The other four were obviously his patsies; not one carried any political clout at all. Sailing for France on 4 December, the president reached Brest nine days later. He then spent nearly a month touring Europe. Often he was acclaimed by adoring throngs. His earlier call in the Fourteen Points for self-determination

---

*Americans apparently do not like to have the president tell them how to vote in Congressional elections. FDR tried the same tactic in the Democratic primaries of 1938; he too got bashed.

was highly popular with many sectors of nationalism in Europe. But what did the slogan mean? How could it be implemented? What was a "nation"? Other members of the American contingent were bothered by Wilson's high-blown cant; one of them commented privately: "I am disquieted to see how hazy and vague our ideas are. We are going to be up against the wiliest politicians in Europe. There will be nothing hazy or vague about their ideas." The most biting comments about Wilson came from the premier of France, Georges Clemenceau. For openers: "God gave us the Ten Commandments and we broke them. Wilson gives us the Fourteen Points. We shall see." And, to Colonel House: "I can get on with you. You are practical. I understand you, but talking to Wilson is something like talking to Jesus Christ!" In 1925: "Wilson was a noble figure, but he did not appreciate the facts or the significance of European history." Clemenceau, on that point, was correct. And, if nobody knew concretely what the United States wanted, Clemenceau knew precisely what France needed: The old-style balance of power, but with a much elevated position for his country. Particularly, France must sap the strength of Germany.

Most details of the Treaty of Versailles need not detain us. Some, however, were to play giant in coming decades. As a summary judgment, the document was abhorrent. It stripped away territories from Germany. It divided up the Austro-Hungarian Empire, meanwhile bestowing the garland of nationhood on such non-nations as Czechoslovakia. In addition, it imposed massive indemnities on the defeated powers. Good economists were quick to see the defects in this program. Apart from exports of gold—neither Germany nor Austria had any in 1919—or the granting of credit by foreigners, international debts must be paid by the transfer of goods. But none of the intended beneficiaries of these indemnities was willing to accept increased imports; on the contrary, they wanted to increase their exports.* Nor should Article 10, Section 1 be overlooked:

> The Members of the League undertake to respect and preserve as against external aggression the territorial integrity and existing political independence of all Members of the League. In case of any such aggression or in case of any threat or danger of such aggression the Council shall advise upon the means by which this obligation shall be fulfilled.

The president saw this provision as the keystone of the peace settlement; Eugene Debs would refer to the League of Nations as "the new capitalist international." Two considerations seem clear. Wilson became obsessed with the menace posed by the Bolshevik revolution in Russia in November, 1917;

---

*This contradiction was eased for a few years by some idiotic processes: Americans make loans to Germans; Germany pays indemnities to Britain and France, which then repay war loans from the U.S. (See Chapter 22 for the role of the Morgan banking interests as beneficiaries of this chain of lending.)

some consequences of his mania will be examined shortly. Also, with considerable encouragement from Mrs. Wilson, he took special note of the "yellow peril," meaning Japan.

As usual, foreign policy was linked with domestic difficulties. On the very eve of the declaration of war, the president is said to have spoken to a reporter as follows:

> Once lead this people into war, and they'll forget there ever was such a thing as tolerance. To fight you must be ruthless and brutal, and the spirit of ruthless brutality will enter into the very fiber of our national life, infecting Congress, the courts, the policeman on the beat, the man in the street.

One scholar has questioned that the president uttered such a paragraph; another has rebutted that it seems in character for Wilson. If you take the latter view (I do), it must be said that the chief executive hedged by making it a self-fulfilling prediction. He was under heavy pressure from that renowned war-monger Theodore Roosevelt: "He who is not with us, absolutely and without reserve of any kind, is against us, and should be treated as an alien enemy." Wilson contributed to the hysteria. During the war he declaimed, "Woe be to the man that seeks to stand in our way in this day of high resolution when every principle we hold dearest is to be vindicated and made secure." (See the statements by our ambassador to England against "hyphenated Americans," mid-Chapter 22.)

Worked to a frenzy by the invective from high office, masses of Americans found release in an orgy of bigotry and violence. It reached its peak in the four years 1916–1920. It had many sources and took many forms, all ugly. Immigrants were beaten up by mobs. German-language instruction was abolished in many school districts. Socialists and pacifists ran the risk of being tarred and feathered. Radical publications were denied the use of the mails. Leaders of the Socialist party were sent to the county workhouse for advocating resistance to conscription; Eugene Debs later went to the federal prison at Atlanta on a similar charge. The federal government tried to get better organization into the repression: on 7 September, 1917, it made simultaneous raids on radical headquarters across the nation.

One might hope that peace would mean a return to sanity, but events did not move that way. A manic does not swiftly recover his balance, and mania was rife. Other reasons can be detected for the persistence of hysteria. The Democratic party continued to need it. Having suffered a humiliating defeat in 1918, they had no wish to walk the plank again. Their plight declined further as servicemen returned home to find no jobs. The federal government itself compounded this difficulty by an abrupt reversal of fiscal policy. In the last half of 1918, its expenditures were $9 billion in excess of its receipts. For the next six months, the treasury showed a surplus of $831 million. Inevitably this retraction caused a drastic reversal of wholesale prices, which fell by 33 per cent from 1920 to 1921. By the latter year an estimated 5 million workers were unemployed.

The Democrats had badly lost the election of 1920. Their last-ditch fight was composed of two main appeals. The administration tried to rally the people to the Treaty of Versailles, especially to the League of Nations. Wilson took the position, understandably, that a mass of amendments and reservations to the treaty would nullify it totally. A majority of the Senate believed, yet more understandably, that the president had abandoned altogether too many traditional American precepts.* Knowing that he would lose in the Foreign Relations Committee, Wilson took the issue to the voters. On 4 September, 1919, he began his famous "swing around the circle" in the West, making 37 speeches in 29 cities. Before the month ended, his gamble was lost when he collapsed in Colorado. He was hurried back to the White House. On 2 October he had a stroke. For several months his activities were at best limited; the vice president was a nobody, and rumors circulated that Mrs. Wilson was making important decisions.

With the president incapacitated, with his retirement certain, with the economic situation shaky, the Democrats had their backs to the wall. Some of their leaders turned vicious. The wolf whose name might endure in infamy was the attorney general, A. Mitchell Palmer. He set in motion the ignoble procession known as the "Palmer raids" against radicals, which he hoped would launch his career toward the White House. Although Palmer wanted the publicity he got, perhaps he ended up with more ignominy than he deserves. He had, if not justification, at least a plausible excuse. Since April numerous efforts had been made to send bombs through the mails to public officials. The front of Palmer's own house was smashed by a bomb (the bombardier was killed). Confronted by such lethal anarchy, few can remain calm. Observers of Canadian affairs may well recall that, after a sequence of bombings, two kidnappings, and a murder in October, 1970, the provincial and federal governments were provoked into policies that the same men would not have undertaken in quieter moments.

Depending on how one chooses to define a "raid," dating of the Palmer raids will differ. It suffices to say that they ran from the autumn of 1919 to the spring of 1920. An early momentous event came just before Christmas when 249 immigrants, alleged radicals, were deported to Russia. The brutalities had scarcely begun. On New Year's Day simultaneous raids were conducted in 33 cities. The number of persons arrested was large; estimates vary from 2,700 to 6,000. They were treated most viciously. In Hartford, any visitor to a supposed revolutionary in jail was himself arrested. Detroit packed them in like sardines:

---

*Particularly such as our time-tested reluctance to make prior commitments to foreign disputes and our belief that the Monroe Doctrine was a divine precept. Wilson, often hailed as an upholder of the American way, had a pronounced tendency to depart from it, especially in foreign affairs.

for a week more than a hundred men were kept in a bull-pen that measured 30 feet by 24. These actions, like others before and since, should make us wonder at the chauvinistic paeans to "the American sense of fair play," or the cheerleading that says Americans are devoted to law as well as to order, or the flabby assertion that we have lived by a "politics of consensus." In moments of strain we have the Stamp Act Riots, race riots, anti-draft riots, the Palmer Raids, the Watts Riot of 1965.

The national elections of 1920 must be seen in this context—the sagging economy, the mood of resentment mounting to hysteria. When the presidential polls had been tallied, they revealed that the total votes had shot upward by about 30 per cent. The increase was due in large measure to the enfranchisement of women by the 19th Amendment in August 1920. To a Democrat, the results were horrible. Support for his party remained at the level of 1916, whereas the Republican vote almost doubled. The GOP not only recaptured the marginal elector who had gone Progressive in 1912 and Democratic in 1916, it also won normally Democratic districts. Its candidate Warren G. Harding got more than 60 per cent of the votes; the Democrats a mere 34 per cent, as their tally actually decreased in all sections except the seaboard East and the South. They had brought the drubbing on themselves in considerable measure. For president they had put forward an unknown. The vice presidential nominee was a brash youngish man who had been assistant secretary of the navy. His name was Franklin Delano Roosevelt. Whether his purpose was to win the approval of Woodrow Wilson or not, he sought during the campaign to champion the League of Nations, and in the process fell into some indiscretions. The proposed federation, he said, could be controlled by the United States: Consider the banana republics of Latin America—weren't at least a half dozen of those votes in his side pocket?

Other generalizations can be advanced about national politics during this decade. Seemingly the business cycle did not have much effect on how people voted. Recessions of some magnitude occurred in 1924 and 1927. The number of unemployed in the first of these years rose to 2 million, and it nearly reached that figure in 1927 (due in large part to Ford's shutdown for six months to make the changeover from Model T to Model A). The Republicans continued to prove that they had a semi-permanent presidential majority; as long as they could hold their own ranks together, they could win the White House. Tactically they were shrewd, knowing how to capitalize on such events as a general strike in Seattle and a policeman's strike in Boston—the latter event gave Governor Calvin Coolidge of Massachusetts a chance to break the strike, appear as the champion of law and order, get his name on the front pages, and thus become the Republican nominee for the vice presidency in 1920. His boss, President Harding, was a likable cuss. It is hackneyed to refer to him as the worst chief executive in American history, but recent scholarship makes this verdict debatable. I confess to some prejudice because it was the conservative Harding, not the liberal Wilson, who pardoned Debs. But

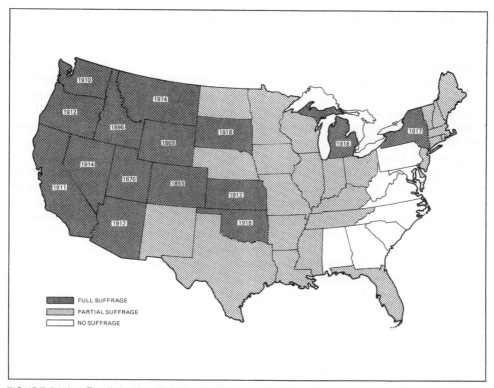

FIGURE 24-1. *The Adoption of Women's Suffrage as of 1919*

Harding was not a bad sort. He was addicted to his friends, whiskey, poker, and having a mistress. He installed as secretary of state Charles Evans Hughes, who in spite of his august demeanor maneuvered the achievements of the Washington Naval Conference of 1921–1922 (late in Chapter 24). Every republic gets the president it deserves, and Harding suited the national mood. Mercifully for him he died before the corrupt leasing of oil reserves at Teapot Dome, Wyoming, and at Elk Hills, California, became public knowledge. Although one result of these scandals was to send a member of the cabinet to prison, the faith of most Americans in the Republican party was not shaken.*

Its ascendancy was challenged in 1924. With support from the dwindling corps of Socialists, the railroad unions, and modest help from other branches of trade unionism, a rejuvenated Progressive party put forward

---

*One of my deep desires is to see a nation admit its vices as well as commemorating its virtues. A series of stamps should be done along this order: Polluted Meat, 1777; Crédit Mobilier; Teapot Dome; deep-freeze scandals during Truman administration, and so on into an obvious series of candidates in the seventies.

LaFollette of Wisconsin. Its platform was blunt: "The great issue before the American people today is the control of government and industry by private monopoly. . . . Through control of government, monopoly has steadily extended its absolute dominion to every basic industry." LaFollette, a hard worker with his hands on facts, an adept politician, was a strong candidate. Coolidge, hardly a charismatic personality, ran for re-election, with a nobody. The Democrats found two nobodies to put forward. One senator from California, a Progressive Republican, wrote to his sons that the issue separating the two major parties was "whether the entrance to the office of J. P. Morgan and Company should be on Wall or Broad Street."

Apart from the independent Progressive move, the zest of the campaign was provided by the Ku Klux Klan. This nativist movement, like its forebears such as the Know-Nothings and the American Progressive Association, was sired by hatred out of fear. The enemy might be blacks, or Jews, or adulterers, or Catholics; for natives of the southern Midwest, the last named were the most dangerous. This issue exploded into national politics in 1924 because a prominent candidate for the Democratic nomination, Governor Alfred E. Smith of New York, was Catholic. His forces introduced a resolution condemning the Klan. It lost by one vote, and he did not get the nomination. We can fairly say that Americans in this decade tended to vote from the viscera, not from the brain. The xenophobia in the Democratic national convention seems a close index to the national temper; Congress had just enacted a new immigration law that clearly discriminated on ethnic grounds. In 1926 the Imperial Wizard and Emperor of the Klan made the viewpoint clear (Document 25-3). These resentments were not confined to any region of the country; they were not rural or small town or big city; they were not defined by social class. William Allen White, great editor of a small-town newspaper in Kansas, ran for governor while opposing the Klan: ". . . the way the Catholics and Jews and colored people were persecuted in Kansas was a dirty shame, and I couldn't rest under it." After his defeat he had this to say about attitudes among trade-unionists, many of them coal miners:

> Here was a funny thing: labor in the Middle West is shot through with the Ku-Klux Klan. It voted for Coolidge . . . because he was right on the Pope. I didn't get much of it because I was wrong on the Pope. . . . Certainly nothing has hit labor such a smash in my memory in politics as the Ku-Klux Klan. . . . It will be a decade before labor recovers what it has lost by flirting with the Ku-Klux Klan.

The Democratic showing in the election of 1924 was more dismal than in 1920: its presidential candidate won only 30 per cent of the popular votes. But Coolidge did not do as well as Harding had done in the preceding election, getting only 54 per cent of the electorate. The wide swing went to LaFollette, who had nearly 5 million votes. He drew more heavily from Democratic than from Republican supporters. His appeal was mainly to the Midwest and the Pacific coast; in California the Democrats were obliterated. Lastly, note that this campaign (not FDR, who in some tomes is made to appear like God at the Creation) brought into prominence a phrase that has passed into the language. The pro tem Committee of One Hundred headed by the editor of the *Nation* announced that it would support the Progressives with this sentence: "We believe that the time has come for a new deal."

In 1928 no third party of substance came forward. Coolidge, although he had been elected only once, chose to doze through the coming contest without having his name in the headlines: his laconic phrase was "I do not choose to run." The Republican candidate was Herbert Hoover, resident in California but a native of the Midwest, a mining engineer who had made a fortune in developments that girdled the globe. His venture into public affairs came as director of American relief efforts in Europe after World War I. Then he became chief of the Department of Commerce, where his aim was to encourage cooperation among companies. This sally had its good side and its bad. Any tinkerer will know the importance of standardizing such commodities as nuts and bolts or lavatory washers by reducing the number of sizes. On the other side, any consumer will know the perils of making it easy for erstwhile competitors to standardize prices. At last Al Smith got the Democratic nomination. He got stomped; Hoover did better than Coolidge had done four years earlier, almost as well as Harding had done in 1920. His 58 per cent of the vote eclipsed Smith's 41 per cent. The anti-Catholic South went strongly against Smith, who lost the normally Democratic Atlanta, Birmingham, Oklahoma City, Dallas, and Houston. But the story must not be allowed to end there. In the North, Smith swung 112 counties away from the GOP; 77 of them had a Catholic preponderance. (See Figure 24-2.)

If we seek to understand how the Republican dominance in presidential elections gave way to a semi-permanent Democratic majority after 1932, these forces become prominent: the movement to cities, where Democratic machines had long been influential and now became dominant; the altered religious and ethnic mix of the population, increasingly felt as immigrant groups moved onto the political stage; the stigma that the GOP was "responsible" for the Great Depression; the Republican persistence in nominating men who were safe but dull, which became fatal when the Democrats found a candidate who was safe but colorful.

The Harding-Coolidge administrations did record achievements, and some follies, in foreign affairs. It has been fashionable to deprecate the Washington Naval Conference of 1921–1922. The humorist Will Rogers gibed that in days of rhetoric "not a rowboat was sunk." Many historians have taken the opposing tack and argued that the agreements went too far in leaving the United States defenseless before its enemies. These judgments are unfair. To defer an arms race is perhaps not the ultimate in human endeavor, but it is

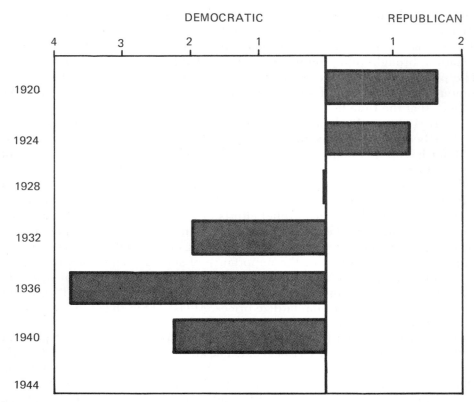

FIGURE 24-2. *Net Pluralities in Twelve Largest Cities (millions of votes)*

certainly an improvement over our experience in recent decades. The sessions at Washington began on 12 November, 1921. When Secretary of State Hughes got up to speak, nothing much was expected. His proposal of a ten-year "holiday" on the construction of capital ships rocked both press and public as well as delegates and ministries. He wanted not only to suspend the laying down of new battleships but he also offered to destroy thirty American battleships that were partially completed or already afloat; in exchange, he told other naval powers what they would have to do. The final intent was to leave his own country, Britain, and Japan with capital ships in the ratio of 5: 5: 3. In this category, France and Italy would be allowed a third the quota of Great Britain and the United States. He had needed only a few minutes to annihilate (verbally) sixty-six battleships totalling nearly 2 million tons. Let those snort who will, the treaty served at least to postpone a breakneck scramble for military advantage. A companion document, called the Nine-Power Treaty, secured the formal consent of other powers to two long-standing American objectives in China: citizens of all foreign nations could participate on the same terms in the economic development of that country, and China would be allowed to develop an independent suzerainty.

The brutalities of the American diplomacy of the time are well-known. By 1924 United States agents were directly managing the finances of ten Latin-American nations. Nicaragua is an example. The United States in 1912, acting under the jurisdiction of its self-proclaimed Roosevelt Corollary to the Monroe Doctrine (1904), had sent a detachment of marines there, with the explanation that the act was required to insure proper fiscal arrangements (especially collection of import duties plus payments on schedule to European bondholders). American troops remained in Nicaragua as an army of occupation until 1933,* when they were finally withdrawn by President Hoover. Earlier Hoover had told the Hondurans: "We have a desire to maintain not only the cordial relations of governments with each other but also the relations of good neighbors." Thus two phrases conventionally tied to FDR—the New Deal and the Good Neighbor Policy—did not originate in his administration at all.

To recapitulate, agreements made at the Washington Conference had obvious defects when they were made; the concurrence on naval limitations did not touch such significant weapons as destroyers and submarines. Weaknesses in the Nine-Power Treaty became obvious with time; a lack of will to enforce by other signatories made it easy for Japan to brush it away. But the agreements signed in 1922 did ease the situation for a few years, and both the Compromise of 1850 and Crittenden's proposals in 1861 should remind us that deferring a showdown can be a good idea. So, retrospectively, American policies in the Pacific and in Latin America may seem badly flawed, but they were not silly. American actions toward Europe were silly.

Further discussion here can be limited to three sets of actions: the Dawes Plan, the World Court, and the Kellogg-Briand Pact. The first arose from the provision in the Treaty of Versailles requiring Germany to pay massive reparations to Britain and France. Dawes' proposal of 1924 began from a recognition that Germany could not meet the payments, so the annual stipend was reduced. So far, so good. But then the Plan restricted the Reich to payment of this obligation only from funds arising from the transfer of Deutschemarks within Germany. This was lunacy. How were the foreign creditors to redeem their credits if their governments imposed rules that prevented imports from Germany? American fumbling with the World Court was equally inane. Elements in the United States had been arguing that although the Senate would not vote to join the League of Nations, it could at

---

*Smedley Butler, major general (retired) of the Marine Corps, spoke about 1940 at the War Memorial in Indianapolis, Indiana: "I spent much of my adult life wandering around in Latin America, grabbing a government by the neck and shouting, 'Be a democracy, damn you, be a democracy.'"

least adhere to a judicial body with authority to rule on some international disputes. In 1926 the Senate voted several qualifications to its acceptance. These included a stipulation that the United States could withdraw at any time; that Congress would determine the American share of expenses of the World Court; that the body could not consider any dispute involving the United States without American consent; "nor shall adherence to the said protocol and statute be construed to imply a relinquishment by the United States of its traditional attitude toward purely American questions." Having adopted these reservations, the Senate did not take action on the total issue until 1935. Then, for want of the necessary two-thirds vote, the proposal lost.

The colossal folly has been saved for last. The Peace Pact of 1928 should not be likened to the naval pacts of 1922. One helped to stave off an arms race; the other in different circumstances was a stimulant to an already maddened illusion. A commitment to outlaw war will do no good unless governments want to live at peace. Evolution of the Kellogg-Briand Pact can be dated from the arrival in the United States of the French foreign minister in early 1927, but the idea goes earlier. Two Americans in particular, a Chicago lawyer and a professor at Columbia University, had been agitating for a world agreement to outlaw war. They won approbation from the chairman of the Senate Foreign Relations Committee, William J. Borah. Here we encounter, to be trite, a comedy of errors. A top French emissary arrives on these shores, and he has two aims. First, quite reasonably, he wants protection against another invasion by Germany, to which end he seeks to involve the United States in advance. Also the two nations have disagreed about the payment of war debts (Chapter 22 on war loans; early Chapter 28), and he is looking for a way to mend matters. He chooses an inept way. In a public speech to the people of the United States, he states: "France would be ready publicly to subscribe, with the United States, to any mutual engagement tending, as between those two countries, to outlaw war." Policy-makers in Washington were, to say the least annoyed. President Coolidge felt that some barn-stormer from Europe had tried to go over his head to the electorate. Secretary of State Kellogg, who had succeeded at the department when Hughes left in 1925, was irked. Bilateral agreement? Absolutely not.

Then, on May 20–21, a miraculous event helped crystallize (among other things) Franco-American popular ideals about peace and friendship. The young Charles A. Lindbergh flew nonstop and solo from Long Island to Le Bourget Aerodrome outside Paris in 33 hours, 30 minutes, and was hailed as an international hero. No term of negotiations could have done so much for Franco-American negotiations; instantaneously many citizens felt that nothing was too good for their French brothers. Kellogg wrote that, instead of a bilateral treaty, the United States would prefer "an effort to obtain the adherence of all the principal powers of the world to a declaration renouncing war as an instrument of national policy." Now France cooled. She and Britain finally signed, but with a mass of qualifications. Of the fifteen initial signatories, three agreed at once: Japan, Germany, and Italy. The treaty allowed for additional names. USSR was the first to be added.

Out of this convoluted mess another question emerges. What did Lindbergh symbolize for the American people? Did he represent the "rugged individualism" to which some Americans still pledged alliance (Document 24-3)? Or did his achievement foreshadow the future dominance of the machine in a world where the individual would hardly figure at all, as we shall see in later chapters?

With strict moral instruction from those schoolmarms in the White House, Roosevelt and Wilson, many citizens had gotten their feet a good way off the ground and up the success ladder before World War I. The ascent of many financial astronauts was accelerated after an exceptionally hysterical war fever was concluded in the Armistice. Millions went into orbit; the most real of all realities for them was the vicarious (and sometimes vicious) world of make-believe. (This frame of mind, the dominance of fantasy, was splendidly depicted by James Thurber in his short story "The Secret Life of Walter Mitty.") I have placed much responsibility on the pre-war presidents for their contributions to this descent into self-deception. It is rather hard to make a similar charge of personal accountability against Harding or Coolidge. For two generations, Harding's reputation was probably lower than that of any other president. It was rather hard to see why, since his call for a return to "normalcy" exactly caught the mood of a nation tired of political tempests and national heroics. Personally, I side with the columnist who applauded Coolidge for saying nothing, content to sleep through his six years in the White House. The voters did not want him to do anything, so he did very little. When he did act, his behavior was insipid or destructive—as witness the Kellogg-Briand Pact.

SOME NOTABLE EVENTS

1917 Lever Act, 10 August, imposes food rationing.

1918 *Hammer* v. *Dagenhart* invalidates child labor laws.

1919 Paris Peace Conference, 12 January–28 June.
Bomb plots against public officials, April.
Communist parties (several) founded in U.S.
Schenck v. *U.S.*; Holmes on the "clear and present danger" of seditious speech.
Volstead Act, 28 October, outlaws alcoholic beverages.
Palmer raids against alleged radicals begin in earnest, 21 December; last about two months.
Ads begin to appear showing a woman holding a cigarette.

1920 Congressional resolution ratifies peace with Germany.
Transportation Act (also called Esch-Cummins Act), 28 February.
Nineteenth Amendment provides for woman suffrage.
Studebaker stops making horse-drawn vehicles.

1921 Treaty of peace with Germany, 25 August.
Immigration restriction act passes as emergency measure.

1922 Fordney-McCumber tariff compromises business and farm interests.
Treaty of Washington (also called Naval Limitation Treaty, also Five Power Treaty), 21 August.

1924 Congressional resolution for cancellation of oil leases at Teapot Dome and Elk Hill, 8 February.
Immigration Act (National Origins Act), 26 May, establishes immigrant quotas.

1926 Senate votes reservations on U.S. adherence to World Court, 27 January.

1927 Coolidge explains U.S. intervention in Nicaragua, 10 January.
McNary-Haugen grain surplus bill vetoed by Coolidge, 25 February.
Lindbergh flies the Atlantic, 20–21 May.
Sacco and Vanzetti executed, 23 August; many call it political scapegoating.
"Good Neighbor Policy" toward Latin America begins.

1928 Kellogg-Briand Peace Pact, signed by 15 nations on 27 August.

Ways to Study History XXIV

Cling to doubt. Thorstein Veblen, in an essay published more than fifty years ago, declared that skepticism was the beginning of wisdom (Chapter 25). Charles Sanders Peirce argued that the crucial breakthrough of scientists in the nineteenth century was the development of truly detached intellects (Document 25-2). Nature, so Theodore Dreiser asserted, has ways of taking revenge on the cocksure (Chapter 25).

Veblen further argued that skepticism is especially common among persons who have imbibed deeply of two cultures, since they cannot fully accept the values of either. I know not whether Robert H. Ferrell can be termed a "marginal man" in this sense, but certainly he has exhibited the common sense of the proverbial man from Missouri: You got to show me. His study *Peace in Their Time* (1952) shows how the Kellogg-Briand Pact of 1927 came to be drafted and ratified. It begins with the assumption that many phenomena are not what their surface says they are. If the Pact had not helped to confirm and advance the tendency of Americans toward self-delusion, Ferrell's book might be one of the funniest of all works about our history.

The conclusions can only be summarized here. To shore up its defenses against Germany, France wanted a nonaggression pact with the United States. American diplomats were too shrewd for that trap. Then the French foreign minister appealed over their heads to the American people. Although piqued, the executives in Washington were swayed by Charles Lindbergh's nonstop flight across the Atlantic. Feeling unable to say No to the French, the United States counterproposed that all major nations should sign a treaty forswearing warfare. So war would be illegal; but in signing, one nation after another made reservations and qualifications. In Ferrell's words, "The result was that the secretary of state, when he finally 'delivered the goods,' delivered a great amount of wrapping paper."

Document 24-1

Woodrow Wilson never achieved a precise and realistic statement of what he hoped to gain by American entry into World War I. But his oft-cited Fourteen Points seem less adequate in that respect than the Four Points he announced at Mount Vernon, Fourth of July, 1918.

The destruction of every arbitrary power anywhere that can separately, secretly, and of its single choice disturb the peace of the world; or, if it cannot be presently destroyed, at the least its reduction to virtual impotence.

The settlement of every question, whether of territory, of sovereignty, of economic arrangement, or of political relationship, upon the basis of the free acceptance of that settlement by the people immediately concerned. . . .

The consent of all nations to be governed in their conduct towards each other by the same principles of honor and of respect for the common law of civilized society that govern the individual citizens of all modern states in their relations with one another; to the end that all promises and covenants may be sacredly observed, no private plots or conspiracies hatched, no selfish injuries wrought with impunity, and a mutual trust established upon the handsome foundation of a mutual respect for right.

The establishment of an organization of peace which shall make it certain that the combined power of the free nations will check every invasion of right and serve to make peace and justice the more secure by affording a definite tribunal of opinion to which all must submit and by which every international readjustment that cannot be amicably agreed upon by the peoples directly concerned shall be sanctioned.

Document 24-2

The legislative process can be as tortuous as a snake. Some aspects of the procedures that resulted in rejection of the Treaty of Versailles have just been discussed. But glimpses of the precise terms in which the Senate of the United States stated its "reservations" about the League of Nations may also be useful. These are extracts from the resolution that came to vote on 19 March, 1920; the tally was 49 for and 35 against ratification; the motion to adhere to the treaty therefore failed of the necessary two-thirds majority.

1. The United States so understands and construes article 1 that in case of notice of withdrawal from the League of Nations, as provided in said article, the United States shall be the sole judge as to whether all its international obligations and all its obligations under the said covenant have been fulfilled, and notice of withdrawal by the United States may be given by a concurrent resolution of the Congress of the United States.

2. The United States assumes no obligation to preserve the territorial integrity or political independence of any other country by the employment of its military or naval forces, its resources, or any form of economic discrimination. . . .

4. The United States reserves to itself exclusively the right to decide what questions are within its domestic jurisdiction and declares that all domestic and political questions relating wholly or in part to its internal affairs, . . . are solely within the jurisdiction of the United States. . . .

5. The United States will not submit to arbitration or to inquiry by the assembly or by the council of the League of Nations, provided for in said treaty of peace, any questions which in the judgment of the United States depend upon or relate to its long-established policy, commonly known as the Monroe doctrine; said doctrine is to be interpreted by the United States alone and is hereby declared to be wholly outside the jurisdiction of said League of Nations. . . .

Document 24-3

Herbert Hoover was the first president since John Quincy Adams to have spent a major portion of his adulthood abroad. He might also be labelled the first career businessman to occupy the White House. Although he had served in government for a decade by 1928, he had never held elective office. His lack of intimacy with the domestic scene, especially with American politics, contributed to his downfall: no true politician would have shown his dedication to rigid principles. Compare Hoover's campaign speech in 1928 with President Cleveland's philosophy in 1889 (Document 18-1).

When the war closed the most vital of all issues both in our own country and throughout the world was whether governments should continue their war-time ownership and operation of many instrumentalities of production and distribution. We were challenged with a peace-time choice between the American system of rugged individualism and a European philosophy of diametrically opposed doctrines—doctrines of paternalism and state socialism. The acceptance of these ideas would have meant the destruction of self-government through centralization of government. It would have meant the undermining of the individual initiative and enterprise through which our people have grown to unparalleled greatness. . . . Even if governmental conduct of business could give us more efficiency instead of less efficiency, the fundamental objection to it would remain unaltered and unabated. It would destroy political equality. It would increase rather than decrease abuse and corruption. It would stifle initiative and invention. It would undermine the development of leadership. It would cramp and cripple the mental and spiritual energies of our people. . . . For a hundred and fifty years liberalism has found its true spirit in the American system, not in the European systems. . . .

The Life of the Mind, 1898–1929

In *The Theory of the Leisure Class,* Thorstein Veblen explained some aspects of the boom-times mentality of the twenties, some years before they occurred. Every person has an instinct of workmanship, which leads him to be productive and to strive for skillfulness. But he also wants to display the fruits of his labors after he has created them. As long as his product does not greatly exceed his actual needs, these two desires do not conflict. But eventually certain people acquire more goods than they can display, and they need the services of others to consume the excess. Wives are the most immediately available vicarious consumers, causing in part the fist-thumping repugnance at "permitting my wife to work." A producer is not available to consume for another. Servants who perform no useful work, and hangers-on who are supported in luxury, also consume in the service of their benefactor.

The possession of a mob of vicarious consumers might be gratifying to their master, but these functionaries have no opportunity to satisfy their own instincts of workmanship. Often they try to fill this gap by devising a complicated ritual about the trivialities of their lives, and spending time and energy in conforming to it, and watching out for the deviations of others. The cut of a coat, the pronounciation of a word, or the breed of a lap-dog acquire great importance in such a society, though they never quite manage to alleviate its boredom. However, it is worthwhile examining the workings of these and other cultural preoccupations, for it is here that we can begin to see important ingredients of the "roaring" twenties mentality.

By the beginning of the twentieth century the profits of the industrial system had permitted a number of consumers to live ever more luxuriously. Even the original producer need no longer be useful, as he had acquired so very much wealth that further labor on his part had become superfluous. Edith Wharton, the novelist who best portrayed this segment of society, came out of it herself; her family and friends were both astounded and disdainful when she chose to cease being merely decorative and begin a career as a writer. She deplored the pettiness, the ostentation, and the worship of money which flourished around her, but she apparently didn't recognize that these attributes are inevitable in a world of drones. Although usually ironic and precise, Wharton's vision seems clouded by one of the most pervasive features of American life before 1929—nostalgic yearning for an unreal ideal.

In *The House of Mirth* (1905) Wharton's picture of futility among the very rich is most finely drawn. It focuses on a heroine, Lily Bart: although her deceased father lost all his money, Lily continues to be acceptable to society; she is so beautiful and "accomplished" that everyone assumes she will soon make a rich marriage, and then the hostesses of the house parties which she interminably attends will find her a powerful friend and a fearsome opponent. But, because of a delicacy of feeling which those around her do not share, she muffs her opportunity to marry a rich clod. Later, after the husband of her best friend makes some money for her in the stock market, the friend drops Lily from her list. Although tolerant of her husband's infidelities, this woman will not permit any alienation of cash. Later, another friend saves her own reputation at the expense of Lily Bart's. Since a reputation for chastity is the only female attribute which rivals wealth in the marriage market, her fortunes plummet. The hostesses of her circle realize that they need never fear her, and drop her; she winds up a seamstress at a hat shop. There her lower-class co-workers pay her little heed, for "she had 'gone under,' and true to the ideal of their race, they were awed only by success—by the gross tangible image of material achievement." Emulating the rich, the poor worship prosperity.

Another novel published five years earlier, *Sister Carrie,* is Theodore Dreiser's classic portrait of another archetypal American woman with an instinct for the main chance. Carrie Meeker comes to Chicago from the farm to better her condition, but soon, to escape from the grinding monotony of her job at a shoe factory and from the pinch-penny soul of her brother-in-law, she becomes the mistress of a traveling salesman. He introduces her to physical comforts which she had never experienced before, and, more importantly, to acquaintances who outdistance him in wealth and social position. One of these, George Hurstwood, the manager of one of Chicago's most fashionable saloons, lives with an open-handed ease which enchants Carrie, while her beauty and freshness attract him equally. Unhappy with his wife and feeling unneeded by his children, he elopes with Carrie to New York, where they live as man and wife. He buys an interest in another saloon, and they seem to mark time for several years, but inwardly he is dying. In Chicago he was a hail-fellow to many men; in New York he barely manages to remain a cog. Soon enough he loses his business and is no longer even solvent. He sinks into the routine of the unemployed who quickly becomes unemployable, and then to the Bowery bum who depends on soup kitchens even to live.

In the meantime Carrie prospers. The possibilities of New York, which had made Hurstwood feel insignificant, enchant her; she turns to the stage, and before very long has become a famous comic actress, a star. Yet despite the vitality which charmed so many and led to her success, she is a vapid woman. Incapable of genuine emotion, she only occasionally wonders whether life might contain more lasting pleasures than pretty clothes and admiration. The novel dooms Hurstwood to the living death which society imposes on failures and Carrie to the frivolous life which it offers as a prize.

The possibility that any prize might be forthcoming for a woman who had been the mistress of two men shocked *Sister Carrie*'s readers; not for another 20 years could chastity safely be flouted in literature. Yet sexual laxity, although necessary to the book's structure, is but a trivial part of its message. The larger themes, of heartlessness, of hollowness, were perceived by many others of the pre-depression era. T. S. Eliot was one. Though he was an expatriate, his poetry should best be understood within its American context. Nostalgia permeates his work, nostalgia for an implied heroic past which did not whimper. To him everything in the modern era seems stale and tired, with people responding with mechanical formalities to a mechanical world.

> *For I have known them all already, known them all:—*
> *Have known the evenings, mornings, afternoons,*
> *I have measured out my life with coffee spoons;*

In this vision man is a wind-up toy programmed to trudge in circles; he is no longer able to control his destiny or regulate his purposes. His eyes are the only part of him that still lives, and eyes can only view the surfaces of his constantly repeated surroundings, which he can neither change nor understand. If the American Dream of progress and faith in the future was both mythical and unattainable, so much worse would be the fate of those who awakened from it without finding a palpable substitute. The officially authorized Dream required that present pleasures must be subordinated to future perfection, but unfortunately, a realization that such perfection would not be forthcoming in the future was not necessarily, or even probably, an adequate release to allow a modern man to relax and savor the moment. Instead, he would become an Ahab who outlived the whale, a man with no obsession, with nothing at all (See Chapter 14 on Melville.) In such a vision of life as T. S. Eliot's, the most profoundly held emotion is boredom.

The philosopher John Dewey believed that many of America's problems stemmed from the fracturing of work and learning, and that this situation could be eased by a new kind of school. In former days, children learned most of their major lessons by watching and helping their parents or other working adults. Thus the need to learn certain things was immediately apparent, and doing them well produced tangible rewards. But in a society where work went on outside the home, and most people were coming to believe it desirable to separate working and living areas still further, this was no longer possible. To be useful in this changed society, the schools could no longer teach "academic" subjects in a vacuum. In the Laboratory School in Chicago, Dewey devised a system in which all subjects related to a common theme, the themes being different forms of useful labor. Thus a group might be learning about the production of bread. They would raise different kinds of grain, and read and talk about the ways various societies in the past had managed these tasks. Then they would have to thresh and mill grain, and figure out the most efficient ways to measure it. Finally they had to learn processes of baking. While the children were learning about history, mechanics, sociology, and mathematics, all of these lessons were but means to ends, as they would be to actual producers.

This system worked. Children learned faster, remembered longer, and realized that a purpose lay behind their schooling. Unfortunately, the system never became widespread. It would have been extremely expensive. The costs of the extra equipment it required could have been met, but Americans would never entertain the expense of revamping the whole teacher-training establishment. To use the Laboratory School's methods, a teacher needed a wide and generous education, and a mind flexible enough to permit doubt and error. Most teachers were simply drilled in a few irrefutable "facts" to which they clung desperately in the sea of their own ignorance. Their only possible goal was to pound these "facts" into the minds of their charges. To provide a different kind of education would mean luring the very best minds into becoming teachers, and paying them accordingly. At a time when hyped up production of goods was America's pride, and "If you're so smart, why ain't you rich?" one of its common jibes, this could not possibly happen.

Despite its inadequacies, schooling was still regarded as something holy. Children in the black rural South didn't even have the advantage of a semi-regular school run by a graduate of a teacher training academy; if they were lucky, a student at one of the black colleges might wander into the district in the summer time, hawking a little reading and writing for a pittance. W. E. B. DuBois, later to be a noted historian and militant leader, was one of those teachers, and in *The Souls of Black Folk* he recorded his impressions. He saw endurance, and, amazingly, hope. The people he encountered were poor and ignorant, but they had learned to mitigate poverty with laughter, and they hoped that his poor "school" could expand their knowledge of the world. Being black, they were despised, but faith helped to keep them from despising themselves. Although the sturdy white yeoman farmer (already fast disappearing) would have disdained the comparison, they represented most of the virtues which he had been taught to think resided exclusively in himself.

It was becoming increasingly difficult to write of those virtues, and of the optimism which accompanied them, without resorting to the past tense. Willa Cather, who wrote movingly and generously of the farm and small town, always set her stories on these themes in times when the frontier cast its hopeful glow upon them. Although too honest a novelist to give way wholly to nostalgic sugarcoating, Cather's frontier tales have a vitality which would not ring true in the early twentieth century. She recognised that rural life, especially on the frontier, could destroy everything gentle or subtle, but she stressed the ways in which it nurtured strength and hope.

Cather's optimism was always in the form of a memoir. Her novels of her contemporary times present a much sadder picture. In *The Professor's House* the protagonist finally realizes that his life, seemingly so rewarding, has been trickled away in paths he would not have chosen. *A Lost Lady* disintegrates precisely when the dreams of the frontier, represented by her pioneering husband, are no longer possible.

These attitudes—boredom, nostalgia, a sense of futility, a loss of faith—form a personality which we have come to describe as modern. Although they became widespread only after World War I, Herman Melville shared them in the middle of the nineteenth century (Chapter 14). Nonetheless, the year 1920 serves as a useful dividing line in the American mind. Sinclair Lewis published his acid account of American small town life, *Main Street,* in that year. After the 1920 census a majority of the nation's inhabitants resided in urban areas. The Volstead Act established a creaky mechanism to enforce national prohibition. Women across the country were enfranchised in time to help elect Warren Harding. Radio Station KDKA, Pittsburgh, began regular broadcasts. In *This Side of Paradise* F. Scott Fitzgerald trumpeted the start of what was to be called the Jazz Age. Each of these events was something of an exclamation point. The changes which they punctuated had been occurring for some time, but after 1920 it was difficult for even the ostrich to ignore them.

Sinclair Lewis' *Main Street* lampooned the gods of middle America. The small town, where solid goodness was supposed to live, he saw as narrow and fearful. If you would be different, escape or die. Yet its inhabitants were not evil, in Lewis' view; they had been molded by an environment which twisted generosity into gossip and hunger for beauty into cheap sentimental prints. Small-towners lacked the security to afford luxuries, especially the luxury of diversity and change. Lewis showed how the robust optimism of the frontier

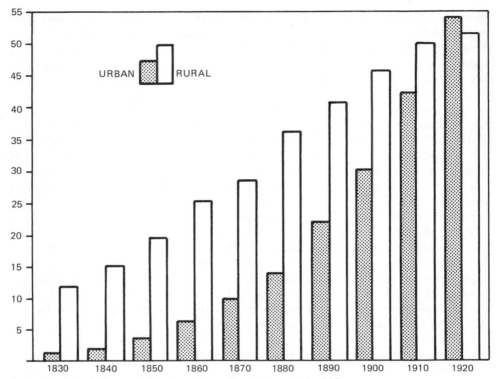

FIGURE 25-1.   *Urban and Rural Population in Millions, 1830–1920*

had stagnated, and fear of the future made time-honored respectabilities a haven.

One of the small town's oldest terrors was the city, by now so visibly swamping the country. National prohibition was one of the last thrusts the country could make against the urban menace. By the time of the passage of the 18th Amendment, most rural states were already dry, and dry counties dotted the wet states. Enforcement here did not pose much of a problem, because local opinion supported abstention from alcohol. But enforcing the national law was to be impossible. Gangsters flourished, and respect for all law weakened. Drinking bad liquor acquired the special tingle reserved for the forbidden, and many drinkers learned to be both guilty and coy about its use. The supply of liquor continued undiminished, but only a scattering of aristocrats could use it in a civilized manner.

The prohibitionists did not foresee the results of their noble experiment. One which shocked them the most was the increasing number of women using alcohol. Prohibitionists had always been allied with women suffragists, and the Prohibition Party had endorsed women's suffrage as early as the 1870's, believing all women to be natural prohibitionists. Their disappointment could not have been greater than that of the dedicated women who labored for decades for the right to vote. Suffragists had hoped that it would result in a massive change in American life, that women's votes would be cast for peace and reform. They did not realize that but few women felt their interests to differ from those of their husbands. The only appreciable result of the suffrage was the destruction of feminism for two generations. For some time feminists had decided to ignore other issues and concentrate their energies on getting a Constitutional Amendment passed which would guarantee women the right to vote. That accomplished, they had few immediate goals. When they discovered that postwar American women were more interested in assuming heretofore masculine privileges (alcohol, tobacco, comfortable clothing, gaiety) than in forcing men to live according to the ideals of Victorian womanhood, most ruefully retired from activism. One who did not retire was birth control advocate Margaret Sanger, who worked within this changed context. Some Victorian feminists had favored birth control in the form of continence, not for the sake of limiting reproduction so much as to free women from the imposition of sex. They got nowhere. Mrs. Sanger realized that while few modern women any longer regarded sex as a burden, large families had become economically and socially undesirable in many households. Her efforts to eliminate the laws which made dissemination of birth control information and devices a crime were not very successful, but she performed a real service, both in letting people know that limitation of conception was possible, and in lifting the smokescreen of prudery which had surrounded the subject.

The uninhibited playfulness, the relaxation of moral norms, which popularly characterize the "roaring" twenties accompanied modern man's sense of futility. In part this resulted from the new media (see mid-Chapter 23) which burgeoned at this time, but some of the liveliest participants in the Jazz Age ascribed it to the war. American reaction to World War I was a combination of fervent self-righteousness and optimistic exuberance: a mixture typical in the past and not to be repeated again. There is still something of Tom Sawyer in a people who try to make the world safe for democracy by calling sauerkraut "liberty cabbage." But the real war—the war of mud and disease and mounds of corpses blotted out by the anonymity of artillery and gas rather than by a cavalier's shining sword—blighted innocence. The old simple convictions could not survive such gangrene. The pain of loss and disillusion touched closest to those who had borne the physical brunt of collapse—the veterans—but it was also severe for anyone with high hopes and wide eyes—alert young people, many adventurous children of the wealthy, and especially the ambitious and well educated. So there were many who felt driven to abandon naive high hopes and golden ideals, and they tried to forget their dismay at the loss by devoting themselves to a desperate pursuit of sensation.

But all was not so easy: the merrymakers had been reared to honor purpose and accomplishment. Even if idealism seemed ludicrous and achievement unattainable, they felt guilty at living without either. Two responses were common. The first was to escape to Europe, where hedonism was more respectable. American bustle, the outward sign of American optimism, had always seemed faintly ridiculous on the Continent anyway, and there were plenty of other exiles to cavort with. More importantly, the other Americans in Europe were presumably escaping from the same guilts, and their presence could therefore not reinforce anybody's self-hatred. Everyone was playing hooky together. But most of the revellers eventually went back to school, and often found that they had missed too many lessons. Europe was gay, but finally arid. To the expatriates, too many of the instinctively known features which make a society rich and rounded seemed remote or missing. Even the novels which came out of the exiled experience were about, not Europe, but the group of expatriates which shuttled between the Ritz Bar and the Riviera. Only Hemingway was able to write meaningfully about an actually foreign culture, but to do so he had to live in Spain long enough to make its symbols his own, and that meant not playing quite the same glamorous game. The returned exile had a double problem: the guilts that drove him away in the first place, and a new sense of isolation from a land once familiar that had changed in his absence. It is not surprising that alcoholism was rampant, and suicide and madness common. The only solution lay in a relearning process. America had to be rediscovered, and guilt recognized and put aside.

The second common response of guilty consciences was to lampoon abandoned gods. This produced useful social comment and delightful wit, and it was probably much more healthy than running away. It is no accident that the *New Yorker,* which for decades was to be America's finest comic magazine, started in the twenties. We laugh at things that don't scare us; if unreasonable fear persists, laughter might help exorcise it.

The majority of Americans weren't invited to the party of the intellectuals. H. L. Mencken called them the booboisie, and they provided plenty of opportunities for mirth. While attempting to cling to the old and the known, they acquired new and sensational devices for doing so. Aimee Semple MacPherson, the Scopes trial, and the Ku Klux Klan were much better targets for wit than sober churches or staid WCTU meetings. But these phenomena were manifestations of serious problems. Doubt and a sense of futility were not the exclusive property of the intellectuals; the death of old dreams was apparent to anyone who dared look at corpses. Most people dared not, for no alternative foundation to sanity presented itself. Their only hope was to turn back the clock.

The amazing success of Aimee Semple MacPherson, evangelist and faith healer, is symptomatic. First, she worked in Los Angeles, the symbolic and actual end of the line. California is as far as you can go; in the twenties many went. If the pot of gold isn't under a palm tree, you have nowhere else to look. Second, she achieved an enormous following by means of the radio. Depersonalization was stripping religion of much of its meaning, while sensation became more varied and less pungent. Third, her preaching in the flesh has been described as a wholly sensuous experience. Theologic content was nil, completing the descent from Edwards through Finney and Moody. (Perhaps Billy Graham represents still a further decline, but I doubt it.) The rich decor of Angelus Temple, and the flamboyant presence of the preacher counted for everything. As long as she mouthed soothing syrup which could be taken for old time religion she was satisfying both nostalgic hunger and the thirst for thrills.

The attitudes of the people of Tennessee which led them to prosecute John Thomas Scopes for teaching evolution were more consciously a clinging to old ways. When all the other established patterns of belief seemed to be crumbling, the dicta of religion must be held to the more rigidly. Furthermore, the heresy which most people associated with Darwin—that man was descended from the apes—was especially terrifying, as it erased a sense of superiority precious to people who doubt their own adequacy in a changing world. Actually, of course, neither Darwin nor Scopes (who believed that "evolution is easily reconciled with the Bible") mentioned the question of the origin of the human species at all. Most of the people of Tennessee—and of the rest of the South, and of the rural Midwest—were fundamentalists. They believed that the Bible was literally true. Most of them who had heard of evolution disbelieved it. But enacting and enforcing a law to prevent its teaching made them a laughing stock. The American Civil Liberties Union believed the law an outrage; they volunteered to finance the defense in a test case. Scopes, a biology teacher in Dayton, Tennessee, agreed to be prosecuted; the local merchants foresaw a great opportunity for civic boosterism. When Clarence Darrow, the agnostic antichrist to rural America, agreed to speak for the defense, and William Jennings Bryan, the defender of the faith, came into the case for the prosecution, the stage was set for Armageddon. Newspapers throughout the nation gave the Scopes trial front page coverage, usually only to reinforce the image of the South as a region populated by superstitious yokels. The trial climaxed when Bryan took the stand as an expert on the Bible, and Darrow hopelessly tangled him into a web of his own illogic. Scopes was convicted, (his conviction was later overturned on a technicality) the town of Dayton had its week of hoopla, fundamentalists felt vindicated by Bryan's oratory, and the rest of the country laughed.

The fears which lead people to barricade themselves against knowledge are more pitiable than amusing. During this period the same trepidations led to a more dangerous manifestation than anti-evolutionary efforts. The Ku Klux Klan, which for several years was the real power in several cities and states, arose out of terror and resentment (Document 25-3). We think of the Klan as an anti-black organization, but during the period of its greatest power anti-Catholicism was its most important tenet, with hatred of immigrants a strong subcurrent. Klansmen also attempted to enforce chastity and sobriety, and vocally supported certain Protestant churches. The nature of prejudice is worth some analysis in an attempt to explain the attractiveness of these beliefs: We hate and fear that which we find significantly different; if our own lives are frustrated and unsatisfactory for reasons which we cannot fathom, and our destiny seems to be out of our own control, then hatred of some other group provides a scapegoat. If we can then band together with others who feel the same way, and discharge our anxiety and hatred in a group, our sense of inadequacy will be lessened. Of course this behavior has no effect on the causes of our dissatisfaction, and is inevitably cruel to the persecuted group, but it may make us feel better if it temporarily releases significant frustrations.

The Klan had other attractions. Torchlight parades, burning crosses, masks, and secret rituals were all very exciting. For most of its members, that was excitement enough; they were never involved in actual violence. But for a few they were just an appetizer. Klansmen unquestionably perpetrated lynchings, burnings, and beatings. This violence, more than its unsavory racist and xenophobic beliefs (shared by a great many non-members), brought the Klan into disrepute. But the real outcry came when the Invisible Empire attempted to control politics. In several states and cities they succeeded. Those officials who were not themselves Klan members had to toe the Klan line to keep their posts. This brought the wrath of a batch of ejected politicians down upon the organization, and also exposed its flimsiness. For, possessing power, the Klan had no idea how to use it. Klan leaders soon began wrangling. Combined with financial tangles and scandals about the private morality of many of its luminaries, this infighting was enough to finish the Klan off. Its members drifted away, and by 1928 the organization no longer had any power.

The trial and execution of Nicola Sacco and Bartolomeo Vanzetti crystallized both the prejudices which spawned the Ku Klux Klan and the increasingly vocal opposition to them. The defendants were Italians, Catholics, and above all anarchists. They were convicted of murder in 1921, on faulty procedures. The defendants were convinced that they were being persecuted because they were Italian and radical. Vanzetti wrote to the governor of Massachusetts in 1927, "People don't seem to understand that Italians are unpopular anyway, especially if they are poor and laboring people. Their habits are not the habits of ordinary Americans, and they are suspected. They don't get the same chance before an American jury that an American would get. The jury cannot help being prejudiced against them, and then if on top of that the Italians turn out to be radicals, they have no show at all." By the time of the execution a great many Americans, and practically all the vocal intellectuals, agreed with Vanzetti, and exerted themselves to prevent the death of innocent men (Figure 26-3). They circulated petitions, marched in protest, took out newspaper ads. But the very publicity further circulated the defendants' radical tenets and solidified hatred of them as anarchisfs while it steadily eroded belief in their guilt in the crime of murder. Thus one group said that Sacco and Vanzetti must be freed, because they had been unjustly convicted of crimes they did not commit, and the rest of the people felt that they must be executed, since to release them would be to condone sins which were unfortunately not illegal.

In the year that Sacco and Vanzetti were executed, Marcus Garvey, leader of the first black movement with widespread lower class support, was deported. Unlike the Urban League and the NAACP, which strived for justice and equality within the American context, and catered almost exclusively to the middle classes of both races, Garvey's Universal Negro Improvement Association stressed racial pride, total segregation, and encouraged a return to Africa. At its peak its membership lay between 100,000 and 200,000, but as Garvey said, "No one will ever know accurately the membership of the Universal Negro Improvement Association, because every second Negro you meet, if not an actual member, is one in spirit." By the twenties American blacks had tried several roads toward the American dream. In the Deep South the subjugation of their working class members was complete. Lynchings declined drastically, but perhaps only because the population they were designed to impress had become sufficiently cowed. W. J. Cash suggests that the entry of the factory system into the South helped to discourage lynchings. Factory owners needed an orderly labor force according to Cash: "For that reason above all, therefore, the masters everywhere are against all excitements and disorders—against whatever operates to fix the attention and emotions of the workman powerfully enough to hinder him from falling swiftly into his robot groove when the whistle blows." In exchange, the factory workers got a "white only" guarantee for their jobs. Many blacks migrated north. There they found less legal segregation of public facilities, and frequently higher paying jobs. But they were crowded into stinking ghettos which made segregation a stronger reality, if not a legality, than in the South, and where their larger pay envelopes were offset by higher costs. Attempts to move out of their inadequate quarters or to use "unsegregated" facilities such as public swimming pools frequently brought on race riots. During World War I some 400,000 black men had joined the army, and some of them had gone overseas, but their patriotism (in this war as in all others before or since) brought no changes in their degraded position in the United States.

Clearly the white man's homilies didn't work for blacks. (They often didn't work for whites either, but this was not quite so obvious.) Moreover, as Garvey was the first leader to realize, it was humiliating for blacks to attempt to shape themselves upon white models, even if their efforts had met with success. They must find pride in being what they were—black. This entailed despising and avoiding everything white. As later groups have discovered

The Cleveland Museum of Art, Hinman B. Hurlbut Collection

FIGURE 25-2. *George Bellows,* Stag at Sharkey's

Stag at Sharkey's is an oil painting by George Bellows, vintage 1907. Bellows was twenty-seven years old, a migrant from Ohio to New York, where he studied with a well-known artist. Sharkey's gym was located across the street, and the young painter went there frequently, but he did not just quiescently loiter. The diagonal slashes across this canvas suggest that his imagination had been touched to the quick.

Nothing is gained by categorizing this type of painting as "realistic." A boxer who tried to fight from either of the stances portrayed here might get pasted hard and often. What is conveyed is in the first place an abstract design. It might be fun to trace (with a ruler if necessary) a straight line to show the directional thrust of each element in the picture. Such an exercise might help analyze the architectonics of the painting, but it omits a good deal. Thomas Eakins ("Ways to Study History XIX") was the palpable American ancestor of Bellows, and Eakins said that nature has no lines, only forms and colors.

which have adopted this attitude, such as the Black Muslims and the Black Panthers, it can lead to a greatly increased sense of dignity and honor. It also creates terror and insecurity among white people. Middle-class integrationist associations can be tolerated, even encouraged, but the economic and psychic well-being of many whites (especially those most anxious about their status) is bolstered by the presence of the black man as cheap labor and as a figure of scorn, and any group which says black people need be neither must be squashed. So Garvey was convicted of fraudulent use of the mails, deported (he was a West Indian), and the UNIA crumbled. It left small apparent effect, except perhaps the remnants of a changed consciousness which were to burst forth again in the 1960's.

Sacco and Vanzetti fired up American intellectuals; Garveyism they ignored. By the end of the decade all had abandoned the Jazz Age ebullience which had flourished in the post-war era. Disillusionment with the plasticity of sensationalism accompanied disillusion with idealism. Scott Fitzgerald's *The Great Gatsby* provides an example. His hero, Gatsby, has made a lot of money, and is leading a fabulous life in one of the flossy towns on Long Island, an abode of the very rich who have nothing to do and want to do it with éclat. Their life is paradise under the money-god, the acme of the American dream. Gatsby comes in search of Daisy, a girl whom he had loved when penniless and who married a stupid (but rich) young sportsman instead. She remembers Gatsby with affection, and his present exotic life as a party-giver to the famous titillates her, so his prospects look ripe. But in a stupid, careless automobile accident, she kills her husband's married mistress, and the shiny surface of all their lives cracks to expose the unsavory truth. Daisy and her husband have always been protected by money, and always will be. Neither good nor evil will ever touch them; they are impervious to responsibility or honest feeling. For them life is a party in a house with lots of servants to sweep up the champagne glasses you drop. Gatsby is more human, but he is a fraud. To be a success he had to invent his glamorous past, and even his name. Fitzgerald's novel ends on a note of deep disillusion: Perhaps the mechanistic technology that America has created necessitated mechanistic emotions which kill the soul; perhaps nature is better than people. The narrator surveys Gatsby's house, now deserted, and sees the land as it once had been, before civilization

---

A connection between these two artists is their mutual fascination with spectator sports. For their times and places, this range of subjects was up-to-date for an artist; by venturing into it, he faced the challenge of depicting experiences that were new in the United States with the growth of cities. Men had been brawling in the streets since the beginning of the nation, but sizeable audiences had not paid to watch them do it.

The two generations that span Eakins and Bellows establish another typical stance in American art. On this side of the Atlantic, the human figure had traditionally been fixed in repose, as it were; now an effort was made to combine the static design of the composition with the dynamics of the actors. No chauvinism is intended here; obviously Michelangelo and Rubens had coped with this problem; but now a new and more determined effort to tackle it was being made in America.

FIGURE 25-3. *Grant Wood,* American Gothic   Courtesy of the Art Institute of Chicago

erupted upon it, and visualizes an unspoiled beauty, a "fresh, green breast of the new world" which inspires his awe. The theme of nostalgia for something hopeful but irretrievably broken is restated here, as well as a hint that nature and human warmth will always be more important than artificial contrivances

Fear of technology as a stultifier is also present in the poetry of Hart Crane. His work shows how people are only able to have "experiences" while perceiving pieces of reality and interrelating them. The human mind takes in different kinds of perceptions—sight, smell, taste, sound, touch—at the same time; only by blending these disparate bits of fact does reality emerge, and reality is constantly changing. Mechanical instruments, such as the camera and the phonograph, not only categorize sensations but tend to freeze them in time. This can provide a useful record of events, and can be the medium of great art when a captured instant in time tells a truth which might be lost in motion, but it can also deaden the mind. After becoming habituated to receiving sensations neatly broken down and marshalled in rank, it can be difficult (as much of Crane's poetry suggests) to experience the natural rhythms of life behind a reality which has not been regimented. Moreover, technological aids make it easy to amplify visual and aural images to the point where they become so much noise. Then to experience anything you have to tune out most of the signals being beamed at you, and to repose in silence becomes almost impossible. Rest and peace, ever more desirable, become ever more unattainable. Crane wrote about the power of technology in New York city; he ended his career in suicide.

For many writers nature offered an escape from pointless urban bustle; rebirth seemed possible there. *Barren Ground,* Ellen Glasgow's account of life on a worn-out farm in Virginia, tells of death and of life. Dorinda Oakley's

---

American Gothic (1930) by Grant Wood is as widely known as any American painting of this century. Each word in the title deserves attention. The Gothic contour of the upper window suggests the Middle Ages, and Wood consciously had chosen as his guides the Flemish primitives of the fifteenth century; he wanted to be the Memling (d. 1495) of the Middle West. The curve of the window is accentuated by the man's eyebrows, the woman's hairline. These two people are blatantly American. The pitchfork symbolizes their rural orientation. Worn but scrupulously clean coveralls, meticulous braid on a jumper, a solid unsmiling stoicism—they all typified the Americans who conquered the prairies. Objects in this painting have a chiselled quality, as they do when you escape from urban smog and see the world etched by sunlight.

Wood was born to a poor farming family in Iowa in 1892. He sank so low that he lived for two years with his mother and sister in a 10′ × 16′ shanty in Cedar Rapids. He climbed back to a position of teaching art at the University of Iowa. He insisted that an artist should stick to the realities that he knew best, in this attitude resembling his predecessors Bingham and Homer (Figures 13-6 and 19-4). But shortly before he died of cancer in 1942, he told Thomas Hart Benton (Figure 27-2) "that when he got well he was going to change his name, go where nobody knew him, and start all over again with a new style of painting."

American Gothic with its pitchfork, prim, upright house, its aura of rectitude, might haunt some viewers now with the trilogy that the Third Reich prescribed for German women: *kinder, küche, kirche* ("kids, kitchen, church," or "family, home, and church").

family had inherited a thousand isolated worthless acres, but their ceaseless labor there cannot lift them out of poverty. Work and religion are the only alternatives to insanity. Dorinda herself is young and blooming, eager for life, but soon the betrayal of the characterless young man she loves destroys her capacity for emotional life, and she becomes, inwardly, as barren as the tired tobacco fields. Yet upon the death of her father she realizes that she need not go on in the traditional way, cultivating a bit of stunted tobacco, letting the piney woods take over a few more acres every year; the land is still good for dairying. She succeeds; for her the barren ground of the novel's title brings forth life in a new way. Her own rebirth is more hesitant and less complete. Although her capacity for passion is, like healthy tobacco, no longer possible, she regains affection and tenderness. Something is irretrievably lost, but the person, like the land, will recover what it can.

This view of nature as the refuge and the healer is superficially reminiscent of the Transcendentalists (Chapter 14), but it avoided most of their excesses. Nature was not necessarily lovely: often it was harsh and ugly. Its quiet and its logic were its important features. Nature provided an escape from hurry and from noise, where it was possible to sort out and discard trivialities. It reaffirmed life, and reduced man to a healthy humility in the face of his own weakness when unprotected by his contrivances.

During World War I, many American soldiers formed the vanguard for a wave of disillusionment that veered sharply away from the values held by hometown civilians in the United States. After the Armistice this rift, you might almost call it a chasm in society, deepened and broadened further. Only the trauma of the Great Depression could serve to institute new bridges between American dreams and disillusionment, and between the common man and the intellectual (Chapter 27). The modern intellectual now saw himself as alienated from his society because the culture itself was fragmented and contradictory. Revolt took many shapes. Veblen wrote ironically about the illusions that spurred his countrymen, about conspicuous consumption and emulation in conflict with the instinct of workmanship. John Dewey singled out the separation of schools from work. A dozen fine writers depicted the shallowness and flummery of their neighbors' ambitions. Encroachments by foreigners and Catholics and Jews and blacks stimulated the idiocies of the Ku Klux Klan. Xenophobia was symbolized by the Sacco-Vanzetti trial. Vast areas of religious commitment were contaminated and vulgarized, from the enthusiastical circuses of Aimee Semple MacPherson and Billy Sunday to the succotash of law and theology that constituted the Scopes trial. Occasionally the victims would try to strike back. Perhaps the most momentous of these counter-cultures would seem, in retrospect, to be the Universal Negro Improvement Association, but it had little impact in its brief life.

SOME NOTABLE EVENTS

1899   Thorstein Veblen, *The Theory of the Leisure Class.*
1900   Theodore Dreiser, *Sister Carrie.*
1905   Edith Wharton, *The House of Mirth.*
1914   Robert Frost, *North of Boston.*
1917   T. S. Eliot, "The Love-song of J. Alfred Prufrock."
1918   Willa Cather, *My Ántonia.*
1920   Volstead Act makes prohibition a reality.
       Station KDKA, Pittsburgh, begins regular radio broadcasts.
       Sinclair Lewis, *Main Street.*
       Majority of Americans are urban dwellers.
1921   Sacco-Vanzetti trial.
1922   T. S. Eliot, *The Wasteland.*
       Sinclair Lewis, *Babbitt.*
1923   Aimee Semple MacPherson founds Angelus Temple in Los Angeles.
1925   Scott Fitzgerald, *The Great Gatsby.*
       Ellen Glasgow, *Barren Ground.*
       Tennessee v. *John Thomas Scopes.*
1927   Deportation of Marcus Garvey.
       Sacco and Vanzetti executed.
1929   Hart Crane, *The Bridge.*

Ways to Study History XXV

Be yourself. Obviously this suggestion follows from "Ways to Study History XX" and others. But of all the maxims that lead into these essays on methodology, this one is probably the most difficult to follow. To be human is to have experiences and reactions that—thank the Lord—you do not want to wear on your sleeve. However, the great books reveal an astounding amount about their authors. One of the greatest recent writers explained the matter thus: ". . . the quality that is necessary for the production of the art of literature is simply that of a personality of wide appeal. . . . The quality of literature, in short, is the quality of humanity. It is the quality that communicates, between man and man, the secret of human hearts and the story of our vicissitudes."

In this spirit, a book that ennobles the study of American history is W. E. B. DuBois, *The Souls of Black Folk* (1903). This brief exposition conveys more insight into the hidden life of the United States in the late nineteenth century than a library filled with monographs. Within its few pages are statistics, and autobiography, and biography, and poetry, many songs, sociology, psychology. Yet it adheres; it is a whole. It is a book that no human being could possibly have written, but one did.

DuBois lived for nearly a century. Born black in a small town in western Massachusetts soon after abolition (1868), he survived to die in an independent black state (Ghana) in 1963. In spite of the handicaps imposed because of his color, he did graduate work in Germany and at Harvard; the first volume in the Harvard Historical Monographs is his *The Suppression of the African Slave Trade* (1896). In addition to writing numerous other books, he taught in universities, worked as a magazine editor, helped to organize several groups aimed at overturning the racist system both in the United States and abroad. Nothing patronizing is meant in asserting that he was one of the dozen or so greatest Americans of this century.

Document 25-1

A balanced view of Andrew Carnegie is hard to achieve: his scope was enormous, and both his virtues and his vices bedazzle. Our concern here is limited to his efforts to help the common man to educate himself. In 1889 he was alarmed by demands for social reform, so he published a magazine article entitled "Wealth." In sum it might be labelled as paternalistic feudalism. But he did act upon the precepts published below; in the twenty years preceding his death in 1919, he gave $350 million to promote libraries, formal education, science, and world peace. Many boys remember the local Carnegie Library as a clean, well-lighted place, with books—and warm during cold winters for those too poor to buy fuel.

There remains, then, only one mode of using great fortunes; but in this we have the true antidote for the temporary unequal distribution of wealth, the reconciliation of the rich and the poor—a reign of harmony—another ideal, differing, indeed, from that of the Communist in requiring only the further evolution of existing conditions, not the total overthrow of our civilization. It is founded upon the present most intense individualism, and the race is prepared to put it in practice by degrees whenever it pleases. Under its sway we shall have an ideal state, in which the surplus wealth of the few will become, in the best sense, the property of the many, because administered for the common good, and this wealth, passing through the hands of the few, can be a much more potent force for the elevation of our race than if it had been distributed in small sums to the people themselves. Even the poorest can be made to see this, and to agree that great sums gathered by some of their fellow-citizens and spent for public purposes, from which the masses reap the principal benefit, are more valuable to them than if scattered among them through the course of many years in trifling amounts. . . .

Document 25-2

Charles Sanders Peirce in 1900 published this essay, "The Century's Great Men of Science." Beginning with the question, "How shall we determine that men are great?", he proceeded to distinguish the scientific attitude of his times from that of the preceding century.

The glory of the nineteenth century has been its science, and its scientific great men are those whom I mean to consider here. Their distinctive characteristic throughout the century, and more and more so in each succeeding generation, has been devotion to the pursuit of truth for truth's sake. In this century we have not heard a Franklin asking, "What signifies a philosophy which does not apply itself to some use?"—a remark that could be paralelled by utterances of Laplace, of Rumford, of Buffon, and of many other well-qualified spokesman of eighteenth-century science. It was in the early dawn of the nineteenth that Gauss (or was it Dirichlet?) gave as the reason of his passion for the Theory of Numbers that "it is a pure virgin that never has been and never can be prostituted to any practical application whatsoever." It was my inestimable privilege to have felt as a boy the warmth of the steadily burning enthusiasm of the scientific generation of Darwin, most of the leaders of which at home I knew intimately, and some very well in almost every country of Europe. . . .

To this self-effacement before the grandeur of reason and truth is traceable the greatness of nineteenth-century science, most obviously in mathematics. . . . I must not be led away from my point, to expatiate upon the reposefulness of the new mathematics, upon how it relieves us of that tiresome imp, man, and from the most importunate and unsatisfactory of the race, one's self. Suffice it to say that it is so reasonable, so simple, so easy to read, when the right view has once been attained, that the student may easily forget what arduous labors were expended in constructing the first convenient pathway to that lofty summit, that mastery over intricacies, far beyond that of the eighteenth-century master. . . .

Document 25-3

This brief account of the Ku Klux Klan's purposes, written by Hiram Wesley Evans, the Imperial Wizard, in 1926, relates some of the doubts and fears which led to its foundation. Nostalgia for a heroic past is expressed here, along with the hope that the past could somehow be revitalized. Bigotry arises out of feelings of inferiority, and in this case is strengthened by worship of the pioneering, "old-stock" ancestor. Rigid morality must be clung to, since the shifting ground of ethical ambiguity can only be comfortable to those who find security within themselves.

There is no need to recount the virtues of the American pioneers; but it is too often forgotten that in the pioneer period a selective process of intense rigor went on. From the first only hardy, adventurous and strong men and women dared the pioneer dangers; from among these all but the best died swiftly, so that the new Nordic blend which became the American race was bred up to a point probably the highest in history. This remarkable race character, along with the new-won continent and the new-created nation, made the inheritance of the old-stock Americans the richest ever given to a generation of men.

In spite of it, however, these Nordic Americans for the last generation have found themselves increasingly uncomfortable, and finally deeply distressed. There appeared first confusion in thought and opinion, a groping and hesitancy about national affairs and private life alike, in sharp contrast to the clear, straightforward purposes of our earlier years. There was futility in religion, too, which was in many ways even more distressing. Presently we began to find that we were dealing with strange ideas; policies that always sounded well, but somehow always made us still more uncomfortable.

Finally came the moral breakdown that has been going on for two decades. One by one all our traditional moral standards went by the boards, or were so disregarded that they ceased to be binding. The sacredness of our Sabbath, of our homes, of chastity, and finally even of our right to teach our own children in our own schools fundamental facts and truths were torn away from us. Those who maintained the old standards did so only in the face of constant ridicule.

Document 25-4

Robert Frost (1874–1963) was unquestionably one of the half-dozen greatest American poets of this century. Although he lived the first ten years of his life in San Francisco, his image is inseparable from New England, for reasons that this poem should demonstrate. "After Apple-Picking" was contained in Frost's second book, *North of Boston* (1914) when the author was already 40 years old. He never earned a college degree, and, while he taught for decades in universities, he will always seem remote from academia. He was also apart from modern poetry in that his works do not need the abundance of literary allusions that T. S. Eliot and Wallace Stevens used. Frost won the Pulitzer Prize for American Poetry four times—never without deserving it.

My long two-pointed ladder's sticking through a tree
Toward heaven still,
And there's a barrel that I didn't fill
Beside it, and there may be two or three
Apples I didn't pick upon some bough.
But I am done with apple-picking now.
Essence of winter sleep is on the night,
The scent of apples: I am drowsing off.
I cannot rub the strangeness from my sight
I got from looking through a pane of glass
I skimmed this morning from the drinking trough
And held against the world of hoary grass.
It melted, and I let it fall and break.
But I was well
Upon my way to sleep before it fell,
And I could tell
What form my dreaming was about to take.
Magnified apples appear and disappear,
Stem end and blossom end,
And every fleck of russet showing clear,
My instep arch not only keeps the ache,
It keeps the pressure of a ladder-round.
I feel the ladder sway as the boughs bend.
And I keep hearing from the cellar bin
The rumbling sound
Of load on load of apples coming in.
For I have had too much
Of apple-picking: I am overtired
Of the great harvest I myself desired.
There were ten thousand thousand fruit to touch,
Cherish in hand, lift down, and not let fall.

For all
That struck the earth,
No matter if not bruised or spiked with stubble,
Went surely to the cider-apple heap
As of no worth.
One can see what will trouble
This sleep of mine, whatever sleep it is.
Were he not gone,
The woodchuck could say whether it's like his
Long sleep, as I describe its coming on,
Or just some human sleep.

PART VI

Living with the Permanent Revolution: *1929–*

The Great Depression and Its Politics

President Hoover, like Martin Van Buren a century earlier, can be regarded as a victim of circumstances. Each man had barely entered the White House when a depression hit the economy, and each bore the blade of resentment. But both deserved it, for in their earlier offices they had sanctioned federal policies that helped to bring on and aggravate the financial crises. Van Buren did not argue against the abolition of the Second Bank of the United States, or the application of the Specie Circular. Nor did Hoover as secretary of commerce oppose the Fordney-McCumber protectionist tariff measure or the fiscal program of Secretary of the Treasury Andrew W. Mellon. One of the half dozen or so wealthiest men in the nation, Mellon's fortune stemmed from one of the true "monopolies"; the Aluminum Corporation of America (Alcoa) was the sole seller of its product. He was also a pioneer owner of the Spindletop well and other Southwestern oil properties.* At the treasury, his policy was to

*One year soon somebody will publish a brilliant book about the Mellon family. Of all the large cities in the United States since World War II, none other was dominated by one man as Richard Mellon held sway in Pittsburgh. Wilmington, Delaware was DuPont, but it was family, not individual.

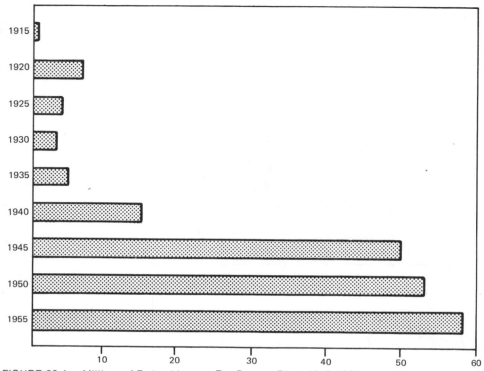

FIGURE 26-1. *Millions of Federal Income Tax Returns Filed, 1915–1955*

run a steady budgetary surplus and pay off the federal debt. At the same time he wanted to cut taxes, especially on fat cats like himself. Due to the rising national income he was able to combine these aims. Forced to compromise in 1924, Mellon came back to win with the Revenue Act of 1926, which cut the maximum surtax on high incomes from 40 to 20 per cent, wiped out the gift tax, cut the estate tax in half. If the major cause of the depression was a maldistribution of income (I think it was), this tax policy that had Hoover's tacit consent must bear a lot of blame.

Hoover's interpretation of the depression did not agree with mine. He had three theses. For months he contended that it did not exist; merely a flurry on the stock market. In his speech accepting the nomination Hoover had said, "We in America today are nearer to the final triumph over poverty than ever before in the history of any land." A campaign slogan had proclaimed, "A chicken in every pot and two cars in every garage." If Hoover was blind, probably he was not deaf; he might have been hearing the pundits of the country. From a Harvard worthy:

The great war produced a number of political revolutions in Europe. It has not yet produced an economic revolution. The only economic revolution now under way is going on in the United States. It is a revolution that is to wipe out the distinction between laborers and capitalists by making laborers their own capitalists and by compelling most capitalists to become laborers of one kind or another, because not many of them will be able to live on the returns from capital. This is something new in the history of the world.

Words of wisdom indeed. Financial analyst Roger Babson (one of the few who sobered up before the crash came) argued for Hoover's election on the grounds that it would assure the prolongation of prosperity. The president of a renowned research organization, the National Industrial Conference Board, proclaimed: "There is no reason why there should be any more panics." Then came the panic.

When it was no longer possible to blink away the hard times, Hoover took two new gambits. He began to admit that the times were troubled, but announced that they would soon cease to be so: "Prosperity is just around the corner." Somehow the corner kept getting farther away. Another Hoover device, baldly chauvinistic, was to proclaim that the American economy had no difficulties of its own. No domestic problem existed; the collapse was strictly an import from the corrupt and decadent foreigners, particularly in Europe. Admittedly, the nationalistic programs of alien nations did not make the American situation easier. However, for the United States as for its president, most dislocations were self-made. The generalization will have to come up in regard to the New Deal, but it is so crucial that it will bear stating more than once. Although Americans can find many episodes in their history to inspire pride, quite a few others should awaken shame. One of the worst episodes is the twelve years from 1929 to 1941. When a majority of the population was confronted with a variety of crises, the national intelligence disappeared in a miasma of rhetoric. An honorable handful spoke for rational and humane actions, but men in power chose not to hear them.

A proper preliminary to further consideration of the economic policies of the Hoover administration is a glance at the international and domestic context. Many nations that relied chiefly on exports of agricultural products or minerals to maintain their foreign balance of payments were confronted now by falling prices on the world market and began to depreciate their currencies. This expedient made the import duties of other countries inadequate, so they in turn resorted to quotas on imports, which by 1933 were systematized by most of the important trading nations plus the British Commonwealth. Next came systematic exchange control—a process whereby the movement of the government's currency into or especially out of the country is impeded or blocked. In the first years of the Great Depression, Great Britain used these devices more than any other nation. She had been subsidizing exports of certain commodities since World War I and now these arrangements were

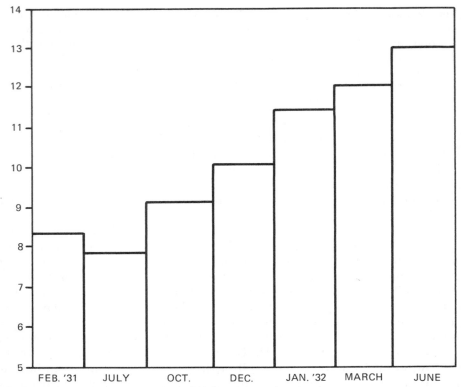

FIGURE 26-2. *Unemployment, 1931–1932 (in millions of workers)*

extended. In addition, a conference at Ottawa, Canada, in 1932 imposed Imperial Preference, which discriminated against goods from without the British sphere. True, these tidal waves from overseas were bad. Maybe the lack of pressure at home was worse. The executive committee of the American Federation of Labor announced in 1931: "Realization of the pernicious effects of wage reductions has prevented a widespread liquidation of wages as we had in the depression of 1921. Growing adherence to the high-wage principle, strengthened by the President's stand against wage cuts, has brought effective support from the leading industrialists of the country." More guff. By the autumn of 1931, when these pronunciamentoes came from the chief labor body, the joke had ended.

Even the president, somewhat to the left of the labor leaders, had recognized a year earlier that the depression was rather serious. He had therefore in October, 1930, appointed the President's Emergency Committee for Employment. One of the three members of this board, a renowned executive of an advertising agency, had expressly warned against use of the word "*un*employment." Two prior attempts had been made to get the Red

Cross to take action, especially in the Appalachian coal fields that had been stricken by drought as well as recession, but this charitable institution refused because depression was "not an Act of God" and thus outside its boundaries. (Who ever put God under their jurisdiction?) Then national action seemed essential, but Hoover hated the idea of laying the problem before Congress. The ultimate funding of the federal relief agency was $157,000, to last for nearly a year. Within that time the farce was ended, the committee disbanded. In the words of a Philadelphia social worker, "As a result of the policy of drift . . . our government will be compelled, by the logic of inescapably cruel events ahead of us, to step into the situation and bring relief on a large scale. . . . Private philanthropy . . . is virtually bankrupt in the face of great disaster." The end of an era seemed in sight.

Until the fall of 1931, it was widely believed that the bad times were similar to periods in the past; no need to get in a flap about the situation. That view became preposterous. Estimates of unemployment varied among contemporaries, and they will therefore continue to vary among historians. The graph in Figure 26-2 shows some that seem reliable, but to most readers these figures will seem ludicrously abstract. An effort should be made to break them down and put them into context. In January, 1932—the height of the season—President Sidney Hillman of the Amalgamated Clothing Workers said that only 10 per cent of his members in New York City had jobs. For the Ford Motor Company, employment went from 128,142 in March, 1929, to 37,000 in August, 1931.

The level of abstraction can be brought to a more concrete level. One of the great athletes of my lifetime has been Stan Musial, who came from a steel town, Donora, in Pennsylvania. With a population in March, 1932, of 13,900, it had 277 persons with jobs. His need to escape was severe. But there were worse spots. In Williamson County, Illinois, in the town of Coello, two people had remunerative employment in a population of 1,350. Now we can bring the level of abstraction down to an even sharper focus. At school in the coal fields, a teacher asked a little girl if she was ill. The pupil replied that she was just hungry. The teacher suggested that she go home and eat. The girl said, "It won't do any good . . . because this is sister's day to eat." Do not permit yourself to believe that incidents like this one are chosen at random; millions of people could tell comparable stories.

The point might be reinforced by anecdotes that are doubtless apocryphal and that admittedly are chosen at random. Here are two. Hoover asks Mellon: "Will you lend me a nickel? I want to phone a friend." Mellon answers: "Here are two nickels. Phone all your friends." The other concerns a man who was considered the greatest baseball player of them all, Babe Ruth, who was engaged in his annual holdout for a better contract. In 1932, he wanted $80,000. After training season had been in action for weeks, it became apparent that none of the lesser executives on the New York Yankees could bring Ruth to terms. Negotiations relapsed onto the desk of the brewery head

Ben Shahn. *Scotts Run, West Virginia.*
Tempera on cardboard. 22¼ × 27⅞.
Collection Whitney Museum of American
Art

FIGURE 26-3. *Ben Shahn,* Scotts Run, West Virginia

Ben Shahn had not turned 35 when he burst into the consciousness of the art world in 1932 by exhibiting more than twenty paintings about the Sacco-Vanzetti case (see mid-Chapter 25 on the scapegoat impulse). The series certainly showed indignation. It pointed to stony-eyed judges, to self-righteous review boards. But the content was far from being one-dimensional; Shahn's outrage was toned down by irony and even by touches of humor. Simplicity was present not in the mood but in the technique of the artist. His surfaces tended to be flat; his forms reminiscent of some Picassos in the broad areas of a solid color. His pigment was gouache, a type of water color. In his addiction to this medium, Shahn was the chief exponent since Winslow Homer (Figure 19-4).

Shahn also resembles Homer in that both men served an early term of apprenticeship to a lithographer. But these similarities came in spite of a vast difference in backgrounds. Homer was who also owned the Yankees. When their conference began, Ruth kept repeating that he wanted $80,000. Finally the owner shouted, "Babe, that's more than the president gets." Ruth thought it over: "So what? I had a better season than Hoover."

Most poor folks had gags to jolly each other along; when your limbs are shriveled because you cannot get food, when they shake because you cannot buy fuel, laughter becomes the only essential that can be had. Men of power did not laugh; they began at last to admit that much of the furiously invented propaganda was mere ruse. For eighteen months they had frequently used a line that said—well, while employment has fallen a bit, hourly pay has held up. Then the president of U.S. Steel said: "We are living in a fool's paradise if we think that every steel manufacturer in the U.S. has maintained . . . the current rates of wages; it has not been done." His own company in September, 1931, cut wage rates by 10 per cent. General Electric, U.S. Rubber, major textile and coal firms fell into line. Ford put through a 25 per cent reduction. The railroads got the Brotherhoods to agree to a 10 per cent decrease. In New York and Chicago the building trades accepted 25 per cent less. Every stopper had gone down the drain. Nearly every strike was in protest against these pay cuts. Nearly every strike failed. But resentments made manifest can force adaptations. The United Mine Workers, long one of the routine members of the AFL, declared for "unemployment reserves" in January, 1932. The tradition of voluntarism—trade unions should have nothing to do with government—was caving in. The Federation of Labor in New York state came out for jobless insurance.

The governor, Franklin D. Roosevelt, was already on the scene; in August, 1931, he called it a "social duty" for the state to step in when "widespread economic conditions render large numbers of men and women incapable of supporting either themselves or their families because of circumstances beyond their control which make it impossible for them to find remunerative labor." That was good sense, but its impact did not compare to

---

old-stock Yankee, Shahn an immigrant from Lithuania. Homer painted the seas and the woods, Shahn focused on city playgrounds and the bombed-out debris of war. It had to be the latter man, not the former, who tried to depict the jetsam of the depression in this painting of *Scotts Run, West Virginia* (1937). In his last years Shahn turned from industrial landscape to subjects that must be called religious, whether Moses Maimonides or a wheat field.

The variety of Shahn's work is impressive, from jacket designs for paperbound books to monumental murals. But his ambition was steady: "I have always believed that the character of a society is largely shaped and unified by its great creative works, that a society is molded upon its epics, and that it imagines in terms of its created things—its cathedrals, its works of art, its musical treasures, its literary and philosophical works. One might say that a public may be so unified because the highly personal experience is held in common by the many individual members of the public."

his "forgotten man" speech the next spring (8 April, 1932) when he set forth several planks: (a) protect the purchasing power of farmers; (b) save home-owners from losing their houses by foreclosure of mortgages; (c) negotiate tariff reciprocity to win more foreign markets. Thus early FDR emerged as what he was. These three planks must be supplemented by many others at later points in the story. They do reveal, however, his orientation. It aimed at the solid citizen in danger of being treated badly. Folks should be able to keep what they toiled to earn: farmers their farms, homeowners their homes.

Roosevelt's flexibility appealed to "the boys"; meaning the city bosses, "the pols," the small gang in the smoke-filled room at the nominating convention. FDR's attachment to this crew may seem transparent—they had votes—but that is not enough to say. He liked them; they talked the language he knew best. Following a stunt that Lincoln's managers had used as a device to win the presidency, the Democratic boss of the Bronx had employed it to make Roosevelt governor. He held back every single return from his borough until all the rest of the state had reported. When everybody knew what FDR's deficit was, the Bronx made it up.

Roosevelt knew how to use such tactics—and how to beat them. As delegates arrived at the Democratic national convention in Chicago, June, 1932, local boss Edward J. Kelly thought he had everything set. Passes to enter the galleries of the hall were reserved for supporters of Alfred Smith. They rooted and hooted for their champeeeeeen. A brilliant diversion was begun by Senator Huey Long of Louisiana. Clearly a majority of the members were more or less committed to Roosevelt. But for a century, since its first convention in 1832, the party had required a two-thirds majority to make a nomination. Smith and others had substantial support. So why not try to abolish the two-thirds rule? The rule would remain for another four years, but the controversy stirred so much dust that Roosevelt sneaked through. Astute observers were not enchanted. The hallelujahs for FDR that came later were to come—later. One jaundiced commentator wrote: "I have seen many conventions, but this is one of the worst. It is both the stupidest and the most dishonest." An incisive columnist wrote that Roosevelt's main qualification was that he was a young man who wanted very much to be president.

The pundits got scotched. Radio was used as never before (Chapter 27). The Democratic candidate put together a staff of academics who were at best shrewd and at worst pompous; the mouthpiece turned out to have a flowing mellifluous voice. Even more important in beating the Republicans were the faults they could not conquer: their candidate, and their record. Hoover had too many principles to be a strong contender. In the race for the White House a man has to hang loose and easy. With his starched collars and his immobile jowls, Hoover couldn't swing it. The image he projected from a crystal-set radio was stern and demanding, but personality can be emphasized too much. His record killed his chances.

We can only sample the conditions and actions by which the Hoover administration earned apoplectic aversion. An advertisement for a market in Los Angeles in September, 1932, listed these bargains:

Tomatoes, 8 lbs.	5¢
Potatoes, 18 lbs.	25¢
Oranges, 3 dozen	10¢
Lettuce, per head	1¢
Spring lamb chops, lb.	12¹/₂¢
Hamburger, lb.	5¢

Any shopper today might be thrown into paroxysms of glee by sight of such a list, but imagine what it was doing to potato growers or ranchers in 1932. Another bloc of voters that merits attention is the veterans of World War I. Soon after the Armistice they began agitating for a "bonus." In 1924 they got the bill through Congress—with a hitch; payment was to be deferred for twenty years. With the depression, the vets in many localities started agitating for payment *now*. About mid-May, 1932, they started the spontaneous Veterans Bonus March on Washington. Uncoordinated when they left home, they quickly got organized after they reached the capital and set up several shanty colonies or moved into vacant federal office buildings. A showdown came on 28 July. After some relatively minor skirmishes involving the evacuation of government property, the president ordered the army to come over from Fort Myers, Virginia. The contingent was headed by General Douglas MacArthur, Major Dwight D. Eisenhower, and young George S. Patton. It included four troops of cavalry, four companies of infantry, a squadron of mounted machine guns, six tanks. Before they finished, they had evicted the Bonus Expeditionary Force from its encampments. They had killed two men and sprayed a lot of gas around; total casualties could not possibly be determined. The incident probably offended more voters than any other of Hoover's term in office.

The forcibly retired president would rather sourly comment twenty years later in his *Memoirs*: "As we expected, we were defeated in the election." Surely one of the understatements of the decade. The results in November, 1932, stood thus:

	Popular Votes	Per cent of Popular Vote	Electoral Vote
Democrats	22,809,638	57.41	472
Republicans	15,758,901	39.66	59
Others	1,163,181		

This time, as a wag had said of the Democratic nominee in 1924, Hoover lost by acclamation. He won only six states, all in New England or the Middle

States, all except Pennsylvania on the small side. Roosevelt carried more counties than any preceding presidential candidate: 2,721. Hoover had less than 15 per cent as many. But in regard to popular votes, FDR did not set other records in 1932: Harding had shown better in 1920, and Roosevelt, Lyndon Johnson, and Nixon would set superior marks later. Two addenda to these statistics should be noted. The Socialists again neared the million mark. The Prohibitionists still had a dwindling following. The Communists, who would play a strategic role in the next years, could gather barely 100,000 votes. Second, Roosevelt came to the White House with huge majorities in both houses of Congress: nearly 3 to 1 in the Representatives, nearly 2 to 1 in the Senate.

When Roosevelt became president in March, 1933, his massive party support in Congress would have followed him nearly anywhere he wanted to go. Some of his measures would soon meet strong roadblocks by the federal courts, and it would take time to tear down those barricades. But initially his problem was not that he was obstructed by the legislature; he even got a helping hand from several Republicans. His quandary was that he had no ideas and few commitments. Therefore he seldom knew which direction to take. Much has been made of the Brain Trust that he had gathered around him during the campaign and interregnum. In fact, they had little power (academics usually tend to overestimate the influence they can have as wheelers and dealers in Washington.) Roosevelt very much wanted to be re-elected in 1936. As he saw matters, the route to that goal did not lie with a few professors; it lay with the old machines in the South and in urban centers. He could and did ditch Raymond Moley of Columbia. He would not dream of junking Frank Hague of Jersey City or Ed Flynn of the Bronx or Senator Bankhead of Alabama or Little Joe Robinson of Arkansas or Ed Crump in Memphis. It was Roosevelt who picked John Nance Garner of Texas to be vice president. When the head of the CIO, John L. Lewis, memorialized Garner as "a whiskey-drinking, cigar-smoking, poker-playing, evil old man," he was not wrong. But to FDR, Garner could help to sweep the South, and he was not wrong either.

The celebrated Hundred Days that launched the Roosevelt regime were at best a mixed bag. Look at the first three pieces of "emergency" legislation. A major contention of this book is that breakdown of the banking system is indeed an emergency in a modern society (Document 26-1). The most powerful member of the House of Representatives on monetary matters had reached the point of being deliberately insulting on the floor of that body; in his state, he related, a banker tried to marry a white woman and got lynched.* Every bank in the nation was shut down. Stockholders in member banks of the Federal Reserve had a special reason to want to unload their holdings; the law

---

*This flippant anecdote has racist connotations that are contemptible. But it tells a great deal about attitudes toward bankers at the time.

provided that if a bank was not able to pay off its depositors, each share of stock could be assessed at twice its value. Under these circumstances, it might have been possible to establish public control over the volume of the circulating media. (See Document 26-1.) The president had no inclination to do that. The Emergency Banking Act of 1933 did little beyond setting conditions under which a bank could reopen. Since only one copy of the bill had been prepared, it was read aloud to the House. Forty minutes were allowed for debate. From the convening of Congress until adoption by the Senate took less than eight hours. One commentator approvingly notes: "Not for years had Congress acted with such speed and decision." (When Huey Long used similar tactics in Louisiana, he was either demagogue or dictator.)

The other bills in this lamentable trio should provoke laughter. In sequence, the next was the Economy in Government Act, meant to cut federal salaries pretty much across the board. The president was concerned that the national government, with a debt of $5 billion, would go bankrupt, just as a private household will go on the reefs if it spends beyond its means. An average citizen today might reason that a reduction of incomes is not the right method to combat a depression, but the message did not reach Roosevelt. The third of these vital measures legalized the manufacture of beer with an alcoholic content of no more than 3.2 per cent; a revival of the breweries would doubtless help to add jobs.

In all fairness, the administration's proposals did improve. The remainder of the Hundred Days—in fact, the first two years of the New Deal—can be seen from a perspective suggested at that time by the columnist Walter Lippmann. His thesis was that the more important revolution in American society had happened in 1929, not four years later. Lippmann's preoccupation was with federal policy toward the economy of the nation. He concluded that the crucial question was whether the national government should take responsibility for mitigating or even curing a depression. If it once decided that question in the affirmative, its involvement in the economy would be continuous because a required corollary was that it would intervene in prosperous times as well. For some decades, a few city or state governments had advanced programs of public works to relieve unemployment, but even such a humanitarian governor as Altgeld would not accept this notion during the hard times after 1893. Hoover did accept it, so Lippmann argues, and Roosevelt extended his practices, as Hoover himself would probably have done had he won re-election. By this argument a widely used pamphlet with the title *The New Deal—Revolution or Evolution?* is made absurd. The dichotomy dissolves.

The relation of continuity to change is one of the central questions in historical study. Here is a chance to tackle it. What similarities and dissimilarities exist between the Hoover and Roosevelt administrations? The angle of approach soon will be to ask what policies were instituted at various times to aid special segments of the society. First a couple of matters that seem to me relatively marginal should be at least acknowledged. One is the contrast of personality. Hoover may have seemed dignified and reliable to the wealthy businessmen with whom he had associated for so many years, but to ordinary voters he seemed frigid; he never came across. Even in 1928 he did not run a campaign, he stood for office. It was Republican prosperity and the standing GOP vote that put him in the White House. One might have said about him (as Theodore Roosevelt's daughter did say about Coolidge) that he had been weaned on a pickle. FDR was the opposite, all smiles, his honeyed voice over the radio, homey stories about his dog Fala, the appeal of his wife Eleanor. His affection for striking phrases may often have lured him into nonsense, but it helped to capture the electors. Another implement that has done heavy duty for Roosevelt is the contention that he was a master politician. If the analyst limits his gaze to questions of tactics, this is true. Besides his gift for phrasemaking, FDR knew when to time his moves. Hoover in contrast was often pompous, and he could not sense when the rules of the game had altered. Roosevelt was expert at gaining office, surely the elementary requirement for a politician. By 1932 he had worked at the game full-time for more than twenty years, whereas Hoover was in the novitiate. But when the discussion shifts to a deeper level of meaning and speaks of strategy, the gap between the two becomes less clear. Neither can be put beside Jefferson or Van Buren or Lincoln or Mark Hanna as an architect of a major innovation in the structure of American politics. Neither wanted such a change. Considerable metamorphosis was forced on FDR by protests in streets and shops; he did not promote it and damped its fires on frequent occasions.

On to federal policy. The entire subject of foreign relations and World War II must remain until Chapter 28; moreover, the presentation here of domestic affairs will omit social and intellectual history (Chapter 27); further, it halts at 1940. The main suggestion to be made here is that a modification of the direction of thrust from Washington occurred in the spring of 1935. Here we can only dissect the policy organs actually created to deal with important problems, in this order: (a) farmers, (b) the unemployed, (c) industrialists, (d) bankers and investors, (e) homeowners, (f) hydroelectric power and related public works.

Nowhere do the intellectual deficiencies of the New Deal show worse then in its agricultural program. A common gibe has been that the men in Washington had not worked the land; however, this is a defect that can be overcome. But ignorance becomes lethal when it has a young urbanite in a policy meeting pounding on the table to contend that more must be done for the macaroni growers. Coupled with ignorance was infatuation with an obsolescent myth: the American yeoman, the garden of the world, and the family farm all became an intertwined into a bemusing jumble. Because they embodied such a horde of mistakes, the agricultural policies may be taken as a prototype of the analytical failures of the New Deal. The benefits paid under various schemes in the past forty years have gone overwhelmingly to corporations or to banks or to big ranchers or to the wealthy who own plantations along the delta, and not to operators of the family farm. A later vice president (Richard M. Nixon) was indiscreet when he said that the solution to the farm problem was to eliminate the farmer, but he spoke the historical truth. As the *Canadian Magazine* stated the situation in a feature article in 1971: "Good-bye to the Family Farm." (See also Figure 29-3.)

The idea for "farm parity" stemmed from the head of a manufacturer of farm implements, who declared: "You can't sell a plow to a busted customer." Various schemes were put forward for raising the income of farmers to the point where they could buy the same comparative quantity of industrial goods as on the eve of World War I; that is, farm prices and manufacturing prices should rise or fall together. A technique often proposed was to establish a two-price system, by which alleged surpluses of staple crops would be dumped in foreign markets for whatever sums they would bring, to the end of maintaining a floor under prices in the United States. The McNary-Haugen bill, with other elaborate provisions but resting on this mode of reasoning, had been twice passed by Congress and twice vetoed by Coolidge (1927, 1928). The Hoover administration even before the Great Crash had felt compelled to set up a revolving fund of $500 million to make loans to farm cooperatives. Hoover objected quite rightly that the scheme of foreign dumping would further stimulate overproduction of the staples; he might have said also that it would provoke retaliation.

But this scheme became one leg in the New Deal stool. With it they combined three others: federal price fixing, limitation of acreage planted to certain crops, and marketing agreements. By the Agricultural Adjustment Act (AAA) of 1933, the president was permitted to choose among these alternatives. Emphasis was put on the limitation of acreages for selected staples. Hitches developed. The law did not clear Congress until 12 May, when crops had been planted, shoats and calves had been dropped. So it was deemed necessary to plow wheat and cotton under, to burn fields of corn, to convert animals into fertilizer. Folly ran riot. Often, the more fertilizer, the higher the yield per acre. For corn and wheat, the price more than doubled from 1932 to 1934; the price of cotton did double. But the output per acre of cotton rose slightly. The year 1934 was the beginning of a severe drought and the dust storms that would remain for years; the weather probably had more influence on crop reductions than did the federal actions. Further, the deliberate destruction of foodstuffs while millions of Americans went hungry was hard for folks to understand. Secretary of Agriculture Henry A. Wallace said that he could tolerate his own behavior only "as a cleaning up of the wreckage from the old days of unbalanced production. . . . The plowing under of 10 million acres of growing cotton in August, 1933, and the slaughter of 6 million little pigs in September . . . were not acts of idealism in any sane society. They were emergency acts made necessary by the almost insane lack of world statesmanship during the period from 1920 to 1932." A Republican congressman offered sharp rebuttal:

> I think of all the damnable heresies that have ever been suggested in connection with the Constitution, the doctrine of emergency is the worst. It means that when Congress declares an emergency there is no Constitution. This means its death. It is the very doctrine that the German chancellor is invoking today in the dying hours of the parliamentary body of the German republic, namely, that because of an emergency it should grant to the German chancellor absolute power to pass any law, even though that law contradicts the constitution of the German republic. Chancellor Hitler is at least frank about it.

Only a fool would try to equate FDR with Hitler. But even in the United States, events would run beyond the proclamation of an emergency by Congress, so that presidents took to issuing extraordinary decrees. The case of the "relocation" of Japanese-Americans in World War II will be examined in Chapter 28.

It must be conceded that coercion was not the original intent of AAA. But implementation quickly meant a departure from voluntarism. Power lay with landowners and processing corporations. When young lawyers in the administration tried to maintain some rights for tenants and small farmers, they were angrily purged by their superiors (The victims included Alger Hiss, see Chapter 29). A graduate of an Ivy League law school could be quickly placed in another job; those who were smashed to earth were sharecroppers and other poor folks. Croppers were to get half of federal benefit payments on their portion of the tillage, whereas hired hands were to get nothing. A ruthless landowner had little trouble in reducing a cropper to a hired hand. For years many mortgages, especially in the cotton South, had been in arrears. Banks had not foreclosed because no market existed for the land; their wisest course was to forebear in the hope of eventually being repaid. AAA opened a new opportunity. Banks foreclosed, then withdrew the land from production and collected federal benefits. These were used to displace additional men by buying new machinery. Added efficiency helped to undersell private operators and reduce them to tenancy (see Figure 26-4).

Even earlier, the New Deal had moved to help the jobless. In trying to cope with this tragic difficulty, men in office did come up with creative approaches. The failure was that the administration as a whole did not take these innovations, test them, throw out the bad ones and then expand the useful ones. For instance, the first major statute on unemployment was the Civilian Conservation Corps, which can be used to mark the creation of the multi-purpose program. It aimed to achieve not one goal but many. It benefited society for generations to come by taking idle males off the streets; by the spring of 1934 a quarter of a million families had watched a son or two go off to CCC camp. In addition to the pleasure that wages added to his own life, each youth sent dollars back home. Work in the outdoors helped to maintain

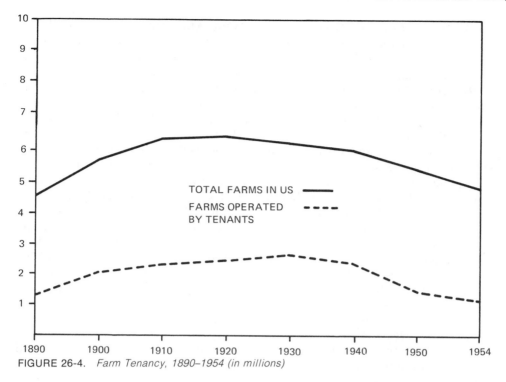

FIGURE 26-4. *Farm Tenancy, 1890–1954 (in millions)*

the health of these young men. The work found for them was creative; the only just criticism might be that it had been too long deferred. Systematic reforestation of the Great Plains and the West was begun by the CCC—but not soon enough to prevent the dust storms of the thirties. (The terror of these storms cannot be exaggerated. An example that sticks in my vision comes from a letter written to *The Nation* in 1937 by a farmwife in Oklahoma. She reported that jackrabbits squatted around her house waiting for food. They could no longer find their own, because they had been blinded by the slashing dust and sand.) A later critic has protested that CCC purposes did not go as far as they should have, with particular reference to schooling of the enrollees. The figures show that he has a point: 5,000 eighth-grade certificates were issued, over 1,000 high-school diplomas. Compared to the number involved, these achievements seem minor. Eight thousand men learned to read and write, but when World War II came, it remained true that millions of conscripts were illiterate.

CCC applied solely to young men. The vast majority of the indigent were sustained at a dismal level by a succession of other bureaus: Federal Emergency Relief Administration (FERA, May, 1933), Public Works Administration (PWA, June, 1933), Civil Works Administration (CWA, November,

1933), Works Progress Administration (WPA, May, 1935). This bewildering succession of agencies, many created by executive orders, has understandably prompted critics to call the New Deal "alphabet soup." Such witticisms may charm; they may also confuse. At their worst, they may divert us from one of FDR's guidelines for administration: namely, to give the same job to several different men and then leave them to cut each other's throats. Thus he ensured that he would be the one person with authority to make a final decision on politically sensitive questions.

Before pushing forward in time, it is advisable to look backward, since our over-all purpose is to compare the Hoover and Roosevelt administrations. The governor of Pennsylvania, one of the states worst beleaguered by distress, wrote to his brother in November, 1931: "I am completely satisfied that the moving impulse behind Hoover's whole handling of the unemployment situation has been his desire to protect the big fellows from additional taxation, as you said." The figures do not dispute this view. In 1930 the federal government actually showed a surplus, and reduced its debt by more than $700 million. A federal surplus might of course suggest heavy taxation, but in this instance it shows that outlays were being trimmed to the bone. Praise the Lord, in 1931, a federal deficit was allowed to the extent of nearly half a billion dollars. A disgruntled Andrew Mellon left Washington. Nor was Hoover pleased; he urged tax increases to bring in another billion dollars a year, together with appropriation cuts to save $350 million. He got no new taxes, and less than half of the cuts he proposed in expenditures. His message to Congress was plaintive: "We cannot squander ourselves into prosperity." Once more, a president was 100 per cent wrong. The childish foibles of these years are hard to understand. Hoover named a former president of the Plumbers' Union to head the United States Employment Service. This official went to address an American Legion conference on unemployment in March, 1931. He exulted in their presence: "I found two of your men jobs this morning in one hour, just using the telephone!" A Legion leader replied, "Fine, I'll give you a list of 750,000 names to place." Hoover's comprehension of the economics of the nation was deplorable; however, as this chapter will try to demonstrate, the leading Democrats did not score much better.

FDR was one of the early advocates of an interstate arrangement for unemployment compensation. The idea was surely a good one, but it lost. He was merely governor of New York. Of more importance on the national scene was Speaker of the House Garner. Bills for federal grants for relief to the needy were knocked down in Congress. I will not pretend to know what went on in Garner's head; perhaps he saw a run for the White House; even though he was 63 years old, he had the asset of 28 years in Congress. In February, 1932, he made an impassioned plea for a balanced federal budget. He left the Speaker's chair to go on the floor and appeal for passage of a federal sales tax. His climax was to ask all members who favored a balanced budget to rise in their seats. But Fiorello LaGuardia succeeded in knocking out the sales tax. A few weeks later Garner had a different proposal: to appropriate some $2.5 billion for public-works projects. About that time Senator Robinson, soon to become the Democratic majority leader, came out with a relief program to total $2.3 billion. The president countered with a proposal of about 15 per cent of that amount, including an onslaught against the Speaker's proposal: "This is not unemployment relief. It is the most gigantic pork barrel ever proposed to the American Congress. It is an unexampled raid on the public treasury. . . ." Such hyperbole should be approached with caution. In Cook County, Illinois, the relief appropriation was running out, and 750,000 job-seekers were seeking in vain. An appeal to the president from Chicago 2 June, 1932, was signed by the head of Marshall Field, three giant meat packers, railroads, International Harvester, the First National Bank, daily newspapers, and mineral processors. Three weeks later the city's mayor appeared in Washington to pose a bleak choice to federal authorities: grant relief to the distressed, or send in the army to put down riots.

The record of both administrations under review in regard to industrialists should make the most gullible wonder. An economist at the Harvard Business School declared bluntly in December, 1930: "We have the dole in America. But the real recipients . . . are not the men who stand for hours before the Salvation Army soup stations." They were, he said, "the great industries of America." Previously noted (late Chapter 24 on the 1928 campaign) was Hoover's fondness for the trade association as a device for reducing competition in an industry. As president he revealed another aspect of his partisanship to big business by sponsoring the Reconstruction Finance Corporation (RFC, January, 1932). This federal agency was designed to make loans to banks, railroads, and other giant corporations in order to save them from disaster. Its president for the first six months was Charles G. Dawes, former vice president of the nation, ambassador to England, re-designer of reparations payments by Germany. He resigned in June and went back to Chicago to tend the affairs of a bank he had organized. His bank got at one swoop an RFC loan of $90 million. Hoover justified such practices by saying that the prosperity of big business would "trickle down" to everybody. One comment on this argument was acidic: To say that the right mechanism for sustaining the poor was to feed the rich was akin to saying that the best way to feed birds was to feed horses.

With the National Recovery Administration (NRA, another product of the Hundred Days), Roosevelt followed this road even farther than Hoover had done. The new president was basically friendly to the agglutinative approach. His experience in Washington during World War I had been with the regulation and coordination of industry, not with forcing it to compete.* He also had served as president of a national trade association, the Construction Council, from 1922 to 1928; this experience, wrote an aide, "taught him that

---

*It also had been focused on the damping of inflation rather than the stoking of deflation; given the circumstances in which FDR now had to operate, he suffered a severe case of "trained incapacity."

purely voluntary self-regulation did not work." Powerful leaders from the Wall Street firm of Lehman Brothers, Jersey Standard, the U.S. Chamber of Commerce, and GE were pushing in the same direction. Textile executives could become metaphoric in their pleas for a shield against deflation: "We are confronted with a condition of rubber money and iron debts. . . ." Spurred by the White House, Congress set up the NRA. The law provided for the producers in each industry to meet in Washington to draw up a code of fair competition. The codes could be enforced by federal sanctions. Predictably, the conferences and the enforcement were dominated by the largest firms. How this collusion worked out can be shown with one illustration, although hundreds of examples could be equally well given. A small lumber yard sold for cash to farmers who carried their purchases away. Its proprietor bought a large shipment of lumber at $24 a thousand feet, planning to sell at $32. Under the Sawmill Code he was required to add 20 per cent for overhead or $6.40, plus $5.20 for handling and delivery, making a total price of $43.60. His farmer-customers could not meet the price; building in the area stopped; the lumber dealer was almost put out of business. After two years these obscenities and NRA powers were cut off by the Supreme Court in the *Schecter* decision, which involved a poultry dealer in Brooklyn. The identity of the plaintiff gave the disillusioned public another barbed jest of the Depression. Taking their cue from the NRA's grotesque poster with its "Blue Eagle" thunderbird symbol, which participants in the detested program were expected to display, writers soon dubbed *Schecter* "the sick chicken case."

While he was trying to coerce the nation with NRA, FDR was also diddling around with monetary policy. We have no reason to think that he ever understood the subject. He was an easy mark for one quack after another. He did not buy every patent medicine, only several. His floundering on the question of the circulating medium was ludicrous. At the beginning of the New Deal, a Cornell professor sold the president on a very old nostrum—"Gresham's law," which can be stated in several ways (see Figure 26-5). One can say that a rise in the price of gold will raise the value of all commodities proportionately, or that an increase in the quantity of money will bring a like rise in the goods. So FDR raised the price of gold. Result: the effect on the general level of prices was very small. In technical language, the velocity of circulation fell. Folks simply took the increased supply of money and tucked it under their mattresses, or put it in banks and let it stagnate there. The fact that some people have more money does not insure that they will want to spend it; the hungry probably will, but the wealthy will spend it only if they see a chance for profit. Simultaneously Roosevelt was considering banking reform. A warehouse full of facts about abuses had been collected. Financiers cheating on their income taxes: one sold $3 million worth of stock in his bank to his wife and later bought back the shares from her. Another banker was caught selling short the stock in his own bank. (To sell short any commodity, including stock in a corporation, is to sell something that you do not own, in the expectation

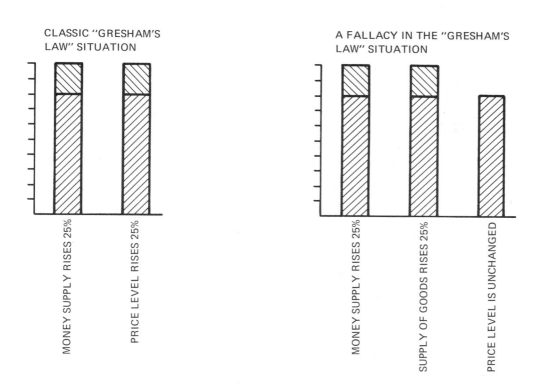

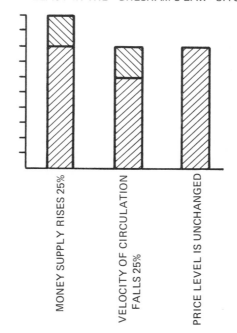

FIGURE 26-5. *Variations on the Quantity Theory of Money and "Greshom's Law"*

that the price in 60 or 90 days will be less than it is today; you sell at today's proffer but deliver at whatever the future price may be. A bank president could find it easy to lower the price of stock in his bank.). Margin buying on the Stock Exchange was financed by the largest industrial firms; Jersey Standard at one time had $100 million loaned (through banks) on call, and its total loans of this type had totalled more than $17.5 billion. So the final day of the Hundred Days saw what was meant to be a lasting statute, and none can gainsay that some of its remedies proved to be useful. The Federal Deposit Insurance Corporation (FDIC) was founded to insure all deposits up to $10,000. No commercial bank which accepted deposits could be connected with a firm selling securities, such as an investment bank or a stockbroker. Interest could not be paid on demand deposits (as in a checking account).

The time has come for a partial assessment. FDR's credit with historians has been exceedingly high. Why? A major reason can be simply stated: They (and most of their students and readers) belonged to precisely the segment of society on whom his administration rained benefits. We might call it the middle 60 per cent of the social strata. The New Deal always had its wealthy supporters, but Roosevelt's name was not popular around the Union League Club, and newspaper publishers did not adore him (count 10 per cent lost). The remaining 30 per cent were the truly disadvantaged, and the president never thought about them much. Their power was negligible, so why bother? But many of them had votes, so they got some benefits too. These tidbits should not be decried. The degree to which folks who have almost nothing can be thankful for a few more crumbs was dramatically expressed two decades later by a black woman in Baltimore. She sang paeans to Roosevelt while assaulting the ingratitude of the contemporary youth. They, she said, don't know what it is to go freeze your butt in an outhouse, and they might be doing it today if it wasn't for That Man.*

Another element in Roosevelt's appeal to many academics can lead to conflicting conclusions. One perspective is offered by a biography (1882) by the English novelist Anthony Trollope about a British prime minister: "He was a statesman for the moment. Whatever was not wanted now, whatever was not practicable now, he drove quite out of his mind." This evaluation would not apply with any richness to Washington, or Hamilton, or Lincoln, but it does seem pertinent to FDR. A harsher analogy can be drawn from a comment by another Englishman, economist John Maynard Keynes: "We are at one of those uncommon junctures of human affairs when we can be saved by the solution of intellectual problems and in no other way." The man who really cut to the quick was the nation's foremost living philosopher, John Dewey (see

---

*The law that seems best to typify the Hundred Days was the Home Owners Loan Act. It contended that men who have worked hard to accumulate property should not be made to give it up under abnormal conditions. The law of 1933, as amended the next year, in effect prohibited foreclosure on a mortgage.

Chapters 25 and 27); under the title "Imperative Need: A New Radical Party," he wrote:

> Events have proved that while those in private control of industry and wealth rule they do not and cannot govern. For government implies order and security at the very least. And what we have is tragic insecurity and essential anarchy. . . . At the time when public officials are calling upon police and militia to keep dairy farmers from emptying milk, the federal government is paying a premium to other farmers for plowing under millions of acres of corn and cotton. If that is not anarchy, no one knows what anarchy is.
>
> This situation continues only because the mass of the people refuse to look facts in the face and prefer to feed on illusions, produced and circulated by those in power with a profusion that contrasts with their withholding of the necessities of life. The day that the mass of the American people awake to the realities of the situation, that day the restoration of democracy will commence, for power and rule will revert to the people.

In 1935 Dewey returned to the attack: "Experimental method is not just messing around nor doing a little of this and a little of that in the hope that things will improve. Just as in the physical sciences, it implies a coherent body of ideas, a theory, that gives direction to effort." A quarter of a century later, a rover boy from the academic-governmental Establishment, acting as an apologist historian of the New Deal, professed to be puzzled by Dewey's protests: "Paradoxically, the New Deal, preferring experiment to abstraction, became repugnant to this theoretical experimentalist."

During the first two years of the Roosevelt administration, the most forward-looking law, the Tennessee Valley Act, put the government into the power and flood control business. This landmark legislation did not get much encouragement from the White House; its chief author was Republican George W. Norris, senator from Nebraska (Chapter 22). Antecedents for such government involvement were several: the Hetch Hetchy struggle in the West for public power; the Muscle Shoals dam in Alabama to produce nitrates during World War I. When war ended, Norris wanted federal operation of the latter development to continue. A bill to that end passed Congress in 1928, vetoed by Coolidge. Another passed in 1931, vetoed by Hoover. These gentlemen would not allow government to compete with free enterprise. Sensing that FDR would not block it, Norris' group made the plan much bolder. Now it would embrace a multi-river system. Further, reverting to the most creative concept of CCC, it would be a multi-purpose enterprise. The easiest part to sell politically was a combination of dams and reforestation as a means to flood control. Tacked on were provisions for recreation areas. The stiffest opposition came to the provisions for hydroelectric power, especially because it was announced that TVA rates could serve as a yardstick for private rates. Leading the objectors was the president of gargantuan Commonwealth and Southern, Wendell Willkie (mid-Chapter 28 on the 1940 campaign). Ironically, after the

FIGURE 26-6. *Norris Dam, Tennessee Valley Authority*

    Norris Dam presides over the Clinch River in eastern Tennessee. Although this river is only about 200 miles long from its origins in southwestern Virginia until its juncture with the Tennessee River, the dam is vital to the complex operated by the Tennessee Valley Authority. This agency, as stated by two authorities, "realized from its beginning in 1933 that its progressive conception of regional development would find appropriate expression only in modern architecture."

    A strong tendency has existed to denigrate American achievements in the visual arts. But this verdict comes from jurors who have defined the subject in too narrow a way. Consider architecture (surely one of the important arts); Frank Lloyd Wright, expressing the expansive view of many American artists, said that two objects that he had wanted to design, without doing so, were a silo and a steamship. Much American genius has expressed itself in novel forms, as exemplified by the statute was enacted, the private companies were among the chief benefactors. As the cost of electricity fell, more families came into the market. When farm homes got current, they bought radios, refrigerators, washing machines. Private profits rose. Two further comments about TVA seem in order. Its outstanding executive subtitled a book: *Democracy on the March.* This ideal was partly realized; it was a semi-autonomous agency of the federal government. But it soon became another swollen bureaucracy, and the notion that it manifested "grass-roots democracy" has been discredited. Even after allowance for this, the TVA can be seen as an advance in several respects. However, it was not replicated. Proposals for similar projects have been repeatedly made, notably for the Missouri valley; repeatedly they have been turned back by Congress. Perhaps the spreading concern for control of the environment will revive them with added zest.

In the spring of 1935 FDR abruptly shifted his course, not quite a total reverse. What ensued is commonly, and justly, called the Second New Deal—if there had been a First. This switch is always referred to, never explained. An effort to that end should be made. Of the two main causes, one must be deferred until Chapter 27: the rise of democracy in the streets, culminating with the formation of the mass CIO unions. The other can be found in Washington, especially in the White House. A task force in the Treasury Department headed by Mordecai Ezekiel had submitted to the secretary and through him to the president a report proposing an increased program of public works to be financed by federal deficits. For some weeks it seemed that Roosevelt was going to advocate this policy. Then he decided it would not be wise politically. Unfortunately perhaps, the report made explicit the alternative to its proposal: prolonged large-scale unemployment. FDR foresaw rough waters for the New Deal. If he could not help to restore full employment, he would have to capture blocs of voters by the advocacy of specialized programs, particularly designed for the working class.*

*This analysis and the documents underlying it (Roosevelt Library at Hyde Park) were offered in a Senior Honors Thesis by William S. Friedman (1965) at Brandeis University. Other interpretations in this chapter rely on facts contained in other Senior Honors Theses done at the same institution by these students: Miriam A. Epstein (1964), Donald Florman (1965), David A. Levine (1963), Daniel Marcus (1962), and J. Victor Samuels (1963).

---

civil engineers who created Norris Dam. The many rivers of eastern America needed bridges, and they offered additional chances to manipulate beauty. Are we to deny an artistic achievement to the Roeblings, father and son, who built Brooklyn Bridge? And what of David B. Steinman, who refashioned it?

Such questions may necessitate some difficult distinctions. Who is an American? The poet T. S. Eliot was born in St. Louis and educated in the United States but lived most of his adult life in England; an analog is W. H. Auden, bred and reared in England, who lived for decades in the United States. Veering back to the subject of unusual genres in the arts, we might consider Donald McKay, the author of the greatest clipper ships in the mid-nineteenth century. A standard source calls him a "Boston shipbuilder." But he came from Nova Scotia, and those formative years provided him with his visions and with many of his techniques.

The Refrigerator

The operation of the mechanical refrigerator depends upon two laws of physics. First, when a liquid evaporates to a gas, it absorbs heat, and when a gas condenses to a liquid, it loses heat. Second, when pressure is increased the "evaporation point" is raised, and the point at which any material will evaporate to a gas or condense to a liquid is higher. Increased pressure at a given temperature will thus condense a gas to liquid, and lower pressure will evaporate a liquid to a gas. Using these principles for refrigeration requires the selection of a refrigerant material which will evaporate to a gas under normal atmospheric pressure inside a freezer (absorbing heat in the process), and which under pressure (hence a higher "evaporation point") will condense to a liquid at room temperature in a coil outside the freezer, giving off the heat it had absorbed inside. A refrigeration plant operates in these phases:

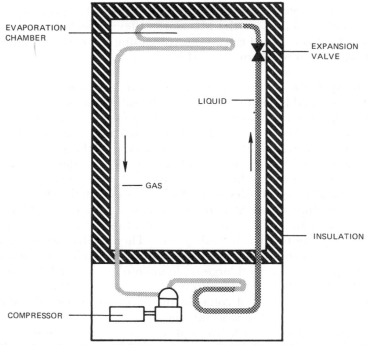

(1) A pump puts the refrigerant under pressure and keeps it in liquid form in a coil outside the freezer; an expansion valve holds it under pressure so that it cannot evaporate prematurely, and the liquid is propelled toward the evaporation chamber.

(2) In the evaporation chamber inside the freezer pressure is relieved; under the lower normal atmospheric pressure the liquid evaporates and absorbs heat.

(3) The refrigerant, now in gas form under normal pressure, is propelled out of the evaporation chamber and toward the compressor.

(4) The refrigerant is compressed by a pump, and under pressure condenses to a liquid and gives off the heat absorbed from inside; it is propelled through the coil outside the freezer, as in phase (1) in the cycle. The refrigerant material is continuously pumped in a steady stream through all phases simultaneously.

Although few American households would today tolerate the inconvenience of the ice box, the importance of mechanical refrigeration does not lie in the domestic sphere. The refrigerated train and truck transport has permitted twentieth century Americans to enjoy a much wider variety of food, especially fruit and vegetables, at all seasons of the year, than was conceivable before their invention.

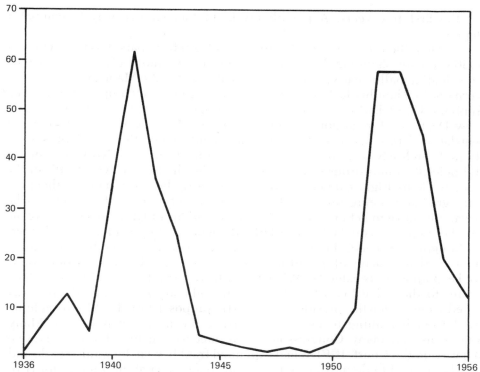

FIGURE 26-7. *Units of Low-rent Federal Housing Completed (in thousands)*

That spring saw three striking new plans. By executive order, no less, the president created the Works Progress Administration (WPA). Disdaining the handout, the agency tried to create jobs on public works. Since the central objective was to put men back to work, they often worked inefficiently in terms of modern technology. Epithets resounded: "Huh, raking leaves!" or "Leaning on a shovel!" These taunts were not only unfair but stupid. In countless towns in the country today you can see a city hall, a library, a bridge, that was built by WPA. Its cultural achievements can be left for the next chapter, as can the groundswell set off by the National Labor Relations Act (NLRA or Wagner Act). The third innovation, and one that Roosevelt had been angling toward for years, was the Social Security Act. In 1931 as a governor he had suggested an interstate meeting to agree on a scheme for compensating the unemployed. That became part of the new law; so did a device for old-age benefits. Undoubtedly over the long run this statute has served to relieve destitution among several segments of society. However, in contrast to WPA with its initial appropriation of nearly $5 billion, Social Security began, not by paying benefits, but by taxing both worker and employer, and thus was deflationary for the first few years. A payroll tax is another strange way to combat a depression.

Then the president decided to rest on his reform oars. His re-election in 1936 was overwhelming: he lost only Maine and Vermont. (The former had its presidential ballot early, giving rise to the jest: "As Maine goes, so goes Vermont.") Then his lack of understanding began to catch up with him. The Supreme Court had certainly behaved outrageously in striking down many New Deal laws for captious reasons; if any court can be accused of "judicial legislation," this one can. On the other hand, many New Deal bills were drafted carelessly or were offensive to the Constitution; the NRA for instance did delegate a monstrous share of power to the chief executive. Details of the famous Court Fight cannot be given here, partly because many of them are only gradually being uncovered, but some points seem established. As he began his move to get more of the bench behind his program by increasing the number of justices on the Court, FDR did not bother to consult his own leaders in Congress. Second, he fabricated an announced reason for his move, claiming that so many of the sitting members were elderly that the Court could not keep up with its calendar. When Chief Justice Hughes was able to produce figures to show that his tribunal was in fact abreast of its work, the rug was jerked from under the president's feet. His proposal lost. In this struggle he erred from beginning to end, and I suspect he need not have lost. Many Americans and many Congressmen were incensed against the conservative majority on the Court. If FDR had explained frankly what he wanted to do and why he wanted to do it, if he had made advance preparations on Capitol Hill, he might have won. Instead he alienated several of his staunchest supporters.

So the president reverted to one of his favorite kicks—balance the budget. The federal debt was actually reduced a little from 1937 to 1938, but unemployment soared from 13.8 per cent to 18.7 per cent of the civilian labor force. What next?—another reverse. The Wagner-Steagall Act (September, 1937) was intended to provide public housing for low-income groups; its results will be examined in Chapter 29. Doing a clear about-face from NRA, Roosevelt appointed a trust-buster to head the anti-trust division of the Justice Department, and a sweeping investigation of the squelching of competition in the economy was launched by the Temporary National Economic Committee. Most important of all, the Fair Labor Standards Act set for workers engaged in interstate commerce both a minimum wage per hour and maximum hours per week. By court decisions plus Congressional action, this law has been frequently upgraded and extended to many additional groups of workers. It must stand as one of the major accomplishments of the New Deal. Elated by the achievement of these reforms, Roosevelt tried to use the Democratic primaries to purge congressmen in his party who had opposed his program. He got scotched. In only one district did he succeed. Our generalization of Chapter 24 (first footnote) still holds.

Our final topic here is Senator Huey Long, for whom my respect is great. Rich kids from the North may well parrot the labels they have heard, calling him power-hungry, a ruthless dictator, or a demagogue. Poor boys from the South are not likely to feel that way about it. The best break that Roosevelt got in the 1936 election was the assassination of Huey Long, because he would have raised cain—all from the left. He had mastered invective: NRA meant "Nuts Running America," or "National Ruin Administration," or "Never Roosevelt Again." Perhaps his larger greatness lay in his years as governor of Louisiana. In a state that had only bogs as roads, he helped pave them. In a state of many bayous, he helped build bridges. In a state of countless diseases, he helped build hospitals. In a state of illiterate adults, he helped to start night schools—for black and white equally.

Critics of his programs need also to be educated on another problem: Many have faulted Long for the rise in the public debt of Louisiana (making it sound like the worst accounts of Reconstruction), but almost any economist today would agree that deficit financing was the right way to fight the depression. Let us end with an anecdote. As governor in 1932, he heard that a bank in Lafayette might fold. With a friend he drove through the night to be right there when banking hours began. Up came a patron to present a check for $18,000 to withdraw his deposits. Huey then waved a state check in the man's face and told him that the state check would more than exhaust the bank's cash. Further, said Long, I got here first. "You agree to leave yours in, and I'll agree to leave the state's in, and nobody'll be hurt." If that was Hitlerism—it was not—the United States needed more of it, in 1932.

Looking back on the Great Depression, it seems clear that neither Hoover nor Roosevelt understood what had provoked it or what to do to cure it. Some of FDR's advisers had the needed insights, but they could never persuade him to implement them in a systematic fashion. He floundered along, shuffling from an advocacy of massive deficits in the federal budget to meet the pressures from blocs of voters, then shifting to a contrary policy of striving to make outgoes match receipts in order to satisfy the dogmas of nineteenth-century economic theory. Meanwhile, citizens suffered. From 1931 to 1940, always at least eight million Americans were unemployed. Social welfare payments and direct relief were far less generous than they would be in 1972. Many employed workers suffered persistent dread that they would lose their jobs. Employers watched the savings of decades disappear like smoke. Farmers saw their land dispersed by dust storms or by floods. By the spring of 1935, Roosevelt despaired of getting the idle segment of the labor force back to work. To save his political neck, he turned to programs that aimed at assuaging large groups in the community. The major reforms of the New Deal stem from this strategic reversal: the Social Security Act, the National Labor Relations Act, the Fair Labor Standards Act. As subsequently broadened in scope, these laws have substantially altered the contours of American society. Considering, however, the strains to which the national life was subjected, it is remarkable that such modest and fairly quiet revisions were sufficient to satisfy the bulk of the electorate.

SOME NOTABLE EVENTS

1929 Black Thursday on New York Stock Exchange, 24 October.

1931 Muscle Shoals bill vetoed by President Hoover, 3 March.

International financial crisis, spring; Great Depression in U.S., autumn.

Japan attacks Mukden, 18 September.

1932 Reconstruction Finance Corporation, 22 January.

Norris-LaGuardia Act, 20 March.

Unemployment in June, 13 million.

Payrolls of Ford fall to 37,000, June; they were 128,142 in March, 1929.

Veterans' Bonus March on Washington, May–July.

Japan recognizes Manchukuo, 15 September.

1933 Emergency Banking Act, 9 March.

Economy in Government Act, 20 March.

Beer (3.2 per cent alcohol) legalized, 22 March.

Federal Emergency Relief Act, 12 May.

Agricultural Adjustment Administration, 12 May.

Tennessee Valley Authority, 18 May.

Truth in Securities Act, 27 May.

London Economic Conference, 12 June–27 July.

Home Owners' Loan Act, 13 June.

Farm Credit Act, 16 June.

Banking Act of 1933 (Glass-Steagall Act), 16 June.

National Recovery Administration, 16 June.

U.S.S.R. recognized by U.S., 16 November.

1934 Gold Reserve Act, 30 January.

Johnson Act, 13 April.

1935 Resettlement Administration, April.

Soldiers' Bonus Bill vetoed by Roosevelt, 22 May.

Schecter Poultry Corporation v. *U.S.*, 27 May.

National Labor Relations Act (Wagner Act), 5 July.

Social Security Acts, 5 August.

Neutrality Act of 1935; Italy invades Ethiopia, 2 October.

1936 Canadian Reciprocal Trade Agreement, 14 May.

Hitler seizes the Rhineland, March.

Spanish Civil War begins, summer.

1937 FDR loses struggle to "pack" the Supreme Court, 5 February–22 July.

Farm Security Administration established, 22 July.

Recession begins, August.

Panay incident, 12 December.

1938 Ludlow resolution for referendum on war beaten in House, 10 January.

Agricultural Adjustment Act of 1938, April 14.

House Committee on Un-American Activities set up, 26 May.

Emergency Relief Appropriation Act, 21 June.

Fair Labor Standards Act, 25 June.

FDR tries to purge his Democratic opponents in Congress; fails.

1939 Administrative Reorganization Act, 3 April.

Hatch Act forbids political activity by federal employees, 2 August.

1940 Alien Registration Act (also called Smith Act), 28 June.

Office of Production Management, 20 December.

FDR says U.S. should become "the great arsenal of democracy."

U.S. unemployment: 7,476,000.

Ways to Study History XXVI

Consult eye-witnesses. Diligent historians for generations have been scouring the countryside to find persons who actually participated in memorable events. In the last twenty years this practice has become far more systematic than ever before. Ways to Study History III briefly examined the use of computers in recent research; the use of tape recorders is another example of how modern tools can be helpful. A taped interview permits more accurate replication of what was said, and preserves it indefinitely. Visitors to the Oral History Project at Columbia University or to the Labor History Archives at Wayne State University can hear what was remembered ten years ago by actors in the crises of fifty years ago.

Incredible gains from this technique are visible in the biography of Huey Long by T. Harry Williams (1970). Long was governor of and then United States senator from Louisiana. Restrained writers had customarily called him a demagogue; the headstrong had used phrases about the Hitler of America. Williams gives a far different portrait of a conventional indigenous type whose distinction was that he had much more than normal style and zeal, and who was, it seems to me, the most creative Southern politician of this century. To reach this picture the author used the traditional sources: manuscripts, public records, periodicals. But also, even though Long was assassinated (an old American habit) in 1935, Williams was able to interview 295 eye-witnesses.

The results refute the old canards. Interviews can bring the past to life.

Document 26-1

Bray Hammond was probably one of the three most acute analysts of the history of American money and banking. He also belongs to the squadron of non-academics, persons not affiliated with any university, who in the last generation contributed so much to our knowledge of our past; his career was spent as a civil servant with the Federal Reserve System, and his research and writing were a pursuit to be indulged on vacations, evenings, weekends. His first-hand knowledge, clear mind, and lucid prose work together in this passage to explain the nature of central banking. Although an explanation of this phenomenon has been made in Chapter 12, the repetition of it here should provide a focus on the Great Depression.

When the System was established and for many years later, the Reserve Banks were usually regarded as a means of "pooling" or "mobilizing" the reserve funds of member banks. To a certain extent this view was correct. But it fell far short of recognizing the full and unique nature of Reserve Bank lending power and Reserve Bank credit. The Reserve Banks are most significant as sources of funds than as reservoirs of funds. In extending credit, either by lending or by purchasing securities, they do not use funds already deposited with them. Their lending power is independent of the funds deposited with them. When they extend credit, they increase both their assets and their liabilities; they originate the funds they lend and the funds they pay for securities.

Anybody who has grasped this interpretation, including the meaning of every word in it, is well on the way to understanding other episodes discussed in this chapter and Chapter 22, as well as in Chapters 28 and 29: in creation of the Open Market Committee in 1933; "monetization of the federal debt" during World War II; why the manipulation of the rediscount rate affected only certain spheres of the economy in recent years.

Document 26-2

The public media have long been harping on the economic theories of an Englishman, John Maynard Keynes. But he did not create all the theories involving government intervention in a national economy, nor did he understand them as well as some Americans who preceded him. Even before Franklin Delano Roosevelt became president, this testimony was offered to the Senate Finance Committee in February, 1933, by Marriner S. Eccles, head of twenty-six banks in Utah and president of several other companies. Besides the analysis reprinted here, he advocated on this occasion federal laws on child labor, minimum wages, unemployment insurance, old-age pensions, plus higher income and inheritance taxes on the wealthy.

Before effective action can be taken to stop the devastating effects of the depression, it must be recognized that the breakdown of our present economic system is due to the failure of our political and financial leadership to intelligently deal with the money problem. In the real world there is no cause nor reason for the unemployment with its resultant destitution and suffering of fully one-third of our entire population. We have all and more of the material wealth which we had at the peak of our prosperity in the year of 1929. Our people need and want everything which our abundant facilities and resources are able to provide for them. The problem of production has been solved, and we need no further capital accumulation for the present, which could only be utilized in further increasing our productive facilities or extending further foreign credits. We have a complete economic plant able to supply a superabundance of not only all of the necessities of our people, but the comforts and luxuries as well. Our problem, then, becomes purely one of distribution. This can only be brought about by providing purchasing power sufficiently adequate to enable the people to obtain the consumption goods which we, as a nation, are able to produce. The economic system can serve no other purpose and expect to survive. . . .

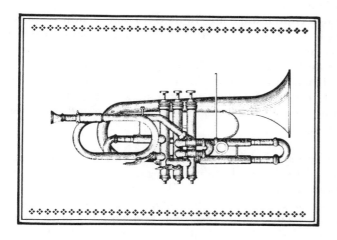

Two Cultures:
Common Men and Intellectuals

In 1959 a renowned English novelist-scientist published a small volume with the title *The Two Cultures and the Scientific Revolution*. His central thesis can be viewed as an ego trip: he implied that he was notable for being conversant with both the humanities and the natural sciences. His self-congratulations were justified in that double-vision is far from common, but he was not unique. To cite only the most famous exemplar, Albert Einstein was a physicist who played the violin and wrote philosophy of quality. Before departing from this theme, an intriguing oddity might be observed. A physicist or chemist is more likely to know something about music and art than is a humanist to know a smidgen about modern science. Between the two, of course, lies mathematics, and therein is the key to the enigma. A person without knowledge of mathematics is barred from contemporary science. This knowledge must be acquired at an early age, whereas a person of any age (perhaps, the older the better) can read a novel or respond to a painting. But his knowledge of any art can be increased if he has pondered the manipulation of numbers. It is not by accident that the highest praise bestowed on a mathematical proof is to call it "elegant."

While the above contentions are limited to a division within the academic community, it appears typical of the much more meaningful polarities in view when we scan a broader horizon, seeking to analyze how the differences between intellectuals and ordinary people enter the panorama. First, an illustration from culture at its lowest. Then, two examples from thought at its highest reaches. Finally, we will look at the democratizing influences: cultural innovations after 1929 that appealed to a wide range of the strata in American society.

Some genre may be more debased than broadcast soap opera, but it is not easy to think of any. This benumbing viper began in Chicago about 1932. Its creators came from various pseudo-intellectual backgrounds; schoolteacher, advertising man, magazine writer, newspaper reporter. Its success was phenomenal. One series, "The Goldbergs," was sponsored continuously by Proctor & Gamble from 1937 until 1945; it had begun as a nighttime show several years earlier but daytime for the housewives seemed to work out better. "Vic and Sade" began in June, 1932, and lasted for thirteen years. One female writer of this pablum made an income estimated at $4,500 a week. Another woman did even better; by the middle of the decade she was earning some $250,000 a year. Later she sold the rights to three of her serials for $175,000. One male writer turned out 100,000 words a week for years.*

The construction of stories was absurd. Any listeners were stultified. Locale was unlikely (usually in small towns). Characters had weird diseases such as temporary blindness or amnesia (did you ever know a person with amnesia?). Children were constantly being killed by automobiles. Men were repeatedly arrested for murder. No woman ever became committed to her lover until he had been crippled. In Thurber's words, the portrait of the American male in soap operas was "Man in a Wheelchair." Such tearjerkers gained audiences running to, in total, some 20 million. A survey reported that 46 per cent of the nation's women were never part of this audience, but think of the other percentage. And how many of the abstainers had daytime jobs? In trying to understand the appeal of the daytime serial, we can begin with its limited demands on audiences. Intellectually it required nothing; anyone could comprehend what it had to say. The pace of action verged toward a dead stop; if a man went to the barber shop for a haircut, the narration of that one haircut could take at least two weeks at the rate of five programs a week. Programs issued no call to a person's physiology; a listener could iron her washing

---

*Facts here gathered in my mother's household have been illuminated by a brilliant series in *The New Yorker* by James Thurber. Journalists have done at least as well as professional historians in interpreting recent America. Many *New Yorker* profiles are superb, and they are exploited often in the pages that follow. Picking almost at random, I think of pieces by S. N. Behrman, Richard O. Boyer, John Hersey, Geoffrey Hellman.

without missing a stroke. Emotionally it was flaccid. In one show a man stopped by to see a lady friend on a hot afternoon. She asked if he wanted anything to drink. He replied that a glass of ice water would be fine. She said: "One cube or two?"

It is probably invalid to say that these programs provided millions of people with vicarious lives. True, many Americans had been made miserable by the depression, and they wanted to flee from reality, but it was not the unemployed and the sharecroppers who owned radios. The common denominator of the soap operas was that they offered so little stimulation to the audience and seemed to offer the average listener some kind of comforting reassurance. But the ability of housewives to get caught up in the juvenilities passes belief. Audiences developed a personal identification with these media "personalities." On one show a man and his beloved got married; the headquarters of the network in New York received moving vans filled with wedding presents. On another, a featured couple was accustomed to talk to each other while in bed—twin beds of course. When the male lead left the show, his replacement continued to talk with his wife while in their beds. An avalanche of letters protested this immorality.

Let us jump from low culture to the highest with what may be the greatest nonfiction work written by an American in the decade after 1929, John Dewey's *Art as Experience*. The operative word is "experience." The fascination of the book is its efforts to define that noun so that it can then define the other noun in the title, with most of its examples being taken from the visual arts. In Dewey's language, we must deny that soap operas promoted any experience whatever (they promoted soap). This topic can be approached by using a coinage that two psychologists devised—a "perfink"—a monstrous term formed by joining sounds from three functions of humans: perception, feeling, thinking. Dewey did not employ this vulgarism, but the concept hints at what he meant by experience; any experience is a "perfink." He went further in saying that it must also involve a muscular response.

Within this framework he tried to resolve a vast range of seeming paradoxes. For instance, he argued that nobody can possibly experience the same painting twice. After the first time, he will be somewhat altered; so also, for him, will be the painting. Here we encounter again the proposition that has been stated above, that all art, all experience, is an interaction of objective with subjective. Obviously this idea was not new with Dewey. The difficulties of distinguishing the *me* from the *not me* are manifold. Dewey stated his conclusion thus: "The moments when the creature is both most alive and most composed and concentrated are those of fullest intercourse with the environment." To be alive, then, is not to be "relaxed" or to "take it easy." Quite the contrary, when speaking about moments of excitement, we use such phrases as "beside myself," "jumped out of my skin," "was transported." A usable analogy to art is religion. An experience in either zone achieves two results: First, it is a temporary loss of Self in that you fuse into external realities.

643

Second, it is a re-creation and hopefully an extension of Self in that you incorporate more external reality into yourself.

From Dewey's premises some corollaries follow. For one, the outside world assumes a vitalizing role in experience. For instance, you may live in a landscape, or more likely in a culture, that lacks diversity; the barrenness will not stimulate you, and you as a person will wither (see the Dewey discussion in Chapter 25). One environment may offer too little stimulation to the sense organs; another may offer too much; another may offer a chaos of sounds and sights and smells. Any of these imbalances can disrupt a human personality; we all have threshholds beyond which we cannot hold ourselves together. A contribution of art is that it gives us a coordinated sequence of sensations, a process. Because it is not helter-skelter, we can make *human* sense of it. Viewed from this angle, great art has an essential similarity to great theology. To phrase the same insight differently, much of the great art has been religious art—for good reason. Another thrust of Dewey's position might be stated thus (he does not so state it): Art may be for itself, but it can never be of itself or from itself. An essential continuity runs from the events of everyday life to the highest realms of esthetics, and this chain cannot be severed.

Thus the comprehension of an artistic work must be an act, not passive; it must be a "perfink." The English writer A. E. Housman said that conceiving a poem was like cutting yourself shaving. Dewey would have pushed this comment further; he would have said that experiencing a poem was like cutting yourself shaving, except that the reader is not cutting himself as deeply as the poet did. Moreover, these cuts can only come from forces that exist in the external world. Without re-creation of sound waves, light waves, palpable objects, flavors, odors, art could not exist. The quality of an artistic work is a function of its success in grasping the greatest variety and tension of these stimuli in order to harmonize them, impart rhythms to them. Here we come to Dewey's definition of a third of those abstract nouns that are so slippery: Art, Experience, and now Imagination:

> Esthetic experience is imaginative. This fact, in connection with a false idea of the nature of imagination, has obscured the larger fact that all *conscious* experience has of necessity some degree of imaginative quality. For while the roots of every experience are found in the interaction of a live creature with its environment, that experience becomes conscious, a matter of perception, only when meanings enter into it that are derived from prior experiences. . . .

The relevance of this argument to the study of history can be highlighted. Imagination can be the distillation from the past of tinctures (occasionally spirits) relevant to the present. It can also be an injection back into the past of perceptions that we have only gained today. The triad of "past-present-future" can be as functional as "thing-thought-word" or the duo "subjective-objective." But the cutting edge of these propositions must be constantly honed anew.

Finally, for present purposes, Dewey's treatise may be taken as a masterly assertion of what all adults know but can seldom express: That each of us develops a Self by forgetting about Self, by reaching beyond Self, by catching hold of a problem that is so engrossing that we become fused with the problem.

Thus far we have seen a sharp contrast between an illustration out of the depths of American culture, versus one from its heights. But the culture also provided some adhesives. Some of them will be examined in the remainder of this chapter. Several musical genre for instance united listeners of many faiths, colors, classes. New technologies made them accessible to a vastly enlarged audience, and audiences were responsive to a vastly expanded repertoire. Chronologically, first phonograph, then radio. For analytic reasons we might distinguish between innovations in the method of communication, and changes in the nature of the music being heard, but it must never be forgotten that both processes happened simultaneously. Persons who are now nearing the age of 50 will not forget the entranced moments of their childhoods when they sat on the floor in the living room winding up with a hand crank the portable RCA Victor phonograph with the foghorn speaker protruding over the top. Depending on the taste of their parents, they might have listened to racist trash as expressed by the Three Black Crows ("Wheah wuz you when the brains wuz handed out?"). But perhaps they listened to Lawrence Tibbett singing arias. The ambivalence of mechanization cannot be denied. More deceits can be imposed on more people in less time. Conversely, more divinity—using the term in a humanistic rather than a theological sense—can be pumped into the human scene.

Radio was the real jump. Statistics on the matter vary greatly, but probably the best ones are those of the National Association of Broadcasters. They report more than 14 million sets in 1930, twice as many a decade later. Put in other terms, one can guess that 75 per cent of all households in the nation had a radio by 1940. Then, as now, most of what the auditors heard was at best diverting. But not all. NBC had begun broadcasting the New York Symphony Orchestra in 1926, added the Boston Symphony a year later, the Philadelphia Symphony in 1929. The latter had a sponsor—Philco. In 1930 CBS began a series on Sunday afternoons with the New York Philharmonic. NBC countered the next year with a Saturday afternoon series by the Metropolitan Opera.* With the aid of radio, the musical firecracker became a

---

*Again, the momentum of change can be exaggerated easily. The quality of performance that could be heard on the radio thirty-five years ago was better than what can be heard now from a live orchestra except on a few stations.

FIGURE 27-1. *Charles Sheeler,* Upper Deck

skyrocket. Before World War I, the country held about 17 symphony orchestras. By 1939 there were more than 270. Equally important, they were no longer locked into the major cities along the Atlantic seaboard; one of the leading orchestras in the country was in Minneapolis under the direction of Dmitri Mitropoulous. Another was about to emerge in Cleveland under George Szell.

Thus the avenues for offering music proliferated, both by electrical devices and by live performances; the latter particularly were closely connected with the growth of cities that multiplied the existence of many types of spectator sports. As audiences grew, the variety of musical forms was greatly expanded. Hymns in church, a fiddle at the square dance, a player piano in the parlor—these had been the tradition. Now millions of Americans began to hear symphonies, chamber music, oratorios. By 1938–1939 some 10 million families every week were listening to one or another of these programs: Metropolitan Opera, NBC Symphony, New York Philharmonic, Ford's Sunday evening hour. The last in 1937 gained an audience more than double what it had drawn in 1935. Perhaps most telling in the long run, in 1938 more than 70,000 schools were piping the NBC Music Appreciation Hour to more than 7 million children, and nothing prevented adults from listening at home.

The presentation of fine music is one thing; creation of it is something else. It is not really a slander against the United States to say that it did not begin to create original music until the late nineteenth century in Louisiana. The new creation was called "Dixieland." Outstanding scholarship has illuminated some aspects of its origins. (1) Its authors were all black. (2) Although persons who have been around the academic world are likely to hate the term, it, like so many innovations, was a product of cross fertilization; it was born in the mating of African conventions with European instruments. Ashanti migrants in particular brought with them certain styles in rhythm that stressed the "snap" or "sprung beat." Their specific notions about the

---

Charles Sheeler was born in Pennsylvania in 1882. Like Ben Shahn (Figure 26-3), he derived a substantial part of his income from photography. By 1921 Sheeler could collaborate with the great photographer Paul Strand to offer a movie, *Manahatta*. With predictable captions from Walt Whitman (whose poem provided the title), this presentation of New York was memorable for its soaring towers and the tempos of the waterfront.

"Tempo" is still there in his mature paintings, but the viewer must search for it. The forms at first glance seem objective and static, as if fashioned from steel with a turret lathe. In *Upper Deck* (1929) Sheeler found the rhythms that are sought by men who work with camera rather than brush. He also resembles them in choosing to use a subdued palette, a preference perhaps derived from reliance on black and white film.

He could never be content with a head-on depiction of a scene as it was. He affirmed that "a picture could have incorporated in it the structural design implied in abstraction, and be presented in a wholly realistic manner." His respect for photography as a realistic medium was in tension with the abstract cubism of modern France and with the geometric rigors of the Italian Renaissance, though many of his aims would be parallel to theirs.

instrumental composition of a band were preserved in the rural South by their descendants, who drifted after the Civil War into New Orleans, the second biggest port in the nation and a highly cosmopolitan place. For their improvised folk music-makers—drums, loosened teeth in jawbones, hunks of cane made into pipes—they substituted clarinets and cornets and pianos. On these strange mechanisms they tried to achieve the tonal effects that they had gotten in the old ways, including their voices. The offspring of this blend was jazz, which came by Africa, out of Europe, into the United States. A magical creature it has been.

But it has had to cope with the folkways of its adopted land, and here it has met with much trouble. The most likely outlet for a black musician in New Orleans was in its seamy underside: saloons and whorehouses. (Why do the people who go to concerts overlook the fact that Johannes Brahms earned his living playing the piano in a brothel?) But the Establishment was squeamish; during World War I, the Navy closed down the red light district in New Orleans. Was there no way for a Negro trombonist to make it playing his horn? Some had already been working on Mississippi riverboats, had been to Memphis and St. Louis and Kansas City and Chicago. They drifted north, a part of the mass migration of blacks that has been unbroken for a half century; the number of Negroes in both the Northeast and the North Central states doubled from 1920 to 1940. We can almost say that as their customers moved, they moved along. Around 1920, few whites enjoyed their thing. Recording companies listed their products in quite distinct "race" catalogs. Back in Red Eye Joe's "down-home" they may have been hot stuff; now they were just another stupid Sam. One of Louis Armstrong's great sessions (reassembled a few years ago on an LP reissue) was cut in five days in 1926 in a garage in Terre Haute, Indiana, Gene Debs' home town.

This ambience was debilitating (anybody who questions that statement should listen to Armstrong's early records compared to his later ones). Jazz, while it had few white customers, was in danger of losing its black customers; blues and its derivatives were tainted by a degraded past in slavery. Specialized markets in music were being swamped as new channels of distribution favored the big mass-market products; now recording firms wanted a large sale to recoup a high investment. Oligopoly and consolidation of companies developed rapidly until a mere three agencies, the Music Corporation of America, William Morris, and the General Amusement Corporation, were by 1940 the bulk of the band business of the country. It almost seems that in this mass-market "packaging," recording companies were systematically badmouthing black musicians. Names of performers were omitted from labels; a famous pianist named Ferdinand "Jelly Roll" Morton on one label became "Fred Morton," on another "Marton"; after he became a star they spelled his name right. But the psychological toll was huge. The clarinet man with Louis Armstrong and His Hot Five in 1926 could improvise with the best in the world, but he called his music "hokum" because he could not play what was written in the score. A trombonist declared that Sidney Bechet was "no musician" because he could not read music.* Such slights abound in the literature of the times—black musicians hating each other, and themselves.

Logically, as entertainers on the make, black musicians applauded the worst white music. They tried, fortunately without perfect execution, to copy it. Armstrong kept proclaiming his adoration of Guy Lombardo. Hack band leaders were applauded as "very modern, almost futuristic"; they could read the score. So could Armstrong, and in another sense as well. He became, not a musician, but a "personality." The star system was being improvised. His early bands were small groups; five performers (not five men, he had a woman too) or seven; the standard Dixieland group was six. The key idea was balance; all other members could nearly match Armstrong in ability. Also crucial was a symmetry in the volume of the instruments. Drums or piano or bass could drown out the others, but didn't. They played subdued rhythm. Trumpet usually carried the melody, trombone below it, clarinet above it doing variations. It was gorgeous. But Armstrong subverted such beauty by surrounding himself with hacks and setting out to be spectacular. Then, sometime around 1930, jazz was cross-bred with pop to invent swing. At its best, as in Benny Goodman's finest cuts, it could be great fun. But it couldn't compare with oldtime Louis playing "Potato Head Blues." Sadder still, young people white and black around 1940 had to learn about Dixieland from white groups because blacks had stopped playing it.

As with music, so with the visual arts. They became available to many more people. Even in fairly large cities, the visitor to an art museum might find nothing beyond reproductions. This was as true in the John Herron Art Institute in Indianapolis as in the Brooklyn Museum. But someone who had never seen anything except plaster casts of discus throwers from ancient Greece could blow his skull when he entered a gallery in the Art Institute of Chicago and confronted Seurat's "Sunday on Grand Jatte Island." Museums had always been created in eccentric ways. The one on Michigan Avenue, which serves the added benefit of blocking the blasts off the Lake in the Windy City, was founded by two self-made millionaires. Besides money, they had taste. They seized upon works by a Spaniard unheard of in the United States, El Greco. They bought early works by Renoir, and the collection now holds a breathtaking assortment of French impressionism. Similarly, the overpowering collection of prints in the Fogg Museum at Harvard was assembled by the wealth and the judgment of one man.

Individualism in the arts (which had first gained momentum in the

---

*Consider (simultaneously) how much America has gained in the glory of spontaneous music and also how, more than they will ever know, Americans have impoverished themselves by putting down the black. I once heard Benny Goodman and the man who had started him on the clarinet, a Negro named Jimmie Noone, take off from "Sweet Georgia Brown." For forty minutes, until both were soaking wet, they swapped choruses, all made up. At the time, 1942, Noone was working as a groundskeeper at Wrigley Field in Chicago. The musical world in the United States could not use him, so it thought—if it thought.

New Britain Museum of American Art, New
Britain, Conn. (Harriet Russell Stanley
Fund). E. Irving Blomstrann, photographer.

FIGURE 27-2. *Thomas Hart Benton*, Arts of the West

Thomas Hart Benton never knew the meaning of the word "serenity." In his paintings there is no repose; you see violent sinuosities of line, screeching oppositions of color, a tumult of action. Trying to depict the enormous variety of life in the United States, he achieved what may be taken as one man's vision of Americans as people on the move. Much of his work, as in this *Arts of the West*, (1932) hovers in the shadowy realm between realism and satire. In cocktail conversations he is often derided (if he is mentioned at all) as the equivalent of Hollywood in the visual arts, but this evaluation is far too glib.

Benton's life (1889–   ) shows the origin of his work. Hailing from the small town of Neosho in southwestern Missouri, he was a son of the (almost) frontier. When he was eighty years old he joined a handful of others to shoot the frothy rapids of an Arkansas river. Besides painting hard, he drank hard and argued hard. In his words, "no American art can come to those who do not live an American life, who do not have an American psychology, and who cannot find in America justification of their lives." (Chapters 24 and 29.)

He was always a tendentious man. He derided the modern city as a "coffin for living and thinking." He himself studied in Paris as a young man, but a quarter century later when he saw Picasso's *Guernica* he scoffed that no decent painting had "come out of France since 1890" (ironically, one of Benton's students about that time was the abstract painter Jackson Pollock). Probably the chief esthetic influence on Benton was the great mural painting of Mexico, but he often tried to adapt its powers to a sheet of canvas on an easel. *Arts of the West*, with its interlocking depiction of a half-dozen scenes, clearly would be suitable for a large wall. Indeed, the recent resurgence of mural painting in the United States might be traced from an effort by Benton in 1930 to portray American activities on a wall at the New School for Social Research in New York City.

1870's) continued after 1929. In that year seven rich collectors founded the Museum of Modern Art in New York. Here also the Whitney Museum of American Art opened in 1930, the first institution to limit itself to esthetic objects created in this country. (Was it possible that the United States could produce beauty?) Colleges and universities busily built up their collections, although unfortunately this activity was concentrated along the East Coast, especially in wealthy Ivy League schools. Notable museums were built in smaller cities; the ones in Buffalo and Dallas and Helena and Youngstown spring to mind. In spite of the continued private or municipal support, the novel element on the scene was federal patronage. This did not take the form of building ponderous new mausoleums in the Corinthian style; even the National Gallery in Washington is the product of philanthropy (the Mellon family, Samuel H. Kress). Rather, federal moneys went to pay room and board for artists. Some of the best painters in the United States today will tell you that the happiest days of their lives were during the Great Depression; they were supported, not handsomely, but well enough to enjoy the sensation of putting pigments on canvas. No time clock; no controls on their messages; for most of them, no students to teach. But WPA workers also ran classes, and started many a pupil on that long climb to a freezing attic studio.

The Art Project of the WPA should remind us that those dreadful years after 1929 were in fact benign for quite a few people (junk dealers and retired servicemen were happy too). It is also a reminder that in the arts, as probably in any human endeavor, personal freedom counts. On the other major projects in the arts—Literature, Music, Theater—more control was imposed. When administration approaches, creativity leaves. These were "group efforts." In every state the writers were required to work on a guidebook to their commonwealth (but see Document 16-3). Some of these tower above others, and any might provide a few useful random facts but none offers much sustenance. The Federal Music Project hit upon a desperate situation. By 1933 some 50,000 professional musicians were out of work, a result not only of the depression but also of movie soundtracks which had knocked countless bands out of the pits. The crude statistics about this project are these. It supported some 15,000 performers. They gave 150,000 programs. They taught a half million youngsters. They collected, on records, about 2,000 folk songs.

What the WPA art projects demonstrated is a truism that every civilized nation in the world knows: that many indispensable forms of culture cannot survive without public subsidy. But now, in the wealthiest country ever, it is difficult in some of the wealthiest cities (Tucson) to get funds for the most basic public culture, the primary schools. If this condition prevails today in regard to the basis of all culture, try to imagine the stresses during the Great Depression. The most striking calamity was the fate of the Federal Theater Project. Started in 1935, it ran until June, 1939. Its budget averaged $7 million a year, and it made only $1 million at the box office. It hired 12,500 performers at an average monthly wage of $83. When it did Sinclair Lewis's "It Can't

Happen Here," the anti-fascist play, opened simultaneously in 21 theaters in 17 states. Eugene O'Neill and G. B. Shaw (notoriously greedy man, he) let the groups do their works for nominal royalties. The Detroit wing did one of the first plays by Arthur Miller. A critic for the New York *Times* called it "the best friend the theater as an institution has ever had in this country."

So what happened? In the spring of 1938 the House Committee on Un-American Activities was set up. In August it began hearings on the Federal Theater Project, which lasted for months. A portion of the hearings went like this, involving the director of the Project and a congressman on the Committee. The director has said that enthusiasm for the Project showed "a certain Marlowesque madness."

> Congressman: "You are quoting from this Marlowe. Is he a
> Communist?" (Laughter.)
> Director: "I was quoting from Christopher Marlowe . . ."
> [colleague of Shakespeare].

This farce knew no boundaries. After Congress, prodded by HUAC, had wiped out the Theater Project, its former director was packing up her office in Washington. She got a phone call from a congressman. She expected sympathy, but no. He was all business, because he wanted to know about future plans for the theater project in his state. She told him that the establishment was defunct. "You voted it out of existence." She told the date: June 30. After a heavy silence, his shocked voice asked, "Was *that* the Federal Theatre?"

No purpose could be served by writing a sentence or so each about a couple of dozen writers; only a few can be mentioned and then two will be discussed more fully. First, another generalization. In spite of, sometimes because of, the misery surrounding them, American authors produced as many inventive works as in any other decade of our history, including 1850–1860 and 1880–1890. Critics have diminished their homeland by deriding or just ignoring some fine authors. Before expanding that contention, a big exception should be noted. Namely, no new major poet emerged in the United States during the thirties and forties. Comparisons here can be made both over time and in space; in France, England, Germany, a few men were proving that poetry could be vitalized. But during this time the United States did not spawn a new figure of the stature of Robert Frost, E. E. Cummings, Wallace Stevens.

Our sense of respect can really go to work if we poke through the prose of the thirties and forties. At the beginning of the decade Dashiell Hammett, in an outburst that lasted through five novels and a sheaf of short stories, proved that the genre of "mysteries" could recount some lasting truths about the human condition. William Faulkner, sitting way off down there in Oxford, Mississippi near the piney woods, made us believe that he could get inside the stream of consciousness of a mute and simple-minded boy, inside the murderous impulses that build up inside a young black man. To my taste at least, Lillian Hellman virtually invented the American stage with "The Little Foxes" (I personally cannot endorse the numerous accolades for Eugene O'Neill, although he obviously had great influence on the American theater). In *U.S.A.*, John Dos Passos published a tedious novel, but the "profiles" in it are often masterly. If you want to learn fast about Morgan, or Ford, or Debs, or Veblen, here is the best place to go. And we have with us still F. Scott Fitzgerald. When he died in 1940, not even nearing his personal mid-century mark, he was writing a novel that featured a movie producer in Hollywood. Published posthumously and unfinished, the book seems to me to be the most credible love story that has been written by an American in this century.

To mention Fitzgerald is call up memories of Hemingway. The two men, in addition to their other abilities with the English language, had the gift of insulting each other. Both living in Paris during the decade of the expatriate, they were in a bar with friends. Fitzgerald, out of his boyish adulation, blurted, "The rich really *are* different." Hemingway, even younger, found a put-down: "Yeah, they have more money." Fitzgerald subsequently concocted one of his most cutting remarks ever: "Ernest always was willing to lend a helping hand to the man on the ledge a little higher up." Nobody else needs to caricature Hemingway; he did it to himself—his show of virility; his assertive habit of sneaking a snort behind pillars in the galleries of art museums; the rotten novels that he issued in the last half of his life. This included melodramatic claptrap about the Spanish Civil War with a hero who might as well be a Boy Scout master in Traverse City, Michigan, and another book (also about a soldier, officer of course) called *Across the River and Into the Trees* which soon brought the rejoinder *Across the Street and Into the Phone Booth.* Particularly after he killed himself, it became easy to make fun of Hemingway. But a dozen or so of his short stories make us know that as a practitioner of that art almost nobody is fit to play in the same league, that on some days he could make angels and devils dance across the page, that he ranks with Joyce and Kafka and Frank O'Connor.

If his short stories are so ultimately satisfying, why do his novels, including the early ones which are the best ones, seem so dull? One aspect of a tenable explanation might be this: A short story can be compelling even though it deals with only a limited range, confined by number of characters, by space, by time. If it reveals two or three personalities as they existed at a given moment, the reader goes home satisfied. It can be static. But a longer work must present temperaments that are changing, or it becomes trying; if it remains static it reminds you of a record that has cracked, and you begin to fidget at hearing chords repeated. Perhaps Hemingway somewhat reflected the worst weaknesses of Freudianism, in that he seemingly did not believe that a person could change. In a novel of 300 pages, the reader simply ceases to care about what happens to his characters; nothing will happen.

If we conclude that Hemingway's defects were flaws in his character, not in his craft, we might venture the same remark about the outstanding new novelist to appear in the decade, John Steinbeck. But the application would be different. Steinbeck's worst problem was that he could seldom get outside the syndrome that was exposed by Twain so accurately in *Huck Finn* (Chapter 19): the cruelty-sentimentality complex. On one end, we have rather heavy handed cruelty and violence: When a woman gripped by spite goes out with garden shears to cut the heads off chrysanthemums, the symbolic meaning approaches the butchery of another woman (in a novel of the same era) who cuts off her nipples with garden shears. Conversely, we have sentimentality: Steinbeck was prone to slobber over the cute Mexicanos, always happy no matter how dire their malnutrition. But, again as with Hemingway, a man's personal foibles, even his literary faults, should not wall us off from his works. Hemingway—in his use of monosyllables, and even more in his telling of tales strictly by means of dialogue (or interior monologue), did a lot to purify the American language, to scrap the used-up razor blades of "picturesque" verbiage that had no cutting edge. Although Hemingway had revived Mark Twain's technique of using a first-person narrator, he did use many descriptive passages. Steinbeck almost abolished these when he became mature. Although he had written five earlier novels, his first success came with *Of Mice and Men* (1937). His own explanation was that he was trying to write simultaneously the short novel and the play; the book seems to read like a movie script. It has dialogue, plus stage directions, plus nothing else. He stripped it almost bare.

Already in January, 1937, Steinbeck was working on his best work, *The Grapes of Wrath*. Eighteen months later, exhausted, he staggered toward the finish line, and the bound volume came out in 1939. Soon it became a movie that was a big success at the box-offices. It deserved to be, still does, still is. Of all the wide range of books that I have asked students to read for courses about the United States in the twentieth century, the two with the sharpest impact on the most students have been this one and *The Autobiography of Lincoln Steffens* (1931). Two qualities made *The Grapes of Wrath* distinctive. The least noticed has been its innovation in technique. A few pages earlier we looked at Dewey's scheme of art as representing a fusion of subjective with objective. Steinbeck, with astounding audacity, proved that the formula does not always apply; he split the two in the most glaring fashion that one can imagine. He alternated a subjective chapter, then an objective one, a subjective, and so on. His "plot" is about one family, the Joads, and their friend Preacher Casey, who migrate from Oklahoma to become itinerant farmers in California. His larger story tells what happened to millions of poor people in the Southwest during the dust storms and the depression. He convinces readers that he knew what he was writing. If art is disciplined passion, this novel has both elements. Steinbeck stated them while he was doing his research:

> I must go over into the interior valleys. There are five thousand families starving to death over there, not hungry but just actually starving. The government is

trying to feed them and get medical attention to them, with the Fascist group of utilities and banks and huge growers sabotaging the thing all along the line, and yelling for a balanced budget. . . .

Do you know what they're afraid of? They think that if these people are allowed to live in camps with proper sanitary facilities they will organize, and that is the bugbear of the large landowner and the corporation farmer. . . .

Although the Resettlement Administration did found more decent camps for migratory pickers, more than three decades would pass before any sizable number of these workers could establish joint action against growers. (See Chapter 29 on Cesar Chavez).

The central point here is that the Great Depression brought a united front among representatives of various social groups who normally never thought about each other. Steinbeck was far from unique. Steelworkers met lawyers; some sociologists began to suspect that poverty cannot be solved by jargon; writers went to lumbering camps and coal towns to see how common folks lived; photographers and artists dipped into segments of the nation that they had ignored earlier (Figure 26-3). Disaffection from the power sector was extreme and ubiquitous among intellectuals. The young novelist Thomas Wolfe wrote to his mother about the hard times in autumn, 1931: "No one seems to be doing anything about it, everyone is standing around with his mouth open as if he expected the gates of heaven to open the next moment and rain milk and honey all over him. People talk about 'the pendulum swinging backward' and 'conditions are bound to change'—This is foolish talk: conditions are not *bound* to change unless something is done to change them, and at present it seems that any change will be for the worse. . . . I think we are at the end of a period." A few months later, Edmund Wilson, one of the naton's most distinguished younger critics, let fly: "The attitude of the Menckenian gentleman, ironic, beer-loving and 'civilized,' . . . attitude of old-American-stock smugness, . . . the liberal attitude that American capitalism was going to show a new wonder to the world by gradually and comfortably socializing itself and that we should just have to respect it in the meantime . . . the attitude of trying to get a kick out of the sheer size and energy of American enterprises, irrespective of what they were aiming at . . . they are no use in our present predicament, and we can see how superficial they were."

This alienation from the Establishment of many intellectuals came to play a signal role in one of the most astonishing innovations of the decade—formation of unions, organized by industry rather than by craft, in the heartlands of mass production. When labor organizers moved surreptitiously among rubber workers in Akron, auto workers in Flint, shoe workers in St. Louis, they carried with them a small battalion of trained publicity men to turn out pamphlets and plant press releases in the local papers. A trade union might even hope for a square shake on the front pages of some metropolitan dailies. Always before in the United States the onset of depression had meant the decimation of labor organization. Ten unemployed men on every corner had meant an abundance of strikebreakers; companies had not feared strikes because they could not sell their products anyway; the rise in unemployment rates had meant a drop in monthly dues to local and national unions. With the going so rough, many organizations had disappeared. But in the Great Depression, union membership grew by as much as 4 million.* Familiarity with the cause of the working class by so many artists, writers, and movie people helped to acclimate other portions of the public to some of labor's bizarre strategies and tactics, which might otherwise have caused panic or streams of blood instead of the few trickles that developed. Black liberationists after World War II would call this style "democracy in the streets" (mid-Chapter 29). Oldtime buddies in the Industrial Workers of the World would talk about "direct action"; Jimmie Higgins in the hiring hall might counsel "hitting the bricks." Call it how you will, it bore little resemblance to the standard middle-class fantasy about the republic as being orderly lines of voters waiting placidly for their turn at the polls on election day.

If hundreds, thousands, of intellectuals took part in a rising pro-labor movement that furthered the humanization of American factories, their role should not be exaggerated. Some politicians also acted with honor and compassion, and a few have been immortalized in such labels as "the Wagner Act." But recognition that other groups in the society had power and used it should never divert us from the central truth: The glory days of labor progress during the Great Depression would not have happened if democracy had not taken to the streets. For decades the public demonstration in the United States had been a formalized ritual trumped up by the Establishment—flagwaving parades during Wilson's days in the White House, stuffy claptrap on the Fourth of July. When a worker charged at a militiaman, carrying a fistful of bolts and throwing them, the norms of polite society had little bearing.

Marches and meetings began, for understandable reasons, among the unemployed. A wave of public protests was often coordinated by Communists, who formed the National Unemployment Council immediately after the financial crash. Crowds stormed the city hall in Cleveland, Philadelphia, Los Angeles. By 6 March, 1930, the organization felt strong enough to call International Unemployment Day. New York witnessed a parade of 110,000, Detroit of 100,000. By February, 1932, a nationwide demonstration brought forth an estimated half million. Three separate petitions, each with more than a million names, were presented to Congress. Demands did not vary much: improved relief programs, unemployment compensation. Other organizations

---

*The drama of this transition was enormous, but the change was far from universal. As late as 1940 the owner of a half dozen mines around Glen Ferris, West Virginia, was quoted publicly on a strike against his operations: "Put a million dollars on a shelf for a year and you still have a million dollars. Put our employees on a shelf for a year and all you have is a pile of bones."

began to suspect that history was passing them by. The stodgy AFL with its history of "voluntarism" finally declared for unemployment benefits. The Socialists in 1932 set up their own organization for the jobless, and in 1936 it merged with the other national outfit to form the Workers' Alliance. Reliable information about these developments is very hard to find. Guesses at the original membership of the Workers' Alliance range from 93,000 to 500,000. By 1938 it could claim 1,500 locals in 45 states. Although the figures given here can be challenged, the impact of this militancy is beyond question. Recalling the prominence of strikebreakers in earlier mutinies, their obscurity after 1929 seems amazing.

Another breakthrough during the Great Depression was the relatively friendly governmental climate offered to trade unions. Reforms in the 48 states cannot be reported in this space; anyway, three federal laws seem preponderant. The change of tone became manifest before the New Deal. The two Congressional sponsors of the Norris-LaGuardia Act had advocated it long before its enactment in 1932. Key provisions were these: Yellow-dog contracts forbidding unions could not be enforced by federal courts (see late Chapter 23 on unions and the courts). Damage suits against unions were restricted. The statute also contained a policy statement. Since under present conditions, the individual employee could not affect the terms on which he worked, it was mandatory that "he should have full freedom of association, self-organization and designation of representatives of his own choosing, to negotiate the terms and conditions." These terms were virtually used verbatim in the two New Deal provisions that proved vital to the growth of collective bargaining: Section 7 (a) of the law establishing the NRA in 1933, and the National Labor Relations Act of 1935.

At this juncture, we encounter the phenomenon of a snowball rolling down a hill—cumulative effects. Section 7 (a) was meant by most of the officials who administered it to be a fake. In most industries it was a fake. But not in all. Of the three unions that benefited from the law in the two years of its existence, two were in the garment trades. They were led by Sidney Hillman (Amalgamated Clothing Workers, ACW) and by David Dubinsky (International Ladies' Garment Workers Union, ILGWU). The third was John L. Lewis's United Mine Workers (UMW). Even before 1929, these three unions, all in sick industries, had been stricken. The UMW had been almost wiped out. More blows fell after 1929. These three organizations (note that all were organized by industry rather than by craft) wobbled and reeled. Then came Section 7 (a). The leaders saw a chance to recoup. Their organizers swarmed into textile towns and coal camps. Lewis's henchmen had a simple slogan: "FDR wants you to join the union." Membership skyrocketed.

Per capita dues flowed into the coffers of ACW, ILG, UMW. A remarkable decision was made. Old-style time-servers might have simply voted themselves higher salaries and built larger mansions at Miami. But eight national unions, now affluent compared to former times, chose to put some of their unaccustomed wealth into breaking the open shop in mass-production industries. Heading the pack strode the massive bulk of Lewis. Himself corrupt through his career in the labor movement and a hopeless autocrat, he apparently overnight caught the altered tempo of the shops. The man should not be idealized (nor should the working class, for that matter). Countless times his thugs had beaten up dissidents at local meetings; no challenge to the regime was permitted; one socialist who wanted to democratize the UMW was expelled from it four times. But about 1933 Lewis sensed that a tidal wave of rebelliousness was sweeping through factories as well as mines. He would have agreed with Lenin, who after the Russian Revolution was asked: How do you make a revolution? His reply: You get in front of it and run like crazy to stay there. This anecdote belittles both Lenin and Lewis, but it does give a sense of the dynamics of a social explosion. At best the talk about "all that Mr. Roosevelt did for the poor" should be taken with a grain of salt; most of it is hokum. What the poor got, they took; nobody gave it.

An uproar surging in from the shops was the last thing in the world desired by the bureaucrats accustomed to running the AFL. They, together with the members of most AFL affiliates, wanted peace and quiet and steady work. They had no plan to cope with a mass upsurge, but they could not altogether ignore it. Plant after plant throughout the nation was being spontaneously organized by the men and women who worked in it. Sometimes literally wringing their hands, the AFL grannies figured out a format—the federal local. This device was merely a corral to hold the roundup until it could be divvied among ranch owners. That is, the skilled workers would be apportioned among craft unions; then the others in the factory could shift for themselves. Typical was a rubber plant in Akron, where some 4,500 workers set up an independent industrial union. They foolishly applied to the AFL for a charter. Within a few weeks they had been sorted out among 19 craft locals. In bargaining against a giant corporation, such divisions might be advantageous to a few dozen skilled employees; for most of the workers they can only be disastrous. Eugene Debs had understood that back in 1893 (mid-Chapter 20). Beginning about 1934, laborers in giant mills—often with little or no guidance or help from on top, sometimes with resistance from on top—had arrived at an organizational form suited to their needs.

Some academics who rail against "oversimplification" by the common man (whoever he is) have been guilty of oversimplifying the processes being considered here. They seize hotly upon the glib phrase by Samuel Gompers: More, Here, Now. But even that phrase, rightly understood, implied better wages and shorter hours. No general discussion of grievances over working conditions is possible because variations from industry to industry, from district to district, from one establishment within an industry to another, were the crux of the problem. Again, some examples must suffice. Coal miners suffered from silicosis, and many became paraplegics for life when underground timbering gave way. Glass and chemical and rubber factories exuded noxious fumes. An advance taste of hell was imparted to workers by the heat in the open-hearth department. In these jobs, men died young. I have seen young auto workers lie on the floor and retch from exhaustion. With the assembly line, man was adapted to the machine, not the machine to the man. The author of the finest study of the sit-down strike in Flint that crumpled the resistance of General Motors wrote: "It was the speed-up that organized Flint, as it was the one element in the life of all the workers that found a common basis of resentment. Wives who feared the intervention of the union vented their execration on the speed-up which left their husbands trembling and exhausted after their work and narrowed the life of the family to the mere acts of physical continuance." The same tale was told over and over. To these stories of physiological hardship must be added the deprivation of the spirit. Persons who have never been exposed to a world outside that of the whitecollar white apparently find it hard to realize that industrial and manual workers of every ethnic background need dignity just like the rest of the world. Let us consider an item from the file of the CIO Packinghouse Workers in Chicago; an exact copy of a grievance submitted at the Armour plant reads thus:

> the string department carries an offensive odor to the extent that it is very hard to find a formular that will take it out of the skin. We have tried everything within our Power, to prevent this awful odor. When a worker takes a street car Every Body tries to get away from this awful smell. So we of the string department are asking the Company to place in our Department a wash room with three showers.

The CIO was built, partly by anger at the lofty policies decreed by top management, partly by gripes against commonplace slurs by petty foremen.

Historians like me are tempted by the dramatic episode, especially when it can be linked to a famous name. So this account cannot omit the clash of giants on the floor of the national AFL convention, during a debate on organizational policy in November, 1935, when Lewis struck the also gargantuan president of the Carpenters in the face. Such a public display of aggression was indeed remarkable since these two despots ordinarily let others do their fighting for them. What provoked them to turn to violence? The Carpenters' boss is perhaps easy to explain; it would not be nasty to label him a hooligan who was desperate to protect both his union's jurisdictional lines and the outlook from which it was derived. For Lewis, with his penchant for histrionics, the turmoil was a way to dramatize the cause of industrial unionism. To an ability at fisticuffs he added a genius for invective. At this 1935 convention eight AFL unions decided to found the Committee for Industrial Organization (CIO), but they would not go the ultimate of full separation from the AFL. Subsequently when CIO chiefs were discussing the situation, it was suggested that they should delay action to explore further into the mind of AFL president William Green. Lewis was jocular: "Explore the mind of Bill Green? Why, Bill and I had offices next door to each other for ten

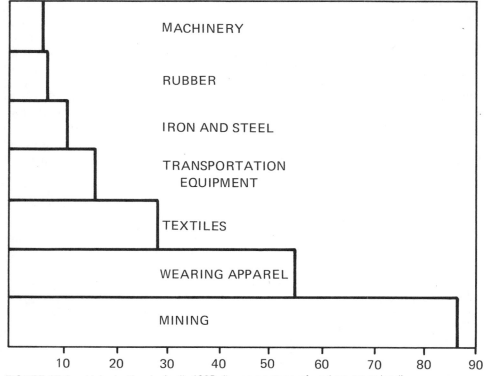

FIGURE 27-3. *Unionization in April, 1935, (by percentage of workers organized)*

years. . . . I have done a lot of exploring in Bill's mind and I give you my word there is nothing there." Maybe another warning is needed against romanticizing Lewis. Several of his associates have pointed to a self-serving motive for his role in the CIO: to keep his control in the UMW. By this account, hundreds of young rebels were challenging for power throughout the mine districts. Lewis siphoned them off by giving them paid jobs on the staff of the Steelworkers Organizing Committee.

The historian who speculates about the motives of any individual (including himself) is risking his life and his sacred honor; it is not a smart thing to do. Whatever the motives were, the results were the wonder of the world. In autos, organization was next to nothing before 1933, and due in considerable part to Roosevelt's devious behavior, progress under the Blue Eagle was slight. The Big Three had hardly been breached. Scattered locals existed in minor companies: White Motors in Cleveland, Auto-Lite in Toledo, some tool-and-die firms in Detroit. But by 1937 both GM and Chrysler had signed exclusive bargaining agreements. Ford did not topple until 1941. As of April, 1935, the percentage of employees in other industries covered by trade-union agreements is shown in Figure 27-3. Within ten years, by 1945, 80 per cent of the workers in all of these industries except textiles were protected by collective agreements.

The giant corporations never did fold up and surrender, but they were forced to make concessions. In retrospect, two episodes seem crucial. The first began on December 26, 1936, in Flint, Michigan, when the workers simply locked themselves in the plant at Fisher Body. No general ever devised better strategy. The company had only two sets of dies to stamp out bodies. Flint handled Buick, Oldsmobile, Pontiac. Fisher of Cleveland did all Chevrolets. As the strike went on, sometimes violently, for six weeks, it was the steadfastness of the ordinary worker that finally won a settlement, although the union produced several leaders of outstanding ability. But one man deserves special mention, Governor Frank Murphy. He was Catholic in a non-Catholic state. He was a Democrat in a Republican state. Now pressure was put on him to send in the National Guard to drive the strikers out of the plants. He must have been strongly tempted, but he let events run their course. Finally on 11 February the bastion of the open shop signed an agreement with the United Auto Workers (UAW). In less than three weeks a major subsidiary of U.S. Steel had signed with the Steelworkers Organizing Committee (SWOC).

These occurrences do not mean that smaller—still huge—firms would at all times follow the lead of the biggest manufacturer in the industry. So-called "Little Steel" fought back bitterly, highlighted by the attacks of South Chicago police outside the Republic plant in South Chicago that caused the death of ten strikers and injury to untold numbers. Ford remained unorganized for years, during which time its Service Department committed thousands of indecencies not to say crimes. Partly because of these strongholds of anti-unionism, the insurgency of industrial workers ran out of steam by about 1938. It revived briefly during World War II, and then was jettisoned by union chieftains.

A final word. The president of the United States was indifferent if not hostile to these efforts to improve the status of the industrial worker. He did champion the Social Security Act. FDR signed but clearly did nothing to promote the National Labor Relations Act. On the Fair Labor Standards Act of 1938 he was neutral. What has been more important in the long run was his unwillingness to use the new power structure of organized labor to alter the regularities of the American party system. In spite of his alleged affinities to Sidney Hillman, Roosevelt was always more comfortable with Ed Flynn and Ed Kelly and Jimmy Byrnes and Sam Rayburn. The mother of a former student of mine once asked, when confronted with some evidence about FDR: "Why did such a marvelous man allow so many terrible things?" It does make a chap wonder.

The persisting ditch between Mr. Citizen and Mr. Egghead had become a moat by 1929. Happily, the next decade framed new bridges between these

Courtesy of the Pennsylvania Academy of
Fine Arts

FIGURE 27-4. *Horace Pippin,* John Brown Going to His Hanging

John Brown Going to His Hanging can be viewed in several ways. Done by Horace Pippin, a black, finished in 1942, it can be seen as a manifestation of yet another upsurge in the campaign for black equality. During World War II quite a few Americans of all derivations and beliefs were horror-stricken by the brutalities that the fascist nations were inflicting on alien minorities. This awareness helped to make them aware of injustice in the United States. It also prompted them to comb the nation's past for heroes who had tried to smash the oppressions.

John Brown was not a happy choice for this role. He was, however, a master of self-righteousness. At his trial in 1859 he had declared: "I never did intend murder, or treason, or the destruction of property, or to excite or incite slaves to rebellion, or to make an insurrection." The unvarnished truth is that he had committed every one of these crimes: murder, treason, destruction of differing segments of society. The germs of a new community can be seen in several areas of culture during the Great Depression. In music a new form appeared as Dixieland jazz, which had appeal to both highbrow and lowbrow. The technology of radio and phonograph made popular music as well as more conventional types available to millions of listeners. The visual arts were offered to wider audiences by a proliferation of museums. Book publishing also had its revolutions. Monthly book clubs infiltrated the middle classes in particular. Novels were converted into films, and original screen plays added to the steady flow of movies. Nearly all Americans knew the Marx Brothers, Chaplin, Jean Harlow, Clark Gable, Gary Cooper. Perhaps most telling of all as an adhesive between formerly divorced groups was the broader base of public support behind the effort to organize the mass-production industries. Civic-minded academics and journalists found little to like about the craft unions of the American Federation of Labor, but they had less difficulty in identifying with the industrial unions of the Congress of Industrial Organizations. As employees in the dominant sectors of the economy were struggling to become unionized, the policies of the federal government usually amounted to benevolent neutrality (which was in itself an advance over the hostility of earlier times). Similarly, the indifference of federal authorities toward attempts to invigorate a higher culture can be seen in their acquiescence while the Federal Arts Projects atrophied away.

---

property, incitation to revolt. Nonetheless, this painting contains historical truth, not about John Brown perhaps, but about the rising militancy of many blacks during the war. Pippin said of his own art, "Pictures just come to my mind, and then I tell my heart to go ahead."

Pippin's three paintings that memorialized John Brown were also a landmark in the revival of the artistic primitives (see Figure 14-1). In this sense they were a bridge over the chasm between the intellectuals and the common man. While saluting Pippin's superb work, we might be puzzled to understand how he conquered his craft. Born in 1888 he went to a one-room country school in Pennsylvania. By his account he was already in trouble with the teacher by the time he was seven because he illustrated his spelling papers with sketches. In consequence he would be kept after school to prepare a respectable paper. When he got home he would be whipped for being late. But he persisted, until at last about 1937 he won some recognition. Within nine years he was dead.

Ways to Study History XXVII

Cross-examine the eye-witnesses for bias. This maxim can be explored by a reverse route through an anecdote. A few years back, no history of Tanganyika had ever been written. The region had just gained its freedom from the British Commonwealth; it would be an independent sovereignty in Africa. The British Colonial Office decided to throw open for scholarly use its records relating to Tanganyika (full independence in December 1961; united with Zanzibar and smaller islands in 1964 to form Tanzania).

An experienced anthropologist had spent several years doing field work in Tanganyika. He now saw an opening to do a firmly based history of that country. His earlier field work had been financed to a large degree by the Social Science Research Council. Chancing to encounter at a conference a grants officer from the SSRC, he asked if they would allow him a modest sum to go to England for a summer to explore the available Colonial Office records. In this fashion he could gain a better estimate of whether his long-term undertaking was feasible. In the language of the natural scientists, he proposed a pilot project; on a firing range the sergeant might call it a trial run. The grants officer, knowing the previous accomplishments of the applicant, was highly encouraging. A formal application was submitted. The anthropologist rented a house in England, made airplane reservations for his entire family—and then he got jolted. A word about procedures in foundations. Any request is normally submitted to outside "referees"; that is, other persons of standing who submit opinions about its worth. This rejection contained an opinion from a referee who leaned heavily against the applicant's reliance on Colonial Office papers because they were "prejudiced sources."

My colleagues chatted for a year trying to recall whether any of them had ever seen an unbiased source. We may doubt that one exists. Historical truth is approached by getting the available primary sources, weighing them against each other, and trying to correct for distortions. No eye-witness is fully trustworthy.

CHAPTER 28

How to Get into a War: Installment II

From 1929 to 1939, the United States faced two major problems. The first: To cure the crushing unemployment—of manpower, of machinery, of money. Whether we think of muscle, of mind, of machines, of bank deposits, the amount of idleness was still appalling as late as 1940. On this score, in spite of raucous (but unsupported) assertions to the contrary, the New Deal failed. Some New Dealers had workable ideas, but their ideas were not usually the ones that were used. The second problem: To stop the spread of fascism without fighting a world war. On this score also, the New Deal failed. Need it have done so badly? Failure to cure unemployment is clearly quite distinct from failure to prevent war. The first could certainly have been alleviated by domestic policies dependent on no outside nations. The second required some cooperation from at least three foreign powers: the U.S.S.R., Great Britain, France. In regard to the latter two countries, that cooperation was never proffered. But Americans have little cause to boast of their record in those terrible years. And Main Street, not the White House, must bear the blame, or most of it.

Ironically, a World Disarmament Conference was scheduled for Geneva on 2 February, 1932. The fascist dictator of Italy, Benito Mussolini, had just named his son-in-law as the new foreign minister. That diplomat called on President Hoover in 1931. Henry Stimson, secretary of state, left a memo of the meeting:

> The President . . . gave us a summary of the attitude of the American man on the street. For a hundred and fifty years we had kept out of Europe; then in 1917 we had been dragged into a great war. We had spent forty billions of dollars in the war, and we had added ten billions more in the shape of loans after the war. We were spending a billion dollars a year on our disabled men. And yet Europe was in a worse condition than she was before the war. This, he said, led to despair as to Europe and European affairs on the part of the ordinary American citizen, and now he just wanted to keep out of the whole business. This was the general attitude of the American public, and he did not see how the United States could take the leadership in any direction.

Hoover was right in his assessment. American foreign policy for the next decade must be read in the light of this statement. But two addenda are needed. That catch-all word "isolationism" will conceal more than it reveals. Second, he was wrong about where the initial crisis would occur; his warnings like Washington's were against political commitments in Europe, whereas the United States was more concerned with economic involvements in Asia.

In the autumn of 1931, a conjunction of circumstances combined to give Japan a relatively free hand. England had just abandoned the gold standard and was trying madly to juggle its finances. The U.S.S.R. was absorbed in its Five-Year Plan and the consequent popular resistance. Civil strife in China was multiplied by a Yangtze flood. Naval construction in the United States and Britain had lagged, while Japan steadily built to its limits under the Washington Treaty of 1922. So in September the Japanese army staged an incident at Mukden and followed with an invasion of Manchuria. For three months the United States, hoping it could strengthen the moderates in Japan, sent only private protests. At last the secretary of state, Henry L. Stimson, declared that the nation would not recognize any government that infringed American rights, the Open Door (end of Chapter 21), or the Kellogg-Briand Pact (end of Chapter 24). Neither Britain nor France would support these doctrines—a division among the antifascist governments that would be re-enacted many times before World War II. Stimson made a strong plea for international cooperation, but one wonders. Already he had told China: "We have not attempted to go into the question of right and wrong. . . . we are not taking sides." For such a moralizing nation, the matter of right and wrong would seem to be critical. By 3 March, 1932, the British ambassador in Washington was writing to the foreign minister: "I know that the Americans are dreadful people to deal with. They cannot make firm promises, but they jolly you along with fair prospects and when you are committed they let you down."

Another generalization may be ventured. It is usually malarkey to speak of "the" foreign policy of the United States. Nearly always there are several in operation, often unknown to the practitioners of a contradictory policy. Manchuria offers an illustration. By April, 1932, Stimson was telling the cabinet that it was "almost impossible" to avoid thinking of war against Japan. He warned that the American navy was not equal to the task of "meeting Japan." President Hoover rejoined that reasons existed for not having an "offensive Navy." When Stimson went off (unofficially of course) for talks with other powers at the League of Nations in Geneva, Hoover cut the ground from under him. At the president's instructions, the undersecretary of state announced that in regard to Manchuria our "government's policy excluded sanctions of economic pressure or military force." Japan set up a puppet government in Manchuria, named it Manchukuo, recognized its legality. The League of Nations issued an innocuous report. On one point Stimson had his way with Hoover, but his victory can hardly be regarded with unqualified enthusiasm. Congress enacted a law for Philippine independence. The president vetoed it because the secretary urged that it would unleash further Japanese expansion. As to that, he was undoubtedly right. During the interregnum between administrations, President-elect Roosevelt seemed to be friendly to Stimson's stiff attitude. Further support for a tough line came from messages sent by the American ambassador in Japan: "There is no bluff in her attitude."

The first diplomatic problem to confront the new president was an International Economic Conference slated to convene in London in June. This episode exemplifies three aspects of the years beginning with 1933: one personal, one intragovernmental, one intergovernmental. (1) FDR had a penchant for secrecy. He sometimes tried sneaky tactics when a candid statement of the truth would probably have worked better (end Chapter 26). Perhaps more frequently, he would assign the same job to two or three men, and leave them free to carve each other's backs. By this mechanism, the only man who could make the final decision was the president. Thus the secretary of state was the formal head of the American delegation to the London Conference. But soon FDR also dispatched an assistant secretary of state as his personal representative. Who had power to speak for the United States? The president. (2) The government in Washington was severely divided on monetary policy. Congress had opened the door for devaluation of the dollar. Although this step was not taken until the Gold Reserve Act of January, 1934, the clauses in both public and private contracts that provided for payment in a fixed quantity of gold had been declared null and void. One faction was pressing for immediate devaluation, arguing that if the price of gold went up, the prices of all other commodities would rise also, and thus domestic production would be encouraged. Opponents screamed that the determining element was the quantity of foreign trade, which could best be expanded by a stabilization of international exchange rates. The latter was the goal of the

London meetings. The former was Roosevelt's decision. While several commentators have complained that he "scuttled" the Economic Conference, he was probably justified. To quote his grounds at the time, "The sound internal economic system of a nation is a greater factor in its well-being than the price of its currency in changing terms of the currencies of other nations." So far, so good, but, the domestic monetary policies of the New Deal for the next two years were at best mediocre. (3) While the impact of Roosevelt's actions on the home economy might be graded LP—low pass—its political impact on the world arena was ghastly—pronounced F. The backbiting within the American delegation was supplemented by squabbles in public among the United States, Britain, and France. Meanwhile the blatantly militarist nations could sit by as delighted spectators. A quick summation might be in place. The countries soon to be the Allies were demonstrating daily that they could not manage their own economies. They had admitted privately to fascist diplomats that their electorates were so polarized that the government was paralyzed. Now they added a public exhibition of how embittered the intergovernmental fracas had become.

My intention is not to saddle FDR, or the State Department, or the American people with sole blame for the next eight years. But when the international order fell in ruins, the United States had wrought its share of the damage.

In November, 1933, the administration did take a promising step. Twenty-six years after the Bolshevik Revolution in Russia, our government acknowledged that it had occurred. The initial opposition in Washington to recognition of the U.S.S.R. had been ideological; President Wilson at the time of the Versailles Conference was obsessed by this new menace to a world made safe for democracy. A rationale had to be found, and it was: The Reds would not pay their debts; they had confiscated American property without compensation. Even after the United States had withdrawn its tiny invading army from Siberia, Secretary of State Hughes continued to harp on these themes.* It took FDR and his advisers to cut through the verbiage. They were urged by some forceful proponents: executives of GE hoped to sell dozens of generators to a new customer, while International Harvester foresaw a giant market for its farm machinery. (Similar influences, especially from wheat farmers, operated on the Canadian recognition of Red China in 1970.) Fittingly, one of the loudest opponents of recognition was the AFL, on the grounds that the U.S.S.R. did not have "free" trade unions; advocates of recognition replied

---

*The hypocrisy was distinct. When the United States enacted prohibition, it rendered worthless hundreds of millions of dollars in private property. When it abrogated the gold clause in all contracts, it greatly reduced the value of many forms of property. But when private American rights were disturbed by Mexico (oil fields) or the U.S.S.R. (railroads), our policy-makers became frenetic with moral outrage.

with sharp questions about the degree of freedom in Lewis' Mine Workers or Hutcheson's Carpenters. The extent to which the governments of the U.S. and the U.S.S.R. lived up to their respective commitments in the exchange of ambassadors will remain in dispute, but it is worth while to know what they agreed to. As stated by President Roosevelt to Peoples Commissar for Foreign Affairs Maxim Litvinov, the Russians would undertake the following:

1. To respect scrupulously the indisputable right of the United States to order its own life within its own jurisdiction in its own way and to refrain from interfering in any manner in the internal affairs of the United States, its territories or possessions.
2. To refrain, and to restrain all persons in Government service and all organizations of the Government or under its direct or indirect control, including organizations in receipt of any financial assistance from it, from any act overt or covert liable in any way whatsoever to injure the tranquillity, prosperity, order, or security of the whole or any part of the United States. . . .

FDR made a reciprocal pledge to Litvinov. This opening might hopefully have led to an antifascist alliance before the situation degenerated into all-out war.

But almost immediately Congress began to move against the other potential partners in such a coalition, in particular Great Britain and France. The Johnson Act of 13 April, 1934, forbade all dealings within the U.S. in the securities of any government that had gone in default to this country on the payment of its war debts from World War I. Inside two months, Finland was the only nation that owed the United States from World War I which had not defaulted. The next harmful move was the Neutrality Act of 1935. This measure was opposed by both FDR and Secretary of State Cordell Hull. They both favored an embargo on arms shipments to belligerents, but they wanted the president to have discretion to ban shipments only to the aggressor but not necessarily to the victim. What they got was a mandatory decree, which passed each house by a virtually unanimous vote. The statute was to run for only six months; when it came up for renewal in February, 1936, Roosevelt sought amendments that would meet his original desires. He failed.

Events were rolling downhill fast. Hitler in March, 1935, repudiated unilaterally the Treaty of Versailles by instituting compulsory military service; long before, Germany had left the League of Nations. Probably noting the American embargo on arms exports, Mussolini launched his armies into Ethiopia on 3 October. In December the foreign ministers of Britain and France came up with the Hoare-Laval Pact that proposed to give more than half of Ethiopia to Italy.* The agreement cost Samuel Hoare his post, but

---

*One of the many disgusting features of this era is the willingness of Britain and France to give away property that did not belong to them; witness also the agreements at Munich, September, 1938.

British foreign policy did not alter appreciably, and Mussolini got the "living space" or *lebensraum* that he and Hitler constantly demanded. Two verbal challenges to these aggressive moves need to be noted. FDR spoke to Congress of the expansionist nations:

> They have therefore impatiently reverted to the old belief in the law of the sword, or to the fantastic conception that they, and they alone, are chosen to fulfill a mission and that all the others among the billion and a half human beings in the world must and shall learn from them and be subject to them.

Litvinov spoke on the sacrifice of Ethiopia in July, 1936:

> I say we do not want a League that is safe for aggressors. We do not want that kind of League, even if it is universal, because it would become the very opposite of an instrument of peace.

When Litvinov spoke, Hitler's intentions were clear. On 7 March, 1936, his troops had moved into the Rhineland. German documents captured later make it clear that if France had resisted the occupation, Hitler's generals had orders to withdraw. France might well have resisted if she had believed she would be supported by England and the United States. By herself, she did not. Thus we arrive at a question that may not be answerable but that must be asked: What was the last possibly day that fascist encroachments could have been stopped without a world war? Some historians put it here. I think they are too early by about thirty months; my date would be Munich. Again, Litvinov had his say about the fall of the Rhineland: "One cannot fight for the collective organization of security without taking collective measures against the violation of international obligations. We, however, do not count among such measures collective capitulation to the aggressor." The Soviet slogan for the next three years would be "collective security."

Japan had struck. Italy had struck. Germany had struck. The pace accelerated. Next the fascists in Spain would strike. In a country long ruled by monarchy, the Catholic church, and nobility, a new republic had been formed. The former rulers found this situation intolerable, so armed insurrection was hurled against the regime. The rebels, headed by Francisco Franco, were supplied with war-planes and other modern munitions by Germany and Italy. The Republic got some material aid from the U.S.S.R., but the supply bases for the opposition were much closer. American policy in this crisis, if can be called by so dignified a term, was predetermined. Congress had made its position clear by its refusal to modify the Neutrality Act; on 6 January, 1937, it forbade exporting munitions "for the use of either of the opposing forces in Spain." The administration had no choice but to impose an embargo on all shipments of armaments to Spain, either to the Republicans or the insurrectionists. Inaction by the federal government was vociferously approved by many elements in American society, not least by the ordinary citizen who wanted chiefly to stay clear of troublesome situations. Of the many elements in the power structure whose voices spoke with affection of the Franco rebellion, probably none were heard more widely than several prelates of the Roman Church. Their view was represented at high levels in the Roosevelt administration; one adherent was Joseph P. Kennedy, American ambassador to Great Britain and father of a future president. To many Americans their government, once proud of its republicanism, was permitting, perhaps encouraging, the lynching by fascist Italian and German arms of a fellow republic. The intellectuals found their greatest moral issue since the Civil War in the United States. Never again after the Spanish civil war would the forces of good seem so clearly arrayed against the forces of evil. But Washington left no doubt as to its contrary attitude. A movement had started in many European countries to recruit International Brigades, volunteers from abroad to fight Franco in Spain. The contingent from the United States was called the Abraham Lincoln Battalion. The few hundred Americans who sneaked abroad to join it were mainly intellectuals; those of working-class or middle-class background were inconsequential. The survivors returning to their homeland were subjected to endless persecutions—revocation of passports, discriminations in their search for work. In spite of the sacrifices made in Spain by thousands of Spaniards and their foreign allies, the Republic would fall in 1939.

Japan struck again in July, 1937, ramming into China determined on conquest. Having already given notice that she would not continue to adhere to the Naval Limitation Treaty of 1922, she threw her strengthened martial might across the Sea of Japan. The onslaught included the bombing of Nanking and other cities. This action was sharply protested by the United States: "any general bombing of an extensive area wherein resides a large populace engaged in peaceful pursuits is unwarranted and contrary to principles of law and humanity." Three comments might be made. (1) Italy had earlier bombed civilians in Ethiopia, and Franco had done so in Spain. (2) These atrocities were regarded with horror even in the allegedly "isolationist" Midwest of the United States. (3) Within a few years (starting in World War II), the American air force would be bombing civilians in several countries, and the typical citizen would view it as normal behavior.

The transition from 1937 to the present seems to me great, but it should not be exaggerated. In 1937, most Americans wanted only to be left alone to worry out their private affairs, as three episodes will reveal. They were simultaneous, almost. The first can use a brief preface. One student of FDR has written: "As a foreign policy maker, Roosevelt during his first term was more pussyfooting politician than political leader." With qualification, this judgment will hold for most of his second term. But in fairness it must be said that he did send up trial balloons several times; he did make some gestures at diplomatic leadership. To illustrate, on 5 October, 1937, the president was in

Chicago to make a speech, where he said: "The peace, the freedom and the security of ninety per cent of the population of the world is being jeopardized by the remaining ten per cent who are threatening a breakdown of all international order and law." And: "We are adopting such measures as will minimize our risk of involvement, but we cannot have complete protection in a world of disorder in which confidence and security have broken down." He suggested that the "peace-loving nations" should "quarantine the aggressor." These pronouncements, if we can judge by the press, were greeted by fire and ice. So Roosevelt pulled his hand from the flames, his foot from the water.

Meanwhile the aggressors, far from being quarantined, were pushing forward on several fronts. The Japanese, advancing rapidly in China, flaunted their contempt for the United States on 12 December, 1937. The USS *Panay,* a gunboat, was at anchor in the Yangtze. Although she flew the American flag, she was attacked by bombers and sunk. American merchant ships nearby were also attacked. Officials in Washington were furious. Secretary of the Navy Claude Swanson wanted war. Harold Ickes, secretary of the interior, pondered the matter: "I confess that Swanson's point of view cannot be lightly dismissed. Certainly war with Japan is inevitable sooner or later, and if we have to fight her, isn't this the best time?" The American mood decreed otherwise. Within days, nearly everybody had lost interest. The hysteria of 1898 was not present in 1937; folks wanted just to go about their personal affairs. When Japan on Christmas Eve offered to pay the full indemnity asked by the United States and to take action against the responsible naval officer, the controversy closed.

But it did force action that indicated for a third time just how the country felt. The Ludlow Amendment to the Constitution had been in the congressional hopper for some time. It provided that, except in case of invasion, war could not be declared without prior approval by a referendum of the nation's voters. The audacity of this move to strip the president and Congress of their traditional powers was astounding. A House committee had been keeping the amendment bottled up. After the *Panay* incident, a petition to bring the measure out onto the floor picked up the required names. Strong pressure from the president brought about fifty Democrats back into line, but even so, the Amendment lost only by a vote of 209 to 188. Within two months, German armies moved into Austria. The *Wehrmacht* was rolling onward. Small wonder that Prime Minister Neville Chamberlain would say, "It is always best and safest to count on nothing from the Americans but words." In April he entered an agreement with Italy that recognized Italian interests in the Mediterranean and Africa; he went so far as to promise to persuade other governments to recognize her sovereignty in Ethiopia.

In the United States, appeasement of fascism had prestigious spokesmen. Lindbergh urged that an accommodation with Hitler "could maintain peace and civilization throughout the world as far into the future as we can see." Henry Ford, pursuant to his longstanding anti-Semitism, accepted from

Hitler the highest medal that the Third Reich could grant, the Award of the Grand Cross of the German Eagle. The Midwestern origins of the latter two men might lead to a false inference, so it should be said that, contrary to the divisions of sentiment from 1914 to 1917, the clash of opinion before World War II seems not to have followed any clear sectional lines. Some of the firmest advocates of a vigorous American stand came from the same region as Ford and Lindbergh. The most celebrated small-town editor in the country, William Allen White of Kansas, headed the Committee to Defend America by Aiding the Allies. Senator Norris of Nebraska, with his long record of gallant opposition—to the powers of Speaker Cannon, to private control of Hetch Hetchy, to the sale of the Muscle Shoals power project to Ford, to the Ku Klux Klan—became an outspoken adversary of the fascist nations. While Sinclair Lewis of Minnesota warned of the dangers of fascism in America, his wife Dorothy Thompson was sending home from Europe an impassioned set of daily newspaper despatches about the emergent menace there. To finish off this selective catalog, which proves nothing but which might raise some doubts, the Republican candidate for president in 1940, Wendell Willkie, had his roots in Indiana. His strong antifascist stand certainly did not delight his fellow partisans who wanted to "stay out of it."

Came the point of no return—Munich. At the time the administration was badly off balance. From his smashing re-election in 1936, FDR's popularity had fallen precipitously, due in the large part to the economic recession (late Chapter 26). By the summer of 1938 barely half of the electorate would report in a poll that they would vote for Roosevelt again.

The significance of Czechoslovakia can hardly be exaggerated. With a population of 15 million and the Skoda munitions works, it had an efficient army of 1.5 million men and an air force of 2,000 planes. Its stragetic location is clear. It was the keystone in France's system of alliances. Further, in 1935 it had signed a treaty of mutual assistance with the U.S.S.R. which was to be implemented only *after* the Franco-Czech agreement had been enforced. Chamberlain pulled the whole rug out. If Germany invades Czechoslovakia, he was asked in Commons, and France goes to her defence, will Britain support France? He gave no guarantees. With strong support among persons of German extraction in the Sudetenland, Hitler hoped to pluck off Czechoslovakia in the spring of 1938. The crisis was fended off. By autumn, the *Wehrmacht* obviously was ready to strike. Hurried meetings were held. Britain and France invited Hitler and Mussolini; nobody from Czechoslovakia took part. Hitler got the Sudetenland, undermining the defenses of the smaller nation. The premier of France was horrified at the triumphal greeting given him on his return to Paris; he thought the concessions to Hitler were a disaster. Chamberlain had no doubts. Stepping from the plane in England he waved a document over his head and shouted: "This means peace in our time." He wrote of Hitler: "In spite of the hardness and ruthlessness I thought I saw in his face, I got the impression that here was a man who could be relied upon when he had given his word." The preceding pledge by the chancellor of the Third Reich had been simple: "This is the last territorial claim I shall make in Europe."

The president seemed almost immobilized. During the Munich crisis his chief public actions were appeals to Hitler to act in the interests of peace. After the Munich agreements, Harold Ickes appealed to him to explain to the American people how grave the international situation had become. Roosevelt refused, saying that nobody would believe him. Then in rapid-fire order came calamities that knocked FDR, and millions of other Americans, off the fence. In March, 1939, German troops moved into Prague and controlled all of Czechoslovakia. In August the Nazi-Soviet non-aggression pact was made public.* Thus further unleashed, *blitzkrieg* gashed into Poland, which fell almost overnight. At first the official reaction in Washington to these catastrophes was to withdraw the nation farther into a shell. The Neutrality Act of 1939 (4 November) forbade all American merchant vessels to enter into certain declared war zones. When the Allies entered the war at the invasion of Poland, they could not count on getting supplies from us.**

Then the president began to act with a firmer hand. The arms embargo was lifted, with the proviso that Allied ships still had to carry the goods away from U.S. ports. German submarines in the next year had a field day on the Atlantic—World War I all over again. The British desperately needed warships that could convoy the freighters. With a heretofore atypical audacity, Roosevelt made the destroyer-bases deal in September, 1940, (at the height of a tough campaign for re-election). The British leased to the United States for 99 years a string of naval and air bases from Newfoundland to British Guiana. They were paid with 50 destroyers of the 1200-ton type, designated "over-age" (were they?). Fortunately for FDR, his opponent for the presidency approved of the destroyer-bases swap. Wendell Willkie hailed from Elwood, Indiana, but since 1933 he had been president of one of the largest electric-power companies in the country (Ickes jested that he was "a simple barefoot Wall Street lawyer.").

---

*For many years, this agreement was hardly debated in scholarly circles; everybody denounced it. Such condemnation seems far too narrow. The Soviet Union had been waving the wand of joint security for years, to see it rejected by Britain and France. It knew that Hitler had ambitions to drive eastward; he had said so in *Mein Kampf* (1925). It saw his armies take Czechoslovakia, and knew they were about to take Poland. The temptation to buy time was strong. What the U.S.S.R. bought was about two years.

**Here mention must be made of hearings before the Nye Committee of the Senate, which beginning in 1934 had taken testimony about the relation to World War I of American business, especially munitions manufacturers and investment bankers (see Chapter 22). Strictures against the Nye hearings by several historians arise from a failure to make the following simple distinction: While these Congressional sessions provide incontrovertible testimony that many American companies from 1914 to 1918 had an unwholesome effect on diplomacy and made exorbitant profits, that disclosure did not really show that the situations prior to American entry into the two wars were analogous. Of course this fear or possible inference of the time might have inhibited earlier American involvement prior to World War II.

However, his views on foreign relations were quite similar at this time to those of FDR. Given slight alternatives as to policy, voters plunked for experience. Roosevelt had a 5 million majority in the popular vote; the electoral vote was 449 to 82. The campaign was as dishonest as most. Self-proclaimed radicals chanted:

> *I hate war, so does Eleanor*
> *But we won't be safe til everybody's dead.*

The president solemnly intoned, "I have said this before, but I shall say it again and again: Your boys are not going to be sent into any foreign wars."

Did everybody suspect that almost everybody was lying? By November, 1940, no outlet was open for the United States to avoid entering World War II except total retreat into the Western Hemisphere, and probably even that strategem would have failed. Events might well have resembled the course of American entry into the earlier Great War—conflict on the oceans followed by an open pronouncement of hostilities. Already by 1941 the United States was involved in an undeclared naval war. But crucial facts about that war were concealed from the American people. One instance, (notorious later) was an attack on a German submarine by an American destroyer, the USS *Greer*. Roosevelt publicly denied that American forces had precipitated any armed clashes. In fact U.S. vessels had been "homing" on Nazi U-boats and radioing their position to British and French warships.

Options had existed. Now they were gone. No alternatives were left. Congress reluctantly and belatedly accepted this truth. FDR had a brilliant idea after the election; befitting him, it was shifty. To avoid aggravating the lingering resentments about unpaid war debts, the United States would lend goods instead of money to the Allies. One senator denounced the resultant bill as "the New Deal's Triple-A foreign policy; it will plow under every fourth American boy." Roosevelt called the charge "the most untruthful, as well as the most dastardly, unpatriotic thing that has ever been said." The bill passed, with an appropriation of $7 billion. However, Congress was nowhere close to voting a declaration of war or to committing American armed forces. Without the attack on Pearl Harbor at the end of 1941, the tenuous threads of American neutrality might have held for at least a year longer. Doubtless eventually they would have been severed by damage to American interests on the oceans—but when?

The Republicans charged that the president connived at the Japanese attack on December 7. This accusation needs to be evaluated, if only because it would serve as the basis for Congressional hearings after the war that would win Republican control of both Houses in 1946. Many people believed it—one sign of the growing distrust within the country—and evidence pointing in that direction is easy to find. These things seem reasonably certain: Roosevelt by the autumn of 1941 was clearly committed to thwarting the expansionist powers; nobody can know whether he was so committed to the degree that he might have asked for a declaration of war without violent provocation by the enemy. In highest circles the opinion was general that war against Japan had to come, a view that we have heard stated in Washington since the invasion of Manchuria (early Chapter 28). Also many officials realized the advantages to this country if Japan did attack. In October, 1941, the United States imposed a special alert on its forces in the Far East. Stimson, now secretary of war, wrote in his diary: ". . . so we face the delicate question of the diplomatic fencing to be done so as to be sure that Japan was put in the wrong and made the first bad move—overt move!" The head of Navy Plans thus described the alert: "It was an attempt to retain the peace as long as possible and to make sure that when war came that it would be initiated by Japan and not by the U.S." Certainly many aspects of American behavior encouraged the Japanese to be the aggressor: the lagging economy, the surging rifts in the body politic, the decision to leave the Philippines by 1946, the reduction in force of America's Pacific fleet during 1941 to build up power in the Atlantic. But none of this constitutes a plot with Japan; nothing here constitutes treason. The most positive verdict that can be rendered on the Republican indictment is the old Scottish judgment—Not proven. Personally I think it is despicably false, and that the men who returned the indictment knew it to be false.

However, other charges are true: carelessness in high places, and a grossly inefficient bureaucracy including civilian and military branches. The lack of system was incredible. Intelligence staffs overseas were picked by the local commanding officer; their contact with G-2 in Washington was at best sporadic. A top Japanese diplomatic code called Magic had been broken. But almost nobody in Washington was allowed to see the decoded messages, and the favored few had the paper taken from their hands almost the moment they got it. Nobody knew who saw it, so they made false assumptions about who had what information. The Navy had the key to Magic, and it did not share its secret with the Army. Another possible source of information in Hawaii was radar, but there were only mobile sets that could not detect low-flying planes, could not detect beyond 130 miles, could not detect within 30 miles. Then, for defense, planes could have flown patrols around Hawaii. To be effective, such patrols would have had to go as far out as 800 miles. The planes were not available. Military authorities had asked for another 180 B-17's; unfortunately, that number of B-17's did not exist in the entire United States. A scream has been heard repeatedly: "Roosevelt was warned." So he was, notably by the American ambassador in Tokyo. The warnings, however, were general, and were hardly needed: everybody knew Japan's aggressive intentions. But when and where would she strike?

Serious errors were made. Japan's striking capacity was falsely estimated because it was thought she would have to use land bombers based on Formosa, and she did not have planes that could make the round trip. So she used aircraft carriers. The consequences for the United States were disastrous. Eight battleships were damaged or destroyed at Pearl Harbor, plus three light cruisers and other invaluable matériel. At least nine hours elapsed before the Japanese assaulted the Philippines. They found the American planes lined up conveniently, wingtip to wingtip, so they wiped out half of the bombers and two thirds of the fighters. The explanation of this folly seems to be that orders had been given to transfer the B-17's to a new and safer air strip. But the facility was not yet fully prepared for large bombers, and B-17's were a precious item in December, 1941.

Looking back at 7 December, 1941, we might ponder a few generalizations. Decision-makers were not getting the information they needed to act intelligibly, or to act at all.* Zany though it was, Naval Intelligence was getting most of its information about the foreign policy of the United States by decoding Japanese messages sent in Magic. A crucial part of the matter was the tendency of a bureaucracy to smother its messages in noise, to generate memoranda that convey no information at all but that are intended to create the illusion that "*I* at least am busy." (Persons familiar with large universities will know the pattern: the only scholars who get any books read, much less written, are those who drop nearly all of their incoming communiqués into the waste basket unopened.) In the words of the most thoughtful student of this disaster, Roberta Wohlstetter: "In short, we failed to anticipate Pearl Harbor not for want of the relevant materials, but because of a plethora of irrelevant ones."

The position of the United States was desperate, but not hopeless. Negatively, in the Pacific both its navy and its air force had been for practical purposes wiped out. Military hardware within this country was in short supply, partly because such intensive efforts had been made to ship equipment to Great Britain; American troops in training were using telephone poles as simulated artillery. Although the size of the armed forces had increased four times, still it counted only some 2 million. Positively the country had three assets that were tangible. Its people nearly equalled in numbers the populations of Germany and Japan combined, and were relatively healthy in spite of depression ravages. Second, its productive potential from already existing plant was huge. Ironically, because of idle capacity of both manpower and machinery—such a scandal for years—size of the armed forces and output of military goods could expand greatly without undue disruption to civilian output. The Liaison Conference that ruled Japan had estimated that the American potential for waging war was seven or eight times that of their own country, but stupidly they paid only "lip service" to this ratio. A canny prognosis was made by the commander of the Japanese navy:

---

*Japan had similar frictions. Her foreign minister complained on the eve of war against the United States that the "high command refused to divulge figures on the numbers of our forces, or any facts relating to operations."

If you tell me that it is necessary that we fight, then in the first six months to a year of war against the U.S. and England I will run wild, and I will show you an uninterrupted succession of victories; I must also tell you that should the war be prolonged for two or three years, I have no confidence in our ultimate victory.

Third, even though France had been knocked out, the United States had two allies who were still functioning: Great Britain and the U.S.S.R. Without them America's maneuvering room would have disappeared. She would have had no choice but to withdraw into the Western Hemisphere while the Axis ran wild elsewhere.

It remained to convert these three assets into kinetic energy as quickly as may be. As in our consideration of earlier wars, the analysis here will focus on policy and strategy, with little attention to battles and tactics. (The memory of those beastly frays will never be lost to the participants: Midway, the Coral Sea, Guadalcanal, Taiwan, Okinawa, Anzio, Cassino, Omaha Beach, the Bulge.).

American policy was sound—to destroy the military power of the Axis. Nothing less would suffice. But as this policy was spelled out, it became less satisfactory. Conferring at Casablanca on 14 January, 1943, FDR and Churchill announced their aim as "unconditional surrender." In Roosevelt's words: "It does not mean the destruction of the population of Germany, Italy, or Japan, but it does mean the destruction of the philosophies in those countries which are based on conquest and the subjugation of other people." No other approach could have been taken to the Nazis. Theirs was a despotic regime from top to bottom. The removal of a few men at the top would not do the job; the entire political machine had to be smashed. Japan was different. Members of its ruling strata, both industrialists and civil servants, were not thoroughly committed to militarism. A conditional surrender might well have been considered. Crucial to the conditions would be the absolute disbandment of all armed forces and the destruction of all implements of war. Another limitation on Allied policy was its lasting flirtation with the shoring up of pre-war colonialism—the chief obstructionist being Britain and the chief areas in contention being the Far East, the Middle East, and the Balkans.

Strategy also was generally sound. The struggle against Germany was to take first place over the Pacific war. Weird reasons have been given to explain this choice. According to a 1965 study: "This priority was maintained on the sound assumption that Germany without Japan would be as strong as ever, whereas Japan without Germany could not stand long." Neither half of this alleged assumption will hold water. Japan for "six months to a year" did mighty well without German aid. The chief reason for concentration against Germany is that she was an immediate threat to the homelands of two of the Allies, Japan to none. In retrospect, invasion of the British Isles was turned back by the air battles of the autumn of 1940. Clearly it was vital to Britain and the United States that the Soviet Union should not fall, which would release

German might for piratical adventures elsewhere. Thoughtful men have never spent a more tense winter than 1942–1943: if the British had not held at El Alamein, if the Russians had not held at Stalingrad, the Third Reich with Japan might have controlled the Euro-Asian land mass plus Africa.

One error in strategy seems obvious; another is becoming increasingly clear. The first is the Italian campaign. It was a fiasco. Each German soldier tied up ten Allied soldiers. Losses were exorbitant; possible gains could not be decisive. In this instance, FDR allowed himself to be lured by Churchill into buying a white elephant; if the invasion of France had been undertaken sooner, the end of the war would have come earlier. The other questionable strategy was heavy reliance on strategic bombing. Substantial chunks of evidence suggest that bombing of this type has minimal military effect, (Document 28-3; also Chapter 30). The U.S.S.R. did not use strategic bombers. This abstinence was not prompted by humanitarianism; they simply did not believe that strategic bombing was an economical and efficient way to win a war.

Strategy is devised by men. The ranking generals in the army at the outbreak of war were peacetime and stodgy; quickly younger men were jumped over their heads. With remarkably few exceptions, the men commanding armies and fleets during World War II were intelligent and forceful, right up to Chief of Staff George C. Marshall and Chief of Naval Operations Ernest J. King. Of course the generals did load the game in their own favor; the results were fine for them, but lethal for combat soldiers. Of all the Allied armies, ours was the only one that did not rotate units in and out of the front lines. It rotated individual men. Result: If you were in a combat unit early in the war, your chances of survival were slight. Every paratrooper I knew was convinced that the war would last longer than he would. When the second Allied invasion of France pushed northward from Toulon on 15 August, 1944, all three American divisions involved had already made two or more amphbious landings. One sergeant in that landing spoke:

> I came in at Sicily brand-new. I didn't know my tail from third base. I was only 19. I was only a private then, too. Then pretty soon one guy gets knocked off and pretty soon another guy gets knocked off and another guy and another guy and pretty soon I'm the oldest guy in the squad and so they make me the squad leader.
>
> Then Salerno and some of my new guys get knocked off, and I keep getting more and more new guys, and they keep getting knocked off. They pulled us out of Cassino and shipped us to Anzio, and it was the same old story. I guess I must have had about five different squads.
>
> I don't know how I happened to hang around all this time. Maybe I'm just lucky.

An infantryman might still see "the whites of their eyes," but for many combatants, modern warfare was vastly less personal than its antetypes. A former bombardier recalled: "I remember distinctly seeing, from our great height, the bombs explode in the town, flaring like matches struck in fog. I was completely unaware of the human chaos below."

The depersonalization of warfare obviously was made possible by innovations in technology. Equally obviously, the industrial strength of the United States was a main factor in its contribution to Allied victory. The saying was common: "The war is being won on the assembly lines in Detroit." Battlefields played a part, but the common lore at home often tended to slight that element. And in truth it was the miracles of production in factories and on farms that enabled the armed forces to be so lavish in squandering matériel. No purpose could be served here in piling up statistics, but we can look at two critical items: warplanes and shipping. At the time of Pearl Harbor, the annual rate of plane output was 25,000. The president called for 60,000 in 1942. By the war's end, the nation had produced nearly 300,000 planes. The approach to shipping was to take over the designs of an old-fashioned British tramp steamer, to be known as the Liberty ship. Construction of such a vessel in 1941 required 355 days. When 1942 ended, the time had been reduced to 56 days. One shipyard achieved a time of 14 days. At war's end the United States had bottoms on the oceans totalling 36 million tons.

Except for its gaudy, ghastly finale, the conflict was a war of attrition. Victory in Europe meant a steady pounding forward, terminating at Hitler's aerie, Berchtesgaden. Japan was conquered by sweeping sea battles and by a sweaty malignant murderous process of island-hopping, to Okinawa at the threshhold of the final objective. Nobody was sure what would happen next. Would it be necessary to go for the jugular by invading the industrial plains around Tokyo? Universal opinion in Japanese military intelligence in Washington was that Japan would surrender by the autumn (for reasons to be considered below) without an invasion, but nothing was certain. For years, men far from the battle zones had been working toward what would become American policy.

The story of the atomic bomb could reasonably be started at any of several episodes, such as Einstein's papers early in the century that announced his famous relativity formula: $e = mc^2$, (where e stands for the amount of energy released, m for the mass being exploded, and c^2 for the velocity of light squared); matter, accelerated beyond the speed of light, could become pure energy. This account must be foreshortened, so it starts with January, 1939, when two scientists in Berlin split the uranium atom. Those few residents of the United States who understood much about nuclear energy were galvanized by thinking about the new potential for destruction in Hitler's hands. The power released from one atom may be negligible, but what if thousands or millions of atoms could be harnessed into a chain reaction? Significantly, these *cognoscenti* were all recent immigrants, from Germany, Italy, Denmark, a startling number of Jews from Hungary. Ironically, J. Robert Oppenheimer did not attain his later prominence in connection with the atomic bomb

Atomic Power

An axiom of pre-atomic physics stated that matter is neither created nor destroyed: that is, although atoms can combine with each other to form many different kinds of molecules, the atoms themselves remained unchanged. But early in this century it was discovered that certain elements do break down into others, in the process releasing a great deal of energy. The relationship between matter and energy is expressed in Einstein's formula, $E = MC^2$. The amount of energy (E) released by the breakdown of an element is equivalent to the mass (M) of the substance multiplied by the square of the speed of light (C^2).

Thus a very large amount of energy is produced by the disintegration of a small amount of matter. This energy is released from the nucleus of the atom.

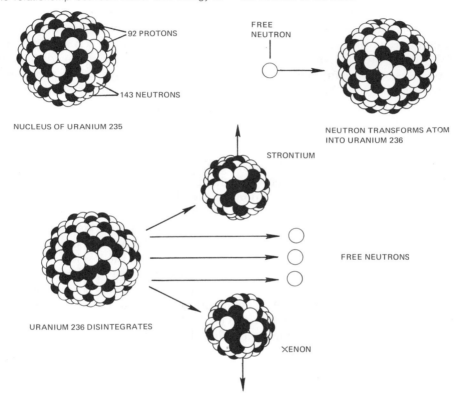

92 PROTONS

143 NEUTRONS

NUCLEUS OF URANIUM 235

FREE NEUTRON

NEUTRON TRANSFORMS ATOM INTO URANIUM 236

STRONTIUM

FREE NEUTRONS

URANIUM 236 DISINTEGRATES

XENON

(1) The nucleus of the Uranium 235 atom contains 92 protons (which carry a positive charge) and 143 neutrons (which have no charge). Since the protons are all straining away from each other (as if they were the positive poles of 92 magnets) a very great amount of energy is needed to hold the nucleus together.

(2) The atom is bombarded with free neutrons. When a neutron becomes attached to the nucleus, it contains 92 protons and 144 neutrons, becoming Uranium 236.

(3) Uranium 236 is a very unstable element and will disintegrate spontaneously into other products, for example strontium and xenon, and release several free neutrons. All of these particles are traveling at enormous speed, and as they hit other parts of the reactor they transmit their energy in the form of heat. The free neutrons go on to break up other Uranium atoms, thus creating the famous "chain reaction" and enormous release of energy.

because of his scientific attainments, which were, so good witnesses say, slight. His distinction came from the fact that in 1930 he was instructor in the only course anywhere in the United States concentrating on nuclear energy (at the California Institute of Technology).

Eminent scientists including Einstein and Leo Szilard immediately tried to emphasize to Roosevelt the devastation that Germany might cause by developing a new weapon. The administration's response was lethargic—a few *thousands* of dollars for research. Not until the summer of 1941 were resources poured into developmental work, for which the code name was Manhattan Project. On 2 December, 1942, a team at the University of Chicago set off the first chain reaction. In the preceding year, resources had been hurled into the effort; at its height, the Manhattan Engineer District employed 539,000 persons at sites in many parts of the nation (The luminaries would turn out to be Los Alamos, New Mexico and Oak Ridge, Tennessee.). By the end of 1944, the director could report that they hoped to have a functional bomb by 1 August, 1945, with an explosive force of 10,000 tons of TNT.

Germany surrendered on 7 May, 1945. Now the problem narrowed down to an overriding question: How could Japan be knocked out of the war? Three alternatives: by (1) direct assault, (2) strangulation coupled with inducements, (3) use of atomic weapons as they became available. Estimates of losses in an invasion varied greatly. Marshall said that casualties should not exceed 30,000 in the first month; Stimson thought the total operation would cost a half million to a million casualties; Douglas MacArthur commanding in the Pacific pointed out that losses could be cut greatly if the Soviets launched a prior attack in Siberia. But why take such risks when possibility (2) seemed well on its way to success; military intelligence estimates were that Japan would surrender by October, 1945, even without use of atomic weapons whose very existence was quite unknown even to Vice President Truman. Naval blockade plus conventional bombing plus the desire for self-preservation of the Emperor and the interlocking bureaucracies were thought to be doing the trick. As early as the autumn of 1944, the Japanese navy was so short of fuel that many of her ships sunk in the Battle of the Philippine Sea could not have made it back home anyway. Shellcases were being made from substitute metals. A shortage of cement had resulted in shoreline fortifications that were nothing but barbed wire, while the only weapons there were machine guns. Mass famine impended. An official government study had predicted that rice supplies for 1945 would fall 14 million tons short of bare subsistence requirements. Stocks of rice for civilians were 40 per cent below the 1941 level, and would yield less than 1,500 calories a day per capita. The movement of Japanese shipping was next to zero. Admiral King and William D. Leahy, the president's personal military adviser, thought the country would surrender to conventional air and naval attacks. But even to invest Japan in this way for a few months would be costly. Although the United States had full sea and air control, she could not prevent the sacrifice of Japanese pilots and planes in suicidal blows in which the enemy filled a plane with dynamite and dived it down the smokestack of an American aircraft carrier. These maniacal youth boasted that they were *kamikaze*—Divine Wind. The wind was lethal.

The further story of the atomic bomb cannot be understood without noting arrival on the stage of the United Nations and Harry S. Truman. Franklin Roosevelt did not live to see the achievement of one of his chief ambitions: the United Nations. FDR died 12 April, 1945; the San Francisco conference that founded the U.N. met from April 25 to June 26. But now Truman was president, and he was not inclined to let foreigners tell him how to use the new American super-weapon. Truman had almost sidled onto the scene. Republicans would never cease taunting that he had tried to run a dinky haberdashery and couldn't make a success of that. As protégé of the corrupt Democratic boss of Kansas City, he had entered the Senate in 1935. Fortune smiled when he became head of a committee to investigate war contracts awarded by the federal government, and he started to get some notice. As the presidential election approached in 1944, Roosevelt feared that Henry A. Wallace had made too many enemies as secretary of agriculture and as vice president. He lopped off a possible drag on the ticket by giving the second spot to Truman, who now succeeded him. As president Truman would win many admirers who bragged that he came out fighting. But often he headed toward the wrong opponent, at the wrong time in the wrong place. He had the compulsion to assert himself often found in men from his background. With notable exceptions, his appointments were dismal, sometimes disastrous. He was too combative for the nation's good.

Truman, Stalin, and Churchill met at Potsdam on 7 July to coordinate strategy for the defeat of Japan. Fourteen days later Truman got the extended report on the successful A-bomb test at Los Alamos on 16 July. Stimson's diary describes a conversation with Churchill on 22 July in which the prime minister said: "Now I know what happened to Truman yesterday. I couldn't understand it. When he got to the meeting after having read this report he was a changed man. He told the Russians just where they got on and off and generally bossed the whole meeting." Atomic diplomacy had begun. Churchill was delighted. Facing a general election at home and a shaky British Empire abroad, he thought that prompt use of the new weapon might not only crush the Japanese but also deter the Soviets. These attitudes rested on an assumption about when another nation, especially the U.S.S.R. could produce an A-bomb. James P. Byrnes, who had become secretary of state on 2 July, said "seven to ten years, at least, to produce a bomb." The general heading the Manhattan Project estimated "no less than five years and probably well over ten." The time actually required was just over four years.

When scientists involved in the Project learned that a bomb had worked, seven of them drew up the Franck Report which called for demonstrating the bomb's power before U.N. representatives on a "barren island." But a contrary decision had already been reached. The president and Stimson had decided that an exclusively civilian group should be formed to advise Truman on use of the bomb. Twelve men were named to the Interim Committee, with Stimson as chairman and Byrnes as the president's agent. They reached three conclusions: (a) Use the bomb as soon as possible. (b) Drop it on a military target surrounded by houses and other highly vulnerable buildings. (c) Give no prior warning. The objective was to effect a holocaust. On these questions, 36 votes were cast. Only one dissent was recorded, on (c).

Not all professional military men are professional militarists. The chief of the air force thought that use of the A-bomb was not needed to win the war because with conventional bombing "we're driving them back to the stone age." Eisenhower, learning at Potsdam of the bomb, said he would hate to see the United States be the first to use such a horrible weapon. After the war, Leahy was bitter: "My own feeling was that in being the first to use it, we had adopted an ethical standard common to the barbarians of the Dark Ages. I was not taught to make war in that fashion and wars cannot be won by destroying women and children." The Strategic Bombing Survey (Document 28-3) concluded: ". . . certainly prior to 31 December, 1945, and in all probability prior to 1 November, 1945, Japan would have surrendered even if the atomic bombs had not been dropped, even if Russia had not entered the war and even if no invasion had been planned or contemplated." From this judgment, says a recent scholar, "there can hardly be a well-grounded dissent."

But each side had its hard-nosed tough guys. In the United States the crucial (in a sense the only important) intransigeant was Truman, who had been rigid on two issues where he should have given ground: He continued to wave the threadbare flag of "unconditional surrender," and he refused to announce the possibility that the Imperial dynasty might be preserved after a surrender. Conversely, several men in Japan's high command seem lunatic. The country was under the sway of the Supreme War Council: the prime minister and foreign minister along with the two ranking officers in the army and navy. Even after the second atomic bomb was dropped, on Nagasaki on 9 November, three of the six members still voted against surrender; they were ready to fight it out on the beaches until the last Japanese was dead (records of the Japanese War Crimes Trials provide an abundance of evidence). Only the intervention of the Emperor broke the tie. When the surrender was announced, some units of the armed forces rebelled at the humiliation. The secretary of war was so mortified he killed himself. Particularly in retrospect, madmen should not be regarded as if they were sane.

Of the many comments made by men who took part in these climactic episodes, two should be quoted. Stimson wrote:

> The face of war is the face of death; death is an inevitable part of every order that a wartime leader gives. The decision to use the atomic bomb was a decision that brought death to over a hundred thousand Japanese. No explanation can change that fact and I do not wish to gloss it over.
>
> But this deliberate, premeditated destruction was our least abhorrent alternative. . . .

The general commanding the Strategic Air Force was addicted to a West Point maxim: "Seize the high ground" (dating back to a Chinese slogan of 500 B.C.). He cabled a friend in Washington: "Personal. Have looked at good photos of Hiroshima today. The atomic bomb disposes of all high ground."

Failure to use the atomic bomb would have prolonged the war. Thousands of American lives, perhaps millions of Japanese lives, would have been lost. The price of abstinence would have been high. Perhaps no commander-in-chief—least of all in a republic—could abstain from using a new weapon that might save the lives of American boys. Doubtless some men on the Interim Committee were hostile to Japan because the war had been activated by a sneak attack on Pearl Harbor and because American prisoners of war in Japanese hands had been badly mistreated. Doubtless some of the members of this Committee were swayed by racial bias (James Byrnes). It has been said, with considerable evidence, that the bomb was used to forestall any voice by the Soviet Union in the postwar governance of Japan. These assertions do not add up to a justification. The price of using the atomic bomb was high, and most of that price would be paid after the war.

Accompanying their efforts to reverse the flow of unemployment, efforts which never were very successful, the Roosevelt administration had to try to arrest the spread of fascism—hopefully without getting involved in a major war. The League of Nations was patently powerless to prevent the encroachments of the fascist powers—Germany, Italy, and Japan gobbled up chunks of foreign soil while but feeble gestures were made to stop them. In Spain, the reactionary movement led by General Franco and aided by Germany and Italy overthrew a republican government.

Despite the feeling among many Americans that the nation should not involve itself with troubles in Europe, the government realized that close cooperation among non-fascist states was needed to contain this menace, and in 1933 took a step in this direction by recognizing the government of the Soviet Union. Yet attempts to solidify alliances with Great Britain and France were unavailing. By the time of the Munich Agreement in 1938, war was inevitable.

The United States still tried to maintain a posture of public neutrality, while providing supplies for the Allies in Europe. Americans were sure to declare war eventually, but if Japan had not attacked Pearl Harbor on December 7, 1941, entry might have been postponed for as long as a year. Once formally at war, the massive productive capacity of the United States was mobilized for a steady effort, a constant attrition which pushed Germany and Japan under relentless force. New technology was developed as well, climaxing in a weapon which harnessed the power of the atom for destructive purposes.

SOME NOTABLE EVENTS

1931 Hoover proposes moratorium on intergovernmental debts from World War I.

1931–
1932 Japan occupies Manchuria, starting 18 Sept. with Mukden incident.

1932 Stimson's note to Japan and China, 7 Jan.

Stimson's letter to Senator Borah about Manchukuo, 24 Feb.

Japan recognizes Manchukuo, 15 Sept.

1933 Hitler named chancellor of Germany, 30 Jan.

Treaty of Tangku ends Manchurian War, 31 May.

International Economic Conference gathers in London, 12 June.

U.S. recognizes U.S.S.R. 16 Nov.

FDR announces new policy on Latin American relations, 28 Dec.

1934 Platt Amendment on Cuba abrogated, 29 May.

Trade Agreements Act, 12 June.

All governments owing debts to U.S. from World War I except "brave little Finland" have defaulted by June 15.

Tydings-McDuffie Act grants independence to Philippines, but not effective until 4 July, 1946.

Japan denounces Washington Naval Treaty of 1922 on 29 Dec.

1935 Neutrality Act, 31 Aug.

Hoare-Laval Plan for Ethiopia, 10 Dec.

1936 Germany invades Rhineland, 7 March.

1936–
1939 Spanish Civil War, ending with fascist victory.

1937 Neutrality Act, 1 May.

Japan invades China, 7 July.

FDR's "quarantine the aggressor" speech in Chicago, 5 Oct.

Peel Report advocates partition of Palestine.

U.S. gunboat *Panay* sunk by Japanese in China, 12 Dec.

1938 Ludlow Amendment narrowly beaten in House of Representatives, 10 Jan.; vote is 209 to 188.

Germany annexes Austria, 12–13 March.

Mexico expropriates U.S. and British oil properties.

Munich agreements cede about half of Czechoslovakia to Germany, 29–30 Sept.

1939 Germany seizes remainder of Czechoslovakia, March.

Germany invades Poland, 1 Sept.

Neutrality Act of 1939 forbids entry of U.S. merchant vessels into war zones, 4 Nov.

Two scientists at Kaiser Wilhelm Institute in Berlin split the uranium atom.

1939–
1940 Russo-Finnish War, 14 Oct.–12 March.

1940 Germany conquers Norway, 9 April–11 June.

The Netherlands, Belgium, and France fall to Germany, 10 May–10 July.

Battle of Britain is fought in the air. RAF loses nearly a thousand planes, Germany twice as many, 8 Aug.–31 Oct.

U.S. makes "destroyers-bases" deal with Britain, 3 Sept.

Germany, Italy, and Japan sign ten-year military and economic alliance, 27 Sept.

U.S. embargo on shipments of scrap iron and steel to Japan takes effect, 16 Oct.

1941 FDR's "Four Freedoms" speech, 6 Jan.

Lend-Lease Act, 11 March.

Germany invades U.S.S.R. 24 June; FDR promises aid the same day.

Atlantic Charter issued by FDR and Churchill; submitted to Congress on 21 Aug.

Pearl Harbor attacked, 7 Dec.; Congress declares war the next day.

686

1941–
1943 Allies retake Africa, 18 Nov.–13 May.
1942 Japanese expansion in Pacific reaches its maximum, early May.

U.S.S.R. assumes counteroffensive, 19 Nov.
1943 Allies take Sicily, 10 July–17 Aug.

Allies begin invasion of Italy, 3 Sept.
1944 D-Day (Operation Overlord); Allies invade western France, 6 June.

Allies invade southern France, 15 Aug. (Operation Dragon).
1945 Germany surrenders, 4 May.

Potsdam Conference, 7 July–2 Aug.

Atomic bomb on Hiroshima, 6 Aug.; called "Little Boy."

Plutonium atomic bomb ("Fat Man") dropped on Nagasaki, 9 Aug.

U.S.S.R. declares war on Japan, 9 Aug.

Japan surrenders, 14 Aug.

Ways to Study History XXVIII

Collaborations can succeed. This assertion has been made rather negatively in Ways to Study History XXI; it should now be re-substantiated. Perhaps the finest of all reference works on the history of the United States is the *Dictionary of American Biography,* edited by Allen Johnson and Dumas Malone (20 volumes plus two Supplements, 1928–1958). Hundreds of contributors have written about thousands of eminent citizens for this series. These volumes have held up amazingly well. Although the final volume in the basic set was issued in 1935, a complete revision today would not require the revision of more than 10 per cent or at most 20 per cent of the information. By such gradual accretions is our knowledge of the past being built up.

The problems confronted by the editors of this compendium can hardly be exaggerated. Its predecessor in the English language had been the *Dictionary of National Biography,* about residents of the British Isles, (22 volumes, 1885–1901). The subjects for many entries had been chosen not for their impact on the country's life but for their family attachments. Likewise authors had been picked for their connections instead of for their scholarship. Many of the careers recounted had not been carefully researched; some entries were either adulatory or condemnatory rather than being detailed narratives.

Who were the significant persons in American history? How much space should each receive? Who is best qualified to write about her (or him)? Because of their skill in meeting these questions, the editors have endowed us with an invaluable guide to our past. More than one instructor has prepared a good lecture while using no other resource than the *D.A.B.* Of course no work of this magnitude can be perfect. There is reason to believe that rascals succeeded in sneaking onto its pages sketches of imagined persons who never existed.

Document 28-1

Some commentators cannot separate Woodrow Wilson from the Fourteen Points. Similarly FDR is often identified with "the Four Freedoms." Acknowledging that the stock in trade of most politicians is words, it nonetheless appears that wars call forth an unusual amount of rhetoric.

Every realist knows that the democratic way of life is at this moment being directly assailed in every part of the world—assailed either by arms or by secret spreading of poisonous propaganda. . . .

As men do not live by bread alone, they do not fight by armaments alone. Those who man our defenses, and those behind them who build our defenses, must have the stamina and courage which come from an unshakable belief in the manner of life which they are defending. . . .

In the future days, which we seek to make secure, we look forward to a world founded upon four essential human freedoms.

The first is freedom of speech and expression everywhere in the world.

The second is freedom of every person to worship God in his own way everywhere in the world.

The third is freedom from want, which, translated into world terms, means economic understandings which will secure to every nation a healthy peacetime life for its inhabitants everywhere in the world.

The fourth is freedom from fear—which, translated into world terms, means a world-wide reduction of armaments to such a point and in such a thorough fashion that no nation will be in a position to commit an act of physical aggression against any neighbor—anywhere in the world.

That is no vision of a distant millenium. It is a definite basis for a kind of world attainable in our own time and generation. That kind of world is the very antithesis of the so-called new order of tyranny which the dictators seek to create with the crash of a bomb.

Document 28-2

In the spring of 1942, the Army removed from the
West Coast 110,000 residents of Japanese ancestry to "relocation centers" in the interior. In
1944, *Korematsu* v. *U.S.*, this military action was
upheld 6-3 by the Supreme Court.

*It is said that we are dealing here with the case of imprisonment of a citizen in a
concentration camp solely because of his ancestry, without evidence or inquiry concerning his
loyalty and good disposition towards the United States. Our task would be simple, our duty clear,
were this a case involving the imprisonment of a loyal citizen in a concentration camp because of
racial prejudice. Regardless of the true nature of the assembly and relocation centers—and we
deem it unjustifiable to call them concentration camps with all the ugly connotations that term
implies—we are dealing with nothing but an exclusion order. To cast this case into outlines of
racial prejudice, without reference to the real military dangers which were presented, merely
confuses the issue. Korematsu was not excluded from the Military Area because of hostility to him
or his race. He was excluded because we are at war with the Japanese Empire, because the
properly constituted military authorities feared an invasion of our West Coast and felt constrained
to take proper security measures, because they decided that the military urgency of the situation
demanded that all citizens of Japanese ancestry be segregated from the West Coast temporarily,
and finally, because Congress, reposing its confidence in this time of war in our military
leaders—as inevitably it must—determined that they should have the power to do just this. There
was evidence of disloyalty on the part of some, the military authorities considered that the need
for action was great, and time was short. We cannot—by availing ourselves of the calm
perspective of hindsight—now say that at that time these actions were unjustified.*

Document 28-3

The United States Strategic Bombing Survey
was a federal team sent to Japan to study the
results of the atomic explosions. The first paragraph here describes some general effects; the
second relates specifically to Hiroshima.

*Penetrating rays such as gamma-rays exposed X-ray films stored in the basement of a
concrete hospital almost a mile from ground zero. Symptoms of their effect on human beings
close to the center of the explosion, who survived other effects thereof, were generally delayed for
two or three days. The bone marrow and as a result the process of blood formation were affected.
The white corpuscle count went down and the human processes of resisting infection were
destroyed. Death generally followed shortly thereafter. . . .*

*Approximately 60,000 to 70,000 people were killed, and 50,000 were injured. Of
approximately 90,000 buildings in the city, 65,000 were rendered unusable and almost all the
remainder received at least light superficial damage. The underground utilities of the city were
undamaged except where they crossed bridges over the rivers cutting through the city. All of the
small factories in the center of the city were destroyed. However, the big plants on the periphery
of the city were almost completely undamaged and 94 percent of their workers unhurt. These
factories accounted for 74 percent of the industrial production of the city. It is estimated that they
could have resumed substantially normal production within 30 days of the bombing, had the war
continued. The railroads running through the city were repaired for the resumption of through
traffic on 8 August, 2 days after the attack. . . .*

The Forbidden Fruits of Affluence

Looking back, it is easy to regard the New Deal as a succession of missed opportunities. More harshly, perhaps more selfishly, stated, many of the problems before the country today have continued because of neglect or indifference by New Dealers. Inflation would be easier to control if a more astute approach to monetary arrangements had been taken in 1933. The mess of the cities could have been relieved somewhat, whereas the Federal Housing Act of 1938 along with freeway construction and other governmental policies have intensified the disease. Racial violence has been endemic to American life, but FDR would not lift a finger, much less wave it, to lance this abscess. Instead of action to elevate the status of women, the nation got a symbol; Eleanor Roosevelt was permitted to serve as ritualistic testimony to the sanctity of motherhood. Perhaps our current politics will serve the country just as badly, but the Roosevelt administration should not be credited with any genius at thinking a problem through, and then building its conclusions into a workable set of institutions.

True, the Great Depression finally ended, but it took the massive spending of the war years to do the job. The soft spots in the economy were merely camouflaged, not eliminated, and they reappeared as soon as war production was curtailed and wartime restrictions were lifted. During the war, two goals were met: employment stayed high, and prices and wages were controlled to prevent galloping inflation. Had this not been done, the costs of scarce consumer goods would have jumped drastically. But soon after VJ Day, the restrictions were lifted, and prices were set free to find their "natural level." Since few factories had yet converted to peacetime production, and since demand had been greatly increased by four years of deprivation, the immediate postwar years saw massive inflation, which a laissez-faire government felt privileged to impede only when it could perceive a "national emergency." World War II had the same influence as other American wars in sending the price level soaring. But after 1933 the federal authorities had even more powerful tools that they could swing in more than one direction. In that year the Federal Reserve Board had started a so-called Open Market Committee that could buy and sell securities on the public exchanges. Using this mechanism, the second great war was financed to a considerable extent by "monetizing the federal debt." This phrase may imply an arcane operation, but what happened was child's play. The Federal Reserve Board printed paper money; the Treasury printed bonds, and they swapped pieces of paper. With such tactics, anybody can be a financier.

Even taking account of the rising price level since 1940, the growth of American prosperity has been impressive. Figures in current prices, billions of dollars, climbed thus:

	1950	1955	1960	1965	1970
Gross National Product	285	398	504	685	924
Personal Incomes	228	311	401	539	804
Federal Expenditures	42	65	77	97	195

The absolute growth of the economy was not accompanied by an equitable distribution of income. As in the past, by far the largest share of the increase went to those who were well-off already. In 1967, the Internal Revenue Service gleaned $1.5 billion dollars in taxes from people earning less than $3,000— exactly the amount which had been allocated to the various poverty programs. And the poverty programs cannot be regarded as mechanisms for returning tax money to those who needed it most, since almost all of their expenditures went to pay for physical plant or the salaries of middle-class administrators. The farm subsidy program provides another example of an attempt to aid the poor which became twisted into a handout for the rich. Half of the $3.5 billion distributed in 1969 went to the richest 15 per cent of the farmers; 20 of the wealthiest got as much as 350,000 of the poorest.

Accompanying the stagnation of poverty was the decay of one of the sacred cows of the American Way, the small businessman. Starting a business has never been easy; most go broke within a year of their hopeful beginnings. But in the decades after World War II the giants of commerce and manufacturing coelesced their power to a degree that had never been possible before. About 200 corporations (out of 200,000) controlled 60 per cent of manufacturing. Three made 95 per cent of the cars, and the largest garnered two billion dollars in after tax profits in one year. Price fixing, wage fixing, and a bland disregard for the consumer's desire for quality and service naturally proceeded from this agglutination of power. Large companies did not restrict themselves to expansion in their original line. The conglomerate, in which many separate companies in unrelated fields are united only by common ownership, is becoming increasingly common. International Telephone and Telegraph, for example, owns among other things Sheraton (hotels), and Bobbs-Merrill (publishing). Aside from the advantages of future profits presumably to be derived from the good management of the executives of the parent company, conglomeration offers two advantages. First, shrewd accounting often allows enormous tax savings. Second, the diverse nature of the various businesses prevents awkward investigation under anti-trust laws, which might become troublesome if a large company tried to gobble up its direct competitors.

Unemployment accompanied inflation. Factories which engaged in war production had been operating under the "cost plus" system, whereby the government paid their expenses, plus 6 per cent. Naturally they had no incentive to keep expenses down, and often hired more men than efficiency demanded. When the sugar plums of government contracts were no longer forthcoming, employers were quick to trim away their surplus manpower. The re-entrance of ex-GIs into the labor market aggravated the problem.

Clearly, careful governmental management was necessary to smooth out economic turbulence. But the actions the government took were both haphazard and repressive. Wages did not escalate as fast as prices (in the four years following the war the cost of living rose an astounding 70 per cent) and the inevitable strikes occurred. Truman tried to stop them by throwing the weight of the federal government on the side of the employer. During the coal strike of 1946, the railroad workers walked out. The president forced them to return to the job by threatening to use the military to run the trains, and broke a coal strike by actually operating the mines with government personel for two months. The numerous strikes, 5,000 in 1946 alone, produced some real gains for workers of many industries, in fringe benefits and improved working conditions as well as in fatter pay envelopes. But inflation more than kept pace, and the constant round of labor disputes provoked much anti-labor feeling which worked to the advantage of the Republican party.

By 1946 the Republicans had won control of both houses of Congress, and used their mandate to pass the Taft-Hartley law. Many union activities were proscribed, and union officials had to sign an affadavit affirming that they were not Communists. Most importantly, the law permitted the president to obtain an injunction postponing any strike for sixty days, which could be extended another twenty. If the dispute continued, he could recommend to Congress any action which he believed to be "appropriate." Most Americans approved the measure. The reforming impulses which had arisen during the depression were clearly yielding to prosperity and the desire for quiet, and the status quo.

On 22 June, 1944, the president signed a major law intended to promote social mobility—the "GI Bill of Rights." In a significant provision, it established a system of federal payments to veterans who wished to continue their education. The resulting flood of new students drastically changed the character of American universities. First, they mushroomed in both size and number. Second, they changed from enclaves catering to the children of the rich into institutions which the middle classes and part of the working classes entered as a matter of course. Given parallel changes which had been occurring in the business world, this broadened educational base was essential. In former years the restriction of higher education to the few didn't matter much. A degree might be the entrée into a few professions, but to little else. In business practical experience counted for much more. But organizations were steadily growing larger, and bureaucratic systems were dominating patterns of advancement. It was more difficult to work your way up through the ranks. The bureaucracy demanded a standard ticket of admission to the executive class, and found it in the form of a university degree. Thus the GI Bill provided a very important service to the many veterans who got not only an education but an all-important diploma.

Most soldiers, like most other Americans, wished to settle into a life where satisfactions were formed chiefly on the personal level. Family, home, enough money to live comfortably—these were the things that mattered. Americans rejected the disruptions inherent in social reform, and were content to forego the satisfactions of public achievement. Thus Truman's re-election in 1948 seems almost as remarkable in retrospect as it did at the time. Both the right and the left wings of the Democratic party had split away, and were expected to take votes from the president. As it happened, the traditional American reluctance to support splinter parties kept the vote for each independent candidate down to about a million apiece. Truman fired his sharpest oratorical barbs not at Thomas E. Dewey, the Republican candidate, but at the Republican 80th Congress, which he excoriated as "do-nothing." But nothing was precisely what the American people wanted done. Probably Truman's appeal was simply himself. He presented an image that retained a nostalgic attractiveness—the little man from down home who zested in battling giants. The people who voted for him could pretend that they were in favor of change and social progress, while they actually prevented those dangers by returning the same hidebound congressmen.

While Truman's election remains somewhat anomalous, that of Dwight

D. Eisenhower in 1952 meshes perfectly with the mood of the times. He retained the enormous popularity which his war record had given him, and his political antecedents were so hazy that he had no bloc of enemies. (A group of liberal Democrats had tried to persuade him to run for the Democratic nomination in 1948; he had never belonged to any political party, and no one was quite sure which one he supported. The perfect candidate.) Eisenhower was soothing, a benign father figure. Nothing drastic was going to happen as long as he was in charge, and the country could go about its business without being shaken up by a lot of turmoil in Washington. His meandering speeches, his passion for golf, his air of stolid rectitude, all inspired love and trust. He probably could have defeated any possible Democratic candidate, and Adlai Stevenson was a piece of cake. The voters thought of Stevenson as an intellectual, a fatal political image. Moreover, his personal platform combined a demand for far-reaching domestic reforms, which most Americans did not want, along with a belligerent attitude in foreign affairs, which most Americans rightly thought was likely to get the country involved in dangerous and unprofitable disputes. Eisenhower, on the other hand, fulfilled his campaign promise to end the Korean War, and although the State Department and the CIA were constantly meddling in the affairs of other countries throughout his two terms, the people didn't know about it, and so didn't have to fret about it (Chapter 30).

The United States fretted about very little during the fifties. Prosperity continued steadily, and few of the prosperous many wanted their consciences pricked by reminders about those for whom respectable middle-class goals were unattainable. Those who persisted in agitating for social change were effectively silenced by the bugbear of Communism. Joseph McCarthy, junior senator from Wisconsin, has been depicted as the center of the witch hunt for Communists, but others all across the country participated. A posture of hostility toward the Soviet Union had been maintained ever since the end of World War II, and American Communists were believed to be all potential spies under orders from Moscow. The age of McCarthy might better be called the age of suppression by Harry S. Truman and such federal agencies as the FBI and the Bureau of Immigration and Naturalization. In the most tyrannical act since the relocation of Japanese-Americans, Truman—not McCarthy—infringed upon his authority as president to decree at his sole discretion on 25 November, 1946, that all federal employees must be "of complete and unswerving loyalty to the United States. . . ." The most detestable phase of the witch hunt began on that day, and held its momentum until John and Robert Kennedy decided to limit its excesses. For a decade, Americans who had nonconforming ideas were faced with a dilemma: keep your mouth shut, or lose your job and occasionally get your head bloodied.

The McCarthy hearings were just the most visible aspect of this repression of dissent. While they were proceeding, the assumption seemed to

FIGURE 29-1   *Centers of U.S. Population, 1870-1970*

be that anyone whose opinions were even slightly left of center was a putative Communist. McCarthy put on a show for a credulous audience by claiming that the government was riddled with subversives, by hauling hundreds of private citizens before a committee where he could examine their political associations. He found a certain number of actual ex-Communists who were willing to accuse their associates of dark deeds, and describe sinister cabals which they had allegedly taken part in. Americans were ready to believe that there was a Communist under every bush, and many governmental and private organizations took steps to uproot the bushes.

Although McCarthy himself did not participate in it, the trial of Alger Hiss for perjury in 1950 typifies the techniques and attitudes of the scare crusaders. Hiss was a former New Dealer (mid-Chapter 26 on AAA) who had worked at the San Francisco Conference which had founded the United Nations. He was convicted of perjury because he denied before a Congressional Committee that he had passed government secrets to the Russians in the thirties. The evidence against him depended on the testimony of one self-declared former Communist who at this point was engaged in hauling former associates before the House Un-American Activities Committee (HUAC). Hiss said that he had once known the man (then going under another name) but was unaware of his Communist affiliation and knew nothing about any espionage. Although a number of dignitaries testified to Hiss' good character, he was convicted. When accused of Communism, a man was guilty until proven innocent, and even then his reputation was smudged.

For the next four years HUAC summoned hundreds of suspected Communists to appear. A few, like Chambers, had pre-arranged to present a list of their former associates and acquaintances, but most preserved a stolid silence, giving the Fifth Amendment's safeguards against self-incrimination as grounds for refusing to answer any questions. Most Americans thought that "taking the Fifth" was self-incrimination enough, but at least witnesses could be protected from a charge of either perjury or contempt of Congress.*

The hearings were a disgraceful spectacle, and subjected both the witnesses and others who feared that they might be called up to unjustifiable badgering, and in some cases to outright persecution. But the activities of other self-appointed Communist hunters around the country were probably more damaging still. In Hollywood, people with known liberal sympathies were driven out of the entertainment industry. For years the only way blacklisted writers could make a living was by having a friend pass off their scripts as his own work—sometimes receiving a fair price, sometimes a pittance. Since the banished writers were among the best in the business, the quality of films plummeted. Not until the sixties was there a significant break in the diet of swill which Hollywood spewed forth. In industry, but particularily in colleges and schools, compulsory loyalty oaths proliferated. Disgraceful enough in themselves, they caused direct hardship to those who refused to sign them and lost their jobs, but their real evil lay in the climate of fear which they engendered. Few dared question the government, or the institutions of the nation, or the established order of things. Teachers in particular didn't dare encourage a doubting spirit among their students.

The students themselves did not seem to mind. Since the placid world of the white middle-class 1950's could satisfy all their ambitions, drastic change could only be for the worse. Few people any longer hoped for personal satisfaction from their jobs, which were "good" when they provided a large enough salary and no worries away from the office. One worked, not to eat, but to get a suburban house, television, a new wardrobe twice a year, a car every three, refrigerator, freezer, transistors, record players, speedboats, and electric toothbrushes. Nothing was expected to last long, and when it broke down no one could be found to fix it. But for the prosperous discarding old things

---

*Use of the Fifth Amendment was not universal. A few witnesses tried to refuse to answer on the grounds that the First Amendment's guarantee of freedom of speech and assembly protected their political beliefs and affiliations from Congressional probing. A few made the Committee look as foolish as it was. Pete Seeger, for example, was asked whether he was a Communist. He replied, "I'm just an old banjo plucker."

FIGURE 29-2. *Henry Hill, G. H. Knoles House*

The home of Dr. and Mrs. George H. Knoles was designed by Henry Hill of the San Francisco firm of Hill and Kruse. Knoles and his wife were looking ahead toward his retirement from the History Department at Stanford University, so they bought several acres on the Pacific Ocean about ten miles south of Carmel, California. The house was placed some 150 feet downward from the highway, on a saddle with a small hillock forming a windbreak between the cottage (for its size would not warrant a more haughty name) and the prevailing westerlies. To the southwest one sees white water along the coast as the breakers explode; to the northwest, coves and hills sweeping to the sea. Seen from California Route 1 above, the triangular shape of the dwelling is striking. The three angles were almost dictated by the forementioned windbreak in tandem with the nature of the views. Materials were stone, redwood, and glass—all rugged to suit the nature of the site. They also conform to what architects call "the interpenetration of space" between indoors and outdoors.

Design of this quality would merit attention anywhere. But new wealth has made California the postwar seedbed for domestic architecture, as Massachusetts was in 1800 or Illinois in 1900. For centuries, Americans had lurched heedlessly across the continent, plundering it as they went. California was clearly the end of the line. A goodly number of its residents seem to have awakened to the reality that they can no longer flee westward, so perhaps they should beautify their home grounds.

provided an opportunity for the gratification of consuming new ones, the only gratification which futile well-paid jobs could offer.

Two important myths prospered with post-war society. One was simply an updated version of the Myth of the Self-Made Man. Everyone could move ahead; everyone could have all the tempting things that television and the magazines presented so enticingly. But now wealth was earned, not by virtue and application, but by personal appearance and a mysterious new entity known as "personality."* If only you used the right toothpaste, kept clean and neat, and smiled brightly you would, if male, get a good job and its accoutrements, and, if female, acquire husband-with-job. Then, if female, you continued by keeping that extention of yourself, your house, properly burnished with all the "right" products—meaning the most recently advertised. Naturally, the cosmetics industry became a giant during these years, and has continued to grow by constantly discovering new ways in which people are unwittingly offending others in their personal habits. Of course the myth did not come true for all, or even most, Americans, but even the defeated continued to believe in it.

The other myth was almost completely new. Americans, like everyone else, had always found satisfactions in family life, but now the Family rose to a high spot in the American pantheon. It consisted of parents and young or adolescent children; the aged had no place in it. This group lived in a private suburban home, supported financially solely by the labors of the father in some other place. The mother cared for the house and children. The Family spent their free time enjoying a variety of activities together; everyone was happy. This new myth, fostered unremittingly by both advertising and entertainment, was partially a response to changing American demography. The age of both men and women at marriage had fallen drastically after the war, and the birth rate had risen. These new families needed housing, and residential suburbs mushroomed in response. There was no room in these subdivisions for either grandparents or productive labor, and no escape from the house for women. As more and more people began living under these conditions the myth developed that they were ideal.

And for many people, suburban private life did offer real satisfactions. The most famous of the post-war subdivisions were the Levittowns on Long Island and in Pennsylvania. They provided cheap, small houses with identical floor plans, taking advantage of every possible economy of scale. The Pennsylvania Levittown housed 70,000 on eight square miles. William Levitt stated the firm's founding premise: "People like people." Suburbs much on the Levittown model, most more expensive, some much more esthetically pleasing, have become ubiquitous. Americans are so accustomed to them that they find it difficult to recognise how great a change they represent. Older residential neighborhoods often display just as much drab sameness, but the

---

**The term "personality" is a perfectly valid one in the study of psychology. But starting in the late forties it became one of the cult words of the popular culture, in the sense of the phrase, "He has a nice personality." Although quite undefinable, "personality" accounted for everything from a child's experiences in kindergarten to the selection of presidents.

similar houses were not erected by one builder at one time. Each individual chose to construct a house quite like his neighbors, because he was familiar with it, because he could afford it. Since a tract was not developed all at once, there was no need to bulldoze out every natural wrinkle on the surface of the land. Moreover, earlier builders had not yet been inoculated by city planning. They didn't realize that residential, commercial, and manufacturing regions must be in as strict quarantine as if they had been infectious diseases. Thus in an earlier era many people could walk to work; everyone could do at least their routine shopping within a block or two of where they lived. As a neighborhood aged, the first floors of some houses would become stores, and certain streets developed into shopping promenades where the residents shopped, strolled, chatted.

In a modern suburb all is changed. The builder has economically uprooted every tree, flattened every hill. Manufacturing is banned, as is all commercial activity except the goods and services the residents need. Thus a mass exodus of wage earners from the neighborhood during the day. The shopping center supposedly fills the functions of the commercial street without its inconveniences—traffic, noise, jostling, parking problems. But the shopping center is merely what its name suggests, a place to buy things. The addition of restaurants, movie theaters, and entertainment cannot disguise its character. Many of the people present on a shopping street are merely out for a walk; others incorporate minor errands. But I can't imagine going to a modern shopping center for such a purpose. Moreover, nearly everyone there has driven in a private car. The planners cluster stores and services because they are supposedly incompatible with houses; they have succeeded in placing them too far from most homes to be conveniently accessible to pedestrians. Even people who live close enough to walk usually prefer to drive: the walk, through treeless, cookie cutter residential streets, is so boring. Despite these disadvantages, almost all Americans want to live in a dormitory suburb; ownership of a private, detached house is a powerful symbol of status and stability. Fewer and fewer can now afford it. Increasingly, poorer families are turning to mobile homes, which allow them to achieve the pride of ownership at a reasonable cost. Assembly line techniques allow trailers, mobile homes, and modular houses to be constructed much more cheaply than a traditional house, without the restrictions imposed by suburban housing codes. Since a mobile home can be placed on a very small site, their owners in some towns can largely sidestep the rocketing land costs which have afflicted all American metropolitan areas in recent years. In 1972, over 80 per cent of all new houses costing less than $20,000 were mobile homes.

The proliferation of the Levittowns and their successors represented a malaise more profound than anything mentioned above. True, they satisfied the hunger for "a home of my own." But they provided no real privacy, and no opportunities to express individuality in more than superficial ways. Few Levittowners really wanted privacy—they needed a community which would hide its lack of intimacy behind a mask of geniality. For intimacy was impossible in a society so fluid; suburban houses are designed with an eye for the inevitable resale.

Some Americans were excluded even from the minimal rewards of docility—prosperity and privacy. The largest single group was shut out because they were black. In the fifties it was still easy for white sympathizers with the black cause to continue in the myopic posture which they had maintained for generations: the problem was Southern. Liberal Northerners shook their heads sadly over segregation, and were outraged at tales of lynching and night riding. Occasionally a specific case might arouse their wrath, as with the Scottsboro case of 1932. Briefly, nine young blacks had been accused of raping two white vagrant girls in a freight car. The girls might be vagrants and probably prostitutes, but they were White Women, the Flower of the South; their testimony assured the defendants' conviction. The NAACP and other groups stepped in for the defense, and the case received much outraged publicity in the North, where its obvious inequities allowed many people to smirk self-righteously about the barbarities of the South. Since most lynchings occurred with the connivance of local authorities, perpetrators were seldom caught and even more rarely punished. It seemed logical to permit federal power to fill this void in justice with a proposed anti-lynching bill, but some Southern senators resisted; they filibustered (on the grounds not of supporting lynching, but of protecting states rights) and defeated the bill. Again, the North pointed an accusing finger. In 1948, in a direct bid for the black vote, Truman eliminated segregation where he could: in the armed forces. These had contained separate black units, often commanded by white officers, since the Civil War. This order had few important practical effects (except the one it was designed to bring about, black votes for Truman), but it indicated the attitude of the federal government.

In the early fifties white Americans still believed that the racial problems of the United States were Southern problems; John Doe was simply blind to the presence of all black people. In *Invisible Man* Ralph Ellison tried to open their eyes to the violent maelstrom beneath a black man's attempts to move up in the South, and to the equally grim picture of his life in the North. Higher education in the black South resembled the old plantation, except that Uncle Tom had been promoted to overseer; the white man remained preeminent. In the North, Ellison saw black solidarity as a mask concealing a perpetual snarl, resulting from a life both physically and emotionally precarious. And white society, which had created these conditions, had simultaneously blinded itself to them. Wishing to reject the black man, white people refused to look at him. But the Southern black was to be constantly in front of their eyes. In 1954 the Supreme Court decided that the Southern system of racial segregation in the public schools was unconstitutional. Racial segregation had been challenged before, and the court had declared it acceptable as long as the facilities provided were "equal." At that time Justice John Marshall Harlan dissented, on grounds which should have been used in 1954; he stated simply that the Constitution is color-blind, segregation is wrong, and it must be stopped. The court was less direct in 1954. The justices based their decision on psychological reasoning which stated that it made black children feel inferior to attend segregated schools, and that such schools were inherently unequal and must be integrated. This left them wide open to the plea of some white parent that it made his child feel inferior to attend integrated schools. But the decision can be criticized on more significant grounds. It decreed integration, but only eventually. The process was to take place "with all deliberate speed," which meant that only token black children were admitted to specific white schools.

Thus Southern schools had plenty of room within which to maneuver. At first some reacted with an outraged refusal to give an inch; they would not permit any integration. Prince Edward County, Virginia, took the desperate step of closing its schools entirely for some years. A number of localities set up "private" schools for whites only, but this expedient was largely thwarted when the courts prevented the states from diverting any public funds to such institutions. Most schools neither integrated nor refused to do so, but simply sat back and waited for a court order directed at them specifically. Then the reaction varied. It might be political suicide to approve or assist integration, but some officeholders indicated their willingness to comply with federal orders, as long as their constituents knew they were being forced. Then the processes of change usually occurred quietly enough.

But often a state governor would attempt to resist federal power; this first occurred in Little Rock, Arkansas, in 1957. At that time virtually all of the Deep South remained segregated. The Little Rock Board of Education set up a plan for gradual integration, which was to begin with the admission of nine black students to Central High School. The federal district court approved. But a group of white mothers petitioned a state court to stop the proceedings, on the grounds that integration would result in violence, and Governor Orval Faubus supported them. He sent the National Guard to the high school, ostensibly to maintain order, but actually to keep the black students out. They were smuggled in after a federal judge ordered him to remove the troops. But then a white mob stormed the school, and the children had to be removed for their own safety. President Eisenhower was outraged, and his reaction showed the rest of the South that it could not resist federal authority indefinitely. He sent a thousand paratroopers to Little Rock to secure orderly desegregation, and for several months the nine black students attended classes under the protection of the army.

This pattern of confrontation over segregated schools was repeated elsewhere, and Southern blacks continued to be external to it. The dispute was between Northern and Southern whites, with Northern middle-class blacks, represented by the NAACP, occasionally participating. But an indigenous Southern black rebellion was proceeding at the same time, led by a minister from Georgia, Martin Luther King. This movement can be dated from

December of 1955, in Montgomery, Alabama, and was precipitated when a tired Negro woman refused to go to her alloted place in the back of a public bus. She was ejected. The black residents of Montgomery responded by boycotting the bus company, which suffered a 65 per cent decrease in revenue, and was forced to capitulate and desegregate the buses on December 21. This episode featured many elements of the black liberation movement in the South that were to be used for the next decade. First, it raised non-violence to a creed. Second, both its leaders and its participants were black, and Southern. Northern whites generally approved, but their aid was superfluous. Third, whites were made conscious of the economic power that blacks had but which they had not exercised in a concerted fashion. Black people acted directly to change a specific wrong, and did not rely on legalistic maneuvering.

The character of Martin Luther King was an important influence in Montgomery, and throughout the Southern struggle. His religious beliefs, devoutly Christian but strongly influenced by Mahatma Ghandi, inspired his followers in a way that a purely secular struggle for civil rights could not have done. King believed that violence was un-Christian, and that gains achieved by violence were ephemeral. On the other hand, an oppressed people need not passively accept the wrongs dealt out to them, or confuse Christian humility with grovelling before white people. He called on black Southerners to pray, to march in unity for their rights, and to resist steadfastly attempts to keep those rights from them. This exhortation was extremely appealing, especially after experience showed that it worked. Often the demonstrators' non-violence was met by a mob, and by clubs and dogs, but King himself was there to take the blows along with his followers. Direct action worked.

Other groups, notably the Student Non-Violent Co-ordinating Committee (SNCC) and the Congress of Racial Equality (CORE) imitated King's techniques. By the early sixties most Northerners had seen the Southern strife on television; the contrast between the orderly, often singing demonstrators and the rock- and bottle-throwing mobs who met them evoked much sympathy. A few expressed their feelings by going south and working in the movement. Their presence enraged even liberal-minded white Southerners. Many Southerners had thought all along that racial troubles were caused by "outside agitators"; the presence of white Northerners seemed to confirm this mistaken notion. And those who sympathized with the black cause rightfully resented the patronizing Northern assumption that prejudice and injustice were restricted to the South. Yankee do-gooders had been anathema since abolitionist times. Eventually this well-meant aid was rejected by the black organizations. They had first welcomed white participation, then accepted it when restrained to subservient positions, then realized that it was often harmful and never necessary. Black people themselves had the power to change the conditions under which they lived; they needed only to organize and be determined to use their power.

Their strength lay in numbers; an efficient, orderly way to express numerical strength is at the polls. By the mid-sixties legal segregation had been crushed through most of the South, but blacks were still disfranchised. Voter registration drives became the crux of the Civil Rights Movement. Early in 1965 Martin Luther King began a campaign to register black voters in Selma, Alabama, a town with an almost even racial split. Ninety-nine per cent of the whites were registered; one per cent of the blacks. Each day several hundred black residents paraded to the county courthouse, ostensibly planning to register. Each day the sheriff turned them back, either by force or by arresting the marchers on a host of charges. Soon 2,000 people were in jail. On February 18 the state police broke up a sympathy demonstration in a nearby town, and one of the participants was killed. King called for a protest march to Montgomery, which was halted by state police a few miles outside Selma. The troopers used whips, clubs, and tear gas to disperse the marchers. The whole deplorable scene was broadcast on national television. It provoked outrage and a number of spontaneous sympathy demonstrations. Four hundred white clergymen flew into Selma to participate in the march. When one of them was murdered by a group of local toughs the tension and protest intensified. Even segregationist Southern newspapers deplored the violence, and realized that such senseless brutality only ensured the passage of tougher federal civil rights measures. On March 17 King won out, and the march to Montgomery took place; four months later the voter registration bill which the South had been opposing became law.

Except for the assassination of Martin Luther King in 1968, the events in Selma were the last ones in the Southern struggle for liberation which won widespread publicity and sympathy in the North. In August of 1965 Northern liberals were joggled out of their complacency by a five-day riot in Watts, a black ghetto in Los Angeles. Throughout the century black laborers had been streaming north, bringing few skills and less money. They qualified for only the most menial jobs, and since most employers followed a policy of "last hired, first fired" with regard to black labor, many were unable to obtain any work at all when times were hard. White bigotry confined blacks in squalid ghettos, where they were charged high rents for poor housing, where recreation facilities were nonexistent, where schools were ramshackle and overcrowded. School segregation was almost as rigid in the North as in the South, but its maintenance did not require legal support. Rigid residential segregation did the job.* When attempts were made to halt *de facto* school segregation by busing children to different schools, white mothers reacted with as much fury as had their counterparts in Little Rock. They rarely dared oppose desegregation as such, but usually based their protest on the need to preserve "neighborhood schools"—which amounted to the same thing.

---

*Residential segregation was not necessarily the rule in the South. One civil rights worker told of conducting a voter registration drive in a small town where residential integration was so absolute that door-to-door canvassing was useless—it was impossible to tell whether a black or white family lived in any given house. They finally solved the problem by consulting the city directory, where white heads of households were designated "Mr." or "Mrs." and blacks received no title.

Superficially, the Watts ghetto was a much more livable place than its counterparts in the East. Its housing was newer, and consisted mostly of detached houses rather than tenements. But since poor blacks could live in no other area, rents were extremely high. Three and four families often had to crowd into a house built for one. Bus service was almost nonexistent, even sparser than for the rest of southern California. Indeed, inferior city services have been a distinguishing mark of black ghettos across the nation. There were very few employers in Watts, as it was built as a residential suburb. It contained no hospitals, no movie houses, almost no opportunities for recreation. Moreover, a high proportion of its residents were unemployed. Accumulated anger at these conditions broke forth in a frenzy of destruction. The same pattern repeated itself in other large Northern cities over the next few years, with the expression of stored fury triggered by some small event, usually a petty act of repression on the part of the police.

But the woeful state of the ghettos had existed for generations. Why were the late sixties the time when they suddenly caught fire? The answer lies in changing expectations. Southern blacks were winning gains, and white liberals were vocally promoting programs to end poverty and discrimination. Yet paper changes were making no visible dent in the asphalt reality, and it was clear that most Northerners bitterly resented any changes which might affect them personally. The white working class were especially afraid, understandably. They enjoyed greater job security than black workers; any moves toward equality or status seemed to threaten what they felt to be a hard-earned relative security or privilege (often at the expense of blacks). Living in neighborhoods adjacent to the ghetto, lower-class whites felt that the brunt of any residential or school desegregation upheaval would fall upon them, while distance and expense protected the middle classes from any unsettling changes involved with a black influx. Often the children of immigrants who had themselves known ghetto conditions, the white working class cherished the notion that hard work and upright behavior had allowed them to advance, but they rejected the notion that poor blacks should want to do likewise.

Yet the fury of the ghetto riots was not turned outward, to white neighborhoods whose residents sat trembling in the midst of a growing arsenal of handguns, but inward, upon the ghetto itself. The destruction was not mindless. First, poor people have been as much conditioned by advertising as rich; they want the good things they see in the commercials. They took them. Moreover, inner city stores are notorious gougers of the credit-dependent poor, who regarded looting as a justifiable reprisal. Second, much property, both business and residential, was destroyed by fire. It appears that these fires were not set at random, but were a deliberate attempt to demolish the records of loan companies and other credit-granting institutions. Third, of the people who died, almost all of them were black and many of them women and children. The evidence indicates that the overwhelming majority of those shot were killed not by snipers, but by police and national guard. Of the people who died in the Detroit riot in 1967, there is no reason to ascribe even one death to a sniper.

The riots were a reaction of the black community to conditions which oppressed them as a group. Throughout the fifties and sixties a few avenues of escape persisted for individuals, the most visible of which was athletics. Professional spectator sports are an urban phenomenon; they require a large, concentrated population to support them. Their participants are highly visible models for the young, and throughout the century boys have looked to sports as an escape from an intolerable and otherwise locked-in environment. A black child knows he can never be president, but he might hope to be Willy Mays. Mays entered major league baseball in 1951, only four years after Jackie Robinson had officially broken the color bar. For the next twenty years Mays remained one of its most thrilling players, standing close to Babe Ruth on the all-time home run list, and remaining a culture hero even after age had blunted his skills. Henry Aaron has been a less colorful superstar. A few years younger than Mays, he has already passed Mays and broken Babe Ruth's home run record. Yet until that feat his exploits never received much publicity, and his name was probably unknown to those who are unfamiliar with baseball. Although it has provided an entrée into the middle class for many blacks, athletics too knows discrimination. White players who are less than great have an edge over their black counterparts; thus the percentage of black all-stars in the major team sports is greater than the overall percentage of black major leaguers. In football, certain positions, especially quarterback, are reserved for whites. White coaches and owners are no less bigoted than whites in general, and they run sports.

But black athletes are not supposed to speak of these things, or of any "controversial" subject. They should be suitably grateful for the opportunities which athletics has given them, and keep their mouths shut about politics. Muhammad Ali broke this rule and paid a heavy price. A very vocal and vivid man, Ali became heavy-weight champion of boxing in February, 1964, and shortly thereafter announced that he had converted to the Black Muslim faith. This provoked both anger and ridicule, and for years sports writers engaged in a put-down of both Ali and black people in general by persisting in calling him by his abandoned "white" name, Cassius Clay. But he continued as both a great fighter and a consummate entertainer, leaving his enemies no loophole through which to do him serious harm. That was provided them in 1967, when he refused induction into the army, stating that his religious convictions made it impossible for him to fight in a war. The World Boxing Association promptly declared his title vacant, in a gross violation of due process, and a Houston jury sentenced him to five years in jail. His appeal dragged on for five years, until finally the Supreme Court issued an injunction forcing the WBA to permit him to compete, and recognized his status as a conscientious objector.

The contrast between the older type of athlete, such as Mays, and a man like Ali parallels the contrast between the old and new black organizations.

The Black Muslims are a strictly segregationist organization which believes that the white man is a sort of Frankenstein's monster created by a black scientist in Africa. He isn't even real. This attitude provides an ironic counterpoint to the persistent white tendency to ignore "invisible" black neighbors. The Muslims' strength has arisen out of the Northern ghettos, particularily in prisons. They tell people who have always considered themselves worthless, "Be proud, be a man, it's good to be black," and alleviate loneliness by group support. Unfortunately, their credo is based on hate, and therefore will never win the support of the whites who hold the power of the nation. Malcolm X, ex-ghetto delinquent, ex-convict, brilliant orator, attempted to establish a breakaway organization which would incorporate both black pride and tolerance for whites, but he was assassinated before he could begin. The Black Panthers are a much smaller, newer group, whose ranks have been greatly thinned by the police and courts. Begun in the San Francisco Bay Area, the organization consists of young men, most of them ex-convicts, many of them ex-drug addicts, who feel that blacks have the right to defend themselves against unprovoked violence. They distrust the operations of the law, which they feel to be rigged against minorities and the poor, and the intentions of whites who attempt to be philanthropic, especially social workers. They have organized free breakfasts for school children and similar projects, which have received very little publicity, but have also been known to march into the legislative buildings in Sacramento armed to the hilt, which has gotten them a great deal of trouble.

Both the Muslims and the Panthers rest their strength in group identity and purpose. But both organizations seem to strike a majority of white Americans with hate and fear. This reaction apparently arises partially out of guilt; fear provokes hate. Whites have oppressed blacks throughout the nation's history, and naturally are apprehensive about the treatment to be meted out if the blacks ever get on top. The sight of a Panther with a gun in his hand brings terror to the surface, and has often provoked a bloody reprisal.

In 1960 the prediction of the upheavals to come would have sounded like an impossible nightmare. John Kennedy was elected president amid feelings of buoyant hope. He presented an image of youth and tinselled glamour, and offered a "New Frontier" to explore. The placid Eisenhower years had conditioned the American people in complacency, but they were growing a little bored. Eisenhower's vice president and chosen candidate for succession, Richard Nixon, lacked the general's personal popularity and grandfatherly aura. Nonetheless, the election was the closest ever, and Kennedy's victory must be regarded as something of a fluke, caused more by Nixon's tactical errors than by anything else. It was certainly not a mandate for change. The Kennedy style blinded his audience to reality, and voters were becoming increasingly willing to act as an audience. Television was becoming their only outlet on the world. Since this medium is perfectly adapted to transmit style and can easily be made to distort content, it was the ideal disseminator of the Kennedy myth. The election itself was probably decided by television, when Kennedy and Nixon met for a series of debates and the former came across as the much more attractive personality. For all JFK's fine words and grandiose programs, his administration accomplished little, which in itself helped to preserve his popularity. Despite their relish of the new air of bustle in Washington, few Americans really wanted change. If there is any harsh reality that lies concealed under the JFK myth, his assassination in November, 1963, assured that it will remain hidden forever, for the image has become far larger than the man.

Lyndon Johnson's image was very different, and did him no good. A consummate politician, he pushed many of Kennedy's social welfare measures through Congress, and at the time of his election in 1964 it seemed that he might become one of the greatest presidents the country had ever had. But even then, while posing as a "peace" candidate, he was planning to increase the involvement of the United States in southeast Asia (Chapter 30). Even before the festering war destroyed his reputation and his career, the American people thought of him as a crafty man, perhaps even a crooked man. His lies caused a credibility gap, but his aura strengthened it. His Texas folksiness, intended to radiate friendly camaraderie, struck middle America as uncouth.

While the war and the demands of minorities for justice were tearing the country apart, the economy boomed throughout the Kennedy and Johnson years. In large part this was caused by the war and defense spending, and by the space program. Electronics, aircraft, rocketry—these industries were buoyed up by a fat cushion of federal money. And the salaries of their well-paid employees helped support a host of other concerns. The gross national product (GNP) went from $214 billion in 1945 to more than a thousand billions of dollars after 1971. But this heart-pounding jump is deceptive in more ways than one. About half of it was only what might be called paper profits, due to the scandalous rate of inflation (Chapter 30 opening). The remainder did indeed represent a rise in the output of goods and services. But, as before, the increase was not disbursed with the well-being of the ordinary citizen in mind. The federal government grabbed off a huge share without any consumer ever seeing the paper money—and most of this portion went for nonproductive or even destructive uses. Much of this newly produced money did not go either for taxes or for consumer expenditures. It went to a handful of huge corporations, who were free to decide whether they wanted to distribute it to their stockholders or to re-invest it in further expansion of their plants (and their power). If put to the latter use, it supplemented governmental deficits as a recurrent boost to the growth of GNP. If passed out as dividends, it might be re-invested by stockholders or it could be spent on consumer goods and services. The amounts involved became mind-boggling. General Motors in 1972 showed net earnings of more than $2 billion. Few states in the union, and fewer national régimes abroad, could approach that figure in total receipts for the year.

The interstate freeway program also pumped dollars into the economy,

FIGURE 29-3. *Combines on a Wheat Ranch*

This photograph by P. M. Burn of the Calgary *Herald* shows combines sweeping across the wheat fields of the Red Maples Farms in Alberta. Although this picture was not taken in the United States at all, it belongs here for three reasons. It typifies the mechanization of today's agriculture; these combines are threshing while they reap. The scene calls to mind the *Wehrmacht* tanks grinding across the plains of Poland. Second, nature does not respect the international boundary. The bonanza farms of southern Alberta do not differ much from those of Montana or western North Dakota. Perhaps the chief difference is the presence in the Canadian province of chinooks, warm westerly winds that come over the Rockies and cause the temperature to skyrocket; this photograph was taken under such conditions at the beginning of December, 1969. To recoup wheat that had been thought lost to the snows, Red Maples Farms mobilized the three combines it owned plus five borrowed from neighbors.

Third, the proprietors of this spread live in Texas. Although Canadian anxiety about the intrusion of American capital has focussed on a few areas—oil and natural gas, minerals, manufacture of consumer durables—in fact American money is found in many other spheres of the economy. Of foreign investment in Canada, in 1900 Britain furnished 85 per cent and the U.S. 14 per cent. By 1922 the British share had dwindled to 47 per cent, while the U.S. held the majority. By 1946–47 the American portion had swollen to 72 per cent. By 1963 the U.S. controlled 97 per cent of all capital used to make autos in Canada, 90 per cent in rubber manufacture, 66 per cent in electrical goods, 54 per cent in chemicals.

and if Johnson's various poverty programs did little for the poor, they were clearly a boon to the thousands of social workers, researchers, and teachers whom they employed. But tangible factors cannot serve as a full explanation of the economic boom, for the psychology of prosperity was its strongest support. In prosperous times people spend money and invest money optimistically. They are more than willing to believe that good times will go on forever, and that attitude helps create a self-fulfilling prophecy. Inflation occurs, but means little to the fully employed, who can expect their salaries to keep pace. For the poor, especially the aging, times worsen as the value of the dollar shrinks, but their influence has always been small. For the majority, growth has become an intoxicant, not subject to question by human values. This benign economic climate nurtured a strange new crop—political and social radicalism.

Radical opinion had been silent; in the mid-sixties it began to speak loudly, in a growing number of voices which often shouted for different things. This was not a regrowth of dormant Communism, although capitalism was a frequent target. The Old Left had deplored the uses to which the system had been put, but felt that in proper hands it was a necessary tool. The New Left distrusted government and had a distaste for organized power, even their own. Its members believed that the system, the structure, of society had to be dismantled, for it forced even the well-meaning to become manipulators of others and destroyers of freedom. Arthur Miller is not a partisan of the New Left, but in his play "Death of a Salesman" he presented a classic portrait of the manipulated man. Willy Loman has tried all his life to cooperate with a system which traps him, drains him, and discards him. As soon as he makes the last payment on his refrigerator the door handle falls off. He finishes paying for his house, and dies. The only pride that a futile life has allowed him is the belief that he was "not only liked, but *well* liked"; the salesman has succeeded in selling himself. None of his "friends" attend his funeral. Loman's pathos is dual: circumstances have made his failure inevitable, and in the end he is not even allowed the delusion of success.

The new radicals rejected the world which created Willy Loman. Most of them were young, and middle class, the children of respectable citizens who had followed the rules and reaped the tangible rewards during the preceding two decades. While the immediate object of youthful anger was the war in Vietnam, a rejection of their parents' values underlay the rebellion. An early rumbling of this movement was heard at the University of California at Berkeley, in 1964. Sparked by resistance to an administrative closing of the campus to outside political activitists, the Free Speech Movement was really a rejection of the modern university. The protesting students at Berkeley felt that the institution had become a factory stamping out graduates without regard to their needs. Education, they insisted, was only valuable when it was interpersonal and flexible. It could not be twisted into a rigid mechanism which poured information into presumably empty heads, and it could not occur in a classroom containing four hundred people. Since sheer size had forced the

University into a rigid bureaucratic mold, many of its students found that it had become valuable to them only as a meeting place where their ideas about the outside world could be formulated; to bar political activity would make it a useless place. The public reacted to the FSM with disbelief and anger. Protesting that students were in school to "learn," and should be grateful for the opportunity, many irate citizens revealed their conception of education as a passive process, with the student as recipient. Since a college diploma had proven itself as the entrance ticket to the middle class, they were bewildered by the uproar.

To understand protesting students, it is necessary to examine the world in which they had grown up. Most came from the regimented world of the middle-class suburb. Their parents, having lived through, if not necessarily experienced, depression and war, still relished security; the next generation took material things for granted, and sought less tangible satisfactions. Love, loyalty, a sense of worth through accomplishment—America provided few opportunities to attain these goals. Instead it offered material wealth and "togetherness." Many young people rejected these trophies, for they were not merely tarnished, they were hollow within. But what should they strive for instead? The university might have offered an answer to some, but had grown too rigid to even hear the question. To others, only immediate sensual gratification, through drugs, through sex, through dancing, seemed worth having. Naturally these activities horrified their elders. As early as the late 1950's, when Elvis Presley wriggled his way into the national consciousness, respectable people prophesied doom. But Dionysian activities such as these do not spark profound change; instead, they absorb the energies of anger. A more serious threat to the norms of American life would come from those who, rejecting society as it was, also turned away from immediate gratification while recognizing that deep changes come slowly. No flare of angry energy could make a better America, and a lifetime of patient effort might do no more than help hold the line. Conditioned by television more than by anything else to live comfortably with sudden change and instant answers, few young Americans had developed the patience to persist in political activities in the face of persistent failure. If the medium is in fact the message, most youthful radicals had been cancelled after a short season.

By 1967 youthful dissent had moved off campus and onto the streets. Having rejected the values of middle-class America, a growing number of young people searched for a different life style, one incorporating more humanity and less money, more love and less war. Although these aims are certainly commendable, they were sought with a naive idealism that doomed itself. Thousands of members of the "love generation" came to San Francisco in the summer of 1967—most of them teenagers, many of them penniless. They slept on the streets, in the parks, jammed together in tiny apartments. Wearing a common uniform of blue jeans and long hair, they were picked up by the police on drug and vagrancy charges, and assaulted, raped, and robbed by assorted hoodlums who found them easy prey. Although the flower children of

Haight-Ashbury were a short-lived breed, youthful disillusion with America could not be squelched so quickly as they were.

The continuing war in Vietnam led more and more people into radicalism, as the government refused to heed the wishes of the majority who wanted it stopped. By the late sixties it had become meaningless to speak of "hawks" and "doves"—every sane person wanted out. Most were not radicals, or advocates of social change, or even especially interested in politics, but governmental arrogance and repressive police measures were moving more and more quiet liberals to the left every day. The Democratic National Convention in Chicago provides an example. Although Hubert Humphrey, the vice president, represented the rejected policies of the Johnson administration, control of party machinery sent him into the convention with enough votes to ensure nomination. A group of New Left youth (wearing the familiar badges of hair and clothing which by this time provoked a reflex reaction of violence on the part of many policemen) came into the city to demonstrate their disavowal of the war. A few intended to instigate trouble; most had peaceful plans. When the police were set loose on the demonstrations, a series of riots ensued which tended to radicalize not only their participants, but millions who saw it on television. Watching young people being attacked with clubs and tear gas seemed to confirm the contention that America was a repressive and brutal place; some parents who had deplored their children's appearance and activities began to sympathize, and then to agree that the nation needed some drastic changes.

A similar process occurred in May of 1970. In that month President Nixon, who had promised to wind down the war, sent troops into Cambodia. Students demonstrated on hundreds of college campuses. At Kent State University in Ohio the National Guard was called in to preserve order; guardsmen killed four students. Several inferences can be drawn from the events which followed. First, radicalism was growing; among the young, few any longer trusted the government; many no longer wanted the prosperous middle-class life that their parents had thought so desirable. Kent State was not a Berkeley with a history of activism: it has always been a quiet school in a conservative area. If violence could happen there, it could happen anywhere. Second, the nation's polarities were hardening. Everyone was angry after Kent State: the left was infuriated at a society which gave terrified boys guns to shoot students, and the right hated the students for "provoking" the guard. Dialogue across this gap was becoming almost impossible.

From the mid-sixties on, a movement for equality was gaining momentum among America's numerical majority—its women. Superficially, the demands of women's liberation could be easily met. Equal pay, equal job opportunities, provision for mothers to escape the deadening nest of suburbia—all sound like simple justice. But women's inferior position had been so long engraved into society and into both male and female psychologies that it will probably take generations for even rough parity to be achieved. Little girls were given dolls when boys received footballs. But the real problem lay in the attitudes they were presented with at the same time. Boys were encouraged to look outward, to explore, to contend with nature and with others. Girls were warned to watch out for dangers, to be fearful, to experience triumphs vicariously. Even before they started school, boys learned to feel humiliated when defeated by a girl, and girls to assume their own inadequacy when competing with boys. With these attitudes engraved so early, it was not surprising that many men refused to promote women, talk seriously with women, or respect women. And women frequently confirmed their low opinion by being unreliable and unambitious at work and petty-minded housewives everywhere else. Having been convinced of their own inferiority, they commenced to demonstrate it.

Two reactions to the liberation movement confirm this complementary state of mind. First, male reaction to female demands has been not anger but ridicule. This has been true throughout the history of feminism, and indicates the depth of male contempt. Second, there are a very large number of women who hasten to dissociate themselves from any sympathy with the movement whenever the subject comes up. In a way this is reminiscent of the slaves who hastened to assure visitors that they loved massa and didn't want to be free. But anti-liberationist women hold their position especially vituperatively when in the presence of someone who disagrees with them; they are sincere about it, as the slave was not. I can only believe that such people have become so convinced of their personal inadequacy that they don't want to see any woman lead a full life which would deprive them of built-in sexual excuses for being maimed.

One tangible change in the lives of many women came about in the early sixties with the development of a more reliable means of birth control. Planned conception had been a goal for decades (mid-Chapter 25 on Feminism), but the means for achieving it were awkward to use and often didn't work. Birth control pills, which operate by preventing ovulation, are more safe and sure; their popularity burgeoned. One result has been the desire for sexual freedom which has accompanied youthful dissent, but a more significant product of the "pill" has been economic. In some regions of the South all black families have about the same income. The ones who manage to subsist on it decently, perhaps provide opportunities for their offspring, are those with few children. As use of birth control pills has spread, more and more women have been able to control their own fertility, to make a conscious decision with an enormous impact on themselves and the future of their progeny. This device has probably had a greater impact on more women than any other event in the century.

It has been claimed that women have an enormous amount of power, which they don't use. This is true, and liberationists try to bring it to bear. One instance in which consumer power, which is mostly female (if unorganized) did make some changes, occurred in the late sixties when the grape pickers of California went on strike. Large-scale fruit and vegetable production in the

United States is dependent on migrant labor to do the harvesting; in California the pickers are almost all Mexican-Americans. They are, like their counterparts elsewhere, desperately poor, uneducated, and helpless before the rich, well-organized growers. Although migrant workers have been considered impossible to unionize, César Chavez attempted it when he organized the United Farm Workers. By the force of personality and faith he persuaded numbers of his fellow Chicanos to band together and resist the coercion of the employers despite great hardship. At first, growers would not even recognize the union as a bargaining agent, much less grant an increase in wages or an improvement in working conditions. Chavez called a strike against what he felt was a vulnerable group, the growers of table grapes. A strong agricultural union would normally be in a very powerful position, as the crops must be picked within a short period of time or the grower will face total loss; no lockout is possible. But for the duration of the strike the grapes were picked: the growers simply brought in a fresh supply of workers who had not heard of the strike. When the union persuaded them to go out as well, the process was repeated. But the union won. Chavez achieved this feat by publicizing the plight of the UFW members to audiences throughout the country, and telling them that all grapes were being picked by duped strikebreakers. He asked them therefore not to buy any. The resulting boycott, probably the most hated weapon the many can employ against the few, cut drastically into grape sales, and forced the growers to capitulate. Strengthened by victory, the UFW then struck the lettuce growers.

Another group, less politically radical than the New Left, more numerous than women's liberationists, began clamoring in the late sixties for a halt to the reckless destruction of the environment. Lakes and rivers were dying, ocean fish were becoming too contaminated to eat, city air was often unbreathable, and there were more people every day. Concern over these conditions snowballed, and protest became widespread. Several factors need be distinguished. First, urban air is probably no dirtier than it was a hundred years ago. One need only read a description of Pittsburgh, or Chicago, or Birmingham, to realize that our ancestors did not live in a healthful environment. Water pollution is certainly much worse now. Second, environmental decay is caused in large part by population pressure. If the population continues to grow, probably not even the severest controls will prevent an environmental disaster. Third, the worst threat to the ecology, aside from overpopulation, is technology (Document 30-2). Laboratories are developing, factories producing, and people using (and discarding) vast numbers of substances, in vast quantities, including many that do not occur in nature. These substances are almost all complicated hydrocarbons, known as organic chemicals. Naturally occurring organic matter can be a normal part of the ecological system; if it is introduced in moderate quantities, bacteria will feed on it and it will decay, thus breaking up into its component parts. But no bacteria have developed to feed on the new artificial substances, which means that they persist unchanged to pervade the waters and animal food chains, and affect them disruptively and unpredictably.

If the nation's mood in 1950 was complacent, and in 1960 ebullient, in 1970 it was despairing. Decreased government expenditures in defense and the space program sent the economy reeling. Unemployment rose, among the highly skilled as well as the disadvantaged. During the prosperous years arcane electronics firms ringed Boston, growing fat on NASA money; in the seventies one after another fell. During the summer of 1971 one Bostonian commented wryly, "If you take a taxi around here the odds are even that the driver will be an unemployed Ph.D in Physics." Simultaneously, inflation galloped on. In classical economics, unemployment and inflation are supposed to balance each other; you can't have both at the same time. The United States (and many other industrial nations) proved that indeed you could. Thus the times were insecure for almost everyone. The employed worried about losing their jobs; the educated saw their ticket to prosperity disintegrate to waste paper; those on fixed incomes felt inflation drag them into poverty.

Poverty, which a host of social welfare programs was designed to eliminate, persisted. Predictable groups were poor. First, black families, usually urban, often fatherless. Second, farm workers, usually migrant. Third, the aged, usually living alone. This was the hard core of poverty, but its edges were swelled by the growing numbers of unemployed and chronically under-employed. Only a drastic redistribution of income could aid them; social patchwork could not do the job. But redistribution the government would not undertake, believing that higher taxes taken from the middle class would throw them out of office.

In the early seventies the Asian war dragged on, despite the obvious will of the people that American military involvement in it should have ended long before it finally did, by slow degrees, during 1973. But governmental un-responsiveness had become accepted, if hated. The institution seemed too big to control, a monolithic machine with locked controls. Even if it were controllable, many Americans had come to fear that its masters would never operate it for the public advantage. Getting elected and preserving the inertia of power were the functions of Washington; the people could be endlessly manipulated and spied upon for those ends, but could not themselves affect the future.

One index of a healthy society is a reasonable balance between past-mindedness and future-mindedness: the past neither idolized nor ignored, the future neither defied nor dreaded. Through most of the American past a balance had been maintained. The very mobility of American society has helped to preserve it, for while physical and social migration has forced many changes, it also made the migrants ardent conservators when they could resist change. The War for Independence itself, although in some ways a genuine "revolution," was sparked in large part by a desire to preserve the ancient

715

FIGURE 29-4.   *Harrison & Abramovitz, Phoenix Mutual Life Building*

rights of Englishmen from encroachment. By the early seventies this equilibrium became precarious. Most Americans distrusted the future; some were gripped by nostalgia for a more satisfactory past, while others discarded it as irrelevant. It is no accident that the hit television series of the time, *All in the Family,* opened with the song "Those Were the Days," while a substantial part of its audience watched to jeer at a man duped into such sentiments.

A combination of nostalgia and insecurity is understandable enough. American society, still unable to solve the pervasive problem of maldistribution of incomes, masked injustice by an apparent prosperity. Abundance of goods was not accompanied by abundance of services or the pleasures which come from doing useful work, and for a large minority even material things were unobtainable. Since a grossly disproportionate number of the dispossessed were also black, they were sometimes able to focus their anger in ways that the rest of the country could understand. But most of the time white people, prosperous people, relished their self-imposed blindness. Young people also threatened to topple established society, but were sidetracked when their efforts produced few visible results. Having become conditioned to the instantaneous—in news, in food, in answers—they found it hard to deal with slow changes. By the 1970's another question had been raised. Had the American economy and government so hardened itself, in the name of efficiency and speed, that slow changes could not take place? Would drastic means be needed to return more control to a greater number of people?

Americans disturbed by the condition of the environment also worried about the deterioration of the inner cities. This building, the Phoenix Mutual Life Insurance Company's headquarters, is part of Constitution Plaza, a complex designed to expunge blight in the core of Hartford, Connecticut. The beauty of the structure is apparent in the photograph; it is also displayed to travellers between New York and Boston. But its significance goes beyond architectural virtuosity. An overhead walkway ties it to the rest of the Plaza. Underground parking eliminates an eyesore which plagues most American cities. Also the complex offers a goodly amount of greenery and open space—a value often overlooked by those who draft urban building codes. Plans for the building emerged from the New York offices of Harrison & Abramovitz, which also had general responsibility for the United Nations Building in New York.

Apart from its contemporary esthetic and social significance, this building suggests several avenues of contemplation. Hartford has long been a center for insurance; its prosperity depends almost wholly on that industry. Its emergence in this connection begins with Hamilton's plan for funding the federal debt (Chapter 9). Another line of speculation might hit upon the importance of the patron in promoting art: Phoenix Mutual is the twenty-fifth largest life insurance company in the nation in terms of assets. Some firms with even more money are erecting monstrosities.

The company's history is reminiscent of the story of the nation. When formed in 1851, it was called the American Temperance Life Insurance Company, and only served clients who abstained from alcohol. Within a decade its directors felt compelled to widen its appeal, took on the present name, and became less particular as to their clients.

SOME NOTABLE EVENTS

1944 Pocket Books begins to capture mass market; starts paperback revolution.

1946 Truman seizes railroads to avert strike, 24 May.

Republicans win both Houses of Congress, 5 Nov.

1947 Veterans enrolled in U.S. colleges reach peak; of 2.5 million students, 1 million are veterans.

Taft-Hartley Act, 23 June.

Ralph Ellison, *Invisible Man.*

1948 General Motors is first giant employer to grant an "escalator clause" (cost-of living adjustment) in collective-bargaining contract.

Henry A. Wallace nominated by left-wing splinter Progressive party for president, 25 July; increases Truman's chance of defeat for re-election in Nov.

Truman executive order for integration of blacks in armed forces, 26 July.

Alger Hiss called a Communist by Whittaker Chambers, 17 Aug.; on 6 Dec. the charge becomes espionage.

1949 Nobel Prize for Literature to William Faulkner.

Arthur Miller play, "Death of a Salesman."

1950 Hiss convicted of perjury, 21 Jan.

Klaus Fuchs confesses in Great Britain as atomic spy, 3 Feb.

Segregation in colleges and railroad cars banned by Supreme Court, 5 June.

Democrats keep control of both Houses of Congress, 7 Nov.

U.S. Census: 150,697,361 (64 per cent urban).

1951 Color telecast, first in U.S., by C.B.S.

Presidents in future limited to two terms by 22nd Amendment, 26 Feb.

McCarthy asserts that General Marshall was part of "Communist conspiracy," 14 June.

1952 Truman seizes steel mills to avert strike, 8 April; action ruled illegal by Supreme Court, 2 June.

Republicans take both Houses of Congress, 4 Nov.

1953 Mark Harris, *The Southpaw.*

Department of Health, Education, and Welfare created.

1954 Nobel Prize in Literature to Ernest Hemingway.

Army-McCarthy hearings, 22 April–17 June.

Democrats win both Houses of Congress, 2 Nov.

Senate censures McCarthy, 2 Dec.; by 67-22.

Newport Jazz Festival founded.

1955 Salk polio vaccine proven effective, 12 April.

AFL-CIO formed by merger, 5 Dec.

Montgomery, Alabama bus boycott led by Martin Luther King, 1–21 Dec.

1956 First transatlantic telephone cable.

$33.5 billion highway act.

1957 First civil rights bill in eighty years; passed 29 Aug.

First nuclear power station in United States opens in Pennsylvania.

1959 Alaska and Hawaii become states.

St. Lawrence Seaway opens, 26 June.

1960 Black students begin sit-ins.

Federal civil rights voting act.

U.S. Census: 179,324,175 (69.9 per cent urban).

Population of world estimated at 3 billion.

1961 "Freedom rides" begin in March.

Roger Maris hits 61 home runs this season; breaks Babe Ruth's 1927 season record (60).

1962 First television transmission by satellite.

1963 Civil rights march on Washington, 28 Aug.

1964 Free Speech Movement at U. of California, Berkeley, starts in Nov.

Poll tax outlawed by 24th Amendment.

Economic Opportunity Act.

1965   Department of Housing and Urban Development created.

Watts riots in Los Angeles, Aug.

Claude Brown, *Manchild in the Promised Land.*

Autobiography of Malcolm X.

General Motors' profits exceed $2 billion.

1966   Minimum wage set by Congress at $1.40 an hour; covers 38 million workers.

Department of Transportation created.

1967   Gross National Product reaches $750 billion.

First effective organizing drive launched among Mexican-American farm workers in California.

1968   Martin Luther King and Robert F. Kennedy assassinated.

Eldridge Cleaver, *Soul on Ice.*

CHAPTER 29 • The Forbidden Fruits of Affluence

Ways to Study History XXIX

Check dictionaries. A prize-winning work about Jacksonian America was based in part on a calamitous error about the meaning of the term "working class" to Yankees during the Jackson administration. The book imparted to the phrase its modern meaning, taking it to signify industrial laborers toiling for an hourly wage. But in fact the nineteenth-century use of the term had a far broader import. If we consider the Knights of Labor at their numerical peak in 1886, for instance, they still took the word "labor" as inclusive of the entire labor force except for bankers, saloonkeepers, and lawyers. By this definition Andrew Carnegie was a member of "the working class."

Historians of the modern period work mainly with words. The more precision we can impart to the meaning of those words, the better. Certainly the monumental achievement in historical lexicography so far as English is concerned is the thirteen volumes of *The New English Dictionary on Historical Principles,* begun in 1888 and finished at last forty years later. These volumes are on "historical principles" in that they trace in meticulous detail the changing meanings of a word over centuries of time; some single entries run for several pages. With its supplement of 1933 the set is nearly always called *The Oxford English Dictionary* or merely *O.E.D.* (now available in various forms). But it has two detriments: few of us can afford to spend hundreds of dollars for the dictionary in its regular large-type edition, and a reference library is not always accessible. Second, it records primarily British historical usages. For contemporary (but not historical) American variants, packaged in one handy volume, my own favorite is *Webster's New World Dictionary of the American Language* (1953). Definitions are brief and straightforward; etymologies, so valuable in understanding a word, are fairly full; many idioms are given. Also the items are presented in one alphabetical series, instead of having what some consider a cumbersome appendix for biographies and so on. This last feature (with all the others) is shared by *The American Heritage Dictionary* (1969), and also by the *The Random House Dictionary of the English Language: The Unabridged Edition* (1967), which has additional virtues but which is more costly and bulkier.

Document 29-1

Doubtless many readers have thought that it was unjust to print the parody, "Eisenhower's Gettysburg Address" (Ways to Study History VI), so they might want to read a portion of an actual address that he delivered to graduation exercises at the national academy for local police officers that is conducted by the Federal Bureau of Investigation. The president was presented with an FBI badge. A fellow speaker was the Rev. Norman Vincent Peale, author of *The Power of Positive Thinking.*

Mr. Hoover and my friends:
   To say that I am honored by this presentation is indeed an understatement. To say that I am astonished and even astounded is perfectly true, particularly when you realize that on the way over here I was telling Mr. Hoover I couldn't think of a single secret we had in Government that hadn't already appeared in the papers. And this one, he just reminded me, has been a well-kept secret.
   I want to say one other thing; that is, that I am moved by the tenor of Dr. Peale's remarks—and just by the way they appealed to me very deeply. He said that there must be an underlying deeply felt religious faith if we are each to bear the burdens that are brought to our particular spot in our lives today, and in view of the tensions and ill-feeling and vituperation and bad words that we read in our papers about each other, sometimes internationally, sometimes closer to home. . . .
   And so I couldn't more emphatically endorse what he says today. As we go about our work and each of us in his own capacity does his best, then I believe if we are to be the great civilization that we are destined to be, we must remember there is a God Whom we all trust. . . .

Document 29-2

The deprived groups in American society loomed somewhat bigger in practical politics when President Johnson admonished in his State of the Union message on 8 January, 1964: "this administration here and now declares unconditional war" against poverty. Some dimensions of the problem were summarized in a report to a senate committee later that year.

When Americans look at themselves today, they cannot help seeing a reflection of growing affluence and optimism. The image is thrown back from every side. . . .

But in spite of this, there remains an unseen America, a land of limited opportunity and restricted choice. In it live nearly 10 million families who try to find shelter, feed and clothe their children, stave off disease and malnutrition, and somehow build a better life on less than $60 a week. Almost two-thirds of these families struggle to get along on less than $40 a week.

These are the people behind the American looking glass. There are nearly 35 million of them. Being poor is not a choice for these millions; it is a rigid way of life. It is handed down from generation to generation in a cycle of inadequate education, inadequate homes, inadequate jobs, and stunted ambitions. It is a peculiar axiom of poverty that the poor are poor because they earn little, and they also earn little because they are poor. For the rebel who seeks a way out of this closed circle, there is little help. The communities of the poor generally have the poorest schools, the scarcest opportunities for training. The poor citizen lacks organization, endures sometimes arbitrary impingement on his rights by courts and law enforcement agencies; cannot make his protest heard or has stopped protesting. A spirit of defeatism often pervades his life and remains the only legacy for his children. . . .

The Decline (and Fall?) of the
American Empire

The military-industrial complex, as President Eisenhower would call it later, did not end with V-J Day, nor did it begin then. Such major companies as DuPont had counted the government as a major customer for a century and a half. They had learned the discretion of hiring retired Army officers to handle their negotiations with federal purchasing agencies. But after 1945 the interlocking became tighter and more extensive. Generals such as MacArthur and Somervell were now common on corporate boards of directors. Conversely, business executives (Wilson of GE, Wilson of GM, McNamara of Ford, countless others) became luminaries in Washington. In this two-way traffic, each man was likely to carry with him the attitudes and values to which he had been conditioned by his earlier environment. Most military men were doubtful that war was good, but nearly all knew that defense appropriations were good. Most tycoons from the corporate sector thought that government was bad, but they all knew that federal purchases from private enterprise were splendid.

During the Eisenhower administration at least two members of the cabinet, both from the upper berths of business, tried to check federal expenditures in order to balance the budget. But they were merely following a hackneyed catch-phrase, and their efforts were futile. Nearly every year, the federal debt grew. When it did not grow fast enough, the economy sagged. Through an epoch that shows astounding prosperity by some time-series, we can find pronounced slumps. The nadirs for unemployment as a percentage of the labor force were in

1949	5.5 per cent
1961	6.7 per cent
1971	5.9 per cent

By the yardstick of the 1930's, these figures seem modest, but they shocked millions who had grown accustomed to figures such as 1.9 per cent in 1945 and 2.5 per cent in 1953. They also shocked the unemployed, many of whom were accustomed to thick steaks plus two or three cars in the driveway.

One palliative was obvious to anybody who could think: Hike government expenditures. Even if public agencies had not borrowed—and they did, in amounts worthy of pharaohs—their capacity to pay their bills was growing dramatically. Receipts by the U.S. Treasury were $44.5 billion at the end of World War II. Then they eased downward to $36.5 billion in 1950. That year saw the beginning of the Korean War, and intensification of the Cold War. By 1960 they were closing in on $100 billion, nearly thrice the figure of a decade earlier. By 1970 they had nearly doubled again. Where did these vast resources come from, and where did they go? They came obviously from taxes, which continued, although perhaps to a lesser degree than earlier, to spare the rich and soak the middle incomes. As to where they went, a large portion was never there at all. The inflated figures of 1960 or 1970 merely reflects the general rise in prices, as can be illustrated by the consumer price index (1967 equals 100):

1950	72.1
1955	80.2
1960	88.7
1965	94.5
1970	116.3

After 1970, as the value of the dollar plummeted (memories of the Continental bills of credit and of the Weimar Republic), the cost to the federal government of each nut and bolt rose. The means of payment came from the many unlucky citizens who could not find a way to evade their taxes, and who were simultaneously suffering from the rising cost-of-living. The rest of the increase in federal receipts tended to find its way into the pockets of millions of civil servants—plus a couple of hundred giant companies.

With so much money at stake, and with such a tightly knit community of military-industrial interests, corruption was inevitable. Taxpayers even paid the bills for the corruption. One giant corporation put out a glossy monthly to boast of its achievements in defense and outer-space products; for these goods, there was only one buyer. The same firm was not damaged by the revelation that one of its vice presidents had been procuring prostitutes for potential customers at a sales convention. A company that became big at home before it became a part of outer space was General Dynamics, which repeatedly bought the expensive back cover of *Scientific American* for its "institutional advertising." Successive administrations in Washington, to justify the taxes that made possible these massive expenditures, needed programs that they could sell to millions of Americans. Hence came the overpowering freeways; any prosperous citizen can drive for hours on a six-lane divided highway in Nevada and see very few other cars. Hence came the more modest anti-poverty programs. But the two largest rat-holes down which to pour the wealth of the middle classes were provided by the Cold War. The outer-space program was not designed for scientic ends but for public-relations: Beat the Russians. Direct military appropriations were bigger yet. Although their efficacy in buoying up the domestic economy can hardly be denied, they might be regarded even in that connection as an evasion of the need to think. Abroad, the results were disastrous, as we shall see.

"A man's pride shall bring him low; but honor shall uphold the humble in spirit." (Proverbs xxix:23) The twenty-five years after Hiroshima heard the American orchestra play paeans until they reached a crescendo. A large part of the audience did not listen. The catastrophic approach to foreign relations that had begun with McKinley was pushed to awesome distances in the years from Truman to Johnson, and it is far from certain that Nixon's gestures towards détente will settle Americans back to earth.

For eighteen vital months from July, 1945, to January, 1947, James F. Byrnes headed the State Department. In that period the Allies of World War II—restive with each other at best, united only on the grand policy of smashing the armed might of the Axis, and even within that policy each of them striving to fry its own kettle of fish—these Allies turned into a pack of wolves slashing at each other's throats. Nobody struck a jugular, but body wounds were frequent. Blood and corruption flowed from bodies, gold from treasuries, hardware exploded from factories. Byrnes had neither the understanding nor the character to cope with this melee. Viewing the origins of the Cold War, he could not grasp what was happening; much less could he offer remedies. To his death he remained a small-town politician in South Carolina, elevated to eminence by FDR in 1941 by an appointment as Justice of the United States, resigning from that body in 1942 to become almost an assistant president. He felt no sympathy for the poor, nothing but antagonism to organized labor, and hatred for blacks. His appointment to be secretary of state was as obnoxious as any imaginable.

Already at Potsdam, the U.S.-U.S.S.R. clash was becoming manifest. Truman and Churchill agreed to keep atomic information to themselves, leaving the Soviet Union out. The first major dispute to become public had to do with central Europe and the Balkans. This vast region, as far west as Berlin, had been conquered by Russian armies. Stalin, knowing too well the pro-Nazi governments that had flanked Russia prior to the war, was determined to establish the *cordon sanitaire* which eventually formed the "iron curtain." But at Potsdam, Truman and Churchill had argued that, as Byrnes would say a month later, "Our objective is a government both friendly to the Soviet Union and representative of all the democratic elements of the country." Byrnes was talking about Poland in September. In December he was in Moscow discussing the matter again with Foreign Minister Molotov, surely (from his record during the war and Cold War) one of the most repugnant diplomats of this century. The upshot was that Byrnes and his advisers accepted (they had little choice) the existing pro-Soviet governments in Bulgaria and Rumania. The Russians, at whatever cost in terms of public relations with the outside world, were determined to maintain friendly regimes in all adjacent nations. To that end they had engulfed Latvia, Lithuania, and Estonia in 1940, and they had invaded Finland and sliced off a chunk of its flesh. Having gained effective control of a half-dozen nations to its west, the U.S.S.R. was not about to let any of them lapse into antagonistic or neutral hands.

In this very early postwar period, the lack of international cooperation on atomic energy proved to be critical. Two countries had decided to keep their secret. But it was not theirs, and there was no secret. The theories that had produced the atomic bomb were known to scientists all over the world; the only job that remained for any government was largely engineering: how to manufacture them. We might make a loose analogy by talking about bomb production in the same way as about building machine tools and the assembly line. This task would be immensely expensive, but it was not intellectually taxing. The arms race was on. The U.S.S.R. had an A-bomb by 1949; Red China by 1964. (Soon enough would follow France, India—Argentina?) Who could tell when every puny impoverished country in the world would have one? Would they still be puny? What if some military boss of a government wanted to play with his new toy? The entire world would continue to live with this menace, growing steadily worse as more nations gained the capacity to build atomic weapons. No reliable evidence has become public as to when or in what terms the Soviet Union protested the American-British secrecy on the topic; perhaps her counterthrust was limited to espionage plus developmental work within her own scientific community. In the Western camp, we know what the leaders thought. Truman's alienation from Byrnes reportedly began in December, 1945, when he thought the secretary was too soft at Moscow. The phrase "iron curtain" had been invented by Hitler's minister of propaganda, but its popularity began with a speech by ex-Prime Minister Churchill near Truman's home town in a suburb of Kansas City:

> From Stettin in the Baltic to Triest in the Adriatic, an iron curtain has descended across the Continent. Behind that line lie all the capitals of the ancient states of central and eastern Europe. Warsaw, Berlin, Prague, Vienna, Budapest,

Belgrade, Bucharest and Sofia, all these famous cities and the populations around them lie in the Soviet sphere and all are subject in one form or another, not only to Soviet influence but to a very high and increasing measure of control from Moscow. Athens alone, with its immortal glories, is free to decide its future at an election under British, American and French observation.

Two twists at the end of this passage deserve special note. One is the singling out of Athens. The other is the positioning of Britain ahead of its Allies in talking about interests in Greece. If the Italian invasion of 1943 had any rational purpose, it was not to defeat the Axis; it was to fence the Russians away from the Mediterranean. When civil war erupted in Greece the next year, it was apparent that one side was pro-Soviet while the other had British support. By 1948 this struggle for the Middle East spanned thousands of miles from Greece to Pakistan. Several elements fed into American policy, and they all pushed in the same direction. One was the devotion to loose abstractions that usually sufficed to conceal from most an underlying paranoia; the operative terms were "national security" and "defense of the Free World." There was also the attachment to free enterprise as embodying "the American way of of life"; *ergo*, remorseless opposition to expansion of the socialist bloc. Third, the genocide against Jews in wartime Europe had determined millions of Americans to see Israel established as an independent state—an aim achieved in 1948. Here was a massive voting faction that was both concentrated in key districts and also nearly 100 per cent united in pursuit of a single goal. In terms of domestic politics, the consequence was to warp American policy throughout the Middle East.

Year by year, disruptions multiplied: within the United States, within other nations, between nations. A few mileposts must suffice, in the hope they will reveal some patterns. In the area of nuclear power, the Atomic Energy Commission (AEC) was set up in August, 1946. Clearly, it has helped to develop some peacetime applications of this magnificent force; equally clearly most of its expenditures have been in the proliferation of military hardware. This federal stance aroused opposition at high levels (although not enough to change it); already in September, 1946, Truman fired from the cabinet his predecessor as vice president, Henry Wallace, who had spoken against American policy toward the U.S.S.R. Within three years, so Truman would announce, the Russians had built their own atomic bomb. His response was to order the AEC to construct the more powerful hydrogen bomb.

While American and Soviet power seemed to be growing, the might of Britain and France was patently crumbling. Before his government was felled by Labor in 1945, Churchill had boasted that he had not become PM to reign over the collapse of the Empire: "What we have, we hold." But England could not hold it. In 1947 a populous subcontinent was partitioned into the states of India and Pakistan, which promptly set to slaughtering each other. Within twenty years, the United Kingdom would hardly have a foreign possession left. Neither would France. In Asia and Africa, the Victorian world fell in ruins. The Soviet Union had troubles even maintaining or enforcing its preponderance in contiguous countries. When they supported separatist groups in Iran on their southern borders, they were frustrated by actions in the United Nations. They turned to consolidating their western borders. Pro-Soviet politicians took full power in Czechoslovakia, either with or without popular approval (the point seems uncertain). The U.S. countered with the Marshall Plan (Document 30-1). Since the Russian zone in occupied Germany encircled Berlin (which had been partitioned among the Allies), they were able to seal off all highway access to the city in June, 1948. The United States countered with the Berlin airlift, by which all supplies for almost a year for the three "Western" zones were flown in.

At this stage, many persons were saying that tensions could hardly become worse. They did become worse—war. They did not become apocalyptic—atomic war. The confrontation of the two great powers had now become global because each of them could threaten the other in many zones. Thus the Korean fray that began in 1950 had as its immediate background American gains in Europe. The recovery of several economies of the western Continent, to which the Marshall Plan made a substantial contribution, was startling in its speed. Then the United States persuaded eleven other countries to join in forming the North Atlantic Treaty Organization (NATO), which from its origins in 1949 was almost entirely a military coalition. For that year, American foreign aid of more than $6 billion was exclusively military. Although the federal government adopted the Technical Co-operation or "Point Four" program to help underdeveloped countries, the first appropriation was a mere $35 million. From Europe the center of conflict in 1950 shifted to the Far East. The question of who was the aggressor in Korea is perhaps as pointless as who fired the first shot at the Boston Massacre: neither the U.S.S.R. nor North Korea nor the United States nor South Korea can be held blameless, and some evidence has become public that the U.S.S.R. may have been distressed at the actions of North Korea. The consequences of the Korean War are more clear than its origins. Specifically, it prompted the United States to transplant its Cold War military ambitions to Asia by making pledges to the Koumintang exiles on Taiwan and by enlarging its aid to the French overlords in Vietnam.

The Korean War cannot be understood without noting the elements of continuity and change in the strategies of three nations—none of them Korean. Lenin made explicit what had always been Soviet policy, that Communism would win ascendance by controlling the contiguous countries of the U.S.S.R., China, and India. The dramatic change had come in China, when Communist armies in 1949 had driven the Chiang Kai-shek regime off the mainland to Formosa (Taiwan). This change in sovereignty was altogether predictable, in spite of George Marshall's brilliant efforts to prevent it by a diplomatic mission in 1945–1946. Red armies had made a steadfast fight against the Japanese invaders for a decade, while Kuomintang bureaucrats had occupied themselves in selling American medical supplies on the black market. In comparison to Russia and China, the American role is more difficult to assess. Was it continuous or did it change? Forty years earlier Theodore Roosevelt had insisted that the United States could not be a major power in the Far East; but was this evaluation more true or less true by 1949?

The American move in 1950 was megalomaniac, but it was not solely that. Improvements in transportation and communications appeared to facilitate effective action at distances that had not been thinkable at the beginning of the century. When Korea was stripped away from Japan at the end of World War II, it was split into two warring sovereignties, pro-Soviet and pro-Western. When hostilities of uncertain origin broke out, Red armies swept quickly southward. The U.N. ordered them to withdraw. They did not, and President Truman sent in American troops. Why? To stake out another theme, the Korean War must be seen as a series of power plays in domestic politics. Several of these have been examined in Chapter 29: a Republican sweep in 1946, the trial of Alger Hiss, the repression of radicals. Perhaps most important, the deaf ears that the public turned to the China White Paper. Issued August, 1949, this policy statement on American "abandonment" of China to the Communists was summarized by Truman's new secretary of state in a sentence: "Nothing that this country did or could have done within the reasonable limits of its capabilities would have changed the result, nothing that was left undone by this country has contributed to it." But still the pressure increased for a scapegoat for the loss of China to "Communism." The Republicans had been out of office too long; nobody can measure their resentment at the finesse with which their man had snatched defeat from the mouth of victory in the presidential race of 1948; they were egged on by a China Lobby eager to reconstitute a China where they could act as they pleased. The secretary's sane argument made few converts. Six months later he tried to expound realities again: "The Communists did not create this condition. They did not create this revolutionary spirit. They did not create a great force which moved out from under Chiang Kai-shek. But they were shrewd and cunning to mount it, and to ride this thing into victory and into power."

He still had no audience. This awareness shoved him into backsliding. For three months after American intervention in June, the forces of the North drove southward. Then the United States, using its naval and air superiority, leaped around them and made a beachhead landing far above the North Korean troops. Question: Should they push on north to destroy the enemy? The Chinese issued a clear warning that they would not allow "imperialists" to approach the Yalu River which formed their boundary. President Truman flew to the Far East to confer personally with the American commander, Douglas MacArthur. When asked, "What are the chances for Chinese or Soviet interference?," the general replied, "Very little. Had they interfered in the first or second months it would have been decisive. We are no longer fearful of their intervention." Sixty days later at the brink of the Chinese border he was met by swarms of Chinese infantry, and so he had provoked Chinese intervention despite Truman's warning. First he appealed publicly for more soldiers to fend off the new adversary and fight on to victory (which seemed to include further provocation of China). Impatient, he presented his position in a letter to the minority leader in the House. It was released to the media. MacArthur was sacked for going over the head of the president. Deservedly so, for if any American tradition deserves to be revered, it is the one that places civil, elective authority above the military. If ever a prominent American behaved like an arrogant fool, it was Douglas MacArthur in 1951 (plus his congressional advocates). After 33,000 American deaths, the war ended by treaty. This result could only be achieved by turning out the Democrats, who had become so confined that they could not negotiate with the enemy.

For the next few years the conflict was literally worldwide, and it cannot be neatly segmented into regional clashes. After the United States exploded its first H-bomb in 1952, it was countered the next year by the Soviet Union. Six months later the American secretary of state began to talk about "massive retaliation" if any Communist power launched a nuclear attack against us. Tongues waggled freely, seldom wisely. The first atomic submarine was launched by the U.S. at the beginning of 1954. That same year saw the temporary—very temporary—settlement of an armed confrontation that had raged in the Far East for fifteen years. Resistance in Vietnam to the Japanese occupation had been strong throughout World War II. When France, longtime overlord in the country (known then as French Indochina), tried to reassert their sovereignty at war's end, they met their masters. The outcome was a conference that climaxed on 21 July with a decision to divide the country. The northern half was conceded to the Vietminh (widely known to be Communist as well as nationalist); the southern half was to be ruled by a government which will be discussed in a moment. It was expected that French influence would remain strong in South Vietnam, but this assumption proved false. The United States did not sign this agreement, but it did agree to do nothing to undermine it. The Geneva Convention prescribed that the United States would not go beyond a quota in placing military men in Vietnam. We will see later when and how this agreement was violated. A counterpunch was made by the United States by the inauguration of the Southeast Asia Treaty Organization (SEATO). The Soviet Union instituted the Warsaw Pact as an anti-NATO combine. It seemed that nothing could impede the oscillation of military might.

Then a Third Force started to emerge. This development had more than one facet. It can be summarized as a revolt against colonialism, but the alleged colonizers included powers in both of the major blocs. When delegates from twenty-nine Asian and African nations met in Indonesia for the Bandung Conference, they seemed to cite France and Britain as the chief oppressors,

Red China as the strongest friend. The British government must have been astonished when its occupation of the Suez Canal in 1956 met with virtually unanimous resentment, including that of the United States, so that it was forced to withdraw. But neither of the major powers could go around whistling cheerfully. Their closest neighbors had to be coerced into compliance. The first test for the United States in Central America came in Guatemala. No known Communists were in the cabinet, but it did lean toward the left and it propagated a program of redistribution of the land. The United States through the medium of the Central Intelligence Agency (CIA) is reputed to have played a strong hand in toppling it by a military *putsch*. For non-Communism, we substituted *caudillismo*. In defense, of course, of the Free World. The Soviet Union also intervened in adjacent countries—crudely, by the use of its own brass knuckles. Insurgents in Poland were crushed in June, 1956. An uprising in Hungary was smashed by early November. Egypt, which can be regarded as part of the Third Force but which might have been susceptible to Russian seduction, was invaded by Israel in October, and beaten. In view of the persistent situation in the Mideast, it becomes impossible to talk about an "aggressor nation." We do know that Israel emerged from this conflict, as from the Six Day War in 1967, with accretions to its territory. American policy had been consistently pro-Israeli rather than neutralist.

Then comes a phase of the Russo-American strife that left the earth altogether. Indeed, it left reality altogether. A distinction must be made clearly here. Sane people can applaud the objective of learning more about different kinds of reality, including those of the external solar system. But this goal could have been accomplished at much lower risks in human life and at much lower costs in productive outlays than have been manifest in the space program. Manned satellites have never been needed to explore the moon; they were a good public-relations gambit for the administration, whatever it happened to be. They bred a new breed of culture heroes; they were a circus. They worked great things for the economies of Waltham, Massachusetts, of Houston, Texas, and of Langston Field, Virginia. Nor should we forget Cape Canaveral/Kennedy. Bread and circuses. The competition with the U.S.S.R. was no longer limited to the arms race; it was also a struggle for prestige. Within four months after the Russian *sputnik* the United States had its first earth satellite in orbit.

The razzmatazz did nothing to solve down-to-earth problems. On May Day, 1960, shortly before the leaders of the Big Four (ignoring of course Red China) were slated to meet in Paris, a U.S. "reconnaisance plane" was shot down when it was clearly violating Soviet air space.* The conference never met. Then along came John F. Kennedy with his own style of hoopla. "And so,

---

*The corruption of language by bureaucrats was one of the worst results of the Cold War. The phenomenon was far from new, but seemingly it became more extreme. The U-2 in question was there to spy.

my fellow Americans: Ask not what your country can do for you—ask what you can do for your country." Dedicating himself to the New Frontier (did it ever exist?), he sparred at extending it overseas by announcing the formation of the Peace Corps. The effect of this flamboyant program on underdeveloped areas was about zero. Its major impact was on young Americans, and it can be dissected into three elements. It extended further the magical aura that Kennedy created among students and other young adults (mid-Chapter 29). It provided junkets abroad for thousands of people who could not have afforded to pay their own way. Most important, it taught quite a few participants that poverty existed in the world, so that when they came home they had a deeper commitment to change their native country.

While the administration was taking this initiative that was on balance positive, it continued a policy that was destructive in the extreme. It went on barging around in Latin America like some piratical state. Admittedly the intentions of many Americans to the countries toward the south had been wanton since the filibustering raids of the antebellum era, but only in this century did lust and greed come to dominate policy in the United States. Thereafter the government had sent occupying forces in Nicaragua, into Santo Domingo, wherever it chose; it had tried to bully Mexico over the confiscation of oil rights. Perpetuation of this attitude, which had relaxed under the New Deal, became obvious in three southern neighbors after World War II: Guatemala, Cuba, the Dominican Republic. The first, by scholarly report, was a screaming scandal; the Boston-controlled United Fruit Company, that mammoth importer of bananas, did not want land reform.

Freight cars of paper have been exhausted in writing about Cuba since the insurrectionists took control in 1959. These pages cannot hope to contribute solid conclusions to the heated debate, but they can lay out some guidelines to a discussion. First, the preceding government had been one of the most wretched tyrannies to be found on the globe. The mass base of the revolt was to be found on sugar plantations, while the organized guerrillas came down from the hills. The leaders of the latter included some avowed Marxists. It is contended, however, that the new government was willing to deal with any foreign power that would negotiate freely with them about economic aid, guaranteed markets for raw sugar, and perhaps munitions. Chiefly for ideological reasons, the Eisenhower administration spurned all Cuban advances. Refugees—some of them decent folk who did not want to live under a Marxist regime, some of them hated as men who had prospered under the earlier regime—swarmed into the United States, particularly Florida (only ninety miles from Cuba). They began to organize, on American soil, a plan to reconquer their homeland. Evidence makes clear that the CIA provided them with training and certain types of equipment. Preparations for the invasion were far advanced when the Kennedy administration took office.

What to do? The White House decided, in a clear breach of neutrality, to allow the invaders to push off. Two distinct types of reasoning are reported as having joined in this conclusion. By one account from an adviser, Kennedy reasoned thusly: We have Cubans here who are illegally armed. It is better to get rid of them in Cuba than in the United States. The true fantasists thought the invasion would succeed because the inhabitants of the island would rise up to sustain it, with the wonderful result that Marxist tyranny would vanish from the Caribbean. This wish fulfillment did not last for twenty-four hours after the invaders hit the beach at the Bay of Pigs. For several years after the fiasco of April, 1961, all parties acted from desperation. Rebuffed by the United States and therefore hopelessly dependent on the U.S.S.R. market for its sugar, Cuba foolishly allowed the Russians to install missile bases within its jurisdiction. At this juncture, in a week that involved the cleanest thinking about foreign policy that an American president had done in the century, Kennedy did not prattle about making the Free World safe. He sounded like Thomas Jefferson talking about New Orleans when he said to the Soviet Union: Get them out. The chief executive who thinks cleanly is the one who wins; Kennedy won. But the United States had not learned its full lesson. Having the preponderance of force in Cuba does not prove that you have it everywhere; in parts of Latin America you may not be able to bring it quickly to bear. When a Marxist party came to power in Chile and began to nationalize American companies, the bleats showed dismay. American industrial and governmental disapproval had no quick effect, but the changes the new government was putting through appalled the power elite in Chile. A group of reactionary army officers, in a brief but bloody coup, ousted the Marxist regime and established a dictatorship. Those Americans who may have been relieved to see a Communist government fall had been given quite a scare.

The worst example of the American big-head was manifest in the Far East. It was punctured in a way so startling as to prompt a quite new question: Are there any Great Powers left? The Soviet Union could not hold control in Poland, Czechoslovakia, or Hungary except by armed intervention. Yugoslavia escaped its aegis altogether. Great Britain was humiliated in India and at Suez, France in Indochina and Algeria. These rebukes to major nations had no precedents in the many years from Napoleon to World War II; any country could lose a war, but to lose to a tiny colony was beyond belief. Perhaps the worst putdown of all was inflicted on the United States in Asia.

Given American precepts combined with the logistics involved, the final dilemma of the United States was quite predictable. But it was not inevitable, inasmuch as federal authorities could have changed their assumptions. Indeed, as these pages will show, they were repeatedly warned what would happen if they were content to move forward when they were already "over their heads in the Big Muddy." They could not learn, and each error led to a worse one. It would be idle to talk here about the tactics of specific engagements. It is not even very sensible to talk much about strategy. The rent that could not be mended was in policy, and this error was irremediable. When the United States set out to put down a nationalist rebellion, being carried on by irregular militia, which had the support of all three mammoth countries in the continent, in a strange terrain halfway around the world, it could not win. This assessment, we now know, was made repeatedly by military intelligence and sometimes by the Joint Chiefs of Staff (JCS). The JCS on occasion argued that the importance of Vietnam to American security was being badly exaggerated. But civilians in high office, captive to their own hollow phrases and spurred by spasms of pique, drove a bad policy to its ultimate ruin.

Although American troubles in the Far East can be traced back to the origins of U.S. engagement there, they certainly became worse after World War II. As late as 1947, many officials in Washington were calm and judicious about the fracas in China. When he was recalled from China in January to be head of the State Department, Marshall reported:

> Between this dominant reactionary group in the Government and the irreconcilable Communists who, I must state, did not so appear last February, lies the problem of how peace and well-being are to be brought to the long-suffering and presently inarticulate mass of the people of China. . . .

He explained that Red propaganda against his own nation was more vicious than that issued by the Kuomintang; he also stated that the "reactionaries in the Government have evidently counted on substantial American support regardless of their actions."

The United States would have both of these last problems replicated in Vietnam, and again we will commence in 1945. Japanese occupation of French Indochina had been resisted by guerrillas during the war. When the French tried to re-assert their control, native resistance continued and movements for independence developed. By the winter of 1949–1950 the French were hard pressed. At this point Washington decided to intervene in support of a backward and corrupt native emperor. When France asked for military aid, the head at the State Department wrote in recommending approval: "The choice confronting the U.S. is to support the legal governments in Indochina or to face the extension of Communism over the remainder of the continental area of Southeast Asia and possibly westward." The domino theory was first advanced by the National Security Council* in February, 1950: If one falls, all will fall. So aid is needed. At this stage the policy objective of the United States had been set, and it was never seriously debated at the top levels of government for seventeen years. When a line of action is obviously failing, you would think it would be questioned. But the policymaking hotshots sent around endless

---

*Membership varied, but at least the president, heads of the State Department, Defense Department, and CIA, plus one or more Presidential Assistants for National Security.

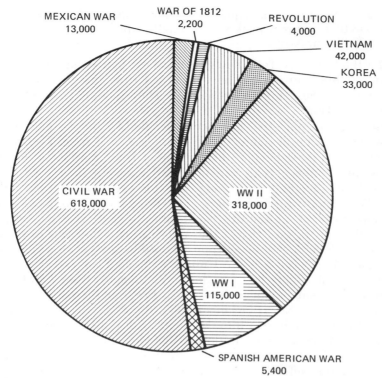

FIGURE 30-1 *Deaths of American Soldiers in Major Wars*

memos about the quantity of manpower required, how much hardware was needed, how to conceal their actions from Congress.

If the Truman team defined a goal, the Eisenhower administration took noticeable steps to implement it. Under the two succeeding Democratic regimes the strides got longer; under Nixon they were shortened. Before we look at decisions that revised American commitments of military forces to the Vietnam conflict, we might look at the scale on which manpower was being used:

1954   Geneva Accord permits U.S. to have 342 men in Vietnam.
1961   948 in Nov.
1962   2,646 on 9 Jan.
         5,576 on 30 June.
1963   16,732 by Oct.
1965   184,314 by 31 Dec.
1966   Army command is asking for 542,588 *ground troops* in Aug.
         469,000 troops authorized in Nov. to be delivered in Vietnam by June.

1968   206,756 *more* men requested by U.S. commander.
1969   543,000 troops is peak U.S. strength, April.
1971   196,000 in Nov.

Except for the last entry, from newspapers, these figures have been taken from the most reliable sources that have emerged from the government such as secret reports to the commander-in-chief. They quantify certain trends that cannot be mistaken.

Although an objective had been specified by the Truman administration, it was visibly implemented under Eisenhower. Waning French power in Indochina was shoved beyond the horizon at Dienbienphu in the spring of 1954. The Joint Chiefs of Staff were not greatly concerned: ". . . with reference to the Far East as a whole, *Indochina is devoid of decisive military objectives and the allocation of more than token* U.S. armed forces *in Indochina would be a serious diversion* of limited U.S. capabilities."—date: 26 May, 1954. Even at this time, the Chiefs said that if the American decision was to intervene in what became Vietnam, atomic weapons should be used even if Red China did not take part. By December, the United States had coerced the French into yielding to us all rights to train South Vietnamese troops and to begin a withdrawal that had not been foreseen a few months earlier. As Vietcong infiltration from the North began in 1955, the U.S. was sending increasing numbers of military advisers into the South. Not until 1959 did the CIA pick up evidence of large-scale infiltration of Vietcong southward. In August, 1960, a national intelligence estimate in Washington stated of South Vietnam: "In the absence of more effective Government measures to protect the peasants and to win their positive cooperation, the prospect is for expansion of the areas of Vietcong control in the countryside. . . ."

Eisenhower out, Kennedy in. The imbroglio worsened. In less than three years, American troops in Vietnam were multiplied sixteen times. That was not enough. The folly of sending them there at all was exaggerated by the folly of using "only limited means to achieve excessive ends." The president resisted the pressures to send in ground forces, but in many other respects he exploited the resources—great but not inexhaustible—of his country. As stated in *The Pentagon Papers* (1971): ". . . the limited-risk gamble undertaken by Eisenhower had been transformed into an unlimited commitment under Kennedy." The tactics employed in the expanding involvement will hardly be credited by armchair Americans. Before the Vietcong took over Hanoi in 1954, American-controlled agents contaminated the oil supply for the municipal transit system so that buses would break down. They were training teams to commit sabotage and assassinations, which they prettied up by vague references to "unconventional warfare." They hid their behavior even from themselves behind a barrage of these fancy phrases. When the Mekong Delta suffered a severe flood in 1961, Kennedy's personal military adviser recommended despatching a "relief task force" of 6,000–8,000 men, while specifying that they be "combat troops" who could be diverted into "other activities."

They inflicted upon each other the most unreal dichotomies. When Kennedy sent Vice President Johnson off to Southeast Asia on a fact-finding mission, the latter reported back on 23 May, 1961: "We must decide whether to help these countries to the best of our ability or throw in the towel in the area and pull back our defenses to San Francisco and a Fortress America concept." They exchanged the most grandiose hopes. The JCS estimated that 40,000 Americans could "clean up the Vietcong threat." A general sent on another mission by the president reported that North Vietnam was "extremely vulnerable to conventional bombing." The Kennedy administration made plans for a military "phase-out" in the belief that the Vietcong would be defeated in the field by 1965.

These high-level maneuvers were taken in strict secrecy, but enough facts leaked out that informed guesses could be made about the direction that American policy was taking. Early in the Kennedy administration full-page advertisements against the Vietnam War began to appear in the New York *Times* (paid for by the signatories, in case anybody cares). Originally these ads seemed to come from 200 to 300 academics in the Boston area, but similar protests were appearing in other newspapers near large universities around the nation. The grounds cited by the protestants can be parceled into three categories: (a) Old Far Eastern hands thought that the war was impossible militarily. We had studied other colonial fights against invaders such as the War for Independence, and we had studied the Asian mainland. Air attacks would do little damage because of the absence of vital targets; ground warfare would be a bottomless well for American troops against opponents who could merge at will into their own turf. (b) Broader in their outlook were the natural scientists, who provided the most numbers for these early petitions. They knew facts about nuclear weapons; many of them had been prominent in the development of the atomic bomb. The fallout from a bomb cannot be barricaded within a wall, and they feared that some "limited little war" would become unlimited war. (c) Broadest of all were those who took a moral or a religious stance. Some affirmed that all men are equal in the eyes of God; others were content to say that it was absurd for the United States to go 7,500 miles to fight a little nation that was not bothering us. Obviously these three groups of petitioners overlap, but there were differences in emphasis. Each from his own point of view, all united on one conclusion: the United States was acting in a shameful fashion that violated its own highest traditions. Probably few citizens listened; in a society that is lost in peacetime concerns, that has been depersonalized to a degree where sympathy for your neighbor does not cross your mind, it took the mounting casualty lists to bring mass protests against the war.

Lyndon Johnson saw to that. In the autumn of 1963, the Kennedy team watched warily while a military coup against the premier of South Vietnam took shape. A watchword was: "Sink or swim with Ngo Dinh Diem." Diem sank. A few days later (22 November) Kennedy was assassinated and Johnson became president. Amazing as it may seem in retrospect, many voters who were devoutly opposed to the Vietnam War nonetheless supported his campaign for reelection. This partisanship did not seem incredible at the time. On domestic matters, Johnson's achievements within a year seemed impressive. While Democrats denounced the Republican nominee as a wild man who might (as stated by a cocktail waitress in a Washington hotel) "land us in a depression and a war at the same time," the president posed as the man of reason and restraint in foreign relations. Also feeding the support for Johnson were his own pronouncements. On 29 August, 1964, a tardy celebration of his fifty-sixth birthday was held at Stonewall, Texas, a few miles from his own ranch. After the guests had eaten two tons of beef, the president spoke: "I have had advice to load our planes with bombs and to drop them on certain areas that I think would enlarge the war and escalate the war, and result in our committing a good many American boys to fighting a war that I think ought to be fought by the boys of Asia to help protect their own land." As he spoke thus, Johnson's team was working out an eventual three-phase plan to expand areas for bombing: to go beyond the supply routes across Laos into South Vietnam until attacks were being made on North Vietnam.*

The administration should not bear sole responsibility for later events; Congress must share the blame by virtue of its passage of the Tonkin Gulf resolution on 7 August, 1964: "That the Congress approve and support the determination of the President, as Commander in Chief, to take all necessary measures to repel any armed attack against the forces of the United States and to prevent further aggression." Johnson took this to be almost the equivalent of a declaration of war, so the context should be examined closely. On 30 July, South Vietnamese commandoes had raided North Vietnamese islands in the Gulf. The raids were controlled by the U.S. commander in Vietnam. When the heads of the State and Defense Departments appeared before the senate committee considering the Tonkin Gulf resolve, they lied in their teeth by saying that they had no prior knowledge of the raids of 30 July. Not until 3 August did North Vietnamese PT boats attack a U.S. destroyer. Congress was so complacent that the motion passed the House by 416-0, the Senate by 88-2. Johnson felt unleashed to do as he pleased—after he won re-election.

Conflicts for power between president and Congress can be traced from the origins of the Republic, when George Washington sought the "advice" of the Senate about a treaty (early Chapter 9). Lincoln had his troubles with Congress; Andrew Johnson's difficulties brought about his impeachment.

---

*A further reason for Johnson's colossal victory at the polls in 1964 was his retention of so many advisers from the Kennedy regime; he appealed to young voters by basking in a reflected glow. But the glow had always been a false dawn. When I heard the names of the Boy Scout troop leaders from Cambridge, Massachusetts, whom Kennedy was calling to the capital as advisers, my personal reaction was, "Can the Republic survive?" The question remains.

These struggles ebbed and waned. They hardly appeared for eight years when Harding and Coolidge occupied the White House. During the first six years of FDR's residence at 1700 Pennsylvania, his bitter clashes were almost wholly with the judicial, not with the legislative, branch. While Roosevelt bought Congress, cajoled it, and lied to it, he seldom came to an open break with any strong segment of it. After he died, presidents asserted their supremacy in blatant ways. Their most popular device was the Executive Proclamation. FDR had used it: the "bases for destroyers" swap with the United Kingdom had never been submitted as a treaty. The approach to Fair Employment Practices in 1941 had taken the same legal form. Truman had used it in announcing the loyalty oath for all employees of the executive branch. He used it again in sending American troops into Korea in 1950. Kennedy employed it in dealing with the Cuban missiles crisis. Without doubt, the president is commander-in-chief of the armed forces. Without doubt, Congress is the only agency that can declare war. Without doubt, the boundaries of authority in a tripartite division of authority must meet, and clash, on hazy borders. But where? Johnson pushed the issue far with the Tonkin Gulf Resolution. Richard Nixon pushed it ever farther, beyond matters of security and defense, after congressional committees and grand juries began to investigate the break-in of the Democratic National Headquarters in the Watergate Hotel in Washington in 1972. Asked by a senate committee in the so-called Watergate Affair to produce records that might be relevant to their inquiry, he refused. Was the president "copping out on the Fifth," or was he legitimately and courageously defending the hallowed separation of powers? Congress thought his behavior had passed the limits of presidential privilege, and intended to topple him from the pedestal he had assumed—a post above the law—by the hoary process of impeachment. But before impeachment and trial could proceed, the Supreme Court entered the picture and forced the president to deliver subpoenaed tapes which finally provided irrefutable evidence of Nixon's personal involvement in obstructing justice, and forced his resignation—much to the relief of the Congress and the people. A severe burden was thus thrown on his successor, Gerald Ford, to reburnish the tarnished imagery of the presidency and to seek a more stable balance of power for his office.

From the end of 1964 forward, America's global power delusions fed on themselves. American authorities in Saigon were warning that the situation was desperate; the South Vietnam government was quivering, quaking, frequently toppling. It seemed likely that the Vietcong would conquer the south and win all the marbles. The U.S. aim for sixteen years would be thwarted. It was decided to use Yankee might to enforce the Yankee will. The prognosticators decreed that bombing "must" force the North to negotiate on American terms. The Joint Chiefs of Staff warned that limited bombing would not do the job. A panel including men from all three major intelligence agencies (CIA, Defense, and State Departments) "did not concede very strong chances for breaking the will of Hanoi." The bombing program went forward. It accomplished little. It was amplified. Still little or nothing. Out of frustration, because they did not have any other approaches to try, the United States entered the ground war in April, 1965. By year's end, American forces approached 200,000; they would not drop back to the same level for six years.

American manpower in South Vietnam did indeed escalate (as we saw from the list a few pages back). But the Vietcong seemed to match us man for man; infiltration from the North also escalated. American fatalities escalated. In the United States, demonstrations against the use of napalm, against the Reserve Officer Training Corps, against conscription, began to take violent forms. Dejection about the war escalated to higher floors; in January, 1966, the head of the Defense Department lamented, "We are in an escalating military stalemate." The president's response was to spread the air attacks to oil storage tanks. The Vietcong responded by decentralizing their petroleum depots, which became almost impossible to bomb. The CIA had estimated in advance, in May, 1966, that air strikes against the oil depots would not halt "infiltration of men and supplies." They were right. A study in August said that infiltration was "undiminished." As American soldiers bled and died, resistance at home to the war mounted. Within the administration, disillusionment spread. The undersecretary of state suggested that we "cut our losses." The U.S. commander in Vietnam was asking for more than 500,000 men. As to conditions in South Vietnam, the head of Defense advised the president in October, 1966, that "pacification has if anything gone backward," that more American troops would probably not change the situation, and that U.S. bombing of the North was having "no significant impact" on the war. While the JCS called for more and more men, the secretary of defense decided to resign; perhaps the impressive Tet offensive in January, 1968, had made up his mind. Lyndon B. Johnson, who had yearned for 100 per cent consensus, saw before him a nation more deeply riven than it had been since the Civil War. On 31 March he revealed that he would not stand for re-election.

His successor, Richard Nixon; was virtually handed the election when the Democrats put forward the weakest candidate they could find. If it were not for the uncovering of Nixon's illegal reelection tactics (including burglary, perjury, and obstruction of justice)—which made him famous as the first American president to be forced from office—the Nixon administration might well have been noted for events abroad, and especially for two typical sequences. One was his shifty handling of the court martial of an army lieutenant convicted of complicity in a massacre of civilians at My Lai, Vietnam. To Americans, three segments of this episode were prominent. First, generals who had defied their orders so they could conceal the outrage were quietly released from charges. Second, former soldiers knew that in time of war many outrages are committed, and it seemed unjust that a subordinate officer was being mistreated for symbolic reasons. Third, why did it have to be an infantryman who took the rap, while pilots flying at 20,000 feet could massacre civilians with impunity?

Another fascinating sequence—and probably a constructive one—in Nixon's career was a major asset in his successful campaign for re-election in 1972. As a congressman his public image had been chiefly projected as a staunch foe of Communism. But as vice president he had acted as an important emissary in the negotiations with North Korea. As president he had instituted sweeping cutbacks in American strength in Vietnam (see the list a few pages back). In 1972 he was equipped to say: The Democrats got you into two wars, and I have helped to get you out of both. By the time of the November election, Nixon had not ended the Vietnam War (a year earlier, after he had been chief executive for nearly three years, American forces in Southeast Asia were still ten times what they had been when Kennedy was assassinated) but it did seem that progress was being made.

Not enough progress to suit George McGovern or millions of others. When the Senator for South Dakota began a sustained drive for the Democratic nomination in January, 1971, few thought he could possibly succeed. But in a convention that was drastically different from those of the past—more women, more blacks, more young people—he became the candidate. After eighteen months of brilliant efforts, his campaign came to pieces. Partly the failure was his fault. In a furor over the man he had picked to run for vice president, McGovern seemed to be weak and shifty, whereas his appeal had been to voters who thought him a forthright and principled politician. When he brought forward a plan for a guaranteed annual income, it came out that his staff had done shoddy homework in elaborating a basically sound idea. But in the end, he had a single-plank platform: Stop the Vietnam War. The president pulled that plank right from under the challenger's feet. He came to dramatic reconciliations with the Soviet Union and the People's Republic of China. He seemed to be striving for a settlement in Southeast Asia. Most telling of all, he reduced the casualty lists from Vietnam. Even as his successes abroad seemed to assure his victory, Nixon felt compelled to make his reelection doubly sure by resorting to the illegal campaign tactics whose exposure eventually cost him his power, but none of this bothered many Americans in 1972.

When Nixon substituted massive bombing raids for ground warfare that had cost thousands of American lives, domestic resistance to his program collapsed. The Nixon ticket in 1972 won one of the greatest victories in presidential history; McGovern won electoral votes only in the Dictrict of Columbia plus one state, Massachusetts. The result showed that most Americans were not concerned about the moral issues involved in Southeast Asia. It demonstrated other persisting truths. The sociology of politics was still changing drastically. Movement of the electorate from rural residence to urban, from cities to suburbs, swelling of ghettoes both black and white, both metropolitan and small-town, the explosive participation of black voters—these were trends for vote-seekers to ponder. The election of 1972 also proved further that the party system in politics had died. Most Americans were independent voters. The president, in spite of his startling triumph, could not carry into office a Republican majority in either branch of Congress. But some truths endure. The strategy of the middle 60 per cent, from FDR to Ike to Nixon, has won elections—even though, as Nixon's experiences have shown, a ruthless pursuit of elections might not suffice to hold on to power.

A negotiated cease-fire in Vietnam took effect at the end of January, 1973. What did it mean? From the announced terms, nobody could be sure. One prognosis was that the North Vietnam-Viet Cong coalition would soon seize control of South Vietnam. A gloomier prediction held that if they tried to do so, the president of the United States would again fill the skies with heavy bombers. The most hopeful outlook could be expressed in the directions of a well-known children's game: Return to Square 1. After more than ten years of American effort, the Vietnam War seemed to have achieved no legitimate purpose. It had been the longest war ever fought by the United States. The nation had lost 56,000 servicemen. It had spent $137 billion. How many of his countrymen, even his supporters, believed Richard Nixon when he said that the truce meant "Peace with Honor?" Or was the widespread evaluation the one stated in a song that called him "the genuine plastic man"?

In twenty years, the American sphere of influence had shrunk immeasurably. She had been staved off in Korea. Humbled in Vietnam. Castro still held power in Cuba. Most bitter of all, not only had Red China been given a permanent seat on the Security Council of the United Nations, but the Taiwan regime had been expelled. The vaunted American empire was drooling away into the sands.

For twenty-five years after the close of World War II, the foreign policy of the United States was dictated by the supposed requirements of the Cold War. By this formula, all Communists in every country were subservient to the Soviet Union. Every encroachment by this insidious ideology had to be repelled. If one portion of the Free World fell victim, its neighbors would fall, then their neighbors, and so on, until the entire globe was writhing under tyrannical regimes. Out of this cant came the disposition in governmental circles to bolster every foreign state, no matter how loathsome, so long as it affirmed its hostility to Communism. The previous American tendency to self-deceit was propelled to new depths. When Russia demonstrated that she had fabricated a nuclear bomb, the arms race began in deadly earnest. Weapon gave way to better weapon, each more murderous than the last, while policy-makers embraced the illusion that the road to peace is to prepare for war. Perhaps equally serious was the fantasy that denied that a new Communist government had effective control of mainland China. True, it had taken fifteen years after the Bolshevik revolution for the United States to establish diplomatic relations with the U.S.S.R. but it took twenty-five years for a sober acceptance of truth to occur in regard to the People's Republic of China. In retrospect, it seems that the first major stand-off of the Cold War was the negotiated settlement of the Korean War in 1953. But neither that culmination, nor the French expulsion from Vietnam, taught the American government to tend its own knitting. The miserable outcome was the longest war in our history, with the most humiliating consequences that the United States has ever sustained in a foreign conflict.

SOME NOTABLE EVENTS

1945 Truman, Attlee, and King agree not to share atomic secrets until U.N. agrees on control plan, 15 Nov.

Second conference of foreign ministers on control treaties, Dec.; major split becomes apparent.

Lend-Lease ends; total $50.6 billion.

1945–
1946 Nuremberg trials of Nazi "war criminals."

1945–
1947 U.S. sends Europe $11 billion in aid under UNRRA programs.

1946 Churchill's "iron curtain" address at Fulton, Mo., accelerates cold war, 5 March.

Atomic Energy Commission established, 1 Aug.

Wallace dismissed from cabinet, 20 Sept., after speech attacking U.S. policy toward U.S.S.R., 12 Sept.

1947 Iran charges U.S.S.R. is intervening in her internal affairs, 19 Jan.

India and Pakistan gain independence.

Communists take control of Hungary, 30 April.

Truman Doctrine toward Greece and Turkey, 12 May.

Marshall Plan announced at Harvard, 5 June.

Department of Defense created to unify armed forces.

1948 Communists take control of Czechoslovakia, 25 Feb.

Congress adopts Marshall Plan, 2 April.

Israel becomes a state.

1948–
1949 Berlin airlift, 21 June-12 May.

1949 U.S. takes lead in negotiating treaty with eleven other countries founding NATO, signed 4 April.

NATO ratified by Senate, 21 July.

"Point Four" program of foreign aid.

Truman announces that U.S.S.R. has atomic bomb, 23 Sept.

1950 Truman orders AEC to develop hydrogen bomb, 31 Jan.

South Korea and North Korea go to war, 24 June.

U.N. orders North Korea to cease its invasion of South Korea, 24 June.

Truman commits U.S. forces to repel North Korea, 26–30 June.

U.N. resolution to unify Korea, 7 Oct.

1951–
1953 Korean peace talks.

1951 Marshall Plan ends; total $12.5 billion, 31 Dec.

1952 Allies sign peace contract with West Germany, 26 May.

H-bomb test succeeds at Eniwetok, 10 Nov.

1953 Stalin dies, 5 March.

H-bomb fabrication announced by U.S.S.R., 20 Aug.

1954 Dulles talks of "massive retaliation," 12 Jan.

Nautilus, first atomic-powered submarine, launched, 21 Jan.

Geneva Pact divides Vietnam; awards northern sector to Vietminh, 21 July.

SEATO formed, 8 Sept.

West Germany awarded sovereignty by Allies, plus right to re-arm and to join NATO, 23 Oct.

1955 President at his request given authority to defend Taiwan, 28 Jan.

Warsaw Pact, 14 May.

Bandung Conference brings together 29 Asian and African nations to denounce colonialism, April.

1956 Cominform dissolved.

British occupation of Suez ends, 13 June.

Soviets crush Hungarian uprising, 24 Oct.–4 Nov.

Israel invades Egypt, 29 Oct.

1957 Soviets launch first *Sputnik*, 4 Oct.

1958 DeGaulle wins power in France.

European Common Market.

U.S. puts its first earth satellite in orbit, 31 Jan.

1959 Castro forces win control in Cuba, 1 Jan.

1960 Big Four summit meetings in Paris collapse, 16 May.

1961 Kennedy announces Peace Corps, 1 March.

Bay of Pigs invasion of Cuba shattered, 17 April.

Berlin Wall starts going up.

1962 U.S. puts its first manned satellite in orbit, 20 Feb.

Cuban missile crisis between U.S. and U.S.S.R. 22–28 Oct.

1963 Supreme Court rules that compulsory prayer in public schools is unconstitutional, 17 June.

1964 Gulf of Tonkin incident off Vietnam, Aug.

China explodes its first atomic bomb, 16 Oct.

1965 U.S. armed forces sent to Dominican Republic, 28 April.

1966 France withdraws from NATO, 1 July.

1967 Arab-Israeli War (the Six Day War), 5–10 June.

Vietnam War protest in Washington by 35,000; more than 600 arrests.

1968 *USS Pueblo* seized by North Koreans in Sea of Japan, 23 Jan.

Vietcong launches Tet offensive against South Vietnam, 30 Jan.

U.S.S.R. and other Warsaw Pact nations invade Czechoslovakia, 20–21 Aug.

1969 U.S. begins to reduce its armed forces in Vietnam, 8 July.

Vietnam War protests across nation draw hundreds of thousands, 15 Oct.

Vietnam War protest in Washington enlists 250,000, Nov. 15.

First draft lottery since 1942 is held, 1 Dec.

1970 Nixon sends U.S. troops into Cambodia, 30 April.

Marxist elected as president of Chile; sworn in 3 Nov.; recognizes Castro regime in Cuba.

1971 South Vietnam-U.S. forces invade Laos, 8 Feb.–24 March.

Vietnam War protests in Washington, 24 April–5 May.

Supreme Court affirms right of newspapers to publish *The Pentagon Papers*, 30 June.

1972 Nixon beats McGovern by wide margin, Nov.

1973 Vietnam cease-fire in effect, Jan.

Watergate investigations intensify, Feb.–Mar.

1974 Clashes and Supreme Court rulings on Executive Privilege.

Nixon resigns the presidency, Aug. 8; Ford asumes office.

Ways to Study History XXX

Learn foreign languages. Even for those of us who try to remain sensitive to the nuances of words, a meaning can become not only altered but warped or even reversed. Sometimes a slight revision in spelling can help to sharpen perceptions. To write *re-creation* can remind us of what the word *recreation* first implied. A *profess-or* was a person who advocated a set of values rather than an objective automaton who simply "told the facts"; the resemblance of the word to *confessor* should remind us of times when all professors were ordained clerics. In saying *dis-concert-ing* we imply a destruction of harmonies, the production of static, of noise. Although he did not use this exact term, the concept was central to John Dewey's *Art as Experience* (early Chapter 27).

Procedures for taking a fresh look at a word become more productive if the analyst employs more than one language. Often a knowledge of Latin will startle us for what it shows about English; one brilliant essay is built around Shakespeare's mixture of words from Latin roots with a basic vocabulary from Anglo-Saxon. Or consider an example from Spanish. *Cuchilla* is a mountain ridge, while *cuchillo* is the blade of a knife. Anybody who has done rock climbing in Puerto Rico or the Rockies or the High Sierras will grasp the point, although climbers in the White Mountains or the Smokies may be less alert to the analogy.

A disheartening phenomenon of recent years is the laxity of graduate schools in requiring foreign languages coupled with the resistance of students to learning them. With an introductory grammar and a decent dictionary, anybody can learn to read historical works in a foreign language by concentrating two hours a day for three months. Don't waste money on cheap dictionaries. In the modern languages that are most useful to students of American history, for French, *Larousse Dictionaire Moderne* (1960) fills the bill; for Spanish, *Appleton's New Cuyas Dictionary* (1966); for Italian, I have Nicola Spinelli's *Dizionario Scolastico* (1964). *The New Cassell's German Dictionary* (1965) is standard.

Document 30-1

As secretary of state in 1947, George C. Marshall chose his address at the commencement exercises of Harvard on June 5 to make this proposal for the economic reconstruction of Europe.

In considering the requirements for the rehabilitation of Europe, the physical loss of life, the visible destruction of cities, factories, mines, and railroads was correctly estimated, but it has become obvious during recent months that this visible destruction was probably less serious than the dislocation of the entire fabric of European economy. . . . The modern system of the division of labor upon which the exchange of products is based is in danger of breaking down. . . .

It is already evident that, before the United States Government can proceed much further in its efforts to alleviate the situation and help start the European world on its way to recovery, there must be some agreement among the countries of Europe as to the requirements of the situation and the part those countries themselves will take in order to give proper effect to whatever action might be undertaken by this Government. It would be neither fitting nor efficacious for this Government to undertake to draw up unilaterally a program designed to place Europe on its feet economically. This is the business of the Europeans. The initiative, I think, must come from Europe. The role of this country should consist of friendly aid in the drafting of a European program and of later support of such a program so far as it may be practical for us to do so. The program should be a joint one, agreed to by a number of, if not all, European nations.

An essential part of any successful action on the part of the United States is an understanding on the part of the American people of the character of the problem and the remedies to be applied. . . .

Document 30-2

A treaty restricting the testing of all nuclear weapons was signed on 5 August, 1963, by the United States, the United Kingdom, and the U.S.S.R. Soon the document was acceded to by 99 other governments including all powerful countries except France and China. The sponsors professed as follows:

Proclaiming as their principal aim the speediest possible achievement of an agreement on general and complete disarmament under strict international control in accordance with the objectives of the United Nations which would put an end to the armaments race and eliminate the incentive to the production and testing of all kinds of weapons, including nuclear weapons,

Seeking to achieve the discontinuance of all test explosions of nuclear weapons for all time, determined to continue negotiations to this end, and desiring to put an end to the contamination of man's environment by radioactive substances,

Have agreed as follows:

Article I - 1. Each of the Parties to this Treaty undertakes to prohibit, to prevent, and not to carry out any nuclear weapon test explosion, or any other nuclear explosion, at any place under its jurisdiction or control:

(a) in the atmosphere; beyond its limits, including outer space; or underwater, including territorial waters or high seas; or

(b) in any other environment if such explosion causes radioactive debris to be present outside the territorial limits of the State under whose jurisdiction or control such explosion is conducted. . . .

Article II - . . . 2. Any amendment to this Treaty must be approved by a majority of the votes of all the Parties to this Treaty, including the votes of all of the Original Parties. . . .

Article III - 1. This Treaty shall be open to all States for signature. . . .

Article IV - This Treaty shall be of unlimited duration. . . .

Bibliography

PART IV

ANDREANO, RALPH, ed. *The Economic Impact of the American Civil War.* Cambridge, Mass., 1962.

ATHERTON, LEWIS. *Main Street on the Middle Border.* Bloomington, Ind., 1964.

BARKER, CHARLES ALBRO. *Henry George.* New York, 1955.

BEER, THOMAS. *The Mauve Decade: American Life at the End of the 19th Century.* New York, 1926.

BOGUE, ALLAN G. *From Prairie to Cornbelt: Farming on the Illinois and Iowa Prairies in the Nineteenth Century.* Chicago, 1963.

BROWN, DEE. *Bury My Heart at Wounded Knee.* New York, 1971.

BUCK, PAUL H. *The Road to Reunion, 1865–1900.* Boston, 1937.

CHARNWOOD, LORD. *Abraham Lincoln.* New York, 1927.

CLARK, VICTOR S. *History of Manufactures in the United States, 1860–1914.* Washington, D.C., 1928.

DESTLER, CHESTER MCARTHUR. *American Radicalism 1865–1901.* New London, Conn., 1946.

FRIEDMAN, MILTON, and ANNA JACOBSON SCHWARTZ. *A Monetary History of the United States, 1867–1960.* Princeton, N.J., 1963.

GATES, PAUL WALLACE. *Fifty Million Acres: Conflicts over Kansas Land Policy, 1854–1890.* Ithaca, N.Y., 1954.

GINGER, RAY. *Age of Excess: The United States from 1877 to 1914.* Second Edition. New York, 1975.

——. *Altgeld's America.* New York, 1958.

HAYS, SAMUEL P. *The Response to Industrialism 1885–1914.* Chicago, 1957.

HICKS, JOHN D. *The Populist Revolt.* Minneapolis, 1931.

HUTCHINS, JOHN G. B. *The American Maritime Industries and Public Policy, 1789–1914.* Cambridge, Mass., 1941.

JOSEPHSON, MATTHEW. *The Politicos, 1865–1896.* New York, 1938.

KIRKLAND, EDWARD CHASE. *Men, Cities and Transportation: A Study in New England History, 1820–1900,* 2 vols. Cambridge, Mass., 1948.

LaFEBER, WALTER. *The New Empire: An Interpretation of American Expansion, 1860–1898.* Ithaca, N.Y., 1963.

LURIE, EDWARD. *Louis Aggassiz: A Life in Science.* Chicago, 1960.

MCKITRICK, ERIC L., ed. *Andrew Johnson and Reconstruction.* Chicago, 1960.

SHARKEY, ROBERT P. *Money, Class, and Party: An Economic Study of Civil War and Reconstruction*. Baltimore, 1959.

STAMPP, KENNETH M. *The Era of Reconstruction 1865–1877*. New York, 1965.

STEINMAN, D. B. *The Builders of the Bridge: The Story of John Roebling and His Son*. New York, 1945.

TAYLOR, GEORGE ROGERS. *The Transportation Revolution, 1815–1860*. New York, 1951.

THERNSTROM, STEPHAN. *Poverty and Progress: Social Mobility in a Nineteenth Century City*. Cambridge, Mass., 1964.

THOMAS, BENJAMIN P. *Abraham Lincoln*. New York, 1952.

UNGER, IRWIN. *The Greenback Era: A Social and Political History of American Finance, 1865–1879*. Princeton, N.J., 1964.

WALL, JOSEPH FRAZIER. *Andrew Carnegie*. New York, 1970.

WEBB, WALTER PRESCOTT. *The Great Plains*. Boston, 1931.

WHARTON, VERNON LANE. *The Negro in Mississippi, 1865–1890*. New York, 1947.

WIEBE, ROBERT H. *The Search for Order, 1877–1920*. New York, 1967.

WILEY, BELL IRVIN. *The Plain People of the Confederacy*. Baton Rouge, 1943.

WOODWARD, C. VANN. *Origins of the New South 1877–1913*. Baton Rouge, 1951.

——. *Reunion and Reaction: The Compromise of 1877 and the End of Reconstruction*. Boston, 1951.

——. *The Strange Career of Jim Crow*. New York, 1955.

——. *Tom Watson: Agrarian Rebel*. New York, 1938.

Primary Sources

ADAMS, HENRY. *The Education of Henry Adams*. Boston, 1918.

BRYCE, JAMES. *The American Commonwealth*, 2 vols. Many editions, first published 1898.

CURRENT, RICHARD N., ed. *Reconstruction, 1865–1877*. Englewood Cliffs, N.J., 1965.

DENNETT, JOHN RICHARD. *The South as It Is, 1865–1866*, ed. Henry M. Christman. New York, 1967.

DIAMOND, SIGMUND, ed. *The Nation Transformed: The Creation of an Industrial Society*. New York, 1963.

FRANKLIN, JOHN HOPE. *Reconstruction after the Civil War*. Chicago, 1961.

GINGER, RAY, ed. *The Nationalizing of American Life 1877–1900*. New York, 1965.

HAMILTON, ALICE. *Following the Dangerous Trades*. Boston, 1943.

HOWELLS, WILLIAM DEAN. *The Rise of Silas Lapham*. Many editions, first published 1885.

HYMAN, HAROLD M., ed. *The Radical Republicans and Reconstruction, 1861–1870*. Indianapolis, 1967.

LYND, STAUGHTON, ed. *Reconstruction*. New York, 1967.

MAHAN, ALFRED THAYER. *The Influence of Sea Power upon History, 1660–1783*. Boston, 1890.

SULLIVAN, LOUIS. *The Autobiography of an Idea*. New York, 1922.

TROLLOPE, ANTHONY. *North America*, ed. Donald Smalley and Bradford Allen Booth. New York, 1951.

TWAIN, MARK. *The Adventures of Huckleberry Finn*. Many editions, first published 1885.

PART V

ALLEN, FREDERICK LEWIS. *Only Yesterday: An Informal History of the Nineteen-Twenties*. New York, 1931.

BAILEY, THOMAS A. *Woodrow Wilson and the Betrayal*. New York, 1945.

——. *Woodrow Wilson and the Lost Peace*. New York, 1944.

BEALE, HOWARD K. *Theodore Roosevelt and the Rise of America to World Power*. Baltimore, 1956.

BLUM, JOHN MORTON. *The Republican Roosevelt*. Cambridge, Mass., 1954.

——. *Woodrow Wilson and the Politics of Morality*. Boston, 1956.

BRODY, DAVID. *Labor in Crisis: The Steel Strike of 1919*. Philadelphia, 1965.

CHALMERS, DAVID M. *Hooded Americanism: The History of the Ku Klux Klan*. New York, 1965.

CHANDLER, ALFRED D., JR. *Strategy and Structure: Chapters in the History of the Industrial Enterprise*. Cambridge, Mass., 1962.

CREMIN, LAWRENCE A. *The Transformation of the School: Progressivism in American Education, 1876–1957*. New York, 1961.

DAVIS, ALLEN FREEMAN. *Spearheads for Reform: the Social Settlements and the Progressive Movements*. New York, 1967.

GALBRAITH, JOHN KENNETH. *The Great Crash 1929*. Boston, 1965.

GELFAND, LAWRENCE E. *The Inquiry: American Preparations for Peace, 1917–1919*. New Haven, 1963.

GINGER, RAY. *The Bending Cross: A Biography of Eugene Victor Debs*. New Brunswick, N.J., 1949.

——. *Six Days or Forever?: Tennessee v. John Thomas Scopes*. Boston, 1958.

GRAEBNER, NORMAN A., ed. *An Uncertain Tradition: American Secretaries of State in the Twentieth Century*. New York, 1961.

HIGHAM, JOHN. *Strangers in the Land: Patterns of American Nativism, 1860–1925*. New Brunswick, N.J., 1955.

HOFSTADTER, RICHARD. *The Age of Reform: From Bryan to F.D.R.* New York, 1955.

KIRWAN, ALBERT D. *Revolt of the Rednecks*. Lexington, Ky., 1951.

LEVIN, N. GORDON. *Woodrow Wilson and World Politics*. New York, 1968.

LEUCHTENBURG, WILLIAM E. *The Perils of Prosperity, 1914–32*. Chicago, 1958.

LINK, ARTHUR S. *Woodrow Wilson and the Progressive Era, 1910–1917*. New York, 1954.

LOWITT, RICHARD. *George W. Norris: The Making of a Progressive, 1861–1912*. Syracuse, N.Y., 1963.

——. *George W. Norris: The Persistence of a Progressive, 1913–1933.* Urbana, 1971.

MAYER, ARNO J. *Political Origins of the New Diplomacy.* New Haven, 1959.

——. *Politics and Diplomacy of Peacemaking.* New York, 1967.

MURRAY, ROBERT K. *Red Scare: A Study in National Hysteria, 1919–1920.* Minneapolis, 1955.

NEVINS, ALLAN, and FRANK ERNEST HILL. *Ford,* 3 vols. New York, 1954–1963.

PRESTON, WILLIAM, JR. *Aliens and Dissenters: Federal Suppression of Radicals, 1903–1933.* Cambridge, Mass., 1963.

PRINGLE, HENRY F. *Theodore Roosevelt.* New York, 1931.

PROTHRO, JAMES WARREN. *The Dollar Decade: Business Ideas in the 1920's.* Baton Rouge, 1954.

SINCLAIR, ANDREW. *Prohibition: The Era of Excess.* Boston, 1962.

SWARD, KEITH. *The Legend of Henry Ford.* New York, 1948.

WILLIAMS, WILLIAM APPLEMAN. *The Tragedy of American Diplomacy.* Cleveland, 1959.

Primary Sources

ANDERSON, SHERWOOD. *Winesburg, Ohio.* New York, 1919.

CATHER, WILLA. *A Lost Lady.* New York, 1923.

——. *The Professor's House.* New York, 1925.

CROLY, HERBERT. *The Promise of American Life.* New York, 1909.

DREISER, THEODORE. *An American Tragedy.* New York, 1925.

——. *Sister Carrie.* New York, 1900.

DU BOIS, W. E. BURGHARDT. *The Souls of Black Folk.* Chicago, 1903.

FITZGERALD, F. SCOTT. *The Great Gatsby.* New York, 1925.

FRANKFURTER, MARION DENMAN, and GARDNER JACKSON, eds. *The Letters of Sacco and Vanzetti.* New York, 1928.

GINGER, RAY, ed. *American Social Thought.* New York, 1961.

GLASGOW, ELLEN. *Barren Ground.* New York, 1925.

JAMES, HENRY. *The Ambassadors.* Many editions, first published 1903.

——. *The Wings of the Dove.* Many editions, first published 1902.

LEVEN, MAURICE, and others. *America's Capacity to Consume.* Washington, D.C., 1934.

LEWIS, SINCLAIR. *Babbitt.* New York, 1922.

——. *Main Street.* New York, 1920.

LIPPMAN, WALTER. *Drift and Mastery.* New York, 1914.

LONDON, JACK. *The Iron Heel.* Many editions, first published 1907.

——. *Martin Eden.* Many editions, first published 1908.

LYND, ROBERT S., and HELEN MERRILL LYND. *Middletown: A Study in Modern American Culture.* New York, 1929.

MOWRY, GEORGE E., ed. *The Twenties: Fords, Flappers & Fanatics.* Englewood Cliffs, N.J., 1963.

STEFFENS, LINCOLN. *Autobiography*. New York, 1931.
WHARTON, EDITH. *The House of Mirth*. New York, 1905.

PART VI

AGEE, JAMES, and WALKER EVANS. *Let Us Now Praise Famous Men*. Boston, 1941.

ALINSKY, SAUL D. *John L. Lewis: An Unauthorized Biography*. New York, 1949.

ALLEN, FREDERICK LEWIS. *Since Yesterday: The Nineteen-Thirties in America*. New York, 1940.

ARNOLD, THURMAN. *The Bottlenecks of Business*. New York, 1940.

——. *The Folklore of Capitalism*. New Haven, 1937.

AUERBACH, JEROLD S. *Labor and Liberty: The La Follette Committee and the New Deal*. Indianapolis, 1966.

BERLE, ADOLF A., JR., and GARDNER C. MEANS. *The Modern Corporation and Private Property*. New York, 1932.

BERNSTEIN, IRVING. *The Lean Years: A History of the American Worker 1920–1933*. Boston, 1960.

BLUM, JOHN MORTON. *From the Morgenthau Diaries: Years of Crisis, 1928–1938*. Boston, 1959.

BURNS, JAMES M. *Roosevelt*, 2 vols. New York, 1956–1970.

BUTOW, ROBERT J. C. *Tojo and the Coming of the War*. Princeton, N.J., 1961.

CLARK, THOMAS D. *The Emerging South*. New York, 1961.

FEIS, HERBERT. *The Road to Pearl Harbor*. Princeton, N.J., 1950.

FINE, SIDNEY. *The Automobile Under the Blue Eagle*. Ann Arbor, Mich., 1963.

GARDNER, LLOYD C. *Economic Aspects of New Deal Diplomacy*. Madison, Wis., 1964.

HAMMOND, PAUL Y. *The Cold War Years: American Foreign Policy Since 1945*. New York, 1969.

HERSEY, JOHN. *Hiroshima*. New York, 1946.

JACOBS, JANE. *The Death and Life of Great American Cities*. New York, 1961.

JOSEPHSON, MATTHEW. *Sidney Hillman*. Garden City, N.J., 1952.

KNEBEL, FLETCHER, and CHARLES W. BAILEY II. *No High Ground*. New York, 1960.

LEUCHTENBURG, WILLIAM E. *Franklin D. Roosevelt and the New Deal 1932–1940*. New York, 1963.

LUBELL, SAMUEL. *The Future of American Politics*. New York, 1952.

LYND, ROBERT S., and HELEN MERRELL LYND. *Middletown in Transition*. New York, 1937.

McKENNA, MARIAN C. *Borah*. Ann Arbor, Mich., 1961.

MILLS, C. WRIGHT. *The Power Elite*. New York, 1956.

——. *White Collar: The American Middle Classes*. New York, 1951.

MORISON, ELTING E. *Turmoil and Tradition: A Study of the Life and Times of Henry L. Stimson*. Boston, 1960.

MORISON, SAMUEL ELIOT. *The Two-Ocean War: A Short History of the United States Navy in the Second World War.* Boston, 1963.

NEVINS, ALLEN. *Herbert Lehman and His Era.* New York, 1963.

PAIGE, GLENN D. *The Korean Decision (June 24–30, 1950).* New York, 1968.

SCHLESINGER, ARTHUR M., JR. *A Thousand Days: John F. Kennedy in the White House.* Boston, 1965.

SHERWOOD, ROBERT E. *Roosevelt and Hopkins.* New York, 1948.

SILBERMAN, CHARLES E. *Crisis in Black and White.* New York, 1964.

SORENSON, THEODORE C. *Kennedy.* New York, 1965.

TINDALL, GEORGE B. *The Emergence of the New South, 1913–1945.* Baton Rouge, 1967.

WOHLSTETTER, ROBERTA. *Pearl Harbor: Warning and Decision.* Palo Alto, Calif., 1962.

ZINN, HOWARD. *SNCC: The New Abolitionists.* Boston, 1964.

Primary Sources

BERNSTEIN, BARTON J., and ALLEN J. MATUSOW, eds. *The Truman Administration.* New York, 1966.

CLARK, WALTER VAN TILBURG. *The Ox-Bow Incident.* New York, 1940.

CRAIG, GORDON A., and FELIX GILBERT, eds. *The Diplomats, 1919–1939.* Princeton, N.J., 1953.

EISENHOWER, DWIGHT D. *Crusade in Europe.* Garden City, N.J., 1948.

ELLISON, RALPH. *Invisible Man.* New York, 1952.

FAULKNER, WILLIAM. *Selected Short Stories.* New York, 1962.

GINGER, RAY, ed. *Modern American Cities.* Chicago, 1969.

HAMMETT, DASHIELL. *The Glass Key.* New York, 1931.

HEMINGWAY, ERNEST. *Short Stories.* New York, 1938.

HULL, CORDELL. *Memoirs,* 2 vols. New York, 1948.

ICKES, HAROLD L. *Secret Diary,* 3 vols. New York, 1953–1954.

MALCOLM X, *Autobiography.* New York, 1964.

MARTIN, RALPH G., and RICHARD HARRITY, eds. *World War II: A Photographic Record of the War in Europe from D-Day to V-E Day.* Greenwich, Conn., 1962.

McGOVERN, GEORGE, ed. *Agricultural Thought in the Twentieth Century.* Indianapolis, 1967.

MILLER, ARTHUR. *Collected Plays.* New York, 1957.

Report of the National Advisory Commission on Civil Disorders. New York, 1968

SHEEHAN, NEIL, and others. *The Pentagon Papers.* Chicago, 1971.

SWADOS, HARVEY, ed. *The American Writer and the Great Depression.* Indianapolis, 1966.

WEST, NATHANAEL. *Miss Lonelyhearts.* New York, 1933.

GENERAL BIBLIOGRAPHY

BAILEY, THOMAS A. *A Diplomatic History of the American People.* Many editions, first published New York, 1940.

BALTZELL, E. DIGBY. *Philadelphia Gentlemen: The Making of a National Upper Class.* Glencoe, Ill., 1958.

BERTHOFF, ROWLAND. *An Unsettled People: Social Order and Disorder in American History.* New York, 1971.

BILLINGTON, RAY ALLEN. *America's Frontier Heritage.* New York, 1966.

——. *Westward Expansion.* New York, 1949.

BRANDON, WILLIAM. *American Heritage Book of the Indians.* New York, 1961.

BRUCHEY, STUART. *The Roots of American Economic Growth, 1607–1861.* New York, 1968.

CASH, W. J. *The Mind of the South.* New York, 1941.

CHANNING, EDWARD. *A History of the United States,* 6 vols. New York, 1905–25.

CLARK, THOMAS D. *Frontier America.* New York, 1959.

COHEN, HENNIG, ed. *The American Culture* and *The American Experience,* 2 vols. Boston, 1968.

DIAMOND, SIGMUND. *The Reputation of the American Businessman.* Cambridge, Mass., 1955.

ELIOT, ALEXANDER. *Three Hundred Years of American Painting.* New York, 1957.

FISCHER, DAVID HACKETT. *Historians' Fallacies: Toward a Logic of Historical Thought.* New York, 1970.

FRIEDMAN, JEAN E., and WILLIAM G. SHADE, eds. *Our American Sisters.* Boston, 1973.

GLAAB, CHARLES N., and A. THEODORE BROWN. *A History of Urban America.* New York, 1967.

HANDLIN, OSCAR, and others. *Harvard Guide to American History.* Cambridge, Mass., 1954.

HOFSTADTER, RICHARD. *The American Political Tradition and the Men Who Made It.* New York, 1948.

IMLAH, ALBERT H. *Economic Elements in the Pax Britannica.* Cambridge, Mass., 1958.

JOHNSON, GERALD W. *The Lines Are Drawn: American Life since the First World War as Reflected in the Pulitzer Prize Cartoons.* Philadelphia, 1958.

JOHNSON, THOMAS H. *The Oxford Companion to American History.* New York, 1966.

KELLY, ALFRED H., and WINFRED A. HARBISON. *The American Constitution.* New York, 1948.

KEY, V. O., JR. *Southern Politics in State and Nation.* New York, 1949.

KOUWENHOVEN, JOHN A. *Made in America: The Arts in Modern Civilization.* New York, 1948.

LARKIN, OLIVER W. *Art and Life in America.* New York, 1949.

LASKI, HAROLD J. *The American Democracy.* New York, 1948.

LORD, CLIFFORD L., and ELIZABETH H. LORD. *Historical Atlas of the United States.* New York, 1944.

MENDELOWITZ, DANIEL M. *A History of American Art.* New York, 1960.

MERK, FREDERICK. *Manifest Destiny and Mission in American History.* New York, 1962.

MORRIS, RICHARD B., ed. *Encyclopedia of American History.* New York, 1953.

NORTH, DOUGLASS. *Economic Growth of the United States.* Englewood Cliffs, N.J., 1961.

NYE, RUSSEL B. *This Almost Chosen People: Essays in the History of American Ideas.* East Lansing, Mich., 1966.

PERSONS, STOW. *American Minds: A History of Ideas.* New York, 1958.

PIERSON, WILLIAM H., JR., and MARTHA DAVIDSON, eds. *Arts of the United States.* New York, 1960.

POSTAN, M. M. *Fact and Relevance: Essays on Historical Method.* Cambridge, England, 1971.

POTTER, DAVID M. *People of Plenty: Economic Abundance and the American Character.* Chicago, 1954.

RATNER, SIDNEY. *American Taxation: Its History as a Social Force in Democracy.* New York, 1942.

SALE, RANDALL D., and EDWIN D. KARN. *American Expansion: A Book of Maps.* Homewood, Ill., 1962.

SHANNON, FRED A. *The Farmer's Last Frontier.* New York, 1945.

SHORTER, EDWARD. *The Historian and the Computer: A Practical Guide.* Englewood Cliffs, N.J., 1971.

SMITH, HENRY NASH. *Virgin Land.* Cambridge, Mass., 1950.

TURNER, FREDERICK JACKSON. *The Frontier in American History.* New York, 1920.

U.S. BUREAU OF THE CENSUS. *Historical Statistics of the United States.* Washington, D.C., 1960.

WARNER, SAM BASS JR. *The Private City: Philadelphia in Three Periods of Its Growth.* Philadelphia, 1968.

WEINBERG, ALBERT K. *Manifest Destiny.* Baltimore, 1935.

WILLIAMS, T. HARRY. *Americans at War: The Development of the American Military System.* Baton Rouge, 1960.

WILLIAMS, WILLIAM APPLEMAN. *American Russian Relations, 1781–1947.* New York, 1952.

WOODWARD, C. VANN. *The Burden of Southern History.* Baton Rouge, 1960.

WYLLIE, IRVIN G. *The Self-made Man in America.* New Brunswick, N.J., 1954.

Primary Sources

APTHEKER, HERBERT, ed. *A Documentary History of the Negro People in the United States.* New York, 1951.

BLAIR, WALTER, ed. *Native American Humor (1800–1900).* New York, 1937.

COMMAGER, HENRY STEELE, ed. *Documents of American History.* Many editions, first published, New York, 1934.

KRADITOR, AILEEN S., ed. *Up From the Pedestal: Selected Writings in the History of American Feminism.* Chicago, 1968.

JENSEN, OLIVER, and others. *American Album.* New York, 1968.

WASHBURN, WILCOMB E., ed. *The Indian and the White Man.* Garden City, N.Y., 1964.

WILLIAMS, WILLIAM APPLEMAN, ed. *The Shaping of American Diplomacy.* Chicago, 1956.

THORP, WILLARD, ed. *A Southern Reader.* New York, 1956.

Index of Defined Terms

Subject Index

Name Index

Latvia, 726
League of Nations, 575, 577–578, 583, 588, 667, 669, 685
Leahy, William D., 682, 684
Lee, Robert E., 385, 389
Lehman Brothers, 628
Lenin, Nicolai, 658, 728
Lesy, Michael, 468–469
Levitt, William, 699
Levittown, 699–700
Lewis, John L., 620, 657–660, 669
Lewis, Sinclair, 593, 651, 673
Library of Congress, 547
Lincoln, Abraham, (Pres. 1861–1865), 382–390, 393, 399, 400, 403, 440, 486, 618, 622, 630, 738
Lindbergh, Charles A., 584–585, 587, 672–673
Lippman, Walter, 621
Lithuania, 726
Little Rock, (Ark.), 702, 704
Litvinov, Maxim, 669–670
Lloyd, Henry Demarest, 474, 493, 497
Lodge, Henry Cabot, 489, 490, 517
Lombardo, Guy, 649
London, 415, 454, 547, 667–668
London *Times*, 517
Long, Huey, 618, 621, 637, 639
Long Island, 584, 601, 699
Los Alamos, (N.M.), 682
Los Angeles, (Cal.), 533, 557, 596, 619, 656, 704
Lost Lady, A, 593
Louisiana, 381, 482, 513, 618, 621, 637, 639, 647
Ludlow Agreement, 672
Lusitania, SS, 542–543

MacArthur, Douglas, 619, 682, 723, 729–730
McCarthy, Joseph, 695–696
McClellan, George B., 385
McCormick Harvesting Machine Company, 420–422
McDowell, Irvin, 385

McGovern, George, 741
McGuffey's Readers, 451
McIntire, Samuel, 503
McKay, Donald, 633
McKinley Tariff Act (1890), 484
McKinley, William, 486–487, 489–490, 494, 498, 725
McNamara, Robert, 723
McNamee, Graham, 559
MacPherson, Aimee Semple, 596, 604
Macy's, 427, 514
Madison, James, (Pres. 1809–1817), 437
Main Street, 593
Maine, 387, 430, 437, 464, 465, 636
Maine, USS, 489
Mahan, Alfred T., 484, 517
Malcolm X, 707
Malone, Dumas, 688
Manchuria, 504, 517, 529, 666–667, 676
Manhattan, (N.Y.), 418, 453, 466, 490, 502, 559
Manhattan Project, 682–683
Marshall Field Company, 427, 467, 627
Marshall, George C., 679, 682, 728, 734, 745
Marshall, John, 544
Marshall Plan, 728
Maryland, 482
Massachusetts, 390, 426, 447, 489, 505, 528, 555, 578, 598, 606, 698, 731, 741
Matthiesen, F. O., 425
Mauldin, Bill, 434
Mays, Willie, 706
Meade, George, 385
Meat Inspection Act, 515
Mellon, Andrew W., 611–612, 615, 626
Mellon, Richard, 611
Melville, Herman, 381, 399, 468, 592–593
Memphis, (Tenn.), 620, 648
Mesabi range, 498, 505–506

Metropolitan Opera Company, 645, 647
Mexico, 429, 438, 440, 498, 536, 552, 573, 650, 668, 732
Meyers, Marvin, 389
Miami, (Fla.), 502, 566
Michigan, 653
Miller, Arthur, 652, 710
Minneapolis, (Minn.), 415, 518, 647
Minnesota, 393, 410, 453, 498, 505, 673
Mississippi, 382, 507, 652
Mississippi River, 533, 648
Missouri, 386, 528, 587, 650
Missouri Compromise, 383
Missouri River, 439
Mitropoulous, Dimitri, 647
Modern Instance, A, 462
Moley, Raymond, 620
Monadnock Building, 467
Monroe Doctrine, 441–442, 444, 485, 516, 577, 583
Monroe, James, (Pres. 1817–1825), 516
Montana, 457, 709
Montgomery, (Ala.), 703, 704
Moody, Dwight, 450–451, 597
Morgan, John Pierpont, 408, 483, 486, 501, 510–511, 512, 529, 538, 555, 653
Morgan, John Pierpont, Jr., 538
Morrill Act, 408
Morton, Ferdinand ("Jelly Roll"), 648
Moscow, 695, 726
Munich, 669–670, 673–674, 685
Murphy, Frank, 661
Muscle Shoals Dam, 631, 673
Museum of Modern Art, 651
Museum of Natural History, 511
Musial, Stan, 615
Music Corporation of America, 648
Mussolini, Benito, 666, 669–670, 673

Nagasaki, 684

Napoleon, (Napoleon Bonaparte), 385, 489, 733
Napoleon III, 441
Nation, The, 625
National Aeronautics and Space Administration, 715
National Association for the Advancement of Colored People, 599, 701, 702
National Association of Broadcasters, 645
National Banking Act, 531
National Broadcasting Company, 559, 645, 647
National Gallery, 651
National Labor Relations Act, 635, 637, 661
National Recovery Administration, 627–628, 636, 657
Nebraska, 456, 458, 486, 572, 631, 673
Nevada, 725
Nevins, Allan, 520
New Empire, The, 446
New England, 404, 426, 450, 464, 487, 550, 554–555, 565, 608, 619
New Hampshire, 517
New Jersey, 520
New Orleans, (La.), 487, 648, 733
New York, 404, 410, 430, 447, 487, 509, 533, 572, 574, 626
New York City, 384, 396, 407, 410, 416, 427, 435, 453, 490, 522, 528, 531, 538, 557, 566, 591, 615, 617, 643, 650–651, 716–717
New York *Herald*, 441
New York Philharmonic, 645, 647
New York Stock Exchange, 499, 565–566, 630
New York Symphony Orchestra, 645
New York *Times*, 652, 737
New Yorker, 434, 596, 642
Newfoundland, 674
Nez Perce Indians, 457

Ngo Dinh Diem, 737
Nicaragua, 526, 583, 732
Nine-Power Treaty, 582–583
Nixon, Richard M., (Pres. 1969–1974), 435, 620, 623, 707–708, 712, 725, 735, 739–742
Noone, Jimmy, 649
Norris Dam, 632–633
Norris, George W., 657, 572, 631, 673
Norris-La Guardia Act, 657
North Atlantic Treaty Organization, 728
North Carolina, 382
North Dakota, 709
North of Boston, 608
Northern Pacific Railroad, 447, 499
Nova Scotia, 633
Nye Committee, 674

O'Connor, Frank, 653
Of Mice and Men, 654
Ohio, 390, 393, 396, 410, 416, 458, 509, 600, 712
Okinawa, 680
Oklahoma, 456, 528, 654
O'Neill, Eugene, 652–653
Oppenheimer, J. Robert, 680
Oregon, 438, 441, 456
Oregon Treaty of 1856, 429
Origins of the New South, 493

Page, Walter Hines, 539
Paine, Thomas, 383
Pakistan, 727
Palmer, A. Mitchell, 577
Panama, 526–527
Panama Canal, 526
Panay, USS, 672
Paris, 584, 650, 653, 673, 731
Paterson, (N.J.), 421
Patton, George S., 619
Payne-Aldrich Tariff (1909), 527–528
Peale, Norman Vincent, 720
Pearl Harbor, 383, 675, 677, 680, 685
Peffer, William A., 494

Peirce, Charles Sanders, 587, 607
Pennsylvania, 390, 403, 410, 416, 437, 474, 521, 528, 533, 554, 615, 620, 626, 646, 663, 669
Pennsylvania, Academy of Fine Arts, 465
Pennsylvania Railroad, 401–402, 417, 493, 513
Pentagon Papers, The, 736
Perry, Matthew B., 447
Peruna, 430
Pierce, Franklin, (Pres. 1853–1857), 383
Philadelphia, 412, 418, 453, 470, 615, 656
Philadelphia Sumphony Orchestra, 645
Philippine Islands, 490, 494, 497, 667, 676–677
Picasso, Pablo, 650
Pinchot, Gifford, 529
Pinkerton Detective Agency, 476
Pippin, Horace, 662–663
Pittsburgh, 401, 521, 574, 593, 611, 714
Platt, Orville, 437–438
Plumb Plan, 555
Plunkett, George Washington, 522
Phoenix Mutual Life Insurance Company, 716–717
Poland, 507, 514, 674, 709, 731, 733
Pollock, Jackson, 650
Ponca Indians, 456
Potsdam, 683–684, 725–726
Potter, David M., 399
Presley, Elvis, 711
Professor's House, The, 593
Prussia, 399
Puerto Rico, 453, 491, 745
Pullman, George M., 480
Pullman Palace Car Company, 479–480
Pure Food and Drug Act (1906), 515

Radio Corporation of America, 559
Rayburn, Sam, 661